THE SECRET DOCTRINE
VOL III.

SECRET DOCTRINE

VOLUME III.

ANNIE BESANT

ANCIENT WISDOM PUBLICATIONS

WOODLAND, CALIFORNIA

Contents

PREFACE

The task of preparing this volume for the press has been a difficult and anxious one, and it is necessary to state clearly what has been done. The papers given to me by H.P.B. were quite unarranged, and had no obvious order; I have therefore taken each paper as a separate Section, and have arranged them as sequentially as possible. With the exception of the correction of grammatical errors and the elimination of obviously un-English idioms, the papers are as H.P.B. left them, save as otherwise marked. In a few cases I have filled in a gap, but any such addition is enclosed within square brackets, so as to be distinguished from the text. In "The Mystery of Buddha" a further difficulty arose; some of the Sections had been written four or five times over, each version containing some sentences that were not in the others; I have pieced these versions together,taking the fullest as basis, and inserting therein everything added in any other versions.

It is, however, with some hesitation that I have included these Sections in the Secret Doctrine . Together with some most suggestive thought, they contain very numerous errors of fact, and many statements based on exoteric writings, not on esoteric knowledge. They were given into my hands to publish, as part of the Third Volume of the Secret Doctrine, and I therefore do not feel justified in coming between the author and the public, either by altering the statements, to make them consistent with fact, or by suppressing the Sections. She says she is acting entirely on her own authority, and it will be obvious to any instructed reader that she makes - possibly deliberately - many statements so confused that they are mere blinds, and other statements - probably inadvertently - that are nothing more than the exoteric misunderstandings of esoteric truths. The reader must here, as everywhere, use his own judgment, but feeling bound to publish these Sections, I cannot let them go to the public without a warning that much in them is certainly erroneous. Doubtless, had the author herself issued this book, she would have entirely rewritten the whole of this division; as it was, it seemed best to give all she had said in the different copies, and to leave it in its rather unfinished state, for students will best like to have what she said as she said it, even though they may have to study it more closely than would have been the case had she remained to finish her work.

The quotations made have been as far as possible found, and correct references given; in this most laborious work a whole band of earnest and painstaking students,under the guidance of Mrs. Cooper-Oakley, have been my willing assistants. Without their aid it would not have been possible to give the references, as often a whole book had to be searched through, in order to find a paragraph of a few lines.

This volume completes the papers left by H.P.B., with the exception of a few scattered articles that yet remain and that will be published in her own magazine Lucifer. Her pupils are well aware that few will be found in the present generation to do justice to the occult knowledge of H.P.B., and to her magnificent sweep of thoughts, but as she can wait to future generations for the justification of her greatness as a teacher, so can her pupils afford to wait for the justification of their trust.

ANNIE BESANT

INTRODUCTORY

"POWER belongs to him who knows;" this is a very old axiom. Knowledge - the first step to which is the power of comprehending the truth, of discerning the real from the false - is for those only who, have freed themselves from every prejudice and conquered their human conceit and selfishness, are ready to accept every and any truth once it is demonstrated to them. Of such there are very few. The majority judge of a work according to the respective prejudices of its critics, who are guided in their turn by the popularity or unpopularity of the author, rather than by its own faults or merits. Outside the Theosophical circle, therefore, the present volume is certain to receive at the hands of the general public a still colder welcome than its two predecessors have met with. In our day no statement can hope for a fair trial, or even hearing, unless its arguments run on the line of legitimate and accepted enquiry, remaining strictly within the boundaries of official Science or orthodox Theology.

Our age is a paradoxical anomaly. It is preëminently materialistic and as preëminently pietistic. Our literature, our modern thought and progress, so called, both run on these two parallel lines, so incongruously dissimilar and yet both so popular and so very orthodox, each in its own way. He who presumes to draw a third line, as a hyphen of reconciliation between the two, has to be fully prepared for the worst. He will have his work mangled by reviewers, mocked by the sycophants of Science and Church, misquoted by his opponents, and rejected even by the pious lending libraries. The absurd misconceptions, in so-called cultured circles of society, of the ancient Wisdom-Religion (Bodhism) after the admirably clear and scientifically presented explanations in Esoteric Buddhism, are a good proof in point. They might have served as a caution even to those Theosophists who, hardened in an almost life-long struggle in the service of their Cause, are neither timid with their pen, nor in the least appalled by dogmatic assumption and scientific authority. Yet, do what Theosophical writers may, neither Materialism nor doctrinal pietism will ever give their Philosophy a fair hearing. Their doctrines will be systematically rejected, and their theories denied a place even in the ranks of those scientific ephemera, the ever-shifting "working hypotheses" of our day. To the advocate of the "animalistic" theory, our cosmogenetical and anthropogenetical teachings are "fairy-tales" at best. For to those who would shirk any moral responsibility, it seems certainly more convenient to accept descent from a common simian ancestor and see a brother in a dumb, tailless baboon, than to acknowledge the fatherhood of the Pitris, the "Sons of God," and to have to recognise as a brother a starveling from the slums.

"Hold back!" shout in their turn the pietists. "You will never make of respectable church-going Christians Esoteric Buddhists!"

Nor are we, in truth, in any way anxious to attempt the metamorphosis. But this cannot, nor shall it, prevent Theosophists from saying what they have to say, especially to those who, in opposing to our doctrine Modern Science, do so not for her own fair sake, but only to ensure the success of their private hobbies and personal glorification. If we cannot prove many of our points, no more can they; yet we may show how, instead of giving historical and scientific facts - for the edification of those who, knowing less than they, look to Scientists to do their thinking and form their opinions - the efforts of most of our scholars seem solely directed to killing ancient facts, or distorting them into props to support their own special views. This will be done in no spirit of malice or even criticism, as the writer readily admits that most of those she finds fault with stand immeasurably higher in learning than herself. But great scholarship does not preclude bias and prejudice, nor is it a safeguard against self-conceit, but rather the reverse. Moreover, it is but in the legitimate defence of our own statements, i.e., the vindication of Ancient Wisdom and its great truths, that we mean to take our "great authorities" to task.

Indeed, unless the precaution of answering beforehand certain objections to the fundamental propositions in the present work be adopted - objections which are certain to be made on the authority of this, that, or another scholar concerning the Esoteric character of all the archaic and ancient works on Philosophy - our statements will be once more contradicted and even discredited. One of the main points in this Volume is to indicate in the works of the old Aryan, Greek and

One Key to all Sacred Books - other Philosophers of note, as well as in all the world-scriptures, the presence of a strong Esoteric allegory and symbolism. Another of the objects is to prove that the key of interpretation, as furnished by the Eastern Hindu-Buddhistic canon of Occultism - fitting as well the Christian Gospels as it does archaic Egyptian, Greek, Chaldean, Persian, and even Hebrew -Mosaic Books - must have been one common to all the nations, however divergent may have been their respective methods and exoteric "blinds." These claims are vehemently denied by some of the foremost scholars of our day. In his Edinburgh Lectures, Prof. Max Muller discarded this fundamental statement of the Theosophists by pointing to the Hindu Shastras and Pandits, who know nothing of such Esotericism.

[The majority of the Pandits know nothing of the Esoteric Philosophy now, because they have lost the key to it; yet not one of these, if honest, would deny that the Upanishads, and especially the Puranas, are allegorical and symbolical: nor that there still remain in India a few great scholars who could, if they would, give them the key to such interpretations. Nor do they reject the actual existence of Mahâtmâs - initiated Yogis and Adepts - even in this age of Kali Yuga.] The learned Sanskrit scholar stated in so many words that there was no hidden meaning, no Esoteric element or "blinds," either in the Purânas or the Upanishads. Considering that the word "Upanishad" means, when translated, the "Secret Doctrine." the assertion is, to say the least, extraordinary. Sir M. Monier Williams again holds the same view with regard to Buddhism. To hear him is to regard Gautama, the Buddha, as an enemy of every pretence to Esoteric teachings. He himself never taught them! All such "pretences" to Occult learning and "magic powers" are due to the later Arhats, the subsequent followers of the "Light of Asia"! Prof. B. Jowett, again, as contemptuously passes the sponge over the "absurd" interpretations of Plato's Timaeus and the Mosaic Books by the Neoplatonists. There is not a breath of the Oriental (Gnostic) spirit of Mysticism in Plato's Dialogues, the Regius Professor of Greek tells us, nor any approach to Science, either. Finally, to cap the climax, Prof. Sayce, the Assyriologist, although he does not deny the actual presence, in the Assyrian tablets and cuneiform literature, of a hidden meaning -

"Many of the sacred texts . . . . so written as to be intelligible only to the initiated"-

yet insists that the "keys and glosses" thereof are now in the hands of the Assyriologists. The modern scholars, he affirms, have in their possession clues to the interpretation of the Esoteric Records.

"Which even the initiated priests [of Chaldaea] did not possess."

Thus, in the scholarly appreciation of our modern Orientalists and Professors, Science was in its infancy in the days of the Egyptian and Chaldean Astronomers. Pânini, the greatest Grammarian in the world, was unacquainted with the art of writing. So was the Lord Buddha, and everyone else in India until 300 B.C. The grossest ignorance reigned in the days of the Indian Rishis, and even in those of Thales, Pythagoras, and Plato. Theosophists must indeed be superstitious ignoramuses to speak as they do, in the face of such learned evidence to the contrary!

Truly it looks as if, since the world's creation, there has

been but one age of real knowledge on earth - the present age. In the misty twilight, in the grey dawn of history, stand the pale shadows of the old Sages of world renown. They were hopelessly groping for the correct meaning of their own Mysteries, the spirit whereof has departed without revealing itself to the Hierophants, and has remained latent in space until the advent of the initiates of Modern Science and Research. The noontide brightness of knowledge has only now arrived at the "Know-All," who, basking in the dazzling sun of induction, busies himself with his Penelopeian task of "working hypotheses," and loudly asserts his rights to universal knowledge. Can anyone wonder, then, that according to present views the learning of the ancient Philosopher, and even sometimes that of his direct successors in the past centuries, has ever been useless to the world and valueless to himself? For, as explained repeatedly in so many words, while the Rishis and the Sages of old have walked far over the arid fields of myth and superstition, the mediaeval Scholar, and even the average eighteenth century Scientist, have always been more or less cramped by their "supernatural" religion and beliefs. True, it is generally conceded that some ancient and also mediaeval Scholars, such as Pythagoras, Plato, Paracelsus, and Roger Bacon, followed by a host of glorious names, had indeed left not a few landmarks over precious mines of Philosophy and unexpected lodes of Physical Science. But then the actual excavation of these, the smelting of the gold and silver, and the cutting of the precious jewels they contain, are all due to the patient labours of the modern man of Science. And it is not to be the unparalleled genius of the latter that the ignorant and hitherto-deluded world owes a correct knowledge of the real nature of the Kosmos, of the true origin of the universe and man, as revealed in the automatic and mechanical theories of the Physicists, in accordance with strictly scientific Philosophy?

ASSUMPTIONS HAVE TO BE PROVEN –

Before our cultured era, Science was but a name, Philosophy a delusion and a snare. According to the modest claims of contemporary authority on genuine Science and Philosophy, the Tree of Knowledge has only now sprung from the dead weeds of superstition, as a beautiful butterfly emerges from an ugly grub. We have, therefore, nothing for which to thank our forefathers. The Ancients have at best prepared and fertilised the soil; it is the Moderns who have planted the seeds of knowledge and reared the lovely plants called blank negation and sterile agnosticism.

Such, however, is not the view taken by Theosophists. They repeat what was stated twenty years ago. It is not sufficient to speak of the "untenable conceptions of an uncultured past" (Tyndall): of the "parler enfantin" of the Vaidic poets (Max Muller); of the "absurdities" of the Neoplatonists (Jowett); and of the ignorance of the Chaldaeo-Assyrian initiated Priests with regard to their own symbols, when compared with the knowledge thereon of the British Orientalist (Sayce). Such assumptions have to be proven by something more solid than the mere word of these scholars. For no amount of boastful arrogance can hide the intellectual quarries out of which the representations of so many modern Philosophers and Scholars have been carved. How many of the most distinguished European Scientists have derived honour and credit for the mere dressing-up of the ideas of these old Philosophers, whom they are ever ready to disparage, is left to an impartial posterity to say. Thus it does seem not altogether untrue, as stated in Isis Unveiled, to say of certain Orientalists and Scholars of dead languages, that they will allow their boundless conceit and self-opinionatedness to run away with their logic and reasoning powers, rather than concede to the ancient Philosophers the knowledge of anything the modern do not know.

As part of this work treats of the Initiates and the secret knowledge imparted during the Mysteries, the statements of those who, in spite of the fact that Plato was an Initiate, maintain that no hidden Mysticism is to be discovered in his works, have to be first examined. Too many of the present scholars, Greek and Sanskrit, are but too apt to forego facts in favour of their own preconceived theories based on personal prejudice. They conveniently forget, at every opportunity, not only the numerous changes in language, but also that the allegorical style in the writings of old Philosophers and the secretiveness of the Mystics had their raison d'être; that both the pre-Christian and the post-Christian classical writers - the great majority at all events - were under the sacred obligation never to divulge the solemn secrets communicated to them in the sanctuaries; and that this alone is sufficient to sadly mislead their translators and profane critics. But these critics will admit nothing of the kind, as will presently be seen.

For over twenty-two centuries everyone who has read

Plato has been aware that, like most of the other Greek Philosophers of note, he had been initiated; that therefore, being tied down by the Sodalian Oath, he could speak of certain things only in veiled allegories. His reverence for the Mysteries is unbounded; he openly confesses that he writes "enigmatically," and we see him take the greatest precautions to conceal the true meaning of his words. Every time the subject touches the greater secrets of Oriental Wisdom - the cosmogony of the universe, or the ideal preexisting world - Plato shrouds his Philosophy in the profoundest darkness. His Timaeus is so confused that no one but an Initiate can understand the hidden meaning, As already said in Isis Unveiled:

The speculations of Plato in the Banquet on the creation, or rather the evolution, of primordial men, and the essay on cosmogony in the Timaeus, must be taken allegorically if we accept them at all. It is this hidden Pythagorean meaning in Timaeus, Cratylus, and Parmenides, and a few other triologies and dialogues, that the Neoplatonists ventured to expound, as far as the theurgical vow of secresy would allow them. The Pythagoran doctrine that God is the Universal Mind diffused through all things, and the dogma of the soul's immortality, are the leading features in these apparently incongruous teachings. His piety and the great veneration he felt for the Mysteries are sufficient warrant that Plato would not allow his indiscretion to get the better of that deep sense of responsibility which is felt by every Adept. "Constantly perfecting himself in perfect Mysteries a man in them alone becomes truly perfect," says he in the Phaedrus.

He took no pains to conceal his displeasure that the Mysteries had become less secret than formerly. Instead of profaning them by putting them within the reach of the multitude, he would have guarded them with jealous care against all but the most earnest and worthy of his disciples. [This assertion is clearly corroborated by Plato himself, who writes: "You say that in my former discourse I have not sufficiently explained to you the nature of the First. I purposely spoke enigmatically, that in case the tablet should have happened with any accident, either by sea or land, a person without some previous knowledge of the subject might not be able to understand its contents." (Plato. Ep., II. 312 Cory. Ancient Fragments. p.304] While mentioning the Gods on every page, his monotheism is unquestionable, for the whole thread of his discourse indicates that by the term "God" he means a class of beings lower in the scale than Deities, and but one grade higher than men. Even Josephus perceived and acknowledged this fact, despite the natural prejudice of his race.

THE SPIRIT OF PLATO'S TEACHING –

In his famous onslaught upon Apion, this historian says;"Those, however, among the Greeks who philosophized in accordance with truth were not ignorant of anything, . . . nor did they fail to perceive the chilling superficialities of the mythical allegories, on which account they justly despised them. . . . By which thing Plato, being moved, says it is not necessary to admit any one of the other poets into 'the Commonwealth,' and he dismisses Homer blandly, after having crowned him and pouring unguent upon him, in order that indeed he should not destroy by his myths, the orthodox belief in respecting one God." [Isis Unveiled, i. 287, 288.]

And this is the "God" of every Philosopher, God infinite and impersonal. All this and much more, which there is no room here to quote, leads one to the undeniable certitude that (a) as all the Sciences and Philosophies were in the hands of the temple Hierophants, Plato, as initiated by them, must have known them; and (b), that logical inference alone is amply sufficient to justify anyone in regarding Plato's writings as allegories and "dark sayings," veiling truths which he had no right to divulge.

This established, how comes it that one of the best Greek scholars in England, Prof. Jowett, the modern translator of Plato's works, seeks to demonstrate that none of the Dialogues - including even the Timaeus - have any element of Oriental Mysticism about them? Those who can discern the true spirit of Plato's Philosophy will hardly be convinced by the arguments which the Master of Balliol College lays before his readers. "Obscure and repulsive" to him, the Timaeus may certainly be; but it is as certain that this obscurity does not arise, as the Professor tells his public, "in the infancy of physical science," but rather in its days of secresy; not "out of the confusion of theological, mathematical, and physiological notions," or "out of the desire to conceive the whole of Nature without any adequate knowledge of the parts."

[The Dialogues of Plato, translated by B.Jowett. Regius Professor of Greek at the University of Oxford, 111 5z3.] For Mathematics and Geometry were the backbone of Occult cosmogony, hence of "Theology," and the physiological notions of the ancient Sages are being daily verified by Science in our age; at least, to those who know to read and understand ancient Esoteric works. The "knowledge of the parts" avails us little, if this knowledge only leads us the more to ignorance of the Whole, or the "nature and the reason of the Universal," as Plato called Deity, and causes us to blunder most egregiously because of our boasted inductive methods.

Plato may have been "incapable of induction, or generalization in the modern sense"; [Op. cit., p.561] he may have been ignorant also, of the circulation of the blood, which, we are told, "was absolutely unknown to him," [Op. cit., p.591] but then, there is naught to disprove that he knew what blood is - and this is more than any Physiologist or Biologist can claim nowadays.

Though a wider and far more generous margin for knowledge is allowed the "physical philosopher" by Prof. Jowett than by nearly any other modern commentator and critic, nevertheless, his criticism so considerably outweighs his laudation, that it may be as well to quote his own words, to show clearly his bias. Thus he says:

To bring sense under the control of reason; to find some way through the labyrinth or chaos of appearances, either the highway of mathematics, or more devious paths suggested by the analogy of man with the world and of the world with man; to see that all things have a cause and are tending towards an end - this is the spirit of the ancient physical philosopher. [This definition places (unwittingly, of course), the ancient "physical philosopher" many cubits higher than his modern "physical" confrère, since the ultima thule of the latter is to lead mankind to believe that neither universe nor man have any cause at all - not an intelligent one at all events - and that they have sprung into existence owing to blind chance and a senseless whirling of atoms. Which of the two hypotheses is the more rational and logical is left to the impartial reader to decide.] But we neither appreciate the conditions of knowledge to which he was subjected, nor have the ideas which fastened upon his imagination the same hold upon us. For he is hovering between matter and mind; he is under the dominion of abstractions; his impressions are taken almost at random from the outside of nature; he sees the light, but not the objects which are revealed by the light; and he brings into juxtaposition things which to us appear wide as the poles asunder, because he finds nothing between them.

The last proposition but one must evidently be distasteful to the modern "physical philosopher," who sees the "objects" before him, but fails to see the light of the Universal Mind, which reveals them, i.e., who proceeds in a diametrically opposite way. Therefore the learned Professor comes to the conclusion that the ancient Philosopher, whom he now judges from Plato's Timaeus, must have acted in a decidedly unphilosophical and even irrational way. For:

He passes abruptly from persons to ideas and numbers, and from ideas and numbers to persons; [Italics are mine. Every tyro in Eastern Philosophy, every Kabalist, will see the reason for such an association of persons with ideas, numbers, and geometrical figures. For number, says Philolaus, "is the dominant and self-produced bond of the eternal continuance of things." Alone the modern scholar remains blind to the grand truth] he confuses subject and object, first and final causes, and in dreaming of geometrical figures is lost in a flux of sense.

SELF-CONTRADICTION OF THE CRITIC –

[Here again the ancient Philosopher seems to be ahead of the modern. For he only "confuses . . . first and final causes" (which confusion is denied by those who know the spirit of the ancient scholarship), whereas his modern successor is confessedly and absolutely ignorant of both. Mr. Tyndall shows Science "powerless" to solve a single one of the final problems of Nature and "disciplined [read, modern materialistic], imagination retiring in bewilderment from the contemplation of the problems " of the world of matter. He even doubts whether the men of present Science possess "the intellectual elements which would enable them to grapple with the ultimate structural energies of Nature." But for Plato and his disciples, the lower types were but the concrete images of the higher abstract ones: the higher abstract ones: the immortal Soul has an arithmetical, as the body has a geometrical beginning. This beginning, as the reflection of the great universal archaeus (Anima Mundi), is self-moving, and from the centre diffuses itself over the whole body of the Macrocosm.] And now an effort of mind is required on our parts in order to understand his double language, or to apprehend the twilight character of the knowledge and the genius of ancient philosophers which, under such conditions [?], seems by a divine power in many instances to have anticipated the truth. [Op. cit., page 523.]

Whether "such conditions" imply those of ignorance and mental stolidity in "the genius of ancient philosophers" or something else, we do not know. But what we do know is that the meaning of the sentences we have italicized is perfectly clear. Whether the Regius Professor of Greek believes or disbelieves in a hidden sense of geometrical figures and of the Esoteric "jargon," he nevertheless admits the presence of a "double language" in the writings of these Philosophers. Thence he admits a hidden meaning, which must have had an interpretation. Why, then, does he flatly contradict his own statement on the very next page? And why should he deny to the Timaeus - that preëminently Pythagorean (mystic) Dialogue - any Occult meaning and take such pains to convince his readers that

The influence which the Timaeus has exercised upon posterity is partly due to a misunderstanding.

The following quotation from his Introduction is in direct contradiction with the paragraph which precedes it, as above quoted:

In the supposed depths of this dialogue the Neo-Platonists found hidden meanings and connections with the Jewish and Christian Scriptures, and out of them they dictated doctrines quite at variance with the spirit of Plato. Believing that he was inspired by the Holy Ghost, or had received his wisdom from Moses, [Nowhere are the Neoplatonists guilty of such an absurdity. The learned Professor of Greek must have been thinking of two spurious works attributed by Eusebius and St. Jerome to Ammonius Saccas, who wrote nothing: or must have confused the Neoplatonists with Philo Judaeus. But then Philo lived over 130 years before the birth of the founder of Neoplatonism. He belonged to the School of Aristobulus the Jew, who lived under Ptolemy Philometer (150 years B.C), and is credited with having inaugurated the movement which tended to prove that Plato and even the Peripatetic Philosophy were derived from the "revealed" Mosaic Books. Valckenaer tries to show that the author of the Commentaries on the Books of Moses, was not Aristobulus, the sycophant of Ptolemy. But whatever he was, he was not a Neoplatonist, but lived before, or during the days of Philo Judaeus - since the latter seems to know his works and follow his methods.] they seemed to find in his writings the Christian Trinity, the Word, the Church . . . and the Neo-Platonists had a method of interpretation which could elicit any meaning out of any words. They were really incapable of distinguishing between the opinions of one philosopher and another, or between the serious thoughts of Plato and his passing fancies. [Only Clemens Alexandrinus, a Christian Neoplatonist and a very fantastic writer.] . . . [But] there is no danger of the modern commentators on the Timaeus falling into the absurdity of the Neo-Platonists.

No danger whatever of course, for the simple reason that the modern commentators have never had the key to Occult interpretations. And before another word is said in defence of Plato and the Neoplatonists, the learned master of Balliol College ought to be respectfully asked: What does, or can he know of the Esoteric canon of interpretation? By the term "canon" is here meant that key which was communicated orally from "mouth to ear" by the Master to the disciple, or by the Hierophant to the candidate for initiation; this from time immemorial throughout a long series of ages, during which the inner - not public - Mysteries were the most sacred institution of every land. Without such a key no correct interpretation of either the Dialogues of Plato nor of any Scripture, from the Vedas to Homer, from the Zend Avesta to the Mosaic Books, is possible. How then can the Rev. Dr. Jowett know that the interpretations made by the Neoplatonists of the various sacred books of the nations were "absurdities"? Where, again, has he found an opportunity of studying these "interpretations"? History shows that all such works were destroyed by the Christian Church Fathers and their fanatical catechumens, wherever they were found. To say that such men as Ammonius, a genius and a saint, whose learning and holy life earned for him the title of Theodidaktos ("God-taught"), such men as Plotinus, Porphyry, and Proclus, were "incapable of distinguishing between the opinions of one philosopher and another, or between the serious thoughts of Plato and his fancies, " is to assume an untenable position for a Scholar. It amounts to saying that, (a) scores of the most famous Philosophers, the greatest Scholars and Sages of Greece and of the Roman Empire were dull fools, and (b) that all the other commentators, lovers of Greek Philosophy, some of them the acutest intellects of the age - who do not agree with Dr. Jowett - are also fools and no better than those whom they admire. The patronising tone of the last above-quoted passage is modulated with the most naive conceit, remarkable even in our age of self-glorification and mutual admiration cliques.

THE CHARACTER OF AMMONIUS SACCAS –

We have to compare the Professor's views with those of some other scholars.

Says Prof. Alexander Wilder of New York, one of the best Platonists of the day, speaking of Ammonius, the founder of the Neoplatonic School:

His deep spiritual intuition, his extensive learning, his familiarity with the Christian Fathers, Pantaenus, Clement, and Athenagoras, and with the most erudite philosophers of the time, all fitted him for the labour which he performed so thoroughly. [The labour of reconciling the different systems of religion.] He was successful in drawing to his views the greatest scholars and public men of the Roman Empire, who had little taste for wasting time in dialectic pursuits or superstitious observances. The results of his ministration are perceptible at the present day in every country of the Christian world; every prominent system of doctrine now bearing the marks of his plastic hand. Every ancient philosophy has had its votaries among the moderns; and even Judaism . . . has taken upon itself changes which were suggested by the "God-taught" Alexandrian . . . He was a man of rare learning and endowments, of blameless life and amiable disposition. His almost superhuman ken and many excellencies won for him the title of Theodidaktos; but he followed the modest example of Pythagoras, and only assumed the title of Philalethian, or lover of truth. [New Platonism and Alchemy, by Alex. Wilder, M.D. pp. 7.4.]

It would be happy for truth and fact were our modern scholars to follow as modestly in the steps of their great predecessors. But not they - Philalethians!

Moreover, we know that:

Like Orpheus, Pythagoras, Confucius, Socrates, and Jesus himself, [It is well-known that, though born of Christian parents, Ammonius had renounced the tenets of the Church - Eusebius and Jerome notwithstanding. Porphyry, the disciple of Plotinus, who had lived with Ammonius for eleven years together, and who had no interest in stating an untruth, positively declares that he had renounced Christianity entirely. On the other hand, we know that Ammonius believed in the bright Gods, Protectors, and that the Neoplatonic Philosophy was as "pagan" as it was mystical. But Eusebius, the most unscrupulous forger and falsifier of old texts, and St. Jerome, an out-and-out fanatic, who had both an interest in denying the fact, contradict Porphyry. We prefer to believe the latter, who has left to posterity an unblemished name and a great reputation for honesty.] Ammonius committed nothing to writing. [Two works are falsely attributed to Ammonius. One, now lost, called De Consensu Moysis et Jesu, is mentioned by the same "trustworthy" Eusebius, the Bishop of Caesaraea, and the friend of the Christian Emperor Constantine, who died, however, a heathen. All that is known of this pseudo-work is that Jerome bestows great praise upon it (Vir. Illust.,55: and Euseb., H.E.., vi.19). The other spurious production is called the Diatesseron (or the "Harmony of the Gospels"). This is partially extant. But then, again, it exists only in the Latin version of Victor, Bishop of Capua (sixth century), who attributed it himself to Tatian, and as wrongly, probably, as later scholars attributed the Diatesseron to Ammonius. Therefore no great reliance can be placed upon it, nor on its "esoteric" interpretation of the Gospels. Is it this work, we wonder, which led Prof. Jowett to regard the Neoplatonic interpretations as "absurdities"?] Instead he . . . communicated his most important doctrines to persons duly instructed and disciplined, imposing on them the obligations of secresy, as was done before him by Zoroaster and Pythagoras, and in the Mysteries. Except a few treatises of his disciples we have only the declarations of his adversaries from which to ascertain what he actually taught.[Op. cit., p.7.]

It is from the biased statements of such "adversaries." probably, that the learned Oxford translator of Plato's Dialogues came to the conclusion that:

That which was truly great and truly characteristic of him [Plato], his effort to realise and connect abstractions, was not understood by them [the Neoplatonists] at all [?].

He states, contemptuously enough for the ancient methods of intellectual analysis, that:

In the present day . . . an ancient philosopher is to be interpreted from himself and by the contemporary history of thought. [Op. cit., iii 524.]

This is like saying that the ancient Greek canon of proportion (if ever found), and the Athena Promachus of Phidias, have to be interpreted in the present day from the contemporary history of architecture and sculpture, from the Albert Hall and Memorial Monument, and the hideous

Madonnas in crinolines sprinkled over the fair face of Italy. Prof. Jowett remarks that "mysticism is not criticism." No; but neither is criticism always fair and sound judgement.

La critique est aisée, mais l'art est difficile.

And such "art" our critic of the Neoplatonists - his Greek scholarship notwithstanding - lacks from a to z. Nor has he, very evidently, the key to the true spirit of the Mysticism of Pythagoras and Plato, since he denies even in the Timaeus an element of Oriental Mysticism, and seeks to show Greek Philosophy reacting upon the East, forgetting that the truth is the exact reverse; that it is "the deeper and more pervading spirit of Orientalism" that had - through Pythagoras and his own initiation into the Mysteries - penetrated into the very depths of Plato's soul.

But Dr. Jowett does not see this. Nor is he prepared to admit that anything good or rational - in accordance with the "contemporary history of thought" - could ever come out of that Nazareth of the Pagan Mysteries; nor even that there is anything to interpret of a hidden nature in the Timaeus or any other Dialogue. For him,

The so-called mysticism of Plato is purely Greek, arising out of his imperfect knowledge ["Imperfect knowledge" of what? That Plato was ignorant of many of the modern 'working hypotheses" - as ignorant as our immediate posterity is sure to be of the said hypotheses when they in their turn after exploding join the "great majority" - is perhaps a blessing in disguise.] and high aspirations, and is the growth of an age in which philosophy is not wholly separated from poetry and mythology.[Op.cit., p.524.]

PLATO A FOLLOWER OF PYTHAGORAS –

Among several other equally erroneous propositions, it is especially the assumptions (a) that Plato was entirely free from any element of Eastern Philosophy in his writings, and (b) that every modern scholar, without being a Mystic and a Kabalist himself, can pretend to judge of ancient Esotericism - which we mean to combat. To do this we have to produce more authoritative statements than our own would be, and bring the evidence of other scholars as great as Dr. Jowett, if not greater, specialists in their subjects, moreover, to bear on and destroy the arguments of the Oxford Regius Professor of Greek.

That Plato was undeniably an ardent admirer and follower of Pythagoras no one will deny. And it is equally undeniable, as Matter has it, that Plato had inherited on the one hand his doctrines, and on the other had drawn his wisdom, from the same sources as the Samian Philosopher. [l'Histoire Critique du Gnosticisme, by M.J. Matter, Professor of the Royal Academy of Strasburg. "It is in Pythagoras and Plato that we find, in Greece, the first elements of [Oriental] Gnosticism." he says. (Vol.i. pp.48 and 50.)] And the doctrines of Pythagoras are Oriental to the backbone, and even Brâhmanical; for this great Philosopher ever pointed to the far East as the source whence he derived his information and his Philosophy, and Colebrooke shows that Plato makes the same profession in his Epistles, and says that he has taken his teachings "from ancient and sacred doctrines." [Asiat. Trans.,i. 579.]

Furthermore, the ideas of both Pythagoras and Plato coincide too well with the systems of India and with Zoroastrianism to admit any doubt of their origin by anyone who has some acquaintance with these systems. Again:

Pantaenus, Athenagoras, and Clement were thoroughly instructed in the Platonic philosophy, and comprehended its essential unity with the Oriental systems. [New Platonism and Alchemy. p.4.]

The history of Pantaenus and his contemporaries may give the key to the Platonic, and at the same time Oriental, elements that predominate so strikingly in the Gospels over the Jewish Scriptures.

SECTION I
PRELIMINARY SURVEY

INITIATES who have acquired powers and transcendental knowledge can be traced back to the Fourth Root Race from our own age. As the multiplicity of the subjects to be dealt with prohibits the introduction of such a historical chapter, which, however historical in fact and truth, would be rejected a priori as blasphemy and fable by both Church and Science - we shall only touch on the subject.

Science strikes out, at its own sweet will and fancy, dozens of names of ancient heroes, simply because there is too great an element of myth in their histories; the Church insists that biblical patriarchs shall be regarded as historical personages, and terms her seven "Star-angels" the "historical channels and agents of the Creator." Both are right, since each finds a strong party to side with it. Mankind is at best a sorry herd of Panurgian sheep, following blindly the leader that happens to suit it at the moment. Mankind - the majority at any rate - hates to think for itself. It resents as an insult the humblest invitation to step for a moment outside the old well-beaten tracks, and, judging for itself, to enter into a new path in some fresh direction. Give it an unfamiliar problem to solve, and if its mathematicians, not liking its looks, refuse to deal with it, the crowd, unfamiliar with mathematics, will stare at the unknown quantity, and getting hopelessly entangled in sundry x's and y's, will turn round, trying to rend to pieces the uninvited disturber of its intellectual Nirvana. This may, perhaps, account for the ease and extraordinary success enjoyed by the Roman Church in her conversions of nominal Protestants and Free-thinkers, whose name is legion, but who have never gone to the trouble of thinking for themselves on these most important and tremendous problems of man's inner nature.

And yet, if the evidence of facts, the records preserved in History, and the uninterrupted anathemas of the Church against, "Black Magic" and Magicians of the accursed race of Cain, are not to be heeded, our efforts will prove very puny indeed. When, for nearly two millenniums a body of men has never ceased to lift its voice against Black Magic, the inference ought to be irrefutable that if Black Magic exists as a real fact, there must be somewhere its counterpart - White Magic.

THE PROTECTORS OF CHINA -

False silver coins could have no existence if there were no genuine silver money. Nature is dual in whatever she attempts, and this ecclesiastical persecution ought alone to have opened the eyes of the public long ago. However much travellers may be ready to pervert every fact with regard to abnormal powers with which certain men are gifted in "heathen" countries; however eager they may be to put false constructions on such facts, and - to use an old proverb - "to call white swan black goose," and to kill it, yet the evidence of even Roman Catholic missionaries ought to be taken into consideration, once they swear in a body to certain facts. Nor is it because they choose to see Satanic agency in manifestations of a certain kind, that their evidence as to the existence of such powers can be disregarded. For what do they say of China? Those missionaries who have lived in the country for long years, and have seriously studied every fact and belief that may prove an obstacle to their success in making conversions, and who have become familiar with every exoteric rite of both the official religion and sectarian creeds - all swear to the existence of a certain body of men, whom no one can reach but the Emperor and a select body of high officials. A few years ago, before the war in Tonkin, the archbishop in Pekin, on the report of some hundreds of missionaries and Christians, wrote to Rome the identical story that had been reported twenty-five years before, and had been widely circulated in clerical papers. They had fathomed, it was said, the mystery of certain official deputations, sent at times of danger by the Emperor and ruling powers to their Sheu and Kiuay, as they are called among the people. These Sheu and Kiuay, they explained, were the Genii of the mountains, endowed with the most miraculous powers. They are regarded as the protectors of China, by the "ignorant" masses; as the incarnation of Satanic power by the good and "learned" missionaries.

The Sheu and Kiuay are men belonging to another state of being to that of the ordinary man, or to the state they enjoyed while they were clad in their bodies. They are disembodied spirits, ghosts and larvae, living, nevertheless, in objective form on earth, and dwelling in the fastnesses of mountains, inaccessible to all but those whom they permit to visit them. [This fact and others may be found in Chinese Missionary

Reports, and in a work by Monseigneur Delaplace, a Bishop in China. "Annales de la Propagation de la Foi".]

In Tibet certain ascetics are also called Lha, Spirits, by those with whom they do not choose to communicate. The Sheu and Kiuay, who enjoy the highest consideration of the Emperor and Philosophers, and of Confucianists who believe in no "Spirits," are simply Lohans - Adepts who live in the greatest solitude in their unknown retreats.

But both Chinese exclusiveness and Nature seem to have allied themselves against European curiosity and - as it is sincerely regarded in Tibet - desecration. Marco Polo, the famous traveller, was perhaps the European who ventured farthest into the interior of these countries. What was said of him in 1876 may now be repeated.

The district of the Gobi wilderness, and, in fact, the whole area of Independent Tartary and Tibet is carefully guarded against foreign intrusion. Those who are permitted to traverse it are under the particular care and pilotage of certain agents of the chief authority, and are in duty bound to convey no intelligence respecting places and persons to the outside world. But for this restriction, many might contribute to these pages accounts of exploration, adventure, and discovery that would be read with interest. The time will come, sooner or later, when the dreadful sand of the desert will yield up its long-buried secrets, and then there will indeed be unlooked-for mortifications for our modern vanity.

"The people of Pashai," [The regions somewhere about Udyana and Kashmir, as the translator and editor of Marco Polo (Colonel Yule) believes (i.x75).] says Marco Polo, the daring traveller of the thirteenth century, "are great adepts in sorceries and the diabolic arts." And his learned editor adds: "This Paschai, or Udyana, was the native country of Padma Sambhava, one of the chief apostles of Lamaism, i.e., of Tibetan Buddhism, and a great master of enchantments. The doctrines of Sakya, as they prevailed in Udyana in old times, were probably strongly tinged with Sivaitic magic, and the Tibetans still regard the locality as the classic ground of sorcery and witchcraft."

The "old times" are just like the "modern times"; nothing is changed as to magical practices except that they have become still more esoteric and arcane, and that the caution of the adepts increases in proportion to the traveller's curiosity. Hiouen-Thsang says of the inhabitants: "The men . . . are fond of study, but pursue it with no ardour. The science of magical formulae has become a regular professional business with them." [Voyage des Pèlerins Bouddhistes. Vol.1.. Histoire de la Vie de Hiouen-Thsang, etc., traduit du chinois en francais, par Stanislas Julien.] We will not contract the venerable Chinese pilgrim on this point, and are willing to admit that in the seventh century some people made "a professional business: of magic, so, also, do some people now, but certainly not the true adepts. Moreoever, in that century, Buddhism had hardly penetrated into Tibet, and its races were steeped in the sorceries of the Bhon, - the pre-lamaic religion. It is not Hiouen-Thsang, the pious, courageous man who risked his life a hundred times to have the bliss of perceiving Buddh's shadow in the cave of Peshwur, who would have accused the good lamas and monkish thaumaturgists of "making a professional business" of showing it to travellers.

THE A B C OF MAGIC -

The injunction of Gautama, contained in his answer to King Prasenajit, his protector, who called on him to perform miracles, must have been ever-present to the mind of Hiouen-Thsang. "Great king," said Gautama, "I do not teach the law to my pupils, telling them, 'Go, ye saints, and before the eyes of the Brahmans and householders perform, by means of your supernatural powers, miracles greater than any man can perform.' I tell them when I teach them the law, 'Live ye saints, hiding your good works, and showing your sins.' "

Struck with the accounts of magical exhibitions witnessed and recorded by travellers of every age who had visited Tartary and Tibet, Colonel Yule comes to the conclusion that the natives must have had "at their command the whole encyclopaedia of modern Spiritualists." Duhalde mentions among their sorceries the art of producing by their invocations the figures of Laotseu [Lao-tse the Chinese philosopher.] and their divinities in the air, and of making a pencil write answers to questions without anybody touching it." [The Book of Ser Marco Polo, i.3x8.]

The former invocations pertain to the religious mysteries of their sanctuaries; if done otherwise, or for the sake of gain, they are considered sorcery, necromancy, and strictly forbidden. The latter art, that of making a pencil write without contact, was known and practised in China and other countries before the Christian era. It is the A B C of magic in those countries.

When Hiouen-Thsang desired to adore the shadow of Buddha, it was not to "professional magicians" that he resorted, but to the power of his own soul-invocation; the power of prayer, faith, and contemplation. All was dark and dreary near the cavern in which the miracle was alleged to sometimes take place. Hiouen-Thsang entered and began his devotions. He made one hundred salutations, but neither saw nor heard anything. Then, thinking himself too sinful, he cried bitterly and despaired. But as he was about to give up all hope, he perceived on the eastern wall a feeble light, but it disappeared. He renewed his prayers, full of hope this time, and again he saw the light, which flashed and disappeared again. After this he made a solemn vow: he would not leave the cave till he had the rapture to at last see the shadow of the "Venerable of the Age." He had to wait longer after this, for only after two hundred prayers was the dark cave suddenly "bathed in light, and the shadow of Buddha, of a brilliant white colour, rose majestically on the wall, as when the clouds suddenly open, and all at once display the marvellous image of the 'Mountain of Light.' A dazzling splendour lighted up the features of the divine countenance. Hiouen-Thsang was lost in contemplation and wonder, and would not turn his eyes away from the sublime and incomparable object." Hiouen-Thsang adds in his own diary, See-yu-kee, that it is only when man prays with sincere faith, and if he has received from above a hidden impression, that he sees the shadow clearly, but he cannot enjoy the sight for any length of time (Max Muller, Buddhist Pilgrims.)

From one end to the other the country is full of mystics, religious philosophers, Buddhist saints and magicians. Belief in a spiritual world, full of invisible beings who, on certain occasions, appear to mortals objectively, is universal. "According to the belief of the nations of Central Asia," remarks I. J. Schmidt, "the earth and its interior, as well as the encompassing atmosphere, are filled with spiritual beings, which exercise an influence, partly beneficent, partly malignant, on the whole of organic and inorganic nature. . . . Especially are deserts and other wild and uninhabited tracts, or regions in which the influences of nature are displayed on a gigantic and terrible scale, regarded as the chief abode or rendez-vous of evil spirits. And hence the steppes of Turan, and in particular the great sand desert of the Gobi, have been looked on as the dwelling place of malignant beings, from the days of hoary antiquity."

The treasures exhumed by Dr. Schliemann at Mycenae, have awakened popular cupidity, and the eyes of adventurous speculators are being turned toward the localities where the wealth of ancient peoples is supposed to be buried, in crypt or cave, or beneath sand or alluvial deposit. Around no other locality, not even Peru, hang so many traditions as around the Gobi Desert. In independent Tartary this howling waste of shifting sand was once, if report speaks correctly, the seat of one of the richest empires the world ever saw. Beneath the surface is said to lie such wealth in gold, jewels, statuary, arms, utensils, and all that indicates civilization, luxury, and fine arts, as no existing capital of Christendom can show today. The Gobi sand moves regularly from east to west before terrific gales that blow continually. Occasionally some of the hidden treasures are uncovered, but not a native dare touch them, for the whole district is under the ban of a mighty spell. Death would be the penalty. Bahti -hideous, but faithful gnomes - guard the hidden treasures of this prehistoric people, awaiting the day when the revolution of cyclic periods shall again cause their story to be known for the instruction of mankind.[Isis Unveiled, i. 599-601, 603, 598.]

The above is purposely quoted from Isis Unveiled to refresh the reader's memory. One of the cyclic periods has just been passed and we may not have to wait to the end of Maha Kalpa to have revealed something of the history of the mysterious desert, in spite of the Bahti, and even the Rakshasas of India, not less "hideous." No tales or fictions were given in our earlier volumes, their chaotic state notwithstanding, to which chaos the writer, entirely free from vanity, confesses publicly and with many apologies.

It is now generally admitted that, from time immemorial, the distant East, India especially, was the land of knowledge and of every kind of learning. Yet there is none to whom the origin of all her Arts and Sciences has been so much denied as to the land of the primitive Aryas. From Architecture down to the Zodiac, every Science worthy of the name was imported by the Greeks, the mysterious Yavanas - agreeably with the decision of the Orientalists! Therefore, it is but logical that even the knowledge of Occult Science should be refused to India, since of its general practice in that country less is known than in the case of any other ancient people.

MAGIC AS OLD AS MAN –

It is so, simply because:

With the Hindus it was, and is, more esoteric, if possible, than it was even among the Egyptian priests. So sacred was it deemed that its existence was only half admitted, and it was only practised in public emergencies. It was more than a religious matter, for it was [and is still] considered divine. The Egyptian hierophants, notwithstanding the practice of a stern and pure morality, could not be compared for one moment with the ascetical Gymnosophists, either in holiness of life or miraculous powers developed in them by the supernatural abjuration of everything earthly. By those who knew them well they were held in still greater reverence than the magians of Chaldaea. "Denying themselves the simplest comforts of life, they dwelt in woods, and led the life of the most secluded hermits," [Ammianus Marcellinus, xxiii.6.] while their Egyptian brothers at least congregated together. Notwithstanding the slur thrown on all who practised magic and divination, history has proclaimed them as possessing the greatest secrets in medical knowledge and unsurpassed skill in its practice. Numerous are the volumes preserved in Hindu Mathams, in which are recorded the proofs of their learning. To attempt to say whether these Gymnosophists were the real founders of magic in India, or whether they only practised what has passed to them as an inheritance from the earliest Rishis [The Rishis - the first group of seven in number lived in days preceding the Vedic period. They are now known as Sages and held in reverence like demigods. But they may now be shown as something more than merely mortal Philosophers.

There are other groups of ten, twelve and even twenty-one in number. Haug shows that they occupy in the Brahmanical religion a position answering to that of the twelve sons of Jacob in the Jewish Bible The Brahmans claim to descend directly from the Rishis.] - the seven primeval sages - would be regarded as mere speculation by exact scholars.[Isis Unveiled, i. 90.]

Nevertheless, this must be attempted. In Isis Unveiled, all that could be stated about Magic was set down in the guise of hints; and thus, owing to the great amount of material scattered over two large volumes, much of its importance was lost upon the reader, while it still more failed to draw his attention on account of the faulty arrangement. But hints may now grow into explanations. One can never repeat it too often - Magic is as old as man. It cannot any longer be called charlantry or hallucination, when its lesser branches - such as mesmerism, now miscalled "hypnotism," "thought reading," "action by suggestion," and what not else, only to avoid calling it by its right and legitimate name - are being so seriously investigated by the most famous Biologists and Physiologists of both Europe and America. Magic is indissolubly blended with Religion of every country and is inseparable from its origin. It is as impossible for History to name the time when it was not, as that of the epoch when it sprang into existence, unless the doctrines preserved by the Initiates are taken into consideration. Nor can Science ever solve the problem of the origin of man if it rejects the evidence of the oldest records in the world, and refuses from the hand of the legitimate Guardians of the mysteries of Nature the

key to Universal Symbology. Whenever a writer has tried to
connect the first foundation of Magic with a particular country
or some historical event or character, further research has
shown his hypothesis to be groundless. There is a most
lamentable contradiction among the Symbologists on this
point. Some would have it that Odin, the Scandinavian priest
and monarch, originated the practice of Magic some 70 years
B.C.. although it is spoken of repeatedly in the Bible. But as it
was proven that the mysterious rites of the priestesses Valas
(Voilers) were greatly anterior to Odin's age, [See Munter
"On the most Ancient Religions of the North before Odin.'
Mémoires de la Société des Antiquaires de France. ii. 230.]
then Zoroaster came in for an attempt on the ground that he
was the founder of Magian rites; but Ammianus Marcellinus,
Pliny and Arnobius, with other ancient Historians, have shown
that Zoroaster was but a reformer of Magic as practised by
the Chaldaeans and Egyptians, and not at all its founder. [
Ammianus Marcellinus, xxvi.6.]

Who, then, of those who have consistently turned their
faces away from Occultism and even Spiritualism, as being
"unphilosophical" and therefore unworthy of scientific thought,
has a right to say that he has studied the ancients; or that, if
he has studied them, he has understood all they have said?
Only those who claim to be wiser than their generation, who
think that they know all that the Ancients knew, and thus,
knowing far more today, fancy that they are entitled to laugh
at their ancient simple-mindedness and superstition; those,
who imagine they have discovered a great secret by declaring
the ancient royal sarcophagus, now empty of its King Initiate,

to be a "corn-bin," and the Pyramid that contained it, a granary, perhaps a wine-cellar! ["The date of the hundreds of pyramids in the Valley of the Nile is impossible to fix by any of the rules of modern science: Herodotus informs us that each successive king erected one to commemorate his reign, and serve as his sepulchre. But Herodotus did not tell all, although he knew that the real purpose of the pyramid was very different from that which he assigns to it. Were it not for his religious scruples, he might have added that, externally, it symbolized the creative principle of Nature, and illustrated also the principles of geometry, mathematics, astrology and astronomy.]

THE TREE OF KNOWLEDGE -

Modern society, on the authority of some men of Science, calls Magic charlatantry. But there are eight hundred millions on the face of the globe who believe in it to this day; there are said to be twenty millions of perfectly sane and often very intelligent men and woman, members of that same society, who believe in its phenomena under the name of Spiritualism. The whole ancient world, with its Scholars and Philosophers, its Sages and Prophets, believed in it. Where is the country in which it was not practised? At what age was it banished, even from our own country? In the New World as in the Old Country (the latter far younger than the former), the Science of Sciences was known and practised from the remotest antiquity. The Mexicans had their Initiates, their Priest-Hierophants and Magicians, and their crypts of

Initiation. Of the two statues exhumed in the Pacific States, one represents a Mexican Adept, in the posture prescribed for the Hindu ascetic, and the other an Aztec Priestess, in a head-gear which might be taken from the head of an Indian Goddess; while the "Guatemalan Medal" exhibits the "Tree of Knowledge" - with its hundreds of eyes and ears, symbolical of seeing and hearing - encircled by the "Serpent of Wisdom" whispering into the ear of the sacred bird.) Bernard Diaz de Castilla, a follower of Cortez, gives some idea of the extraordinary refinement, intelligence and civilization, and also of the magic arts of the people whom the Spaniards conquered by brute force. Their pyramid are those of Egypt, built according to the same secret canon of proportion as those of the Pharaohs, and the Aztecs appear to have derived their civilization and religion in more than one way from the same source as the Egyptians and, before these, the Indians. Among all these three peoples arcane Natural Philosophy, or Magic, was cultivated to the highest degree.

That it was natural, not supernatural, and that the Ancients so regarded it, is shown by what Lucian says of the "laughing Philosopher," Democritus, who, he tells his readers,

Believed in no [miracles] . . . but applied himself to discover the method by which the theurgists could produce them; in a word, his philosophy brought him to the conclusion that magic was entirely confined to the application and the imitation of the laws and the works of nature.

[Internally, it was a majestic fane, in whose sombre recesses were performed the Mysteries, and whose walls had often witnessed the initiation scenes of members of the royal family. The porphyry sarcophagus, which Professor Piazzi Smith, Astronomer Royal of Scotland, degrades into a corn-bin, was the baptismal font, upon emerging from which, the neophyte was 'born again,' and became an adept.' (Isis Unveiled. i. 518, 519.)]

Who then can still call the Magic of the Ancients "superstition"?

In this respect the opinion of Democritus is of the greatest importance to us, since the Magi left by Xerxes, at Abdera, were his instructors, and he had studied magic, moreover, for a considerable time with the Egyptian priests. [Diog. Laert., in "Democrit. Vit."] For nearly ninety years of the one hundred and nine of his life, this great philosopher had made experiments, and noted them down in a book, which, according to Petronius, [Satyric, ix. 3.] treated of nature - facts that he had verified himself. And we find him not only disbelieving in and utterly rejecting miracles, but asserting that every one of those that were authenticated by eye-witnesses, had, and could have taken place, for all, even the most incredible, were produced according to the "hidden laws of nature." [Pliny, Hist. Nat.]. . . Add to this that Greece, the "later cradle of the arts and sciences," and India, cradle of religions, were, and one of them still is, devoted to its study and practice - and who shall venture to discredit its dignity as a study, and its profundity as a science? [Isis Unveiled, I. 512.]

No true Theosophist will ever do so. For, as a member of our great Oriental body, he knows indubitably that the Secret Doctrine of the East contains the Alpha and the Omega of Universal Science; that in its obscure texts, under the luxuriant, though perhaps too exuberant, growth of allegorical Symbolism, lie concealed the corner, and the key-stones of all ancient and modern knowledge. That Stone, brought down by the Divine Builder, is now rejected by the too-human workman, and this because, in his lethal materiality, man has lost every recollection, not only of his holy childhood, but of his very adolescence, when he was one of the Builders himself; when "the morning stars sang together, and the Sons of God shouted for joy." after they had laid the measures for the foundations of the earth - to use the deeply significant and poetical language of Job, the Arabian Initiate. But those who are still able to make room in their innermost selves for the Divine Ray, and who accept, therefore, the data of the Secret Sciences in good faith and humility, they know well that it is in this Stone that remains buried the absolute in Philosophy, which is the key to all those dark problems of Life and Death, some of which, at any rate, may find an explanation in these volumes.

The writer is vividly alive to the tremendous difficulties that present themselves in the handling of such abstruse questions, and to all the dangers of the task. Insulting as it is to human nature to brand truth with the name of imposture, nevertheless we see this done daily and accept it.

OCCULTISM MUST WIN THE DAY –

For every occult truth has to pass through such denial and its supporters through martyrdom, before it is finally accepted; though even then it remains but too often -
A crown

Golden in show, yet but a wreath of thorns.

Truths that rest on Occult Mysteries will have, for one reader who may appreciate them, a thousand who will brand them as impostures. This is only natural, and the only means to avoid it would be for an Occultist to pledge himself to the Pythagorean "vow of silence." and renew it every five years. Otherwise, cultured society - two-thirds of which think themselves in duty bound to believe that, since the first appearance of the first Adept, one half of mankind practised deception and fraud on the other half - cultured society will undeniably assert its hereditary and traditional right to stone the intruder. Those benevolent critics, who most readily promulgate the now famous axiom of Carlyle with regard to his countrymen, of being "mostly fools," having taken preliminary care to include themselves safely in the only fortunate exceptions to this rule, will in this work gain strength and derive additional conviction of the sad fact, that the human race is simply composed of knaves and congenital idiots. But this matters very little. The vindication of the Occultists and their Archaic Science is working itself slowly but steadily into the very heart of society, hourly, daily, and yearly, in the shape of two monster branches, two stray off-shoots of the trunk of Magic - Spiritualism and the Roman Church. Fact works its way very often through fiction. Like an immense boa-constrictor, Error, in every shape, encircles mankind, trying to smother in her deadly coils every aspiration towards truth and light. But Error is powerful only on the surface, prevented as she is by Occult Nature from going any deeper; for the same Occult Nature encircles the whole globe, in every direction, leaving not even the darkest corner unvisited. And, whether by phenomenon or miracle, by spirit-hook or bishop's crook, Occultism must win the day, before the present era reaches "Shani's (Saturn's) triple septenary" of the Western Cycle in Europe, in other words - before the end of the twenty-first century "A.D."

Truly the soil of the long by-gone past is not dead, for it has only rested. The skeletons of the sacred oaks of the ancient Druids may still send shoots from their dried-up boughs and be reborn to a new life, like that handful of corn, in the sarcophagus of a mummy 4.000 years old, which, when planted, sprouted, grew, and "gave a fine harvest." Why not? Truth is stranger than fiction. It may any day, and most unexpectedly, vindicate its wisdom and demonstrate the conceit of our age, by proving that the Secret Brotherhood did not, indeed, die out with the Philalethians of the last Eclectic School, that the Gnosis flourishes still on earth, and its votaries are many, albeit unknown. All this be done by one, or more, of the great Masters visiting Europe, and exposing in their turn the alleged exposers and traducers of Magic. Such secret Brotherhoods have been mentioned by several well-known authors, and are spoken of in Mackenzie's Royal Masonic Cyclopaedia. The writer now, in the face of the millions who deny, repeats boldly, that which was said in Isis Unveiled.

If they [the Initiates] have been regarded as mere fictions of the novelist, that fact has only helped the "brother-adepts" to keep their incognito the more easily. . . . The St. Germains and Cagliostros of this century, having learned bitter lessons from the vilifications and persecutions of the past, pursue different tactics now-a-days. [Op. cit., ii.403.]

These prophetic words were written in 1876, and verified in 1886. Nevertheless, we say again,

There are numbers of these mystic Brotherhoods which have naught to do with "civilized" countries; and it is in their unknown communities that are concealed the skeletons of the past. These "adepts" could, if they chose, lay claim to strange ancestry, and exhibit verifiable documents that would explain many a mysterious page in both sacred and profane history. [This is precisely what some of them are preparing to do, and many a "mysterious page" in sacred and profane history are touched on in these pages. Whether or not their explanations will be accepted - is another question.] Had the keys to the hieratic writings and the secret of Egyptian and Hindu symbolism been known to the Christian Fathers, they would not have allowed a single monument of old to stand unmutilated. [Ibid.]

But there exists in the world another class of adepts, belonging to a brotherhood also, and mightier than any other of those known to the profane. Many among these are personally good and benevolent, even pure and holy occasionally, as individuals. Pursuing collectively, however, and as a body, a selfish, one-sided object, with relentless vigour and determination, they have to be ranked with the adepts of the Black Art.

BLACK MAGIC AT WORK –

These are our modern Roman Catholic "fathers" and clergy. Most of the hieratic writings and symbols have been deciphered by them since the Middle Ages. A hundred times more learned in secret Symbology and the old Religions than our Orientalists will ever be, the personification of astuteness and cleverness, every such adept in the art holds the keys tightly in his firmly clenched hand, and will take care the secret shall not be easily divulged, if he can help it. There are more profoundly learned Kabalists in Rome and throughout Europe and America, than is generally suspected. Thus are the professedly public "brotherhoods" of "black" adepts more powerful and dangerous for Protestant countries than any host of Eastern Occultists. People laugh at Magic! Men of Science, Physiologists and Biologists, deride the potency and even the belief in the existence of what is called in vulgar parlance "Sorcery" and "Black Magic"? The Archaeologists have their Stonehenge in England with its thousands of secrets, and its twin-brother Karnac of Brittany, and yet there is not one of them who even suspects what has been going on in its crypts, and its mysterious nooks and corners, for the last century. More than that, they do not even know of the existence of such "magic halls" in their Stonehenge, where curious scenes are taking place, whenever there is a new convert in view. Hundreds of experiments have been, and are being made daily at the Salpetriere, and also by learned hypnotisers at their private houses. It is now proved that certain sensitives - both men and women - when commanded in trance, by the practitioner, who operates on them, to do a certain thing - from drinking a glass of water up to simulated murder - on recovering their normal state lose all remembrance of the order inspired - "suggested" it is now called by Science. Nevertheless, at the appointed hour and moment, the subject, though conscious and perfectly awake, is compelled by an irresistible power within himself to do that action which has been suggested to him by his mesmeriser; and that too, whatever it may be, and whatever the period fixed by him who controls the subject, that is to say, holds the latter under the power of his will, as a snake holds a bird under its fascination, and finally forces it to jump into its open jaws. Worse than this: for the bird is conscious of the peril; it resists, however helpless in its final efforts, while the hypnotized subject does not rebel, but seems to follow the suggestions and voice of its own free-will and soul. Who of our European men of Science, who believe in such scientific experiments - and very few are they who still doubt them now-a-days, and who do not feel convinced of their actual reality - who of them, it is asked, is ready to admit this as being Black Magic? Yet it is the genuine, undeniable and actual fascination and sorcery of old. The Mulu Kurumbas of Nilgiri do not proceed otherwise in their envoutements when they seek to destroy an enemy, nor do the Dugpas of Sikkim and Bhutan know of any more potential agent than their will. Only in them that will does not proceed by jumps and starts, but acts with certainty; it does not depend on the amount of receptivity or nervous impressibility of the "subjects." Having chosen his victim and placed himself en rapport with them, the Dugpa's "fluid" is sure to find its way, for his will is immeasurably more strongly developed than the will of the European experimenter - the self-made, untutored, and unconscious Sorcerer for the sake of Science - who has no idea (or belief either) of the variety and potency of the world-old methods used to develop this power, by the conscious sorcerer, the "Black Magician" of the East and West.

And now the question is openly and squarely asked: Why should not the fanatical and zealous priest, thirsting to convert some selected rich and influential member of society, use the same means to accomplish his end as the French Physician and experimenter uses in his case with his subject? The conscience of the Roman Catholic priest is most likely at peace. He works personally for no selfish purpose, but with the object of "saving a soul" from "eternal damnation." In his view, if Magic there be in it, it is holy, meritorious and divine Magic. Such is the power of blind faith.

Hence, when we are assured by trustworthy and respectable persons of high social standing, and unimpeachable character, that there are many well-organised societies among the Roman Catholic priests which, under the pretext and cover of Modern Spiritualism and mediumship, hold séances for the purposes of conversion by suggestion, directly and at a distance - we answer: We know it. And when, moreover, we are told that whenever those priest-hypnotists are desirous of acquiring an influence over some individual or individuals, selected by them for conversion, they retire to an underground place, allotted and consecrated by them for such purposes (viz., ceremonial Magic); and there, forming a circle, throw their combined will-power in the direction of that individual, and thus by repeating the process, gain a complete control over their victim - we again answer: Very likely.

BLACK MAGIC AND HYPNOTISM -

In fact we know the practice to be so, whether this kind of ceremonial Magic and envoûtement is practised at Stonehenge or elsewhere. We know it, we say, through personal experience; and also because several of the writer's best and most loved friends have been unconsciously drawn into the Romish Church and under her "benign" protection by such means. And, therefore, we can only laugh in pity at the ignorance and stubbornness of those deluded men of Science and cultured experimentalists who, while believing in the power of Dr. Charcot and his disciples to "envoûté" their subjects, find nothing better than a scornful smile whenever Black Magic and its potency are mentioned before them. Eliphas Levi, the Abbe-Kabalist, died before Science and the Faculté de Médecine of France had accepted hypnotism and influence par suggestion among its scientific experiments, but this is what he said twenty-five years go, in his Dogme et Rituel de la Haute Magie, on "Les Envoutements et les Sorts":

That which sorcerers and necromancers sought above all things in their evocations of the Spirit of Evil, was that magnetic potency which is the lawful property of the true Adept, and which they desired to obtain possession of for evil purposes. . . . One of their chief aims was the power of spells or of deleterious influences. . . . That power may be compared to real poisonings by a current of astral light. They exalt their will by means of ceremonies to the degree of rendering it venomous at a distance. . . .We have said in our "Dogma" what we thought of magic spells, and how this power was exceedingly real and dangerous. The true Magus throws a spell without ceremony and by his sole disapproval, upon those with whose conduct he is dissatisfied, and whom he thinks it necessary to punish; [This is incorrectly expressed. The true Adept of the "Right Hand" never punishes anyone, not even his bitterest and most dangerous enemy: he simply leaves the latter to his Karma, and Karma never fails to do so, sooner or later.] he casts a spell, even by his pardon, over those who do him injury, and the enemies of Initiates never long enjoy impunity for their wrong-doing. We have ourselves seen proofs of this fatal law in numerous instances. The executioners of martyrs always perish miserably; and the Adepts are the martyrs of intelligence. Providence [Karma] seems to despise those who despise them, and puts to death those who would seek to prevent them from living. The legend of the Wandering Jew is the popular poetry of this arcanum. A people had sent a sage to crucifixion; that people had bidden him "Move on!" when he tried to rest for one moment.... well! That people will become subject, henceforth, to a similar condemnation; it will become entirely proscribed, and for long centuries it will be hidden "Move on! move on!" finding neither rest nor pity.[Op. cit.,ii. 239. 241,240.]

"Fables," and "superstition," will be the answer. Be it so. Before the lethal breath of selfishness and indifference every uncomfortable fact is transformed into meaningless fiction, and every branch of the once verdant Tree of Truth has become dried up and stripped of its primeval spiritual significance. Our modern Symbologist is superlatively clever only at detecting phallic worship and sexual emblems even where none were ever meant. But for the true student of Occult Lore, White or Divine Magic could no more exist in Nature without its counterpart Black Magic, than day without night, whether these be of twelve hours or of six months duration. For him everything in that Nature has an occult - a bright and a night side to it. Pyramids and Druid's oaks, dolmens and Bo-trees, plant and mineral - everything was full of deep significance and of sacred truths of wisdom, when the Arch-Druid performed his magic cures and incantations, and the Egyptian Hierophant evoked and guided Chemnu, the "lovely spectre," the female Frankenstein-creation of old, raised for the torture and test of the soul-power of the candidate for initiation, simultaneously with the last agonising cry of his terrestrial human nature. True, Magic has lost its name, and along with it its rights to recognition. But its practice is in daily use; and its progeny, "magnetic influence," "power of oratory," "irresistible fascination," "whole audiences subdued and held as though under a spell," are terms recognised and used by all, generally meaningless though they now are. Its effects, however, are more determined and definite among religious congregations such as the Shakers, the Negro Methodists, and Salvationists, who call it "the action of the Holy Spirit" and "grace." The real truth is that Magic is still in full sway amidst mankind, however blind the latter to its silent presence and influence on its members, however ignorant society may be, and remain, to its daily and hourly beneficent and maleficent effects. The world is full of such unconscious magicians - in politics as well as in daily life, in the Church as in the strongholds of Free-Thought. Most of those magicians are "sorcerers" unhappily, not metaphorically but in sober reality, by reason of their inherent selfishness, their revengeful natures, their envy and malice. The true student of Magic, well aware of the truth, looks on in pity, and, if he be wise, keeps silent. For every effort made by him to remove the universal cecity is only repaid with ingratitude, slander, and often curses, which, unable to reach him, will react on those who wish him evil. Lies and calumny - the latter a teething lie, adding actual bites to empty harmless falsehoods - become his lot, and thus the well-wisher is soon torn to pieces, as a reward for his benevolent desire to enlighten.

The Philosophy Stands on Its Own Merits - Enough has been given, it is believed, to show that the existence of a Secret Universal Doctrine, besides its practical methods of Magic, is no wild romance or fiction. The fact was known to the whole ancient world, and the knowledge of it has survived in the East, in India especially. And if there be such a Science, there must be naturally, somewhere, professors of it, or Adepts. In any case it matters little whether the Guardians of the Sacred Lore are regarded as living, actually existing men, or are viewed as myths. It is their Philosophy that will have to stand or fall upon its own merits, apart from, and independent of any Adepts. For in the words of the wise Gamaliel, addressed by him to the Synedrion: "If this doctrine is false it will perish, and fall of itself; but if true, then - it cannot be destroyed.

SECTION II

MODERN CRITICISM AND THE ANCIENTS

THE Secret Doctrine of the Aryan East is found repeated under Egyptian symbolism and phraseology in the Book of Hermes. At, or near, the beginning of the present century, all the books called Hermetic were, in the opinion of the average man of Science unworthy of serious attention. They were set down and loudly proclaimed as simply a collection of tales, of fraudulent pretences and most absurd claims. They "never existed before the Christian era," it was said: "they were all written with the triple object of speculation, deceiving and pious fraud;" they were all, even the best of them, silly apocrypha. [See in this connection, Pneumatologie des Esprits, by the Marquis de Mirville, who devotes six enormous volumes to show the absurdity of those who deny the reality of Satan and Magic, or the Occult Sciences - the two being with him synonymous.] In this respect the nineteenth century proved a most worthy scion of the eighteenth, for, in the age of Voltaire as well as in this century, everything, save what emanated direct from the Royal Academy, was false, superstitious, foolish. Belief in the wisdom of the Ancients was laughed to scorn, perhaps more so even than it is now. The very thought of accepting as authentic the works and vagaries of "a false Hermes, a false Orpheus, a false Zoroaster," of false Oracles, false Sibyls, and a thrice false Mesmer and his absurd fluid, was tabooed all along the line. Thus all that had its genesis outside the learned and dogmatic precincts of Oxford and Cambridge, [We think we see the sidereal phantom of the old Philosopher and Mystic - once of Cambridge University - Henry More, moving about in the astral mist over the old moss-covered roofs of the ancient town in which he wrote his famous letter to Glanvil about "witches." The "soul" seems restless and indignant, as on that day of May, 1678, when the doctor complained so bitterly to the author of Sadducismus Triumphatus of Scot, Adie and Webster. "Our new inspired saints," the soul is heard to mutter, "sworn advocates of the witches. . . . who against all sense and reason . . . Will have no Samuel but a confederate knave . . . these in-blown buffoons, puffed up with . . . ignorance, vanity and stupid infidelity!" (See "Letter to Glanvil," and Isis Unveiled, i, 205, 206)] or the Academy of France, was denounced in those days as 'unscientific," and "ridiculously absurd." This tendency has survived to the present day.

ALL HONOUR TO GENUINE SCIENTISTS –

Nothing can be further from the intention of any true Occultist - who stands possessed, by virtue of his higher psychic development, of instruments of research far more penetrating in their power than any as yet in the hands of physical experimentalists - than to look unsympathetically on the efforts that are being made in the area of physical enquiry. The exertions and labours undertaken to solve as many as possible of the problems of Nature have always been holy in his sight. The spirit in which Sir Isaac Newton remarked that at the end of all his astronomical work he felt a mere child picking up shells beside the Ocean of Knowledge, is one of reverence for the boundlessness of Nature which Occult Philosophy itself cannot eclipse. And it may freely be recognised that the attitude of mind which this famous simile describes is one which fairly represents that of the great majority of genuine Scientists in regard to all the phenomena of the physical plane of Nature. In dealing with this they are often caution and moderation itself. They observe facts with a patience that cannot be surpassed. They are slow to cast these into theories, with a prudence that cannot be too highly commended. And, subject to the limitations under which they serve Nature, they are beautifully accurate in the record of their observations. Moreover, it may be conceded further that modern Scientists are exceedingly improbable that any discovery will ever conflict with such or such a theory, now supported by such and such an aggregation of recorded facts. But even in reference to the broadest generalizations - which pass into a dogmatic form only in brief popular text books of scientific knowledge - the tone of "Science" itself, if that abstraction may be held to be embodied in the persons of its most distinguished representatives, is one of reserve and often of modesty.

Far, therefore, from being disposed to scoff at the errors into which the limitations of their methods may betray men of Science, the true Occultist will rather appreciate the pathos of a situation in which great industry and thirst for truth are condemned to disappointment, and often to confusion.

That which is to be deplored, however, in respect to

Modern Science, is in itself an evil manifestation of the excessive caution which in its most favourable aspect protects Science from over-hasty conclusions: namely, the tardiness of Scientists to recognise that other instruments of research may be applicable to the mysteries of Nature besides those of the physical plane, and that it may consequently be impossible to appreciate the phenomena of any one plane correctly without observing them as well from the points of view afforded by others. In so far then as they wilfully shut their eyes to evidence which ought to have shown them clearly that Nature is more complex than physical phenomena alone would suggest, that there are means by which the faculties of human perception can pass sometimes from one plane to the other, and that their energy is being misdirected while they turn it exclusively on the minutiae of physical structure or force, they are less entitled to sympathy than to blame.

One feels dwarfed and humbled in reading what M. Renan, that learned modern "destroyer" of every religious belief, past, present and future, has to say of poor humanity and its powers of discernment. He believes mankind has but a very narrow mind; and the number of men capable of seizing acutely (finement) the true analogy of things, is quite imperceptible. [Études Religieuses.]

Upon comparing, however, this statement with another opinion expressed by the same author, namely, that:

The mind of the critic should yield to facts, hand and feet bound, to be dragged by them wherever they may lead him. [Études Historiques.]

one feels relieved. When, moreover, these two philosophical statements are strengthened by a third enunciation of the famous Academician, which declares that:

Tout parti pris a priori, doit etre banni de la science, [Mémoire read at the Academie des Inscriptions des Belles Lettres, in 1859.] there remains little to fear. Unfortunately M. Renan is the first to break this golden rule.

The evidence of Herodotus - called, sarcastically no doubt, the "Father of History," since in every question upon which Modern Thought disagrees with him, his testimony goes for nought - the sober and earnest assurances in the philosophical narratives of Plato and Thucydides, Polybius, and Plutarch, and even certain statements of Aristotle himself, are invariably laid aside whenever they are involved in what modern criticism is pleased to regard as myth. It is some time since Strauss proclaimed that:

WHAT IS A MYTH? -

The presence of a supernatural element or miracle in a narrative is an infallible sign of the presence in it of a myth;

and such is the canon of criticism tacitly adopted by every modern critic. But what is a myth - μυθος - to begin with? Are we not told distinctly by ancient writers that the word means tradition? Was not the Latin term fabula, a fable, synonymous with something told, as having happened in pre-historic times, and not necessarily an invention. With such autocrats of criticism and despotic rulers as are most of the French, English, and German Orientalists, there may, then, be no end of historical, geographical, ethnological and philological surprises in store for the century to come. Travesties in Philosophy have become so common of late, that the public can be startled by nothing in this direction. It has already been stated by one learned speculator that Homer was simply "a mythical personification of the épopée"; [See Alfred Maury's Histoire des Religions de la Grèce. i. 248: and the speculations of Holzmann in Zeitschriftfur Vergleichende Sprach forschung, ann. 1882, p.487. sq.] by another, that Hippocrates, son of Esculapius, "could only be a chimera"; that the Asclepiades, their seven hundred years of duration notwithstanding, might after all prove simply a "fiction"; that "the city of Troy (Dr. Schliemann to the contrary) existed only on the maps." etc. Why should not the world be invited after this to regard every hitherto historical character of days of old as a myth? Were not Alexander the Great needed by Philology as a sledge-hammer wherewith to break the heads of Brahmanical chronological pretensions, he would have become long ago simply "a symbol for annexation," or "a genius of conquest," as has been already suggested by some French writer.

Blank denial is the only refuge left to the critics. It is the most secure asylum for some time to come in which to shelter the last of the sceptics. For one who denies unconditionally, the trouble of arguing is unnecessary, and he also thus avoids what is worse, having to yield occasionally a point or two before the irrefutable arguments and facts of his opponent. Creuzer, the greatest of all the modern Symbologists, the most learned among the masses of erudite German Mythologists, must have envied the placid self-confidence of certain sceptics, when he found himself forced in a moment of desperate perplexity to admit that:

We are compelled to return to the theories of trolls and genii, as they were understood by the ancients; [it is a doctrine] without which it becomes absolutely impossible to explain to oneself anything with regard to the Mysteries. [Creuzer's Introduction des Mystères,iii, 456.] of the Ancients, which Mysteries are undeniable.

Roman Catholics, who are guilty of precisely the same worship, and to the very letter - having borrowed it from the later Chaldaeans, the Lebanon Nabathaeans, and the baptized Sabaeans, [The later Nabathaeans adhered to the same belief as the Nazarenes and the Sabaeans, honoured John the Baptist, and used Baptistm. (See Isis Unveiled, ii.127: Munck, Palestine, p.525; Dunlap, Sid, the Son of Man. etc.)] and not from the learned Astronomers and Initiates of the days of old - would now, by anathematizing it, hide the source from which it came. Theology and Churchianism would fain trouble the clear fountain that fed them from the first, to prevent posterity from looking into it, and thus seeing their original prototype. The Occultists, however, believe the time has come to give everyone his due. As to our other opponents - the modern sceptic and the Epicurean, the cynic and the Sadducee - they may find an answer to their denials in our earlier volumes. As to many unjust aspersions on the ancient doctrines, the reason for them is given in these words in Isis Unveiled:

The thought of the present-day commentator and critic as to the ancient learning, is limited to and runs round the exoterism of the temples; his insight is either unwilling or unable to penetrate into the solemn adyta of old, where the hierophant instructed the neophyte to regard the public worship in its true light. No ancient sage would have taught that man is the king of creation, and that the starry heaven and our mother earth were created for his sake. [i.535.]

When we find such works as Phallicism [By Hargrave Jennings.] appearing in our day in print, it is easy to see that the day of concealment and travesty has passed away. Science, in Philology, Symbolism and Comparative Religion, has progressed too far to make wholesale denials any longer, and the Church is too wise and cautious not to be now making the best of the situation. Meanwhile, the "rhombs of Hecate" and the "wheels of Lucifer," [See de Mirville's Pneumatologie, iii, 267 et seq.] daily exhumed on the sites of Babylonia, can no longer be used as clear evidence of a Satan-worship, since the same symbols are shown in the ritual of the Latin Church. The latter is too learned to be ignorant of the fact that even the later Chaldaeans, who had gradually fallen into dualism, reducing all things to two primal Principles, never worshipped Satan or idols, any more than did the Zoroastrians, who now lie under the same accusation, but that their Religion was as highly philosophical as any; their dual and exoteric Theosophy became the heirloom of the Jews, who, in their turn, were forced to share it with the Christians. Parsis are to this day charged with Heliolatry, and yet in the Chaldean Oracles, under the "Magical and Philosophical Precepts of Zoroaster" one finds the following:

CHALDEAN ORACLES -

Direct not thy mind to the vast measures of the earth;

For the plant of truth is not upon ground.

Nor measure the measures of the sun, collecting rules,

For he is carried by the eternal will of the Father, not for your sake.

Dismiss the impetuous course of the moon; for she runs always by work of necessity.

The progression of the stars was not generated for your sake.

There was a vast difference between the true worship taught to those who showed themselves worthy, and the state religions. The Magians are accused of all kinds of superstition, but this is what the same Chaldaean Oracle says:

The wide aerial flight of birds is not true,

Nor the dissections of the entrails of victims; they are all mere toys, the basis of mercenary fraud; flee from these If you would open the sacred paradise of piety, Where virtue, wisdom, and equity are assembled.

[Psellus, 4: in Cory's Ancient Fragments. 269.]

As we say in our former work:

Surely it is not those who warn people against "mercenary fraud" who can be accused of it; and if they accomplished acts which seem miraculous, who can with fairness presume to deny that it was done merely because they possessed a knowledge of natural philosophy and psychological science to a degree unknown to our schools? [Isis Unveiled, i, 535, 536.]

The above quoted stanzas are a rather strange teaching to come from those who are universally believed to have worshipped the sun, and moon, and the starry hosts, as Gods. The sublime profundity of the Magian precepts being beyond the reach of modern materialistic thought, the Chaldean Philosophers are accused of Sabaeanism and Sun-worship, which was the religion only of the uneducated masses.

SECTION III

THE ORIGIN OF MAGIC

THINGS of late have changed, true enough. The field of investigation has widened; old religions are a little better understood; and since that miserable day when the Committee of the French Academy, headed by Benjamin Franklin, investigated Mesmer's phenomena only to proclaim them charlatanry and clever knavery, both heathen Philosophy and Mesmerism have acquired certain rights and privileges, and are now viewed from quite a different standpoint. Is full justice rendered them, however, and are they any better appreciated? We are afraid not. Human nature is the same now, as when Pope said of the force of prejudice that:

The difference is as great between

The optics seeing, as the objects seen.

All manners take a tincture from our own,

Or some discolour'd through our passions shown,

Or fancy's beam enlarges, multiplies,

Contracts, inverts, and gives ten thousand dyes.

Thus in the first decades of our century Hermetic Philosophy was regarded by both Churchmen and men of Science from two quite opposite points of view. The former called it sinful and devilish; the latter denied point-blank its authenticity, notwithstanding the evidence brought forward by the most erudite men of every age, including our own. The learned Father Kircher, for instance, was not even noticed; and his assertion that all the fragments known under titles of works by Mercury Trismegistus, Berosus, Pherecydes of Syros, etc., were rolls that had escaped the fire which devoured 100,000 volumes of the great Alexandrian Library - was simply laughed at. Nevertheless the educated classes of Europe knew then, as they do now, that the famous Alexandrian Library, the "marvel of the ages," was founded by Ptolemy Philadelphus; that numbers of its MSS, had been carefully copied from hieratic texts and the oldest parchments, Chaldaean, Phoenician, Persian, etc; and that these transliterations and copies amounted, in their turn, to another 100,000 rolls, as Josephus and Strabo assert.

THE BOOKS OF HERMES –

There is also the additional evidence of Clemens Alexandrinus, that ought to be credited to some extent.[The forty-two Sacred Books of the Egyptians mentioned by Clement of Alexandria as having existed in his time, were but a portion of the Books of Hermes. Iamblichus, on the authority of the Egyptian priest Abammon, attributes 1,200 of such books to Hermes, and Manetho 36.000. But the testimony of Iamblichus as a Neoplatonist and Theurgist is of course rejected by modern critics. Manetho, who is held by Bunsen in the highest consideration as a "purely-historical personage," with whom "none of the later native historians can be compared" (see Egypte, i. 97) suddenly becomes a Pseudo-Manetho, as soon as the ideas propounded by him clash with the scientific prejudices against Magic and the Occult knowledge claimed by the ancient priests. However, none of the Archaeologists doubt for a moment the almost incredible antiquity of the Hermetic books. Champollion shows the greatest regard for their authenticity and truthfulness, corroborated as it is by many of the oldest monuments. And Bunsen brings irrefutable proofs of their age. From his researches, for instance, we learn that there was a line of sixty-one kings before the days of Moses, who preceded the Mosaic period by a clearly-traceable civilization of several thousand years. Thus we are warranted in believing that the works of Hermes Trismegistus were extant many ages before the birth of the Jewish law-giver. "Styli and inkstands were found on monuments of the fourth Dynasty, the oldest in the world," says Bunsen. If the eminent Egyptologist rejects the period of 48.863 years before Alexander, to which Diogenes Laertius carries back the records of the priests, he is evidently more embarrassed with the ten thousand of astronomical observations, and remarks that "if they were actual observations, they must have extended over 10.000 years" (p.44). "We learn, however," he adds, "from one of their own old chronological works . . . that the genuine Egyptian traditions concerning the mythological period treated of myriads of years." (Egypte, i, 15: Isis Unveiled, i. 33)] Clemens testified to the existence of an additional 30,000 volumes of the Books of Thoth, placed in the library of the Tomb of Osymandias, over the entrance of which were inscribed the words, "A Cure for the Soul."

Since then, as all know, entire texts of the "apocryphal"

works of the "false" Pymander, and the no less "false" Asclepias, have been found by Champollion in the most ancient monuments of Egypt. [These details are taken from Pneumatologie, iii, pp, 204, 205] As said in Isis Unveiled:

After having devoted their whole lives to the study of the records of the old Egyptian wisdom, both Champollion-Figeac and Champollion Junior publicly declared, notwithstanding many biased judgments hazarded by certain hasty and unwise critics, that the Books of Hermes "truly contain a mass of Egyptian traditions which are constantly corroborated by the most authentic records and monuments of Egypt of the hoariest antiquity." [Egypte, p.143 Isis Unveiled, i. 625.]

The merit of Champollion as an Egyptologist none will question, and if he declare that everything demonstrates the accuracy of the writings of the mysterious Hermes Trismegistus, and if the assertion that their antiquity runs back into the night of time be corroborated by him in minutest details, then indeed criticism ought to be fully satisfied. Says Champollion:

These inscriptions are only the faithful echo and expression of the most ancient verities.

Since these words were written, some of the "apocryphal" verses by the "mythical" Orpheus have also been found copied word for word, in hieroglyphics, in certain inscriptions of the Fourth Dynasty, addressed to various Deities. Finally, Creuzer discovered and immediately pointed out the very significant fact that numerous passages found in Homer and Hesiod were undeniably borrowed by the two great poets from the Orphic Hymns, thus proving the latter to be far older than the Iliad or the Odyssey.

And so gradually the ancient claims come to be vindicated, and modern criticism has to submit to evidence. Many are now the writers who confess that such a type of literature as the Hermetic works of Egypt can never be dated too far back into the prehistoric ages. The texts of many of these ancient works, that of Enoch included, so loudly proclaimed "apocryphal" at the beginning of this century, are now discovered and recognised in the most secret and sacred sanctuaries of Chaldaea, India, Phoenicia, Egypt and Central Asia. But even such proofs have failed to convince the bulk of our Materialists. The reason for this is very simple and evident. All these texts - held in universal veneration in Antiquity, found in the secret libraries of all the great temples, studied (if not always mastered) by the greatest statesmen, classical writers, philosophers, kings and laymen, as much as by renowned Sages - what were they? Treatises on Magic and Occultism, pure and simple; the now derided and tabooed Theosophy - hence the ostracism.

Were people, then, so simple and credulous in the days of Pythagoras and Plato? Were the millions of Babylonia and Egypt, of India and Greece, with their great Sages to lead them, all fools, that during those periods of great learning and civilization which preceded the year one of our era - the latter giving birth but to the intellectual darkness of mediaeval fanaticism - so many otherwise great men should have devoted their lives to a mere illusion, a superstition called Magic? It would seem so, had one to remain content with the word and conclusions of modern Philosophy.

Every Art and Science, however, whatever its intrinsic merit, has had its discoverer and practitioner, and subsequently its proficients to teach it.

WHAT IS THE ORIGIN OF MAGIC? -

What is the origin of the Occult Sciences, or Magic? Who were its professors, and what is known of them, whether in history or legend? Clemens Alexandrinus, one of the most intelligent and learned of the early Christian Fathers, answers this question in his Stromateis. That ex-pupil of the Neoplatonic School argues:

If there is instruction, you must seek for the master. [Strom., VI, vii. The following paragraph from the same chapter.]

And so he shows Cleanthes taught by Zeno, Theophrastus by Aristotle, Metrodorus by Epicurus, Plato by Socrates, etc. And he adds that when he had looked further back to Pythagoras, Pherecydes, and Thales, he had still to search for their masters. The same for the Egyptians, the Indians, the Babylonians, and the Magi themselves. He would not cease questioning, he says, to learn who it was they all had for their masters. And when he (Clemens) had traced down the enquiry to the very cradle of mankind, to the first generation of men, he would reiterate once more his questioning, and ask, "Who is their teacher?" Surely, he argues, their master could be "no one of men." And even when we should have reached as high as the Angels, the same query would have to be offered to them: "Who were their (meaning the 'divine' and the 'fallen' Angels) masters?'

The aim of the good father's long argument is of course to discover two distinct masters, one the preceptor of biblical patriarchs, the other the teacher of the Gentiles. But the students of the Secret Doctrine need go to no such trouble. Their professors are well aware who were the Masters of their predecessors in Occult Sciences and Wisdom.

The two professors are finally traced out by Clemens, and are, as was to be expected, God, and his eternal and everlasting enemy and opponent, the Devil; the subject of Clemens' enquiry relating to the dual aspect of Hermetic Philosophy, as cause and effect. Admitting the moral beauty of the virtues preached in every Occult work with which he was acquainted, Clemens desires to know the cause of the apparent contradiction between the doctrine and the practice, good and evil Magic, and he comes to the conclusion that Magic has two origins - divine and diabolical. He perceives its bifurcation into two channels, hence his deduction and inference.

We perceive it too, without, however, necessarily designating such bifurcation diabolical, for we judge the "left-hand path" as it issued from the hands of its founder. Otherwise, judging also by the effects of Clemens' own religion and walk in life of certain of its professors, since the death of their Master, the Occultists would have a right to come to somewhat the same conclusion as Clemens. They would have a right to say that while Christ, the Master of all true Christians, was in every way godly, those who resorted to the horrors of the Inquisition, to the extermination and torture of heretics, Jews and Alchemists, the Protestant

Calvin who burnt Servetus , and his persecuting Protestant successors, down to the whippers and burners of witches in America, must have had for their Master, the Devil. But Occultists, not believing in the Devil, are precluded from retaliating in this way.

Clemens' testimony, however, is valuable in so far as it shows (1) the enormous number of works on Occult Sciences in his day; and (2) the extraordinary powers acquired through those Sciences by certain men.

He devotes, for instance, the whole of the sixth book of his Stromateis to this research for the first two "Masters" or the true and the false Philosophy respectively, both preserved, as he says, in the Egyptian sanctuaries. Very pertinently too, he apostrophises the Greeks, asking them why they should not accept the "miracles" of Moses as such, since they claim the very same privileges for their own Philosophers, and he gives a number of instances. It is, as he says, Aeachus obtaining through his Occult powers a marvellous rain; it is Aristaeus causing the winds to blow; Empedocles quieting the gale, and forcing it to cease etc.[See Pneumatologie, iii.207 Therefore Empedocles is called κωλυθαυεμοςthe "dominator of the wind." Strom., VI. iii.]

The books of Mercurius Trismegistus most attracted his attention. [Ibid. iv.] He is also warm in his praise of Hystaspes (or Gushtasp), of the Sibylline books, and even of the right Astrology.

There have been in all ages use and abuse of Magic, as there are use and abuse of Mesmerism or Hypnotism in our own. The ancient world had its Apollonii and its Pherecydae, and intellectual people could discriminate then, as they can now. While no classical or pagan writer has ever found one word of blame for Apollonius of Tyana, for instance, it is not so with regard to Pherecydes. Hesychius of Miletia, Philo of Byblos and Eusthathius charges the latter unstintingly with having built his Philosophy and Science on demoniacal traditions - i.e., on Sorcery.

PHERECYDES OF SYROS –

Cicero declares that Pherecydes is, potius divinus quam medicus, rather a soothsayer than a physician," and Diogenes Laertius gives a vast number of stories relating to his predictions. One day Pherecydes prophesies the shipwreck of a vessel hundreds of miles away from him; another time he predicts the capture of Lacedaemonians by the Arcadians; finally, he foresees his own wretched end. [Summarised from Pneumatologie, iii.209.]

Bearing in mind the objections that will be made to the teachings of the Esoteric Doctrine as herein propounded, the writer is forced to meet some of them beforehand.

Such imputations as those brought by Clemens against the "heathen" Adepts, only prove the presence of clairvoyant powers and prevision in every age, but are no evidence in favour of a Devil. They are, therefore, of no value except to the Christians, for whom Satan is one of the chief pillars of the faith. Baronius and De Mirville, for instance, find an unanswerable proof of Demonology in the belief in the co-eternity of Matter with Spirit!

De Mirville writes that Pherecydes

Postulates in principle the primordiality of Zeus or Ether, and then, on the same plane, a principle, coeternal and coactive, which he calls the fifth element, or Ogenos. [Loc. cit.]

He then points out that the meaning of Ogenos is given as that which shuts up, which holds captive, and that is Hades, "or in a word, hell."

The synonyms are known to every schoolboy without the Marquis going to the trouble of explaining them to the Academy; as to the deduction, every Occultist will of course deny it and only smile at its folly. And now we come to the theological conclusion.

The resumé of the views of the Latin Church - as given by authors of the same characters as the Marquis de Mirville - amounts to this: that the Hermetic Books, their wisdom - fully admitted in Rome - notwithstanding, are "the heirloom left by Cain, the accursed, to mankind." It is "generally admitted," says that modern memorialist of Satan in History:

That immediately after the Flood Cham and his descendants had propagated anew the ancient teachings of the Cainites and of the surmerged Race.[Op. cit., iii 208]

This proves, at any rate, that Magic, or Sorcery as he calls it, is an antediluvian Art, and thus one point is gained. For, as he says:-

The evidence of Berosius makes Ham identical with the first Zoroaster, founder of Bactria, the first author of all the magic arts of Babylonia, the Chemesenua or Cham, [The English speaking people who spell the name of Noah's disrespectful son "Ham" have to be reminded that the right spelling is "Kham" or "Cham"] the infamous [Black Magic, or Sorcery, is the evil result obtained in any shape or way through the practice of Occult Arts: hence it has to be judged only by its effects. The name of neither Ham nor Cain, when pronounced, has ever killed any one; whereas, if we have to believe that same Clemens Alexandrinus who traces the teacher of every Occultist, outside of Christianity, to the Devil, the name of Jehovah (pronounced Jevo and in a peculiar way) had the effect of killing a man at a distance. The mysterious Schemham-phorasch was not always used for holy purposes by the Kabalists, especially since the Sabbath or Saturday, sacred to Saturn or the evil Shani, became - with the Jews - sacred to "Jehovah."] of the faithful Noachians, finally the object of adoration for Egypt, which having received its name χημεια, whence chemistry, built in his honour a town called Choemnis, or the "city of fire." [Khoemnis, the pre-historic city, may or may not have been built by Noah's son, but it was not his name that was given to the town, but that of the Mystery Goddess Khoemnu or Khoemnis (Greek form); the deity that was created by the ardent fancy of the neophyte, who was thus tantalised during his "twelve labours" of probation before his final initiation. Her male counterpart is Khem. The city of Choemnis or Khemmis (today Akhmem) was the chief seat of the God Khem. The Greeks identifying Khem with Pan, called this city "Panopolis."] Ham adored it, it is said, whence the name Chammaim given to the pyramids; which in their turn have been vulgarised into our modern noun "chimney." [Pneumatologie, iii, 210. This looks more like pious vengeance than philology. The picture, however, seems incomplete, as the author ought to have added to the "chimney" a witch flying out of it on a broomstick.]

This statement is entirely wrong. Egypt was the cradle of Chemistry and its birth-place - this is pretty well known by this time. Only Kenrick and others show the root of the word to be chemi or chem, which is not Chem or Ham, but Khem, the Egyptian phallic God of the Mysteries.

But this is not all. De Mirville is bent upon finding a satanic origin even for the now innocent Tarot.

He goes on to say:

As to the means for the propagation of this evil Magic, tradition points it out, in certain runic characters traced on metallic plates [or leaves, des lames] which have escaped destruction by the Deluge [How could they escape from the Deluge unless God so willed it? This is scarcely logical.] This might have been regarded as legendary, had not subsequent discoveries shown it far from being so. Plates were found covered with curious and utterly undecipherable characters, characters of undeniable antiquity, to which the Chamites [Sorcerers, with the author] attribute the origin to their marvellous and terrible powers. [Loc. cit., p.210]

The pious author may, meanwhile, be left to his own orthodox beliefs.

Cain, Mathematical and Anthropomorphic -   He, at any rate, seems quite sincere in his views. Nevertheless, his able arguments will have to be sapped at their very foundation, for it must be shown on mathematical grounds who, or rather what, Cain and Ham really were. De Mirville is only the faithful son of his Church, interested in keeping Cain in his anthropomorphic character and in his present place in "Holy Writ." The student of Occultism, on the other hand, is solely interested in the truth. But the age has to follow the natural course of evolution.

SECTION IV

THE SECRESY OF INITIATES

THE false rendering of a number of parables and sayings of Jesus is not to be wondered at in the least. From Orpheus, the first initiated Adept of whom history catches a glimpse in the mists of the pre-Christian era, down through Pythagoras, Confucius, Buddha, Jesus, Apollonius of Tyana, to Ammonius Saccas, no Teacher or Initiate has ever committed to writing for public use. Each and all of them have invariably recommended silence and secresy on certain facts and deeds, from Confucius, who refused to explain publicly and satisfactorily what he meant by his "Great Extreme," or to give the key to the divination by "straws" down to Jesus, who charged his disciples to tell no man that he was Christ [Matthew, xvi. 20.] (Chrestos), the "man of sorrows" and trials, before his supreme and last Initiation, or that he had produced a "miracle," of resurrection. [Mark, v. 43.] The Apostles had to preserve silence, so that the left hand should not know what the right hand did; in plainer words, that the dangerous proficients in the Left Hand Science - the terrible enemies of the Right Hand Adepts, especially before their supreme Initiation - should not profit by the publicity so as to harm both the healer and the patient. And if the above is maintained to be simply an assumption, then what may be the meaning of these awful words:

Unto you it is given to know the mystery of the Kingdom of

God; but unto them that are without all these things are done in parables; that seeing they may see and not perceive; and hearing, they may hear and not understand; lest at any time they should be converted and their sins should be forgiven them.[Mark, iv.11.]

EXOTERIC AND ESOTERIC TEACHINGS -

Unless interpreted in the sense of the law of silence and Karma, the utter selfishness and uncharitable spirit of this remark are but too evident. These words are directly connected with the terrible dogma of predestination. Will the good and intelligent Christian cast such a slur of cruel selfishness on his Saviour? [It is not evident that the words: "lest at any time they should be converted (or: "lest haply they should turn again" - as in the revised version) and their sins be forgiven them" - do not at all mean to imply that Jesus feared that through repentance any outsider, or "them that are without," should escape damnation, as the literal dead-letter sense plainly shows - but quite a different thing? Namely, "lest any of the profane should by understanding his preaching, undisguised by parable, get hold of some of the secret teachings and mysteries of Initiation - and even of Occult powers? "Be converted" is, in other words, to obtain a knowledge belonging exclusively to the Initiated: "and their sins be forgiven them," that is, their sins would fall upon the illegal revealer, on those who had helped the unworthy reap there where they have never laboured to sow, and had given them, thereby, the means of escaping on this earth their deserved Karma, which must thus re-act on the revealer, who, instead of good, did harm and failed.]

The work of propagating such truths in parables was left to the disciples of the high Initiates. It was their duty to follow the key-note of the Secret Teaching without revealing its mysteries. This is shown in the histories of all the great Adepts. Pythagoras divided his classes into hearers of exoteric and esoteric lectures. The Magians received their instructions and were initiated in the far hidden caves of Bactria. When Josephus declares that Abraham taught Mathematics he meant by it "Magic," for in the Pythagorean code Mathematics mean Esoteric Science, or Gnosis.

Professor Wilder remarks:

The Essenes of Judea and Carmel made similar distinctions, dividing their adherents into neophytes, brethren and the perfect . . . . Ammonius obligated his disciples by oath not to divulge his higher doctrines, except to those who had been thoroughly instructed and exercised [prepared for initiation]. [New Platonism and Alchemy, 1869. pp. 7. 9.]

One of the most powerful reasons for the necessity of strict secresy is given by Jesus Himself, if one may credit Matthew. For there the Master is made to say plainly:

Give not that which is holy unto the dogs, neither cast ye your pearls before swine; lest they trample them under their feet, and turn again and rend you. [vii. 6.]

Profoundly true and wise words. Many are those in our own age, and even among us, who have been forcibly reminded of them - often when too late. [History is full of proofs of the same. Had not Anaxagoras enunciated the great truth taught in the Mysteries, viz., that the sun was surely larger than the Peloponnesus, he would not have been persecuted and nearly put to death by the fanatical mob. Had that other rabble which was raised against Pythagoras understood what the mysterious Sage of Crotona meant by giving out his remembrances of having been the "Son of Mercury" - God of the Secret Wisdom - he would not have been forced to fly for his life: nor would Socrates have been put to death, had he kept secret the revelations of his divine Daimon. He knew how little his century - save those initiated - would understand his meaning, had he given out all he knew of the moon. Thus he limited his statement to an allegory, which is now proven to have been more scientific than was hitherto believed. He maintained that the moon was inhabited and that the lunar beings lived in profound, vast and dark valleys, our satellite being airless and without any atmosphere outside such profound valleys; this, disregarding the revelation full of meaning for the few only, must be so of necessity. If there is any atmosphere on our bright Selene at all. The facts recorded is the secret annals of the Mysteries had to remain veiled under penalty of death.]

Even Maimonides recommends silence with regard to the true meaning of the Bible texts. This injunction destroys the usual affirmation that "Holy Writ" is the only book in the world whose divine oracles contain plain unvarnished truth. It may be so for the learned Kabalists; it is certainly quite the reverse with regard to Christians. For this is what the learned Hebrew Philosopher says:

Whoever shall find out the true sense of the Book of Genesis ought to take care not to divulge it. This is a maxim that all our sages repeat to us, and above all respecting the work of the six days. If a person should discover the true meaning of it by himself, or by the aid of another, then he ought to be silent, or if he speaks he ought to speak of it obscurely, in an enigmatical manner, as I do myself, leaving the rest to be guessed by those who can understand me.

The Symbology and Esoterism of the Old Testament being thus confessed by one of the greatest Jewish Philosophers, it is only natural to find Christian Fathers making the same confession with regard to the New Testament, and the Bible in general. Thus we find Clemens Alexandrinus and Origen admitting it as plainly as words can do it. Clemens, who had been initiated into the Eleusinian Mysteries says, that:

The doctrines there taught contained in them the end of all instructions as they were taken from Moses and the prophets,

a slight perversion of facts pardonable in the good Father. The words admit, after all, that the Mysteries of the Jews were identical with those of the Pagan Greeks, who took them from the Egyptians, who borrowed them, in their turn, from the Chaldaeans, who got them from the Aryans, the Atlanteans and so on - far beyond the days of that Race. The secret meaning of the Gospel is again openly confessed by Clemens when he says that the Mysteries of the Faith are not to be divulged to all.

But since this tradition is not published alone for him who perceives the magnificence of the word; it is requisite, therefore, to hide in a Mystery the wisdom spoken, which the Son of God taught. [Stromateis, xii.]

ORIGEN ON "GENESIS" –

Not less explicit is Origen with regard to the Bible and its symbolical fables. He exclaims:

If we hold to the letter, and must understand what stands written in the law after the manner of the Jews and common people, then I should blush to confess aloud that it is God who has given these laws; then the laws of men appear more excellent and reasonable. [See Homilies 7., quoted in the Source of Measures, p.307.]

And well he might have "blushed," the sincere and honest Father of early Christianity in its days of relative purity. But the Christians of this highly literary and civilised age of ours do not blush at all; they swallow, on the contrary, the "light" before the formation of the sun, the Garden of Eden, Jonah's whale and all, notwithstanding that the same Origen asks in a very natural fit of indignation:

What man of sense will agree with the statement that the first, second and third days in which the evening is named and the morning, were without sun, moon , and stars, and the first day without a heaven? What man is found such an idiot as to suppose that God planted trees in Paradise, in Eden, like a husbandman, etc? I believe that every man must hold these things for images, under which a hidden sense lies concealed. [Origen: Huet., Origeniana,167: quoted from Dunlop's Sid. p. 176.]

Yet millions of "such idiots" are found in our age of enlightenment and not only in the third century. When Paul's unequivocal statement in Galatians, iv. 22-25, that the story of Abraham and his two sons is all "an allegory." and that "Agar is Mount Sinai" is added to this, then little blame, indeed, can be attached to either Christian or Heathen who declines to accept the Bible in any other light than that of a very ingenious allegory.

Rabbi Simeon Ben-"Jochai," the compiler of the Zohar, never imparted the most important points of his doctrine otherwise than orally, and to a very limited number of disciples. Therefore, without the final initiation into the Mercavah, the study of the Kabalah will be ever incomplete, and the Mercavah can be taught only "in darkness, in a deserted place, and after many and terrific trials." Since the death of that great Jewish Initiate this hidden doctrine has remained, for the outside world, an inviolate secret.

Among the venerable sect of the Tanaim, or rather the Tananim, the wise men, there were those who taught the secrets practically and initiated some disciples into the grand and final Mystery. But the Mishna Hagiga, 2nd Section, say that the table of contents of the Mercaba "must only be delivered to wise old ones." The Gemara is still more dogmatic. "The more important secrets of the Mysteries were not even revealed to all priests. Alone the initiates had them divulged." And so we find the same great secresy prevalent in every ancient religion. [Isis Unveiled, ii. 350.]

What says the Kabalah itself? Its great Rabbis actually threaten him who accepts their sayings verbatim. We read in the Zohar:

Woe to the man who sees in the Thorah, i.e., Law, only simple recitals and ordinary words! Because if in truth it only contained these, we would even today be able to compose a Thorah much more worthy of admiration. For if we find only the simple words, we would only have to address ourselves to the legislators of the earth.[The materialistic "law-givers," the critics and Sadducees who have tried to tear to shreds the doctrines and teachings of the great Asiatic Masters past and present - no scholars in the modern sense of the word - would do well to ponder over these words. No doubt that doctrines and secret teachings had they been invented and written in Oxford and Cambridge would be more brilliant outwardly. Would they equally answer to universal truths and facts, is the next question however.] to those in whom we most frequently meet with the most grandeur. It would be sufficient to imitate them, and make a Thorah after their words and example. But it is not so; each word of the Thorah contains an elevated meaning and a sublime mystery. . . . The recitals of the Thorah are the vestments of the Thorah. Woe to him who takes this garment for the Thorah itself . . . . The simple notice only of the garments or recitals of the Thorah, they know of no other thing, they see not that which is concealed under the vestment. The more instructed men do not pay attention to the vestment, but to the body which it envelops.[iii. fol. 1526, quoted in Myer's Qabbalah, p.102.]

Ammonius Saccas taught that the Secret Doctrine of the Wisdom-Religion was found complete in the Books of Thoth (Hermes), from which both Pythagoras and Plato derived their knowledge and much of their Philosophy; and these Books were declared by him to be "identical with the teachings of the Sages of the remote East." Professor A.

Wilder remarks:

As the name Thoth means a college or assembly, it is not altogether improbable that the books were so named as being the collected oracles and doctrines of the sacerdotal fraternity of Memphis. Rabbi Wise has suggested the same hypothesis in relation to the divine utterances recorded in the Hebrew Scriptures. [New-Platonism and Alchemy.p.6]

This is very probable. Only the "divine utterances" have never been, so far, understood by the profane. Philo Judaeus, a non-initiate, attempted to give their secret meaning and - failed.

But Books of Thoth or Bible, Vedas or Kabalah, all enjoin the same secresy as to certain mysteries of nature symbolised in them. "Woe be to him who divulges unlawfully the words whispered into the ear of Manushi by the First Initiator."

The "Dark Sayings" of the "Testaments."   Who that "Initiator" was is made plain in the Book of Enoch:

From them [the angels] I heard all things, and understood what I saw, that which will not take place in this generation [Race], but in a generation which is to succeed at a distant period [the 6th and 7th Races] on account of the elect [the Initiates]. [i. 2.]

Again, it is said with regard to the judgment of those who, when they have learned "every secret of the angels," reveal them, that:

They have discovered secrets, and they are those who have been judged; but not thou, my son [Noah] . . . thou art pure and good and free from the reproach of discovering [revealing] secrets. [IXIV.10.]

But there are those in our century, who, having "discovered secrets" unaided and owing to their own learning and acuteness only, and who being nevertheless, honest and straightforward men, undismayed by threats or warning since they have never pledged themselves to secresy, feel quite startled at such revelations. One of these is the learned author and discoverer of one "Key to the Hebrew-Egyptian Mystery." As he says, there are "some strange features connected to the promulgation and condition" of the Bible.

Those who compiled this book were men as we are. They knew, saw, handled and realized, through the key measure, [The key is shown to be "in the source of measures originating the British inch and the ancient cubit" as the author tries to prove.] the law of the living, ever active God.[The word as a plural might have better solved the mystery. God is ever-present; if he were ever-active he could no longer be an infinite God - nor ever-present in his limitation.] They needed no faith that He was, that He worked, planned and accomplished, as a mighty mechanic and architect.[The author is evidently a Mason of the way of thinking of General Pike. So long as the American and English Masons will reject the "Creative Principle" of the "Grand Orient" of France they will remain in the dark.] What was it, then, that reserved to them alone this knowledge, while first as men of God, and second as Apostles of Jesus the Christ, they doled out a blinding ritual service, and an empty teaching of faith and no substance as proof, properly coming through the exercise of just those senses which the Deity has given all men as the essential means of obtaining any right understanding?

Mystery and parable, and dark saying, and cloaking of the true meanings are the burden of the Testaments, Old and New. Take it that the narratives of the Bible were purposed inventions to deceive the ignorant masses, even while enforcing a most perfect code of moral obligations: How is it possible to justify so great frauds, as part of the Divine economy, when to that economy, the attribute of simple and perfect truthfulness must, in the nature of things, be ascribed? What has, or what by possibility ought mystery to have, with the promulgation of the truths of God? [Source of Measures, pp.308, 309]

Nothing whatever most certainly, if those mysteries had been given from the first. And so it was with regard to the first, semi-divine, pure and spiritual Races of Humanity. They had the "truths of God," and lived up to them, and their ideals. They preserved them, so long as there was hardly any evil, and hence scarcely a possible abuse of that knowledge and those truths. But evolution and the gradual fall into materiality is also one of the "truths" and also one of the laws of "God." And as mankind progressed, and became with every generation more of the earth, earthly, the individuality of each temporary Ego began to assert itself. It is personal selfishness that develops and urges man on to abuse of his knowledge and power. And selfishness is a human building, whose windows and doors are ever wide open for every kind of iniquity to enter into man's soul. Few were the men during the early adolescence of mankind, and fewer still are they now, who feel disposed to put into practice Pope's forcible declaration that he would tear out his own heart, if it had no better disposition than to love only himself, and laugh at all his neighbours. Hence the necessity of gradually taking away from man the divine knowledge and power, which became with every new human cycle more dangerous as a double-edged weapon, whose evil side was ever threatening one's neighbour, and whose power for good was lavished freely only upon self. Those few "elect" whose inner natures had remained unaffected by their outward physical growth, thus became in time the sole guardians of the mysteries revealed, passing the knowledge to those most fit to receive it, and keeping it inaccessible to others. Reject this explanation from the Secret Teachings, and the very name of Religion will become synonymous with deception and fraud.

Yet the masses could not be allowed to remain without some sort of moral restraint. Man is ever craving for a "beyond" and cannot live without an idea of some kind, as a beacon and a consolation. At the same time, no average man, even in our age of universal education, could be entrusted with truths too metaphysical, too subtle for his mind to comprehend, without the danger of an imminent reaction setting in, and faith in Gods and Saints making room for an unscientific blank Atheism. No real philanthropist, hence no Occultist, would dream for a moment of a mankind without one title of Religion.

THE GREATEST CRIME EVER PERPETRATED -

Even the modern day Religion in Europe, confined to Sundays, is better than none. But if, as Bunyan put it, "Religion is the best armour that a man can have," it certainly is the "worst cloak" ; and it is that "cloak" and false pretence which the Occultists and the Theosophists fight against. The true ideal Deity, the one living God in Nature, can never suffer in man's worship if that outward cloak woven by man's fancy, and thrown upon the Deity by the crafty hand of the priest greedy of power and domination, is drawn aside. The hour has struck with the commencement of this century to dethrone the "highest God" of every nation in favour of One Universal Deity - The God of Immutable Law, not charity; the God of Just Retribution, not mercy, which is merely an incentive to evil-doing and to a repetition of it. The greatest crime that was ever perpetrated upon mankind was committed on that day when the first priest invented the first prayer with a selfish object in view. A God who may be propitiated by iniquitous prayers to "bless the arms" of the worshipper, and send defeat and death to thousands of his enemies - his brethren; a Deity that can be supposed not to turn a deaf ear to chants of laudation mixed with entreaties for a "fair propitious wind" for self, and as naturally disastrous to the selves of other navigators who come from an opposite direction - it is this idea of God that has fostered selfishness in man, and deprived him of his self-reliance. Prayer is an ennobling action when it is an intense feeling, an ardent desire rushing forth from our very heart, for the good of other people, and when entirely detached from any selfish personal object; the craving for a beyond is natural and holy in man, but on the condition of sharing that bliss with others. One can understand and well appreciate the words of the "heathen" Socrates, who declared in his profound though untaught wisdom, that:

Our prayers should be for blessings on all, in general, for the Gods know best what is good for us.

But official prayer - in favour of a public calamity, or for the benefit of one individual irrespective of losses to thousands - is the most ignoble of crimes, besides being an impertinent conceit and a superstition. This is the direct inheritance by spoliation from the Jehovites - the Jews of the Wilderness and of the Golden Calf.

It is "Jehovah," as will be presently shown, that suggested the necessity of veiling and screening this substitute for the unpronounceable name, and that led to all this "mystery parables, dark sayings and cloaking." Moses had, at any rate, initiated his seventy Elders into the hidden truths, and thus the writers of the Old Testament stand to a degree justified. Those of the New Testament have failed to do even so much, or so little. They have disfigured the grand central figure of Christ by their dogmas, and have led people ever since into millions of errors and the darkest crimes, in His holy name.

It is evident that with the exception of Paul and Clement of Alexandria who had been both initiated into the Mysteries, none of the Fathers knew much of the truth themselves. They were mostly uneducated, ignorant people; and if such as Augustine and Lactantius, or again the Venerable Bede and others, were so painfully ignorant until the name of Galileo [In his Pneumatologie, in Vol. iv., pp. 105-112, the Marquis de Mirville claims the knowledge of the heliocentric system - earlier than Galileo - for Pope Urban VIII. The author goes further. He tries to show that famous Pope, not as the persecutor but as one persecuted by Galileo, and calumniated by the Florentine Astronomer into the bargain. If so, so much the worse for the Latin Church, since her Popes, knowing of it, still preserved silence upon this most important fact, either to screen Joshua or their own infallibility. One can understand well that the Bible having been so exalted over all the other systems, and its alleged monotheism depending upon the silence preserved, nothing remained of course but to keep quiet over its symbolism, thus allowing all its blunders to be fathered on its God.] of the most vital truths taught in the Pagan temples - of the rotundity of the earth, for example, leaving the heliocentric system out of question - how great must have been the ignorance of the rest! Learning the accusations of dealing with the Devil lavished on the Pagan Philosophers.

But truth must out. The Occultists, referred to as "the followers of the accursed Cain," by such writers as De Mirville, are now in a position to reverse the tables. That which was hitherto known only to the ancient and modern Kabalists in Europe and Asia, is now published and shown as being mathematically true. The author of the Key to the Hebrew-Egyptian Mystery or the Source of Measures has now proved to general satisfaction, it is to be hoped, that the two great God-names, Jehovah and Elohim, stood, in one meaning of their numerical values, for a diameter and a circumference value, respectively; in other words, that they are numerical indices of geometrical relations; and finally that Jehovah is Cain and vice versa.

This view, says the author,

Helps also to take the horrid blemish off from the name of Cain, as a put-up-job to destroy his character; for even without these showings, by the very text, he [Cain] was Jehovah. So the theological schools had better be alive to making the amend honorable, if such a thing is possible, to the good name and fame of the God they worship

ASIATIC RELIGIONS PROCLAIM THEIR ESOTERISM OPENLY –

[Op.cit., App. vii. p.296. The writer feels happy to find this fact now mathematically demonstrated. When it was stated in Isis Unveiled that Jehovah and Saturn were one and the same with Adam Kadmon, Cain, Adam and Eve, Able, Seth. etc., and that all were convertible symbols in the Secret Doctrine (see Vol ii. pp. 446, 448, 464 et seq.): that they answered, in short, to secret numerals and stood for more than one meaning in the Bible as in other doctrines - the author's statements remained unnoticed. Isis had failed to appear under a scientific form, and by giving it too much, in fact, gave very little to satisfy the enquirer. But now, if mathematics and geometry, besides the evidence of the Bible and Kabalah are good for anything, the public must find itself satisfied. No fuller, more scientifically given proof can be found to show that Cain is the transformation of an Elohim (the Sephira Binah) into Jah-Veh (or God-Eve) androgyne, and that Seth is the Jehovah male, than in the combined discoveries of Seyffarth, Knight, etc., and finally in Mr.Ralston Skinner's most erudite work. The further relations of these personifications of the first human races, in their gradual development, will be given later on in the text.]

This is not the first warning received by the "theological schools." which, however, no doubt knew it from the beginning, as did Clemens of Alexandria and others. But if it be so they will profit still less by it, as the admission would involve more for them than the mere sacredness and dignity of the established faith.

But, it may also be asked, why is it that the Asiatic religions, which have nothing of this sort to conceal and which proclaim quite openly the Esoterism of their doctrines, follow the same course? It is simply this: While the present, and no doubt enforced silence of the Church on this subject relates merely to the external or theoretical form of the Bible - the unveiling of the secrets of which would have involved no practical harm, had they been explained from the first - it is an entirely different question with Eastern Esoterism and Symbology. The grand central figure of the Gospels would have remained as unaffected by the symbolism of the Old Testament being revealed, as would that of the Founder of Buddhism had the Brahmanical writings of the Puranas, that preceded his birth, all been shown to be allegorical. Jesus of Nazareth, moreover, would have gained more than he would have lost had he been presented as a simple mortal left to be judged on his own precepts and merits, instead of being fathered on Christendom as a God whose many utterances and acts are now so open to criticism. On the other hand the symbols and allegorical sayings that veil the grand truths of Nature in the Vedas, the Brahmanas, the Upanishads and especially in the Lamaist Chagpa Thogmed and other works, are quite of a different nature, and far more complicated in their secret meaning. While the Biblical glyphs have nearly all a triune foundation, those of the Eastern books are worked on the septenary principle. They are as closely related to the mysteries of Physics and Physiology, as to Psychism and the transcendental nature of cosmic elements and Theogony; unriddled they would prove more than injurious to the uninitiated; delivered into the hands of the present generations in their actual state of physical and intellectual development, in the absence of spirituality and even of practical morality, they would become absolutely disastrous.

Nevertheless the secret teachings of the sanctuaries have not remained without witness; they have been made immortal in various ways. They have burst upon the world in hundreds of volumes full of the quaint, head-breaking phraseology of the Alchemist; they have flashed like irrepressible cataracts of Occult mystic lore from the pens of poets and bards. Genius alone had certain privileges in those dark ages when no dreamer could offer the world even a fiction without suiting his heaven and his earth to biblical text. To genius alone it was permitted in those centuries of mental blindness, when the fear of the "Holy Office" threw a thick veil over every cosmic and psychic truth, to reveal unimpeded some of the grandest truths of Initiation. Whence did Ariosto, in his Orlando Furioso, obtain his conception of that valley of the Moon, where after our death we can find the ideas and images of all that exists on earth? How came Dante to imagine the many descriptions given in his Inferno - a new Johannine Apolcalypse, a true Occult Revelation in verse - his visit and communion with the Souls of the Seven Spheres? In poetry and satire every Occult truth has been welcomed - none has been recognised as serious. The Comte de Gabalis is better known and appreciated than Porphyry and Iamblichus. Plato's mysterious Atlantis is proclaimed a fiction, while Noah's Deluge is to this day on the brain of certain Archaeologists, who scoff at the archetypal world of Marcel Palingenius' Zodiac, and would resent as a personal injury being asked to discuss the four worlds of Mercury Trismegistus - the Archetypal, the Spiritual, the Astral and the Elementary, with three others behind the opened scene. Evidently civilised society is still but half prepared for the revelation. Hence, the Initiates will never give out the whole secret, until the bulk of mankind has changed its actual nature and is better prepared for truth. Clemens Alexandrinus was positively right in saying, "It is requisite to hide in a mystery the wisdom spoken" - which the "Sons of God" teach.

That Wisdom, as will be seen, relates to all the primeval truths delivered to the first Races, the "Mind-born," by the "Builders" of the Universe themselves.

THE WISDOM-RELIGION –

There was in every ancient country having claims to civilisation, an Esoteric Doctrine, a system which was designated WISDOM [The writings extant in olden times often personified Wisdom as an emanation and associate of the Creator. Thus we have the Hindu Buddha, the Babylonian Nebo, the Thoth of Memphis, the Hermes of Greece: also the female divinities, Neitha, Metis, Athena, and the Gnostic potency Achamoth or Sophia. The Samaritan Pentateuch denominated the Book of Genesis, Akamouth, or Wisdom, and two remnants of old treatises, the Wisdom of Solomon and the Wisdom of Jesus, relate to the same matters. The Book of Mashalim - the Discourses of Proverbs of Solomon - thus personifies Wisdom as the auxiliary of the Creator. In the Secret Wisdom of the East that auxiliary is found collectively in the first emanations of Primeval Light, the Seven Dhyani-Chohans, who have been shown to be identical with the "Seven Spirits of the Presence" of the Roman Catholics.] and those who were devoted to its prosecution were first denominated sages, or wise men. . . Pythagoras termed this system ηγνωσις των δντων, the Gnosis or Knowledge of things that are. Under the noble designation of WISDOM, the ancient teachers, the sages of India, the magians of Persia and Babylon, the seers and prophets of Israel, the hierophants of Egypt and Arabia, and the philosophers of Greece and the West, included all knowledge which they considered as essentially divine; classifying a part as esoteric and the remainder as exterior. The Rabbis called the exterior and secular series the Mercavah, as being the body or vehicle which contained the higher knowledge. [New Platonism and Alchemy, p.6.]

Later on, we shall speak of the law of silence imposed on eastern chelâs.

SECTION V

SOME REASONS FOR SECRESY

The fact that the Occult Sciences have been withheld from the world at large, and denied by the Initiates to Humanity, has often been made matter of complaint. It has been alleged that the Guardians of the Secret Lore were selfish in withholding the "treasures" of Archaic Wisdom; that it was positively criminal to keep back such knowledge - "if any" - from the men of Science, etc.

Yet there must have been some very good reasons for it, since from the very dawn of History such has been the policy of every Hierophant and "Master." Pythagoras, the first Adept and real Scientist in pre-Christian Europe, is accused of having taught in public the immobility of the earth, and the rotary motion of the stars around it, while he was declaring to his privileged Adepts his belief in the motion of the Earth as a planet, and in the heliocentric system. The reasons for such secresy, however, are many and were never made a mystery of. The chief cause as given in Isis Unveiled. It may now be repeated.

From the very day when the first mystic, taught by the first Instructor of the "divine Dynasties" of the early races, was taught the means of communication between this world and the worlds of the invisible host, between the sphere of matter and that of pure spirit, he concluded that to abandon this mysterious science to the desecration, willing or unwilling, of the profane rabble - was to lose it. An abuse of it might lead mankind to speedy destruction; it was like surrounding a group of children with explosive substances, and furnishing them with matches. The first divine Instructor initiated but a select few, and these kept silence with the multitudes. They recognised their "God" and each Adept felt the great "SELF" within himself. The Atman, the Self, the mighty Lord and Protector, once that man knew him as the "I am," the "Ego Sum," the "Asmi," showed his full power to him who could recognise the "still small voice." From the days of the primitive man described by the first Vedic poet, down to our modern age, there has not been a philosopher worthy of that name, who did not carry in the silent sanctuary of his heart the grand and mysterious truth. If initiated, he learnt it as a sacred science; if otherwise then, like Socrates, repeating to himself as well as his fellow-men, the noble injunction, "O man, know thyself," he succeeded in recognising his God within himself.

THE KEY OF PRACTICAL THEURGY -

"Ye are Gods," the king-psalmist tells us, and we find Jesus reminding the scribes that this expression was addressed to other mortal men , claiming for themselves the same privilege without any blasphemy. And as a faithful echo, Paul, while asserting that we are all "the temple of the living God," cautiously remarked elsewhere that after all these things are only for the "wise," and it is "unlawful" to speak of them.[ii. 317, 318. Many verbal alterations from the original text of Isis Unveiled were made by H.P.B. in her quotations therefrom, and these are followed throughout.]

Some of the reasons for this secrecy may be given.

The fundamental law and master-key of practical Theurgy, in its chief applications to the serious study of cosmic and sidereal, of psychic and spiritual, mysteries was, and still is, that which was called by the Greek Neoplatonist "Theophania." In its generally-accepted meaning this is "communication between the Gods (or God) and those initiated mortals who are spiritually fit to enjoy such an intercourse." Esoterically, however, it signifies more than this. For it is not only the presence of a God, but an actual - howbeit temporary - incarnation, the blending, so to say, of the personal Deity, the Higher Self, with man - its representative or agent on earth. As a general law, the Highest God, the Over-soul of the human being (Atma-Buddhi), only overshadows the individual during his life, for purposes of instruction and revelation; or as Roman Catholics - who erroneously call that Over-soul the "Guardian Angel" - would say, "It stands outside and watches." But in the case of the theophanic mystery, it incarnates itself in the Theurgist for purposes of revelation. When the incarnation is temporary, during those mysterious trances or "ecstasy," which Plotinus defined as

The liberation of the mind from its finite consciousness, becoming one and identified with the Infinite, this sublime condition is very short. The human soul, being the offspring or emanation of its God, the "Father and the Son" become one, "the divine fountain flowing like a stream into its human bed." [Proclus claims to have experienced this sublime ecstasy six times during his mystic life: Porphyry asserts that Appollonius of Tyana was thus united four times to his deity - a statement which we believe to be a mistake, since Apollonius was a Nirmanakaya (divine incarnation - not Avatara) - and he (Porphyry) only once, when over sixty years of age. Theophany (or the actual appearance of a God to man), Theopathy (or "assimilation of divine nature"), and Theopneusty (inspiration, or rather the mysterious power to hear orally the teachings of a God) have never been rightly understood.] In exceptional cases, however, the mystery becomes complete; the Word is made Flesh in real fact, the individual becoming divine in the full sense of the term, since his personal God has made of him his permanent life-long tabernacle - "the temple of God," as Paul says.

Now that which is meant here by the personal God of Man is, of course, not his seventh Principle alone, as per se and in essence that is merely a bean of the infinite Ocean of Light. In conjunction with our Divine Soul, the Buddhi, it cannot be called a Duad, as it otherwise might, since, though formed from Atma and Buddhi (the two higher Principles), the former is no entity but an emanation from the Absolute, and indivisible in reality from it. The personal God is not the Monad, but indeed the prototype of the latter, what for want of a better term we call the manifested Karanatma [Karana Sharira is the "causal" body and is sometimes said to be the "personal God." And so it is, in one sense.] (Causal Soul), one of the "seven" and chief reservoirs of the human Monads or Egos. The latter are gradually formed and strengthened during their incarnation-cycle by constant additions of individuality from the personalities in which incarnates that androgynous, half-spiritual, half-terrestrial principle, partaking of both heaven and earth, called by the Vedantins Jiva and Vijnanamaya Kosha, and by the Occultists the Manas (mind); that, in short, which uniting itself partially with the Monad, incarnates in each new birth. In perfect unity with its (seventh) Principle, the Spirit unalloyed, it is the divine Higher Self, as every student of Theosophy knows. After every new incarnation Buddhi-Manas culls, so to say the aroma of the flower called personality, the purely earthly residue of which its dregs - is left to fade out as a shadow. This is the most difficult - because so transcendentally metaphysical - portion of the doctrine.

As is repeated many a time in this and other works, it is not the Philosophers, Sages, and Adepts of antiquity who can ever be charged with idolatry. It is they in fact, who, recognising divine unity, were the only ones, owing to their initiation into the mysteries of Esotericism, to understand correctly the υπσνσια(hyponea), or under-meaning of the anthropomorphism of the so-called Angels, Gods, and Spiritual Beings of every kind. Each, worshipping the one Divine Essence that pervades the whole world of Nature, reverenced, but never worshipped or idolised, any of these "Gods," whether high or low - not even his own personal Deity, of which he was a Ray, and to whom he appealed.[This would be in one sense Self-worship.]

THE LADDER OF BEING -
The holy Triad emanates from the One, and is the Tetraktys;

the gods, daimons, and souls are an emanation of the Triad. Heroes and men repeat the hierarchy in themselves.

Thus said Metrodorus of Chios, the Pythagorean, the latter part of the sentence meaning that man has within himself the seven pale reflections of the seven divine Hierarchies; his Higher Self is, therefore, in itself but the refracted beam of the direct Ray. He who regards the latter as an Entity, in the usual sense of the term, is one of the "infidels and atheists," spoken of by Epicurus, for he fastens on that God "the opinions of the multitude" - an anthropomorphism of the grossest kind. ["The Gods exist," said Epicurus, "but they are not what the hoi polloi (the multitude) suppose them to be. He is not an infidel or atheist who denies the existence of Gods whom the multitude worship, but he is such who fastens on the Gods the opinions of the multitude."] The Adept and the Occultist know that "what are styled the Gods are only the first principles" (Aristotle). None the less they are intelligent, conscious, and living "Principles," the Primary Seven Lights manifested from Light unmanifested - which to us is Darkness. They are the Seven - exoterically four - Kumaras or "Mind-Born Sons" of Brahma. And it is they again, the Dhyan Chohans, who are the prototypes in the aeonic eternity of lower Gods and hierarchies of divine Beings, at the lowest end of which ladder of being are we - men.

Thus perchance Polytheism, when philosophically understood, may be a degree higher than even the Monotheism of the Protestant, say, who limits and conditions the Deity in whom he persists in seeing the Infinite, but whose supposed actions make of that "Absolute and Infinite" the most absurd paradox in Philosophy. From this standpoint Roman Catholicism itself is immeasurably higher and more logical than Protestantism, though the Roman Church has been pleased to adopt the exotericism of the heathen "multitude" and to reject the Philosophy of pure Esotericism.

Thus every mortal has his immortal counterpart, or rather his Archetype, in heaven. This means that the former is indissolubly united to the latter, in each of his incarnations, and for the duration of the cycle of births; only it is by the spiritual and intellectual Principle in him, entirely distinct from the lower self, never through the earthly personality. Some of these are even liable to break the union altogether, in case of absence in the moral individual of binding, viz.,of spiritual ties. Truly, as Paracelsus puts it in his quaint, tortured phraseology, man with his three (compound) Spirits is suspended like a foetus by all three to the matrix of the Macrocosm; the thread which holds him united being the "Thread-Soul," Sutratma, and Taijasa (the "Shining") of the Vedantins. And it is through this spiritual and intellectual Principle in man, though Taijasa - the Shining, "because it has the luminous internal organ as its associate" - that man is thus united to his heavenly prototype, never through his lower inner self or Astral Body, for which there remains in most cases nothing but to fade out.

Occultism, or Theurgy, teaches the means of producing such union. But it is the actions of man - his personal merit alone - that can produce it on earth, or determine its duration. This lasts from a few seconds - a flash - to several hours, during which time the Theurgist or Theophanist is that overshadowing "God" himself; hence he becomes endowed for the time being with relative omniscience and omnipotence. With such perfect (divine) Adepts as Buddha [Esoteric, as exoteric, Buddhism rejects the theory that Gautama was an incarnation or Avatara of Vishnu, but teaches the doctrine as herein explained. Every man has in him the materials, if not the conditions, for theophanic intercourse and Theopneusty, the inspiring "God" being, however, in every case, his own Higher Self, or divine prototype.] and others such a hypostatical state of avataric condition may last during the whole life; whereas in the case of full Initiates, who have not yet reached the perfect state of Jivanmukta, [One entirely and absolutely purified, and having nothing in common with earth except his body.] Theopneusty, when in full sway, results for the high Adept in a full recollection of everything seen, heard, or sensed.

Taijasa has fruition of the supersensible.[Mandukyopanishad, 4.]

For one less perfect it will end only in a partial, indistinct remembrance; while the beginner has to face in the first period of his psychic experiences a mere confusion, followed by a rapid and finally complete oblivion of the mysteries seen during this super-hypnotic condition. The degree of recollection, when one returns to his waking state and physical senses, depends on his spiritual and psychic purification, the greatest enemy of spiritual memory being man's physical brain the organ of his sensuous nature.

The above states are described for a clearer

comprehension of terms used in this work. There are so many and such various conditions and states that even a Seer is liable to confound one with the other.

THREE WAYS OPEN TO THE ADEPT –

To repeat: the Greek, rarely-used word, "Theophania," meant more with the Neoplatonists than it does with the modern maker of dictionaries. The compound word, Theophania" (from "theos," "God," and "phainomai," "to appear)," does not simply mean "a manifestation of God to man by actual appearance" - an absurdity, by the way - but the actual presence of a God in man, a divine incarnation. When Simon the Magician claimed to be "God the Father," what he wanted to convey was just that which has been explained, namely, that he was a divine incarnation of his own Father, whether we see in the latter an Angel, a God, or a Spirit; therefore he was called "that power of God which is called great," [Acts, viii, 10 (Revised Version).] or that power which causes the Divine Self to enshrine itself in its lower self - man.

This is one of the several mysteries of being and incarnation. Another is that when an Adept reaches during his lifetime that state of holiness and purity that makes him "equal to the Angels," then at death his apparitional or astral body becomes as solid and tangible as was the late body, and is transformed into the real man. [See the explanations given on the subject in "The Elixir of Life," by G.M. (From a Chela's Diary), Five Years of Theosophy.] The old physical body, falling off like the cast-off serpent's skin, the body of the "new" man remains either visible or, at the option of the Adept, disappears from view, surrounded as it is by the Akashic shell that screens it. In the latter case there are three ways open to the Adept:

(1) He may remain in the earth's sphere (Vayu or Kama-loka), in that ethereal locality concealed from human sight save during flashes of clairvoyance. In this case his astral body, owing to its great purity and spirituality, having lost the conditions required for Akashic light (the nether or terrestrial ether) to absorb its semi-material particles, the Adept will have to remain in the company of disintegrating shells - doing no good or useful work. This, of course, cannot be.

(2) He can by a supreme effort of will merge entirely into, and get united with, his Monad. By doing so, however, we would (a) deprive his Higher Self of posthumous Samadhi - a bliss which is not real Nirvana - the astral, however pure, being too earthly for such state; and (b) he would thereby open himself to Karmic law; the action being, in fact, the outcome of personal selfishness - of reaping the fruits produced by and for oneself - alone.

(3) The Adept has the option of renouncing conscious Nirvana and rest, to work on earth for the good of mankind. This he can do in a two-fold way: either, as above said, by consolidating his astral body into physical appearance, he can reassume the self-same personality; or he can avail himself of an entirely new physical body, whether that of a newly-born infant or - as Shânkarâcharya is reported to have done with the body of a dead Rajah - by entering a deserted sheath," and living in it as long as he chooses. This is what

is called "continuous existence." The Section entitled "The Mystery about Buddha" will throw additional light on this theory, to the profane incomprehensible, or to the generality simply absurd. Such is the doctrine taught, everyone having the choice of either fathoming it still deeper, or of leaving it unnoticed.

The above is simply a small portion of what might have been given in Isis Unveiled, had the time come then, as it has now. One cannot study and profit by Occult Science, unless one gives himself up to it - heart, soul, and body. Some of its truths are too awful, too dangerous, for the average mind. None can toy and play with such terrible weapons with impunity. Therefore it is, as St.Paul has it, "unlawful" to speak of them. Let us accept the reminder and talk only of that which is "lawful."

The quotation on p. 56 relates, moreover, only to psychic or spiritual Magic. The practical teachings of Occult Science are entirely different, and few are the strong minds fitted for them. As to ecstasy, and such like kinds of self-illumination, this may be obtained by oneself and without any teacher or initiation, for ecstasy is reached by an inward command and control of Self over the physical Ego; as to obtaining mastery over the forces of Nature, this requires a long training, or the capacity of one born a "natural Magician." Meanwhile, those who possess neither of the requisite qualifications are strongly advised to limit themselves to purely spiritual development. But even this is difficult, as the first necessary qualification is an unshakable belief in one's own powers and the Deity within oneself; otherwise a man would simply develop into an irresponsible medium. Throughout the whole mystic literature of the ancient world we detect the same idea of spiritual Esoterism, that the personal God exists within, nowhere outside, the worshipper. That personal Deity is no vain breath, or a fiction, but an immortal Entity, the Initiator of the Initiates, now that the heavenly or Celestial Initiators of primitive humanity - the Shishta of the preceding cycles - are no more among us. Like an undercurrent, rapid and clear, it runs without mixing its crystalline purity with the muddy troubled waters of dogmatism, an enforced anthropomorphic Deity and religious intolerance.

MAN IS GOD -

We find this idea in the tortured and barbarous phraseology of the Codex Nazaraeus, and in the superb Neoplatonic language of the Fourth Gospel of the later Religion, in the oldest Veda and in the Avesta, in the Abhidharma, in Kapila's Sankhya, and the Bhagavad Gitâ. We cannot attain Adeptship and Nirvana, Bliss and the "Kingdom of Heaven," unless we link ourselves indissolubly with our Rex Lux, the Lord of Splendour and of Light, our immortal God within us. "Aham eva param Brahman" - "I am verily the Supreme Brahman" - has ever been the one living truth in the heart and mind of the Adepts, and it is this which helps the Mystic to become one. One must first of all recognize one's own immortal Principle, and then only can one conquer, or take the Kingdom of Heaven by violence. Only this has to be achieved by the higher - not the middle, nor the third - man, the last one being of dust. Nor can the second man, the

"Son" - on this plane, as his "Father" is the Son on a still higher plane - do anything without the assistance of the first, the "Father." But to succeed one has to identify oneself with one's divine Parent.

The first man is of the earth, earthy; the second [inner, our higher] man is the Lord from heaven. . . . Behold, I show you a mystery.[I.Cor., xv. 47.50.]

Thus says Paul, mentioning but the dual and trinitarian man for the better comprehension of the non-initiated. But this is not all, for the Dephic injunction has to be fulfilled: man must know himself in order to become a perfect Adept. How few can acquire the knowledge, however, not merely in its inner mystical, but even in its literal sense, for there are two meanings in this command of the Oracle. This is the doctrine of Buddha and the Bodhisattvas pure and simple.

Such is also the mystical sense of what was said to Paul to the Corinthians about their being the "temple of God," for this meant Esoterically:

Ye are the temple of [the, or your] God, and the Spirit of [a, or your] God dwelleth in you. [I Cor., iii. 16. Has the reader ever meditated upon the suggestive words, often pronounced by Jesus and his Apostles? "Be ye therefore perfect as your Father. . . is perfect" (Matt., v. 48), says the Great Master. The words are, "as perfect as your Father which is in heaven," being interpreted as meaning God. Now the utter absurdity of any man becoming as perfect as the infinite, all-perfect, omniscient and omnipresent Deity, is too apparent. If you accept it in such a sense, Jesus is made to utter the greatest fallacy. What was Esoterically meant is, "Your Father who is above the material and astral man, the highest Principle (save the Monad) within man, his own personal God, or the God of his own personality, of whom he is the 'prison' and the 'temple.' " "If thou wilt be perfect (i.e., an Adept and Initiate) go and sell that thou hast" (Matt., xix.21). Every man who desired to become a neophyte, a chela, then, as now, had to take the vow of poverty. The "Perfect," was the name given to the Initiates of every denomination. Plato calls them by that term. The Essenes had their "Perfect." and Paul plainly states that they, the Initiates, can only speak before other Adepts. "We speak wisdom among them [only] that are perfect" (I. Cor.ii.6).]

This carries precisely the same meaning as the "I am verily Brahman" of the Vedantin. Nor is the latter assertion more blasphemous than the Pauline - if there were any blasphemy in either, which is denied. Only the Vedantin, who never refers to his body as being himself, or even a part of himself, or aught else but an illusory form for others to see him in, constructs his assertion more openly and sincerely than was done by Paul.

The Delphic command "Know thyself" was perfectly comprehensible to every nation of old. So it is now, save to the Christians, since with the exception of the Mussulmans, it is part and parcel of every Eastern religion, including the Kabalistically instructed Jews. To understand its full meaning, however, necessitates, first of all, belief in Reincarnation and all its mysteries; not as laid down in the doctrine of the French Reincarnationists of the Allan Kardec school, but as they are expounded and taught by Esoteric Philosophy.

Man must in short, know who he was, before he arrives at knowing what he is. And how many are there among Europeans who are capable of developing within themselves an absolute belief in their past and future reincarnations, in general, even as a law, let alone mystic knowledge of one's immediately precedent life? Early education, tradition and training of thought, everything is opposing itself during their whole lives to such a belief. Cultured people have been brought up in that most pernicious idea that the wide difference found between the units of one and the same mankind, or even race, is the result of chance; that the gulf between man and man in their respective social positions, birth, intellect, physical and mental capacities - every one of which qualifications has a direct influence on every human life - that all this is simply due to blind hazard, only the most pious among them finding equivocal consolation in the idea that it is "the will of God." They have never analysed, never stopped to think of the depth of the opprobrium that is thrown upon their God, once the grand and most equitable law of the manifold re-births of man upon this earth is foolishly rejected. Men and women anxious to be regarded as Christians, often truly and sincerely trying to lead a Christ-like life, have never paused to reflect over the words of their own Bible.

JESUS TAUGHT REINCARNATION –

"Art thou Elias?" the Jewish priests and Levites asked the Baptist. [John, i. 21.] Their Saviour taught His disciples this grand truth of the Esoteric Philosophy, but verily, if His Apostles comprehended it, no one else seems to have realised its true meaning. No; not even Nicodemus, who, to the assertion: "Except a man be born again [John,iii, "Born" from above, viz., from his Monad or divine EGO, the seventh Principle which remains till the end of the Kalpa, the nucleus of, and at the same time the overshadowing Principle, as the Karanatma (Causal Soul) of the personality in every rebirth. In this sense, the sentence "born anew" means "descends from above," the last two words having no reference to heaven or space, neither of which can be limited or located, since one is a state and the other infinite, hence having no cardinal points. (See New Testament, Revised Version loc. cit.)] he cannot see the Kingdom of God," answers: "How can a man be born when he is old?" and is forthwith reproved by the remark: "Art thou a Master in Israel and knowest not these things? - as no one had a right to call himself a "Master" and Teacher, without having been initiated into the mysteries (a) of a spiritual re-birth through water, fire and spirit, and (b) of the re-birth from flesh. [This can have no reference to Christian Baptism, since there was none in the days of Nicodemus and he could not therefore know anything of it, even though a "Master."] Then again what can be a clearer expression as to the doctrine of manifold re-births than the answer given by Jesus to the Sadducees, "who deny that there is any resurrection," i.e., any re-birth, since the dogma of the resurrection in the flesh is now regarded as an absurdity even by the intelligent clergy:

They who shall be accounted worthy to obtain that world [Nirvana] [This word, translated in the New Testament "world" to suit the official interpretation, means rather an "age" (as shown in the Revised Version) or one of the periods during the Manvantara, a Kalpa, or Aeon. Esoterically the sentence would read: "He who shall reach, through a series of births and Karmic law, the state in which Humanity shall find itself after the Seventh Round and the Seventh Race, when comes Nirvana, Moksha, and when man becomes 'equal unto the Angels' of Dhyan Chohans, is a 'son of the resurrection' and 'can die no more': then there will be no marriage, as there will be no difference of sexes" - a result of our present materiality and animalism.] . . . . neither marry . . . Neither can they die any more, which shows that they had already died, and more than once. And again:

Now that the dead are raised even Moses shewed . . . He calleth the Lord the God of Abraham, and the God of Isaac, and the God of Jacob, for he is not a God of the dead but of the living. [Luke,xx. 27-38.]

The sentence "now that the dead are raised" evidently applied to the then actual re-births of the Jacobs and the Isaacs, and not to their future resurrection; for in such case they would have been still dead in the interim, and could not be referred to as "the living."

But in the most suggestive of Christ's parables and "dark sayings" is found in the explanation given by him to his Apostles about the blind man:

Master, who did sin, this man or his parents, that he was born blind? Jesus answered, Neither hath this [blind, physical] man sinned nor his parents; but that the works of [his] God should be made manifest in him. [John, ix. 2. 3.]

Man is the "tabernacle," the "building" only, of his God;

and of course it is not the temple but its inmate - the vehicle of "God" [The conscious Ego, of Fifth Principle Manas, the vehicle of the divine Monad or "God".] that had sinned in a previous incarnation, and had thus brought the Karma of cecity upon the new building. Thus Jesus spoke truly; but to this day his followers have refused to understand the words of wisdom spoken. The Saviour is shown by his followers as though he were paving, by his words and explanation, the way to a preconceived programme that had to lead to an intended miracle. Verily the Grand Martyr has remained thenceforward, and for eighteen centuries, the Victim crucified daily far more cruelly by his clerical disciples and lay followers than he ever could have been by his allegorical enemies. For such is the true sense of the words "that the works of God should be made manifest in him," in the light of theological interpretation, and a very undignified one it is, if the Esoteric explanation is rejected.

Doubtless the above will be regarded as fresh blasphemy. Nevertheless there are a number of Christians whom we know - whose hearts go out as strongly to their ideal of Jesus, as their souls are repelled from the theological picture of the official Saviour - who will reflect over our explanation and find in it no offence, but perchance a relief.

SECTION VI

THE DANGERS OF PRACTICAL MAGIC

MAGIC is a dual power: nothing is easier than to turn it into Sorcery; an evil thought suffices for it. Therefore while theoretical Occultism is harmless, and may do good, practical Magic, or the fruits of the Tree of Life and Knowledge,[Some Symbologists, relying on the correspondence of numbers and the symbols of certain things and personages, refer these "secrets" to the mystery of generation. But it is more than this. The glyph of the "Tree of Knowledge of Good and Evil" has no doubt a phallic and sexual element in it, as has the "Woman and the Serpent"; but it has also a psychical and spiritual significance. Symbols are meant to yield more than one meaning.] or otherwise the "Science of Good and Evil," is fraught with dangers and perils.

For the study of theoretical Occultism there are, no doubt a number of works that may be read with profit, besides such books as the Finer Forces of Nature, etc., the Zohar, Sepher Jetzirah, The Book of Enoch, Franck's Kabalah, and many Hermetic treatises. These are scarce in European languages, but works in Latin by the mediaeval Philosophers, generally known as Alchemists and Rosicrucians, are plentiful. But even the perusal of these may prove dangerous for the unguided student. If approached without the right key to them, and if the student is unfit, owing to mental incapacity, for Magic, and is thus unable to discern the Right from the

Left Path, let him take our advice and leave this study alone; he will only bring on himself and on his family unexpected woes and sorrows, never suspecting whence they come, nor what are the powers awakened by his mind being bent on them. Works for advanced students are many, but these can be placed at the disposal of only sworn or "pledged" chelas (disciples), those who have pronounced the ever-binding oath, and who are, therefore, helped and protected. For all other purposes, well-intentioned as such works may be, they can only mislead the unwary and guide them imperceptibly to Black Magic or Sorcery - if to nothing worse.

The mystic characters, alphabets and numerals found in the divisions and sub-divisions of the Great Kabalah, are perhaps, the most dangerous portions in it, and especially the numerals. We say dangerous, because they are the most prompt to produce effects and results, and this with or without the experimenter's will, even without his knowledge. Some students are apt to doubt this statement, simply because after manipulating these numerals they have failed to notice any dire physical manifestation or result. Such results would be found the least dangerous: it is the moral causes produced and the various events developed and brought to an unforeseen crisis, that would testify to the truth of what is now stated had the lay students only the power of discernment.

The point of departure of that special branch of the Occult teaching known as the "Science of Correspondences," numerical or literal or alphabetical, has for its epigraph with the Jewish and Christian Kabalists, the two misinterpreted verses which say that God ordered all things in number, measure and weight; [Wisdom, xi.21. Douay version] and:

He created her in the Holy Ghost, and saw her, and numbered her, and measured her. [Ecclesiasticus, i. 9. Douay version.]

But the Eastern Occultists have another epigraph: "Absolute Unity, x, within number and plurality." Both the Western and the Eastern students of the Hidden Wisdom hold to this axiomatic truth. Only the latter are perhaps more sincere in their confessions. Instead of putting a mask on their Science, they show her face openly, even if they do veil carefully her heart and soul before the inappreciative public and the profane, who are ever ready to abuse the most sacred truths for their own selfish ends. But Unity is the real basis of the Occult Sciences - physical and metaphysical. This is shown even by Eliphas Levi, the learned Western Kabalist, inclined as he is to be rather jesuitical. He says:

Absolute Unity is the supreme and final reason of things. Therefore, that reason can be neither one person, nor three persons; it is Reason, and preeminently Reason (raison par excellence).[Dogme et Rituel de la Haute Magie, i, 361.]

NAMES ARE SYMBOLS –

The meaning of this Unity in Plurality in "God" or Nature, can be solved only by the means of transcendental methods, by numerals, as by the correspondences between soul and the Soul. Names, in the Kabalah, as in the Bible such as Jehovah, Adam Kadmon, Eve, Cain, Abel, Enoch, are all of them more intimately connected, by geometrical and astronomical relations, with Physiology (or Phallicism) than with Theology or Religion. Little as people are as yet prepared to admit it, this will be shown to be a fact. If all those names are symbols for things hidden, as well as for those manifested, in the Bible as in the Vedas, their respective mysteries differ greatly. Plato's motto "God geometrises" was accepted by both Aryans and Jews; but while the former applied their Science of Correspondences to veil the most spiritual and sublime truths of Nature, the latter used their acumen to conceal only one - to them the most divine - of the mysteries of Evolution, namely, that of birth and generation, and then they deified the organs of the latter.

Apart from this, every cosmogony, from the earliest to the latest, is based upon interlinked with, and most closely related to numerals and geometric figures. Questioned by an Initiate, these figures and numbers will yield numerical values based on the integral values of the Circle - "the secret habitat of the ever-invisible Deity" as the Alchemists have it - as they will yield every other Occult particular connected with such mysteries, whether anthropographical, anthroplogical, cosmic, or psychical. "In reuniting Ideas to Numbers, we can operate upon Ideas in the same way as upon Numbers, and arrive at the Mathematics of Truth," writes an Occultist, who shows his great wisdom in desiring to remain unknown.

Any Kabalist well acquainted with the Pythagorean system of numerals and geometry can demonstrate that the metaphysical views of Plato were based upon the strictest mathematical principles. "True mathematics," says the Magicon, "is something with which all higher sciences are connected; common mathematics is but a deceitful phantasmagoria, whose much praised infallibility only arises from this - that materials, conditions and references are made to foundation."

The cosmological theory of numerals which Pythagoras learned in India, and from the Egyptian Hierophants, is alone able to reconcile the two units, matter and spirit, and cause each to demonstrate the other mathematically. The sacred numbers of the universe in their esoteric combination can alone solve the great problem, and explain the theory of radiation and the cycle of the emanations. The lower orders, before they develop into higher ones, must emanate from the higher spiritual ones, and when arrived at the turning-point, be reabsorbed into the infinite.[Isis Unveiled, i, 6, 7.]

It is upon these true Mathematics that the knowledge of the Kosmos and of all mysteries rests, and to one acquainted with them, it is the easiest thing possible to prove that both Vaidic and Biblical structures are based upon "God-in-Nature" and "Nature-in-God," as the radical law. Therefore, this law - as everything else immutable and fixed in eternity - could find a correct expression only in those purest transcendental Mathematics referred to by Plato, especially in Geometry as transcendentally applied. Revealed to men - we fear not and will not retract the expression - in this geometrical and symbolical garb, Truth has grown and developed into additional symbology, invented by man for the wants and better comprehension of the masses of mankind that came too late in their cyclic development and evolution to have shared in the primitive knowledge, and would never have grasped it otherwise. If later on, the clergy - crafty and ambitious of power in every age - anthropomorphised and degraded abstract ideals, as well as the real and divine Beings who do exist in Nature, and are the Guardians and Protectors of our manvantaric world and period, the fault and guilt rests with those would-be leaders, not with the masses.

But the day has come when the gross conceptions of our forefathers during the Middle Ages can no longer satisfy the thoughtful religionist. The mediaeval Alchemist and Mystic are now transformed into the sceptical Chemist and Physicist; and most of them are found to have turned away from truth, on account of the purely anthropomorphic ideas, the gross Materialism, of the forms in which it is presented to them. Therefore, future generations have either to be gradually initiated into the truths underlying Exoteric Religions, including their own or to be left to break the feet of clay of the last of the gilded idols. No educated man or woman would turn away from any of the now called "superstitions," which they believe to be based on nursery tales and ignorance, if they could only see the basis of fact that underlies every "superstition." But let them once learn for a certainty that there is hardly a claim in the Occult Sciences that is not founded on philosophical and scientific facts in Nature, and they will pursue the study of those Sciences with the same, if not with greater, ardour than that they have expended in shunning them. This cannot be achieved at once, for to benefit mankind such truths have to be revealed gradually and with great caution, the public mind not being prepared for them.

THE THREE MOTHERS –

However much the Agnostics of our age may find themselves in the mental attitude demanded by Modern Science, people are always apt to cling to their old hobbies so long as the remembrance of them lasts. They are like the Emperor Julian - called the Apostate, because he loved truth too well to accept aught else - who, though in his last Theophany he beheld his beloved Gods as pale, worn-out, and hardly discernible shadows, nevertheless clung to them. Let, then, the world cling to its Gods, to whatever plane or realm they may belong. The true Occultist would be guilty of high treason to mankind, were he to break forever the old deities before he could replace them with the whole and unadulterated truth - and this he cannot do as yet. Nevertheless, the reader may be allowed to learn at least the alphabet of that truth. He may be shown, at any rate, what the Gods and Goddesses of the Pagans, denounced as demons by the Church, are not, if he cannot learn the whole and final truth as to what they are. Let him assure himself that the Hermetic "Tres Matres," and the "Three Mothers" of the Sepher Jetzirah are one and the same thing; that they are no Demon-Goddesses, but Light, Heat, and Electricity, and then, perchance, the learned classes will spurn them no longer. After this, the Rosicrucian Illuminati may find followers even in the Royal Academies, which will be more prepared, perhaps, than they are now, to admit the grand truths of archaic Natural Philosophy, especially when their learned members shall have assured themselves that, in the dialect of Hermes, the "Three Mothers" stand as symbols for the whole of the forces or agencies which have a place assigned to them in the modern system of the "correlation of forces." ["Synesius mentions books of stone which he found in the temple of Memphis, on one of which was engraved the following sentence: 'One nature delights in another, one nature overcomes another, one nature overrules another, and the whole of them are one'." "The inherent restlessness of matter is embodied in the saying of Hermes: 'Action is he life of Phta': and Orpheus calls nature χολυμηχανος ματηρ , 'the mother that makes many things,' or the ingenious, the contiving, the inventive mother." - Isis Unveiled. i. 257.] Even the polytheism of the "superstitious" Brâhman and idolater shows its raison d'être, since the three Shaktis of the three great Gods, Brahma, Vishnu, and Shiva, are identical with the "Three Mothers" of the monotheistic Jew.

The whole of the ancient religious and mystical literature is symbolical. The Books of Hermes, the Zohar, the Ya-Yakav, the Egyptian Book of the Dead, the Vedas, the Upanishads, and the Bible, are as full of symbolism as are the Nabathean revelations of the Chaldaic Qu-tâmy; it is a loss of time to ask which is the earliest; all are simply different versions of the one primeval Record of prehistoric knowledge and revelation.

The first four chapters of Genesis contain the synopsis of all the rest of the Pentateuch, being only the various versions of the same thing in different allegorical and symbolical applications. Having discovered that the Pyramid of Cheops with all its measurements is to be found contained in its minutest details in the structure of Solomon's Temple; and having ascertained that the biblical names Shem, Ham and Japhet are determinative of pyramid measures, in connection with the 600-year period of Noah and the 500-year period of Shem, Ham and Japhet: . . . the term "Sons of Elohim" and "Daughters" of H-Adam, [are] for one thing astronomical terms,[Source of Measures. p.x.] the author of the very curious work already mentioned - a book very little known in Europe, we regret to say - seems to see nothing in his discovery beyond the presence of Mathematics and Metrology in the Bible. He also arrives at most unexpected and extraordinary conclusions, such as are very little warranted by the facts discovered. His impression seems to be that because the Jewish biblical names are all astronomical, therefore the Scriptures of all the other nations can be "only this and nothing more." But this is a great mistake of the erudite and wonderfully acute author of The Source of Measures, if he really thinks so. The "Key to the Hebrew-Egyptian Mystery" unlocks but a certain portion of the hieratic writings of these two nations, and leaves those of other peoples untouched. His idea is that the Kabalah "is only that sublime Science upon which Masonry is based", in fact he regards Masonry as the substance of the Kabalah, and the latter as the "rational basis of the Hebrew text of Holy Writ." About this we will not argue with the author. But why should all those who may have found in the Kabalah something beyond "the sublime Science" upon which Masonry is alleged to have been built, be held up to public contempt?

In its exclusiveness and one-sidedness such a conclusion

is pregnant with future misconceptions and is absolutely wrong. In its uncharitable criticism it throws a slur upon the "Divine Science" itself.

THE BIBLE AND WORD - JUGGLING -

The Kabalah is indeed "of the essence of Masonry," but it is dependent on Metrology only in one of its aspects, the less Esoteric, as even Plato made no secret that the Deity was ever geometrising. For the uninitiated, however learned and endowed with genius they may be, the Kabalah, which treats only of "the garment of God," or the veil and cloak of truth,

is built from the ground upward with a practical application to present uses. [Masonic Review, July 1886]

Or in other words represents an exact Science only on the terrestrial plane. To the initiated, the Kabalistic Lord descends from the primeval Race, generated spiritually from the "Mind-born Seven." Having reached the Earth the Divine Mathematics - a synonym for Magic in his day, as we are told by Josephus - veiled her face. Hence the most important secret yet yielded by her in our modern day is the identity of the old Roman measures and the present British measures of the Hebrew-Egyptian cubit and the Masonic inch. [See Source of Measures, pp. 47 - 50, et pass.]

The discovery is most wonderful, and has led to further and minor unveilings of various riddles in reference to Symbology and biblical names. It is thoroughly understood and proven, as shown by Nachanides, that in the days of Moses the initial sentence in Genesis was made to read B'rash ithbara Elohim, or "In the head-source [or Mûlaprakriti - the Rootless

Root] developed [or evolved] the Gods [Elohim], the heavens and the earth;" whereas it is now, owing to the Massora and theological cunning, transformed into B'rashith bara Elohim, or, "In the beginning God created the heavens and the earth" - which word juggling alone has led to materialistic anthropomorphism and dualism.] How many more similar instances may not be found in the Bible, the last and latest of the Occult works of antiquity? There is no longer any doubt in the mind of the Occultist, that, notwithstanding its form and outward meaning, the Bible - as explained by the Zohar or Midrash, the Yetsirah (Book of Creation) and the Commentary on the Ten Sephiroth (by Azariel Ben Manachem of the X11th century) - is part and parcel of the Secret Doctrine of the Aryans, which explains in the same manner the Vedas and all other allegorical books. The Zohar, in teaching that the Impersonal One Cause manifests in the Universe through Its Emanations, the Sephiroth - that Universe being in its totality simply the veil woven from the Deity's own substance - is undeniably the copy and faithful echo of the earliest Vedas. Taken by itself, without the additional help of the Vaidic and of Brahmanical literature in general , the Bible will never yield the universal secrets of Occult Nature. The cubits, inches, and measures of this physical plane will never solve the problems of the world on the spiritual plane - for Spirit can neither be weighed nor measured. The working out of these problems is reserved for the "mystics and the dreamers" who alone are capable of accomplishing it.

Moses was an initiated priest, versed in all the mysteries and the Occult knowledge of the Egyptian temples - hence thoroughly acquainted with primitive Wisdom. It is in the latter that the symbolical and astronomical meaning of that "Mystery of Mysteries," the Great Pyramid, has to be sought. And having been so familiar with the geometrical secrets that lay concealed for long aeons in her strong bosom - the measurements and proportions of the Kosmos, our little Earth included - what wonder that he should have made use of his knowledge? The Esoterism of Egypt was that of the whole world at one time. During the long ages of the Third Race it had been the heirloom, in common, of the whole of mankind, received from their Instructors, the "Sons of Light," the primeval Seven. There was a time also when the Wisdom-Religion was not symbolical for it became Esoteric only gradually, the change being necessitated by misuse and by the Sorcery of the Atlanteans. For it was the "misuse" only, and not the use, of the divine gift that led the men of the Fourth Race to Black Magic and Sorcery, and finally to become "forgetful of Wisdom"; while those of the Fifth Race, the inheritors of the Rishis of the Treta Yuga, used their powers to atrophise such gifts in mankind in general, and then, as the "Elect Root," dispersed. Those who escaped the "Great Flood" preserved only its memory, and a belief founded on the knowledge of their direct fathers of one remove, that such a Science existed, and was now jealously guarded by the "Elect Root" exalted by Enoch. But there must again come a time when man shall once more become what he was during the second Yuga (age), when his probationary cycle shall be over and he shall gradually become what he was - semi-corporeal and pure. Does not

Plato, the Initiate, tell us in the Phaedrus all that man once was, and that which he may yet again become:

Before man's spirit sank into sensuality and became embodied through the loss of his wings, he lived among the Gods in the airy spiritual world where everything is true and pure. [See Cary's translation, pp.322, 323.]

MOSES AND THE JEWS -

Elsewhere he speaks of the time when men did not perpetuate themselves, but lived as pure spirits.

Let those men of Science who feel inclined to laugh at this, themselves unravel the mystery of the origin of the first man.

Unwilling that his chosen people - chosen by him - should remain as grossly idolatrous as the profane masses that surrounded them, Moses utilised his knowledge of cosmogonical mysteries of the Pyramid, to build upon it the Genesiacal Cosmogony in symbols and glyphs. This was more accessible to the minds of the hoi polloi than the abstruse truths taught to the educated in the sanctuaries. He invented nothing but the outward garb, added not one iota; but in this he merely followed the example of older nations and Initiates. If he clothed the grand truths revealed to him by his Hierophant under the most ingenious imagery, he did it to meet the requirements of the Israelites; that stiff-necked race would accept no God unless He were as anthropomorphic as those of the Olympus; and he himself failed to foresee the times when highly educated statesmen would be defending the husks of the fruit of wisdom that grew and developed in him on Mount Sinai, when communing with his own personal God - his divine Self. Moses understood the great danger of delivering such truths to the selfish, for he understood the fable of Prometheus and remembered the past. Hence, he veiled them from the profanation of public gaze and gave them out allegorically. And this is why his biographer says of him, that when he descended from Sinai,

Moses wist not that the skin of his face shone . . . And he put a veil upon his face.[Exodus. xxxiv. 29, 33.]

And so he "put a veil" upon the face of his Pentateuch; and to such an extent that, using orthodox chronology, only 3376 years after the event people begin to acquire a conviction that it is "a veil indeed." It is not the face of God or even of a Johovah shining through; not even the face of Moses, but verily the faces of the later Rabbis.

No wonder if Clemens wrote in the Stromateis that:

Similar, then, to the Hebrew enigmas in respect to concealment are those of the Egyptians also. [Op, cit., V, vii.]

SECTION VII

OLD WINE IN NEW BOTTLES

I T is more than likely, that the Protestants in the days of the Reformation knew nothing of the true origin of Christianity, or, to be more explicit and correct, of Latin Ecclesiasticism. Nor is it probable that the Greek Church knew much of it, the separation between the two having occurred at a time when, in the struggle for political power the Latin Church was securing, at any cost, the alliance of the highly educated, the ambitious and influential Pagans, while these were willing to assume the outward appearance of the new worship, provided they were themselves kept in power.

There is no need to remind the reader here of the details of that struggle, well-known to every educated man. It is certain that the highly cultivated Gnostics and their leaders - such men as Saturnilus, an uncompromising ascetic, as Marcion, Valentinus, Basilides, Menander and Cerinthus - were not stigmatised by the (now) Latin Church because they were heretics, nor because their tenets and practices were indeed "ob turpitudinem portentosam nimium et horribilem," "monstrous, revolting abominations," as Baronius says of those of Carpocrates ; but simply because they knew too much of fact and truth. Kenneth R.H. Mackenzie correctly remarks;

They were stigmatised by the later Roman Church because they came into conflict with the purer Church of

Christianity - the possession of which was usurped by the Bishops of Rome, but which original continues in its docility towards the founder, in the Primitive Orthodox Greek Church. [The Royal Masonic Cyclopaedia under "Gnosticism."]

Unwilling to accept the responsibility of gratuitous assumptions, the writer deems it best to prove this inference by more than one personal and defiant admission of an ardent Roman Catholic writer, evidently entrusted with the delicate task by the Vatican.

COPIES THAT ANTE-DATED ORIGINALS -

The Marquis de Mirville makes desperate efforts to explain to the Catholic interest certain remarkable discoveries in Archaeology and Palaeography, though the Church is cleverly made to remain outside of the quarrel and defence. This is undeniably shown by his ponderous volumes addressed to the Academy of France between 1803 and 1865. Seizing the pretext of drawing the attention of the materialistic "Immortals" to the "epidemic of Spiritualism," the invasion of Europe and America by a numberless host of Satanic forces, he directs his efforts towards proving the same, by giving the full Genealogies and the Theogony of the Christian and Pagan deities, and by drawing parallels between the two. All such wonderful likenesses and identities are only "seeming and superficial," he assures the reader. Christian symbols, and even characters, Christ, the Virgin, Angels and Saints, tells them, were all personated centuries beforehand by the fiends of hell, in order to discredit eternal truth by their ungodly copies. By their knowledge of futurity the devils anticipated events, having discovered the secrets of the Angels." Heathen Deities, all the Sun-Gods, named Sotors - Saviours - born of immaculate mothers and dying a violent death, were only Ferouers [In the Ferouers and Devs of Jacobi (Letters F. and D.) the word "ferouer" is explained in the following manner: The Ferouer is a part of the creature (whether man or animal) of which it is the type and which it survives. It is the Nous of the Greeks, therefore divine and immortal, and thus can hardly be the Devil or the satanic copy De Mirville would represent it (See Memoires de l'Academie des Inscriptions, Vol. XXXV11, P. 623, and chap. xxxix. p. 749). Foucher contradicts him entirely. The Ferouer was never the "principle of sensations," but always referred to the most divine and pure portion of Man's Ego - the spiritual principle. Anquetil says the Ferouer is the purest portion of man's soul. The Persian Dev is the antithesis of the Ferouer, for the Dev has been transformed by Zoroaster into the Genius of Evil (whence the Christian Devil), but even the Dev is only finite: for having become possessed of the soul of man by usurpation, it will have to leave it at the great day of Retribution. The Dev obsesses the soul of the defunct for three days, during which the soul wanders about the spot at which it was forcibly separated from its body, the Ferouer ascends to the region of eternal Light. It was an unfortunate idea that made the noble Marquis de Mirville imagine the Ferouer to be a "satanic copy" of a divine original. By calling all the Gods of the Pagans - Apollo, Osiris, Brahma, Ormazd, Bel, etc., the "Ferouers of Christ and of the chief Angels," he merely exhibits the God and the Angels he would honour as inferior to the Pagan Gods, as man is inferior to his Soul and Spirit: since the Ferouer is the immortal part of the mortal being of which it is the type and which it survives. Perchance the poor author is unconsciously prophetic: and Apollo, Brahma, Ormazd, Osiris, etc., are destined to survive and replace - as eternal cosmic verities - the evanescent fictions about the God, Christ and Angels of the Latin Church!] - as they were called by the Zoroastrians - the demon-ante-dated copies (copies anticipées) of the Messiah to come,

The danger of recognition of such facsimiles had indeed lately become dangerously great. It had lingered threateningly in the air, hanging like a sword of Damocles over the Church, since the days of Voltaire, Dupuis and other writers on similar lines. The discoveries of the Egyptologists, the finding of Assyrian and Babylonian pre-Mosaic relics bearing the legend of Moses [See George Smith's Babylon and other works] and especially the many rationalistic works published in England, such as Supernatural Religion, made recognition unavoidable. Hence the appearance of Protestant and Roman Catholic writers deputed to explain the inexplicable; to reconcile the face of Divine Revelation with the mystery that the divine personages, rites, dogmas and symbols of Christianity were so often identical with those of the several great heathen religions. The former - the Protestant defenders - tried to explain it, on the ground of "prophetic, precursory ideas"; the Latinists, such as De Mirville, by inventing a double set of Angels and Gods, the one divine and true, the other - the earlier - "copies ante-dating the originals" and due to a clever plagiarism by the

Evil One. The Protestant stratagem is an old one, that of the Roman Catholics is so old that it has been forgotten, and is as good as new. Dr. Lundy's Monumental Christianity and A Miracle in Stone belong to the first attempts. De. Mirville's Pneumatologie to the second. In India and China, every such effort on the part of the Scotch and other missionaries ends in laughter, and does no harm; the plan devised by the Jesuits is more serious. De Mirville's volumes are thus very important, as they proceed from a source which has undeniably the greatest learning of the age at its service, and this coupled with all the craft and casuistry that the sons of Loyola can furnish. The Marquis de Mirville was evidently helped by the acutest minds in the service of Rome.

He begins by not only admitting the justice of every imputation and charge made against the Latin Church as to the originality of her dogmas, but by taking a seeming delight in anticipating such charges; for he points to every dogma of Christianity as having existed in Pagan rituals in Antiquity. The whole Pantheon of Heathen Deities is passed in review by him, and each is shown to have had some point of resemblance with the Trinitarian personages and Mary. There is hardly a mystery, a dogma, or a rite in the Latin Church that is not shown by the author as having been "parodied by the Curvati" - the "Curved," the Devils. All this being admitted and explained, the Symbologists ought to be silenced. And so they would be, if there were no materialistic critics to reject such omnipotency of the Devil in this world. For, if Rome admits the likenesses, she also claims the right of judgment between the true and the false Avatâra, the real and the unreal God, between the original and the copy - though the copy precedes the original by millenniums.

WHICH WERE THE THIEVES? -

Our author proceeds to argue that whenever the missionaries try to convert an idolater, they are invariably answered:

We had our Crucified before yours. What do you come to show us? [This is as fanciful as it is arbitrary. Where is the Hindu or Buddhist who would speak of his "Crucified'?] Again, what should we gain by denying the mysterious side of this copy, under the plea that according to Weber all the present Puranas are remade from older ones, since here we have in the same order of personages a positive precedence which no one would ever think of contesting. [Op. cit., iv.237]

And the author instances Buddha, Krishna, Apollo, etc. Having admitted all this he escapes the difficulty in this wise:

The Church Fathers, however, who recognised their own property under all such sheep's clothing . . . knowing by means of the Gospel . . . all the ruses of the pretended spirits of light; the Fathers, we say, meditating upon the decisive words, "all that ever came before me are robbers" (John, x. 8), did not hesitate in recognising the Occult agency at work, the general and superhuman direction given beforehand to falsehood, the universal attribute and environment of all these false Gods of the nations; "omnes dii gentium daemonia (elilim)." (Psalm xcv.)[Loc cit., 250.]

With such a policy everything is made easy. There is not one glaring resemblance, not one fully proven identity, that could not thus be made away with. The above-quoted cruel, selfish, self-glorifying words, placed by John in the mouth of Him who was meekness and charity personified, could never have been pronounced by Jesus. The Occultists reject the imputation indignantly, and are prepared to defend the man as against the God, by showing whence come the words, plagiarised by the author of the Fourth Gospel. They are taken bodily from the "Prophecies" in the Book of Enoch. The evidence on this head of the learned biblical scholar, Archbishop Laurence, and of the author of the Evolution of Christianity, who edited the translation, may be brought forward to prove the fact. On the last page of the Introduction to the Book of Enoch is found the following passage:

The parable of the sheep rescued by the good Shepherd from hireling guardians and ferocious wolves, is obviously borrowed by the fourth Evangelist from   Enoch, lxxxix, in which the author depicts the shepherds as killing and destroying the sheep before the advent of the Lord, and this discloses the true meaning of that hitherto mysterious passage in the Johannine parable - "All that ever came before me are thieves and robbers" - language in which we now detect an obvious reference to the allegorical shepherds of Enoch.

"Obvious" truly, and something else besides. For, if Jesus pronounced the words in the sense attributed to him, then he must have read the Book of Enoch - a purely Kabalistic, Occult work, and he therefore recognised the worth and value of a treatise now declared apocryphal by his Churches. Moreover, he could not have been ignorant that these words belonged to the oldest ritual of Inititation.

["Q": Who knocks at the door?

A.: The good cowherd.

Q.: Who preceded thee?

A.: The three robbers.

Q.: Who follows thee?

A.: The three murderers," etc., etc."

Now this is the conversation that took place between the priest-initiators and the candidates for initiation during the mysteries enacted in the oldest sanctuaries of the Himalayan fastnesses. The ceremony is still performed to this day in one of the most ancient temples in a secluded spot of Nepaul. It originated with the Mysteries of the first Krishna, passed to the First Tirthankara and ended with Buddha, and is called the Kurukshetra rite, being enacted as a memorial of the great battle and death of the divine Adept. It is not Masonry, but an initiation into the Occult teachings of that Hero-Occultism, pure and simple.]

And if he had not read it, and the sentence belongs to John, or whoever wrote the Fourth Gospel, then what reliance can be placed on the authenticity of other sayings and parables attributed to the Christian Saviour?

Thus, De Mirville's illustration is an unfortunate one. Every other proof brought by the Church to show the infernal character of the ante-and-anti-Christian copyists may be easily disposed of. This is perhaps unfortunate, but it is a fact, nevertheless - Magna est veritas et prevalebit.

The above is the answer to the Occultists to the two parties who charge them incessantly, the one with "Superstition." and the other with "Sorcery." To those of our Brothers who are Christians, and twit us with the secresy imposed upon the Eastern Chelas, adding invariably that their own "Book of God' is "an open volume" for all "to read, understand, and be saved." we would reply by asking them to study what we have just said in this Section, and then to refute it - if they can. There are very few in our days who are still prepared to assure their readers that the Bible had

God for its author, salvation for its end, and truth without any mixture of error for its matter.

CHARACTER OF THE BIBLE -

Could Locke be asked the question now, he would perhaps be unwilling to repeat again that the Bible is all pure, all sincere, nothing too much, nothing wanting.

The Bible, if it is not to be shown to be the very reverse of all this, sadly needs an interpreter acquainted with the doctrines of the East, as they are to be found in its secret volumes; nor is it safe now, after Archbishop Laurence's translation of the Book of Enoch, to cite Cowper and assure us that the Bible. . .gives a light to every age,
 It gives, but borrows none.

for it does borrow, and that very considerably; especially in the opinion of those who, ignorant of its symbolical meaning and of the university of the truths underlying and concealed in it, are able to judge only from its dead letter appearance. It is a grand volume, a master-piece composed of clever, ingenious fables containing great verities; but it reveals the latter only to those who, like the Initiates, have a key to its inner meaning; a tale sublime in its morality and didactics truly - still a tale and an allegory; a repertory of invented personages in its older Jewish portions, and of dark sayings and parables in its later additions, and thus quite misleading to anyone ignorant of its Esotericism. Moreover it is Astrolatry and Sabaean worship, pure and simple, that is to be found in the Pentateuch when it is read exoterically, and Archaic Science and Astronomy to a most wonderful degree, when interpreted - Esoterically.

SECTION VIII

THE BOOK OF ENOCH THE ORIGIN AND THE FOUNDATION OF CHRISTIANITY

WHILE making a good deal of the Mercavah, the Jews, or rather their synagogues, rejected the Book of Enoch, either because it was not included from the first in the Hebrew Canon, or else, as Tertullian thought, it was disavowed by the Jews like all other Scripture which speaks of Christ [Book of Enoch, Archbishop Laurence's translation. Introduction, p.v.]

But neither of these reasons was the real one. The Synedrion would have nothing to do with it, simply because it was more of a magic than a purely kabalistic work. The present day Theologians of both Latin and Protestant Churches class it among apocryphal productions. Nevertheless the New Testament, especially in the Acts and Epistles, teems with ideas and doctrines, now accepted and established as dogmas by the infallible Roman and other Churches, and even with the whole sentences taken bodily from Enoch, or the "pseudo-Enoch," who wrote under that name in Aramaic or Syro-Chaldaic, as asserted by Bishop Laurence, the translator of the Ethiopian text.

The plagiarisms are so glaring that the author of The Evolution of Christianity, who edited Bishop Laurence's translation, was compelled to make some suggestive remarks in his Introduction. On internal evidence [The Book of Enoch was unknown to Europe for a thousand years, when Bruce found in Abyssinia some copies of it in Ethiopic; it was translated by Archbishop Laurence in 1821, from the text in the Bodleian Library, Oxford.] this book is found to have been written before the Christian period (whether two or twenty centuries does not matter). As correctly argued by the Editor, it is either the inspired forecast of a great Hebrew prophet, predicting with miraculous accuracy the future teaching of Jesus of Nazareth, or the Semitic romance from which the latter borrowed His conceptions of the triumphant return of the Son of man, to occupy a judicial throne in the midst of rejoicing saints and trembling sinners, expectant of everlasting happiness or eternal fire; and whether these celestial visions be accepted as human or Divine, they have exercised so vast an influence on the destinies of mankind for nearly two thousand years that candid and impartial seekers after religious truth can no longer delay enquiry into the relationship of the Book of Enoch with the revelation, or the evolution, of Christianity. [Op. cit., p.xx.]

THE BOOK OF ENOCH AND CHRISTIANITY -

The Book of Enoch also records the supernatural control of the elements, through the action of individual angels presiding over the winds, the sea, hail, frost, dew, the lightening's flash and reverberating thunder. The names of the principal fallen angels are also given, among whom we recognise some of the invisible powers named in the incantations [magical] inscribed on the terracotta cups of Hebrew-Chaldee conjurations. [Loc. cit.]

We also find on these cups the word "Halleluiah," showing that a word with which ancient Syro-Chaldeans conjured has become, through the vicissitudes of language, the Shibboleth of modern Revivalists.[Op. cit., p. xiv., note.]

The Editor proceeds after this to give fifty-seven verses from various parts of the Gospels and Acts, with parallel passages from the Book of Enoch, and says:

The attention of theologians has been concentrated on the passage in the Epistle of Jude, because the author specifically names the prophet; but the cumulative coincidence of language and ideas in Enoch and the authors of the New Testament Scripture, as disclosed in the parallel passages which we have collated, clearly indicates that the work of the Semitic Milton was the inexhaustible source from which Evangelists and Apostles, or the men who wrote in their names, borrowed their conceptions of the resurrection, judgement, immortality, perdition, and of the universal reign of righteousness, under the eternal dominion of the Son of man. This evangelical plagiarism culminates in the Revelation of John, which adapts the visions of Enoch to Christianity, with modifications in which we miss the sublime simplicity of the great master of apocalyptic prediction, who prophesied in the name of the antediluvian patriarch. [Op. cit., p.xxxv.]

In fairness to truth, the hypothesis ought at least to have been suggested, that the Book of Enoch in its present form is simply a transcript - with numerous pre-Christian and post-Christian additions and interpolations - from far older texts. Modern research went so far as to point out that Enoch is made, in Chapter lxxi, to divide the day and night into eighteen parts, and to represent the longest day in the year as consisting of twelve out of these eighteen parts, while a day of sixteen hours in length could not have occurred in Palestine. The translator, Archbishop Laurence, remarks thus:

The region in which the author lived must have been situated not lower than forty-one degrees north latitude, where the longest day is fifteen hours and a half, nor higher perhaps than forty-nine degrees, where the longest day is precisely sixteen hours. This will bring the country where he wrote as high up at least as the northern districts of the Caspian and Euxine Seas . . . the author of the Book of Enoch was perhaps a member of one of the tribes which Shalmaneser carried away, and placed "in Halah and in Habor by the river Goshen, and in the cities of the Medes." [Op. cit., p.xiii.]

Further on, it is confessed that:

It cannot be said that internal evidence attests the superiority of the Old Testament to the Book of Enoch . . . The Book of Enoch teaches the pre-existence of the Son of man, the Elect One, the Messiah, who "from the beginning existed in secret, [The Seventh Principle, the First Emanation.] and whose name was invoked in the presence of the Lord of Spirits, before the sun and the signs were created." The author also refers to the "other Power who was upon Earth over the water on that day" - an apparent reference to the language of Genesis i. 2.[Op cit., p.xxxvii, and xl.] [We maintain that it applies as well to the Hindu Nârâyana - the "mover on the waters."] We have thus the Lord of Spirits, the Elect One, and a third Power, seemingly foreshadowing the Trinity [as much as the Trimûrti] of futurity; but although Enoch's ideal Messiah doubtless exercised an important influence on primitive conceptions of the Divinity of the Son of man, we fail to identify his obscure reference to another "Power" with the Trinitarianism of the Alexandrine school; more especially as "angels of power" abound in the visions of Enoch. [Op cit., pp,x1, and 1i.]

An Occultist would hardly fail to identify the said "Power." The Editor concludes his remarkable reflections by adding:

Thus far we learn that the Book of Enoch was published before the Christian Era by some great Unknown of Semitic [?] race, who, believing himself to be inspired in a post-prophetic age, borrowed the name of an antediluvian patriarch [Who stands for the "Solar" or Manvantaric Year.] to authenticate his own enthusiastic forecast of the Messianic kingdom. And as the contents of his marvellous book enter freely into the composition of the New Testament, it follows that if the author was not an inspired prophet, who predicted the teachings of Christianity, he was a visionary enthusiast whose illusions were accepted by Evangelists and Apostles as revelation - alternative conclusions which involve the Divine or human origin of Christianity. [Op Cit., pp.xli, xlii.]

ENOCH RECORDS THE RACES -

The outcome of all of which is, in the words of the same Editor:

The discovery that the language and ideas of alleged revelation are found in a pre-existent work, accepted by

Evangelists and Apostles as inspired, but classed by modern theologians among apocryphal productions. [Op. cit., p.xlviii.]

The accounts also for the unwillingness of the reverend librarians of the Bodleian Library to publish the Ethopian text of the Book of Enoch.

The prophecies of the Book of Enoch are indeed prophetic, but they were intended for, and cover the records of, the five Races out of the seven - everything relating to the last two being kept secret. Thus the remark made by the Editor of the English translation, that:

Chapter xcii. records a series of prophecies extending from Enoch's own time to about one thousand years beyond the present generation, [Op. cit., p.xxiii.]

is faulty. The prophecies extend to the end of our present Race, not merely to a "thousand years" hence. Very true that:

In the system of [Christian] chronology adopted, a day stands [occasionally] for a hundred, and a week for seven hundred years. [Loc. cit.]

But this is an arbitrary and fanciful system adopted by Christians to make Biblical chronology fit with facts or theories, and does not represent the original thought. The "days" stand for the undetermined periods of the Side-Races, and the "weeks" for the Sub-Races, the Root-Races being referred to by an expression that is not even found in the English translation. Moreover the sentence at the bottom of page 150:

Subsequently, in the fourth week . . . the visions of the holy and the righteous shall be seen, the order of generation after generation shall take place, [xcii.9.] is quite wrong. It stands in the original: "the order of generation after generation has taken place on the earth," etc.; that is, after the first human race procreated in the truly human way had sprung up in the Third Root-Races: a change which entirely alters the meaning. Then all that is given in the translation - as very likely also in the Ethiopic text, since the copies have been sorely tampered with - as about things which were to happen in the future, is, we are informed, in the past tense of the original Chaldean MSS., and is not prophecy, but a narrative of what had already come to pass. When Enoch begins - "to speak from a book" [Op. cit., xcii.4.] he is reading the account given by a great Seer, and the prophecies are not his own, but are from the Seer. Enoch or Enoichion means "internal eye" or Seer. Thus every Prophet and Adept may be called "Enoichion," without becoming a pseudo-Enoch. But here, the Seer who compiled the present Book of Enoch is distinctly shown as reading out from a book:

I have been born the seventh in the first week [the seventh branch, or Side-Race, of the first Sub-Race, after physical generation had begun, namely, in the third Root-Race] . . . But after me, in the second week [second Sub-Race] great wickedness shall arise [arose, rather] and in that week the end of the first shall take place, in which mankind shall be safe. But when the first is completed iniquity shall grow up. [Op.cit.,xcii, 4-7]

As translated it has no sense. As it stands in the Esoteric text, it simply means, that the First Root-Race shall come to an end during the second Sub-Race of the Third Root-Race, in the period of which time mankind will be safe; all this having no reference whatever to the biblical Deluge. Verse 10th speaks of the sixth week [sixth Sub-Race of the Third Root Race] when all those who are in it shall be darkened, the hearts of all of them shall be forgetful of wisdom [the divine knowledge will be dying out] and in it shall a man ascend.

This "man" is taken by the interpreters, for some mysterious reasons of their own, to mean Nebuchadnezzar; he is in reality the first Hierophant of the purely human Race (after the allegorical fall into generation) selected to perpetuate the dying, Wisdom of the Devas (Angels or Elohim). He is the first "Son of Man" - the mysterious appellation given to the divine Initiates of the first human school of the Manushi (men), at the very close of the Third Root-Race. He is also called the "Saviour," as it was He, with the other Hierophants, who saved the Elect and the Perfect from the geological conflagration, leaving to perish in the cataclysm of the Close [At the close of every Root-Race there comes a cataclysm, in turn by fire, or water. Immediately after the "Fall into generation" the dross of the third Root-Race - those who fell into sensuality by falling off from the teaching of the Divine Instructors - were destroyed, after which the Fourth Root-Race originated, at the end of which took place the last Deluge. (See the "Sons of God" mentioned in Isis Unveiled. 593 et seq.)] those who forgot the primeval wisdom in sexual sensuality.

And during its completion [of the "sixth week," or the sixth Sub-Race] he shall burn the house of dominion [the half of the globe or the then inhabited continent] with fire, and all the race of the elect root shall be dispersed. [Op. cit., xcii,xx.]

THE BOOK OF ENOCH SYMBOLICAL -

The above applies to the Elect Initiates, and not at all to the Jews, the supposed chosen people, or to the Babylonian captivity, as interpreted by the Christian theologians. Considering that we find Enoch, or his perpetuator, mentioning the execution of the "degree upon sinners" in several different weeks, [Op.cit., xcii, 7, 11, 13, 15.] saying that "every work of the ungodly shall disappear from the whole earth" during this fourth time (the Fourth Race), it surely can hardly apply to the one solitary Deluge of the Bible, still less to the Captivity.

It follows, therefore, that as the Book of Enoch covers the five Races of the Manvantara, with a few allusions to the last two, it does not contain "Biblical prophecies," but simply facts taken out of the Secret Books of the East. The Editor, moreover, confesses that:

The preceding six verses, viz., 13th, 15th, 16th, 17th, and 18th, are taken from between the 14th and 15th verses of the nineteenth chapter, where they are to be found in the MSS. [Op. cit., note, p.152]

By this arbitrary transposition, he has made confusion still more confused. Yet he is quite right in saying that the doctrines of the Gospels, and even of the Old Testament, have been taken bodily from the Book of Enoch, for this is as evident as the sun in heaven. The whole of the Pentateuch was adapted to fit in with the facts given, and this accounts for the Hebrews refusing to give the book place in their Canon, just as the Christians have subsequently refused to admit it among their canonical works. The fact that the Apostle

Jude and many of the Christian Fathers referred to it as a revelation and a sacred volume, is, however, an excellent proof that the early Christians accepted it; among these the most learned - as, for instance, Clement of Alexandria - understood Christianity and its doctrines in quite a different light from their modern successors, and viewed Christ under an aspect that Occultists only can appreciate. The early Nazarenes and Chrestians, as Justin Martyr calls them, were the followers of Jesus, of the true Chrestos and Christos of Initiation; whereas, the modern Christians, especially those of the West, may be Papists, Greeks, Calvinists, or Lutherans, but can hardly be called Christians, i.e., the followers of Jesus, the Christ.

Thus the Book of Enoch is entirely symbolical. It relates to the history of the human Races and of their early relation to Theogony, the symbols being interblended with astronomical and cosmic mysteries.

88) One chapter is missing, however, in the Noachian records (from both the Paris and the Bodleian MSS.), namely, Chapter 1viii, in Sect X; this could not be remodelled, and therefore it had to disappear, disfigured fragments alone having been left out of it. The dream about the cows, the black, red and white heifers, relates to the first Races, their division and disappearance. Chapter 1xxxviii, in which one of the four Angels "went to the white cows and taught them a mystery," after which, the mystery being born "became a man," refers to (a) the first group evolved of primitive Aryans, (b) to the "mystery of the Hermaphrodite" so called, having reference to the birth of the first human Races as they are

now. The well-known rite in India, one that has survived in that patriarchal country to this day, known as the passage, or rebirth through the cow - a ceremony to which those of lower castes who are desirous of becoming Brahmans have to submit - has originated in this mystery. Let any Eastern Occultist read with careful attention the above-named chapter in the Book of Enoch, and he will find that the "Lord of the Sheep," in whom Christians and European Mystics see Christ, is the Hierophant Victim whose name in Sanskrit we dare not give. Again, that while the Western Churchmen see Egyptians and Israelites in the "sheep and wolves," all these animals relate in truth to the trials of the Neophyte and the mysteries of initiation, whether in India or Egypt, and to that most terrible penalty incurred by the "wolves" - those who reveal indiscriminately that which is only for the knowledge of the Elect and the "Perfect."

The Christians who, thanks to later interpolations, [Those interpolations and alternations are found in almost every case where figures are given - especially whenever the numbers eleven and twelve come in - as these are all made (by the Christians) to relate to the numbers of Apostles, and Tribes, and Patriarchs. The translator of the Ethiopic text - Archbishop Laurence - attributes them generally to "mistakes of the transcriber" whenever the two texts, the Paris and the Bodleian MSS., differ. We fear it is no mistake, in most cases.] have made out in that chapter a triple prophecy relating to the Deluge, Moses and Jesus, are mistaken, as in reality it bears directly on the punishment and loss of Atlantis and the penalty of indiscretion. (The "Lord of the sheep" is

Karma and the "Head of the Hierophants" also, the Supreme Initiator on earth.) He says to Enoch who implores him to save the leaders of the sheep from being devoured by the beasts of prey:

I will cause a recital to be made before me . . . how many they have delivered up to destruction, and . . . what they will do; whether they will act as I have commanded them or not.

OCCULTISTS DO NOT REJECT THE BIBLE -

Of this, however, they shall be ignorant; neither shalt thou make any explanation to them, neither shalt thou reprove them; but there shall be an account of all the destruction done by them in their respective seasons. [Op. cit., 1xxxviii. 99, 100.]

. . . He looked in silence, rejoicing they were devoured, swallowed up, and carried off, and leaving them in the power of every beast for food. . [Loc.cit.,94. This passage, as will be presently shown, has led to a very curious discovery.]

Those who labour under the impression that the Occultists of any nation reject the Bible, in its original text and meaning, are wrong. As well reject the Books of Thoth, the Chaldaean Kabalah or the Book of Dzyan itself. Occultists only reject the one-sided interpretations and the human element in the Bible, which is an Occult, and therefore a sacred, volume as much as the others. And terrible indeed is the punishment of all those who transgress the permitted limits of secret revelations. From Prometheus to Jesus, and from Him to the highest Adept as to the lowest disciple, every revealer of mysteries has had to become a Chrestos, a "man of sorrow" and a martyr. "Beware," said one of the greatest Masters, "of revealing the Mystery to those without" - to the profane, the Sadducee and the unbeliever. All the great Hierophants in history are shown

Buddha he dies at the good old age of eighty, and passes off from life to death peacefully with all the serenity of a great saint, as Barthelemy St. Hilaire has it. Not so in the Esoteric and true interpretation which reveals the real sense of the profane and allegorical statement that makes Gautama, the Buddha, die very unpoetically from the effects of too much pork, prepared for him by Tsonda. How one who preached that the killing of animals was the greatest sin, and who was a perfect vegetarian, could die from eating pork, is a question that is never asked by our Orientalists, some of whom made [as now do many charitable missionaries in Ceylon] great fun at the alleged occurrence. The simple truth is that the said rice and pork are purely allegorical. Rice stands for "forbidden fruit," like Eve's "apple", and means Occult knowledge with the Chinese and Tibetans; and "pork " for Brahmanical teachings - Vishnu having assumed in his first Avatâra the form of a boar, in order to raise the earth on the surface of the waters of space. It is not, therefore, from "pork" that Buddha died, but for having divulged some of the Brahmanical mysteries, after which, seeing the bad effects brought on some unworthy people by the revelation, he preferred, instead of availing himself of Nirvana, to leave his earthly form, remaining still in the sphere of the living, in order to help humanity to progress. Hence his constant reincarnations in the hierarchy of the Dalai and Teshu Lamas, among other bounties. Such is the

Esoteric explanation. The life of Gautama will be more fully discussed later on.] Pythagoras, Zoroaster, most of the great Gnostics, the founders of their respective schools; and in our own more modern epoch a number of Fire-Philosophers of Rosicrucians and Adepts. All of these are shown - whether plainly or under the veil of allegory - as paying the penalty for the revelations they had made. This may seem to the profane reader only coincidence.

To the Occultist, the death of every "Master" is significant, and appears pregnant with meaning. Where do we find in history that "Messenger" grand or humble, an Initiate or a Neophyte, who, when he was made the bearer of some hitherto concealed truth or truths, was not crucified and rent to shreds by the "dogs" of envy, malice and ignorance? Such is the terrible Occult law; and he who does not feel in himself the heart of a lion to scorn the savage barking, and the soul of a dove to forgive the poor ignorant fools, let him give up the Sacred Science. To succeed, the Occultist must be fearless; he has to brave dangers, dishonour and death, to be forgiving, and to be silent on that which cannot be given. Those who have vainly laboured in that direction must wait in these days - as the Book of Enoch teaches - "until the evildoers be consumed" and the power of the wicked annihilated. It is not lawful for the Occultist to seek or even to thirst for revenge: let him wait until sin pass away, for their [the sinners] names shall be blotted out of the holy books [the astral records], their seed shall be destroyed and their spirits slain.[Op. cit., cv.21.]

Esoterically, Enoch is the "Son of man," the first; and

symbolically, the first Sub-Race of the Fifth Root Race.[In the Bible [Genesis, iv and v] there are three distinct Enochs [Kanoch or Chanoch] - the son of Cain, the son of Seth, and the son of Jared; but they are all identical, and two of them are mentioned for the purpose of misleading. The years of only the last two are given, the first one being left without further notice.] And if his name yields for purposes of numerical and astronomical glyphs the meaning of the solar year, or 365, in conformity to the age assigned to him in Genesis, it is because, being the seventh, he is, for Occult purposes, the personified period of the two preceding Races with their fourteen Sub-Races. Therefore, he is shown in the Book as the great grandfather of Noah who, in his turn, is the personification of the mankind of the Fifth, struggling with that of the Fourth Root-Race - the great period of the revealed and profaned Mysteries, when the "sons of God" coming down on Earth took for wives the daughters of men, and taught them the secrets of the Angels; in other words, when the "mind-born" men of the Third Race mixed themselves with those of the Fourth, and the divine Science was gradually brought down by men to Sorcery.

SECTION IX

HERMETIC AND KABALISTIC DOCTRINES

THE cosmogony of Hermes is as veiled as the Mosaic system, only it is upon its face far more in harmony with the doctrines of the Secret Sciences and even of Modern Science. Says the thrice great Trismegistus, "the hand that shaped the world out of formless pre-existent matter is no hand"; to which Genesis is made to reply, "The world was created out of nothing," although the Kabbalah denies such a meaning in its opening sentences.

The Kabalists have never, any more than have the Indian Aryans, admitted such an absurdity. With them, Fire, or Heat, and Motion [The eternal and incessant "inbreathing and outbreathing of Parabrahman" or Nature, the Universe of Space, whether during Manvantara or Pralaya.] were chiefly instrumental in the formation of the world out of pre-existing Matter. The Parabrahman and Mûlaprakriti of the Vedântins are the prototypes of the En Suph and Shekinah of the Kabalists. Aditi is the original of Sephira, and the Prajâpatis are the elder brothers of the Sephiroth. The nebular theory of Modern Science, with all its mysteries, is solved in the cosmogony of the Archaic Doctrine; and the paradoxical though very scientific enunciation, that " cooling causes contraction and contraction causes heat; therefore cooling causes heat," is shown as the chief agency in the formation of the worlds, and especially of our sun and solar system.

All this is contained within the small compass of Sepher Jetsirah in its thirty-two wonderful Ways of Wisdom, signed "Jah Jehovah Sabaoth," for whomsoever has the key to its hidden meaning. As to the dogmatic or theological interpretation of the first verses in Genesis it is pertinently answered in the same book, where speaking of the Three Mothers, Air, Water and Fire, the writer describes them as a balance with the good in one scale, the evil in the other, and the oscillating tongue of the Balance between them. [Op. cit., iii, x.]

One of the secret names of the One Eternal and Ever-Present Deity, was in every country the same, and it has preserved to this day a phonetic likeness in the various languages. The Aum of the Hindus, the sacred syllable, had become the 'Αιψν with the Greeks, and the Aevum with the Romans - the Pan or All. The "thirtieth way" is called in the Sepher Jetzirah the "gathering understanding," because

Thereby gather the celestial adepts judgments of the stars and celestial signs, and their observations of the orbits are the perfection of science. [Op. cit.,30.]

The thirty-second and last is called therein the "serving understanding," and it is so-called because it is

A disposer of all those that are serving in the work of the Seven Planets, according to their Hosts.[Op. cit.,32.]

The "work" was Initiation, during which all the mysteries connected with the "Seven Planets" were divulged, and also the mystery of the "Sun-Initiate" with his seven radiances or beams cut off - the glory and triumph of the anointed, the Christos; a mystery that makes plain the rather puzzling expression of Clemens:

For we shall find that very many of the dogmas that are held by such sects [of Barbarian and Hellenic Philosophy] as have not become utterly senseless, and are not cut out from the order of nature ["by cutting off Christ," [Those who are aware of the term Christos was applied by the Gnostics to the Higher Ego (the ancient Pagan Greek Initiates doing the same), will readily understand the allusion. Christos was said to be cut off from the lower Ego, Chrestos, after the final and supreme Initiation, when the two became blended in one; Chrestos being conquered and resurrected in the glorified Christos - Franck, Die Kabbala, 75: Dunlap, Sod, Vol.11.] or rather Chrestos] . . . Correspond in their origin and with the truth as a whole. [Stromateis,1. xiii.]

In Isis Unveiled, [Op.cit.,II.viii.] the reader will find fuller information than can be given here on the Zohar and its author, the great Kabalist, Simeon Ben Jochai. It is said there that on account of his being known to be in possession of the secret knowledge and of the Mercaba, which insured the reception of the "Word," his very life was endangered, and he had to fly to the wilderness, where he lived in a cave for twelve years surrounded by faithful disciples, and finally died there amid signs and wonders. [Many are the marvels recorded as having taken place at his death, or we should rather say his translation; for he did not die as others do, but having suddenly disappeared, while a dazzling light filled the cavern with glory, his body was again seen upon its subsidence. When this heavenly light gave place to the habitual semi-darkness of the gloomy cave - then only, says

Ginsburg, "the disciples of Israel perceived that the lamp of Israel was extinguished." His biographers tell us that there were voices heard from Heaven during the preparation for his funeral, and at his interment, when the coffin was lowered into the deep cave prepared for it, a flame broke forth and a voice mighty and majestic pronounced these words: 'This is he who caused the earth to quake, and the kingdoms to shake!']

THE KABALAH AND THE BOOK OF ENOCH –

His teachings on the origin of the Secret Doctrine, or, as he also calls it, the Secret Wisdom, are the same as those found in the East, with the exception that in place of the Chief of a Host of Planetary Spirits he puts "God," saying that this Wisdom was first taught by God himself to a certain number of Elect Angels; whereas in the Eastern Doctrine the saying is different, as will be seen.

Some synthetic and Kabalistic studies on the sacred Book of Enoch and the Taro (Rota) are before us. We quote from the MS. copy of a Western Occultist, who is prefaced by these words:

There is but one Law, one Principle, one Agent, one Truth and one Word. That which is above is analogically as that which is below. All that which is, is the result of quantities and of equilibriums.

The axiom of Eliphas Levi and this triple epigraph show the identity of thought between the East and the West with regard to the Secret Science which, as the same MS, tells us, is:

The key of things concealed, the key of the sanctuary. This is the Sacred Word which gives to the Adept the supreme reason of Occultism and its Mysteries. It is the Quintessence of Philosophies and of Dogmas; it is the Alpha and Omega; it is the Light, Life and Wisdom Universal.

The Taro of the sacred Book of Enoch, or Rota, is prefaced, moreover, with this explanation:

The antiquity of this book is lost in the night of time. It is of Indian origin, and goes back to an epoch long before Moses . . . It is written upon detached leaves, which at the first were of fine gold and precious metals . . . It is symbolical, and its combinations adapt themselves to all the wonders of the Spirit. Altered by its passage across the Ages, it is nevertheless preserved - thanks to the ignorance of the curious - in its types and its most important primitive figures.

This is the Rota of Enoch, now called Taro of Enoch, to which de Mirville alludes, as we saw, as the means used for "evil Magic." the "metallic plates [or leaves] escaped from destruction during the Deluge" and which are attributed by him to Cain. They have escaped the Deluge for the simple reason that this Flood was not "Universal." And it is said to be "of Indian origin," because its origin is with the Indian Aryans of the first Sub-Race of the Fifth Root-Race, before the final destruction of the last stronghold of Atlantis. But, if it originated with the forefathers of the primitive Hindus, it was not in India that it was first used. Its origin is still more ancient and must be traced beyond and into the Himaleh, [Pockocke, may be, was not altogether wrong in deriving the German Heaven, Himmel, from Himalaya; nor can it be denied that it is the Hindu Kailasa (Heaven) that is the father of the Greek Heaven (Koilon), and of the Latin Coelum.] the Snowy Range. It was born in that mysterious locality which no one is able to locate, and which is the despair of both Geographers and Christian Theologians - the regions in which the Brahman places his Kailasa, the Mount Sumeru, and the Pârvatî Pamîr, transformed by the Greeks into Paropamisus.

Round this locality, which still exists, the traditions of the Garden of Eden were built. From these regions the Greeks obtained their Parnassus [See Pockocke's India in Greece, and his derivation of Mount Parnassus from Parnasa, the leaf and branch huts of the Hindu ascetics, half shrine and half habitation. "Part of the Par-o-Pamisus (the hill of Bamian), is called Parnassus. "These mountains are called Devanica, because they are so full of Devas of Gods, called "Gods of the Earth:" Bhu Devas. They lived, according to the Puranas, in bowers or huts, called Parnasas, because they were made of leaves; (Parnas)," p.302.] and thence proceeded most of the biblical personages, some of them in their day men, some demigods and heroes, some - though very few - myths, the astronomical double of the former. Abram was one of them - a Chaldaean Brâhman, [Rawlinson is justly very confident of an Aryan and Vedic influence on the early mythology and history of Babylon and Chaldea.] says the legend, transformed later, after he had repudiated his Gods and left his Ur (pur, "town"?) in Chaldaea, into A-brahms [This is a Secret Doctrine affirmation, and may or may not be accepted. Only Abrahm, Isaac and Judah resemble terribly the Hindu Brahmâ, Ikshvâku and Yadu.] (or A-braham "no-brâhman" who emigrated. Abram becoming the "father of many nations" is thus explained. The student of Occultism has to bear in mind that every God and hero in ancient Pantheons (that of the Bible included), has three biographies in the narrative, so to say, running parallel with each other and each connected with one of the aspects of the hero - historical, astronomical and perfectly mythical, the last serving to connect the other two together and smooth away the asperities and discordancies in the narrative, and gathering into one or more symbols the verities of the first two. Localities are made to correspond with astronomical and even with psychic events.

NUMBERS AND MEASURES –

History was thus made captive by ancient Mystery, to become later on the great Sphynx of the nineteenth century. Only, instead of devouring her too dull querists who will unriddle her whether she acknowledges it or not, she is desecrated and mangled by the modern Oedipus, before he forces her into the sea of speculations in which the Sphynx is drowned and perishes. This has now become self-evident, not only through the Secret Teachings, parsimoniously as they may be given, but by earnest and learned Symbologists and even Geometricians. The Key to the Hebrew Egyptian Mystery, in which a learned Mason of Cincinnati, Mr. Ralston Skinner, unveils the riddle of a God, with such ungodly ways about him as the Biblical Jah-ve, is followed by the establishment of a learned society under the presidentship of a gentleman from

Ohio and four vice-presidents, one of whom is Piazzi Smith, the well-known Astronomer and Egyptologist. The Director of the Royal Observatory in Scotland and author of The Great Pyramid, Pharaonic by name, Humanitarian by fact, its Marvels, Mysteries, and its Teachings, is seeking to prove the same problem as the American author and Mason; namely, that the English system of measurement is the same as that used by the ancient Egyptians in the construction of their Pyramid, or in Mr. Skinner's own words that the Pharaonic "source of measures" originated the "British inch and the ancient cubit." It "originated" much more than this, as will be fully demonstrated before the end of the next century. Not only is everything in Western religion related to measures, geometrical figures, and time-calculations, the principal period-durations being founded on most of the historical personages,[It is said in The Gnostics and their Remains, by C.W. King (p.13) with regard to the names of Brahma and Abram: "This figure of the man, Seir Anpin, consists of 243 numbers, being the numerical value of the letters in the name 'Abram' signifying the different orders in the celestial Hierarchies. In fact the names Abram and Brahma are equivalent in numerical value." Thus to one acquainted with Esoteric Symbolism, it does not seem at all strange to find in the Loka-pâlas (the four cardinal and intermediate points of the compass personified by eight Hindu Gods) Indra's elephant, names Abhra - (matanga) and his wife Abhramu. Abhra is in a way a Wisdom Deity, since it is this elephant's head that replaced that of Ganesha (Ganapati) the God of Wisdom, cut off by Shiva. Now Abhra means "cloud," and it is also the name of the city where Abram is supposed to have resided - when read backwards - "Arba (Kirjath) the city of four . . . Abram is Abra with an appended m final, and Abra read backward is Arba" (Key to the Hebrew Egyptian Mystery). The author might have added that Abra meaning in Sanskrit "in, or of, the clouds," the cosmo-astronomical symbol of Abram becomes still plainer. All of these ought to be read in their originals , in Sanskrit.] but the latter are also connected with heaven and earth truly, only with the Indo-Aryan heaven and earth, not with those of Palestine.

The prototypes of nearly all the biblical personages are to be sought for in the early Pantheon of India. It is the "Mind-born" Sons of Brahma, or rather of the Dhyâni-Pitara (the "Father -Gods"), the "Sons of Light," who have given birth to the "Sons of Earth" - the Patriachs. For if the Rig Veda and its three sister Vedas have been "milked out from fire, air and sun," or Agni, Indra, and Surya, as Manu-Smriti tells us, the Old Testament was most undeniably "milked out" of the most ingenious brains of Hebrew Kabalists, partly in Egypt and partly in Babylonia - " the seat of Sanskrit literature and Brahman learning from her origin." as Colonel Vans Kennedy truly declared. One of such copies was Abram or Abraham, into whose bosom every orthodox Jew hopes to be gathered after death, that bosom being localised as "heaven in the clouds" or Abhra.[Before these theories and speculations - we are willing to admit they are such - are rejected, the following few points ought to be explained. (1) Why after leaving Egypt, was the patriarch's name changed by Jehovah from Abram to Abraham. (2) Why Sarai becomes on the same principle Sarah (Gen., xvii.). (3) Whence the strange coincidence of names? (4) Why should Alexander Polyhistor say that Abraham was born at Kamarina or Uria, a city of soothsayers, and invented Asrronomy? (5) "The Abrahamic recollections go back at least three millenniums beyond the grandfather of Jacob, "says Bunsen (Egypt's Place in History. v.35.)]

From Abraham to Enoch's Taro there seems to be a considerable distance, yet the two are closely related by more than one link, Gaffarel has shown that the four symbolical animals on the twenty-first key of the Taro, at the third septenary, are the Teraphim of the Jews invented and worshipped by Abram's father Terah, and used in the oracles of the Urim and Thummim. Moreover, astronomically Abraham is the sun-measure and a portion of the sun, while Enoch is the solar year, as much as are Hermes or Thot; and Thot, numerically, "was the equivalent of Moses, or Hermes," "the lord of the lower realms, also esteemed as a teacher of wisdom," the same Mason-mathematician tells us; and the Taro being, according to one of the latest bulls of the Pope, "an invention of Hell," the same "as Masonry and Occultism," the relation is evident. The Taro contains indeed the mystery of all such transmutations of personages into sidereal bodies and vice versa. The "wheel of Enoch" is an archaic invention, the most ancient of all, for it is found in China. Eliphas Levi says there was not a nation but had it, its real meaning being preserved in the greatest secrecy. It was a universal heirloom.

As we see, neither the Book of Enoch (his "Wheel"), nor

the Zohar, nor any other kabalistic volume, contains merely Jewish wisdom.

THE DOCTRINE BELONGS TO ALL

The doctrine itself being the result of whole millenniums of thought, is therefore the joint property of Adepts of every nation under the sun. Nevertheless, the Zohar teaches practical Occultism more than any other work on that subject; not as it is translated and commented upon by its various critics though, but with the secret signs on its margins. These signs contain the hidden instructions, apart from the metaphysical interpretations and apparent absurdities so fully credited by Josephus, who was never initiated and gave out the dead letter as he had received it. [Isis Unveiled, ii. 350.]

SECTION X

VARIOUS OCCULT SYSTEMS OF INTERPRETA-
TIONS
-OF ALPHABETS AND NUMERALS

THE transcendental methods of the Kabalah must not be mentioned in a public work; but its various systems of arithmetical and geometrical ways of unriddling certain symbols may be described. The Zohar methods of calculation, with their three sections, the Gematria, Notaricon and Temura, also the Albath and Algath, are extremely difficult to practice. We refer those who would learn more to Cornelius Agrippa's works [See Isis Unveiled, ii. 218-300.

Gematria is formed by a metathesis from the Greek word γραμματειαNotaricon may be compared to stenography; Temura is permutation - a way of dividing the alphabet and shifting letters.] But none of those systems can ever be understood unless a Kabalist becomes a real Master in his Science. The Symbolism of Pythagoras requires still more arduous labour. His symbols are very numerous, and to comprehend even the general gist of his abstruse doctrines from his Symbology would necessitate years of study. His chief figures are the square (the Tetraktys), the equilateral triangle, the point within a circle, the cube, the triple triangle, and finally the forty-seventh proposition of Euclid's Elements, of which proposition Pythagoras was the inventor. But with the exception, none of the foregoing symbols originated with him, as some believe. Millenniums before his day, they were well known in India, whence the Samian Sage brought them, not as a speculation, but as a demonstrated Science, says Porphyry, quoting from the Pythagorean Moderatus.

The numerals of Pythagoras were hieroglyphical symbols by means whereof he explains all ideas concerning the nature of things. [De Vita Pythag.]

NUMBERS AND MAGIC –

The fundamental geometrical figure of the Kabalah, as given in the Book of Numbers, [We are not aware that a copy of this ancient work is embraced in the catalogue of any European library; but it is one of the "Books of Hermes," and it is referred to and quotations are made from it in the works of a number of ancient and mediaeval philosophical authors. Among these authorities are Arnoldo di Villanova's Rosarium Philosoph., Francesco Arnuphi's Opus de Lapide, Hermes Trismegistus' Tractatus de Transmutatione Metallorum and Tabula Smaragdina, and above all the treatise of Raymond Lully, Ab Angelis Opus Divinum de Quinta Essentia.] that figure which tradition and the Esoteric Doctrines tell us was given by the Deity Itself to Moses on Mount Sinai, [Exodus,xxv.40.] contains the key to the universal problem in its grandiose, because simple, combinations. This figure contains in itself all the others.

The Symbolism of numbers and their mathematical interrelations is also one of the branches of Magic, especially of mental Magic, divination and correct perception in clairvoyance. Systems differ, but the root idea is everywhere the same. As shown in the Royal Masonic Cyclopaedia, by Kenneth R.H. Mackenzie:

One system adopts unity, another trinity, a third quinquinity; again we have sexagons, heptagons, novems, and so on, until the mind is lost in the survey of the materials alone of a science of numbers. [Sub voce "Numbers."]

The Devanâgarî characters in which Sanscrit is generally written, have all that the Hermetic, Chaldaean and Hebrew alphabets have, and in addition the Occult significance of the "eternal sound," and the meaning given to every letter in its relation to spiritual as well as terrestrial things. As there are only twenty-two letters in the Hebrew alphabet and ten fundamental numbers, while in the Devanâgarî there are thirty-five consonants and sixteen vowels, making altogether fifty-one simple letters, with numberless combinations in addition, the margin for speculation and knowledge is in proportion considerably wider. Every letter has is equivalent in other languages, and its equivalent in a figure or figures of the calculation table. It has also numerous other significations, which depend upon the special idiosyncrasies and characteristics of the person, object, or subject to be studied. As the Hindus claim to have received the Devanagari characters from Sarasvati, the inventress of Sanskrit, the "language of the Devas" or Gods (in their exoteric pantheon), so most of the ancient nations claimed the same privilege for the origin of their letters and tongue. The Kabalah calls the Hebrew alphabet the "letters of the Angels," which were communicated to the Patriarchs, just as the Devanagari was to the Rishis by the Devas. The Chaldaeans found their letters traced in the sky by the "yet unsettled stars and comets," says the Book of Numbers; while the Phoenicians had a sacred alphabet formed by the twistings of the sacred serpents. The Natar Khari (hieratic alphabet) and secret (sacerdotal) speech of the Egyptians is closely related to the oldest "Secret Doctrine Speech." It is a Devanâgarî with mystical combinations and additions, into which the Senzar largely enters.

The power and potency of numbers and characters are well known to many Western Occultists as being compounded from all these systems, but are still unknown to Hindu students, if not to their Occultists. In their turn European Kabalists are generally ignorant of the alphabetical secrets of Indian Esoterism. At the same time the general reader in the West knows nothing of either; least of all how deep are the traces left by the Esoteric numeral systems of the world in the Christian Churches.

Nevertheless this system of numerals solves the problem of cosmogony for whomsoever studies it, while the system of geometrical figures represents the numbers objectively.

To realise the full comprehension of the Deific and the Abstruse enjoyed by the Ancients, one has to study the origin of the figurative representations of their primitive Philosophers. The Books of Hermes are the oldest repositories of numerical Symbology in Western Occultism. In them we find that the number ten [See Johannes Meursius, Denarius Pythagoricus.] is the Mother of the Soul, Life and Light being therein united. For as the sacred anagram Teruph shows in the Book of Keys (Numbers), the number 1 (one) is born from spirit, and the number 10 (ten) from Matter: "the unity has made the ten, the ten, the unity"; and this is only the Pantheistic axiom, in other words "God in Nature and Nature in God."

The kabalistic Gematria is arithmetical, not geometrical. It is one of the methods for extracting the hidden meaning from letters, words, and sentences. It consists in applying to the letters of a word the sense they bear in numbers, in outward shape as well as in their individual sense. As illustrated by Ragon:

The figure I signified the living man (a body erect), man being the only living being enjoying this faculty. A head being added to it, the glyph (or letter) P was obtained, meaning paternity, creative potency; the R signifying the walking man (with his foot forward) going, iens, iturus [Ragon, Maconnerie Occulte, p.426. note.]

Gods and Numbers -

The characters were also made supplementary to speech, every letter being at once a figure representing a sound for the ear, and idea to the mind; as, for instance the letter F, which is a cutting sound like that of air rushing quickly through space; fury, fusee, fugue, all words expressive of, and depicting what they signify. [Ibid., p.432, note.]

But the above pertains to another system, that of the primitive and philosophical formation of the letters and their outward glyphic form - not to Gematria. The Temura is another kabalistic method, by which any word could be made to yield its mystery out of its anagram. So in Sepher Jetzirah we read "One - the spirit of the Alahim of Lives." In the oldest kabalistic diagrams the Sephiroth (the seven and the three) are represented as wheels or circles, and Adam Kadmon, the primitive Man, as an upright pillar. "Wheels and seraphim and the holy creatures" (Chioth) says Rabbi Akiba. In still another system of the symbolical Kabalah called Albath - which arranges the letters of the alphabet by pairs in three rows - all the couples in the first row bear the numerical value ten; and in the system of Simeon Ben Shetah (an Alexandrian Neoplatonist under the first Ptolemy) the uppermost couple - the most sacred of all - is preceded by the Pythagorean cypher: one and a nought - 10.

All beings, from the first divine emanation, or "God manifested," down to the lowest atomic existence, "have their particular number which distinguishes each of them and becomes the source of their attributes and qualities as of their destiny." Chance, as taught by Cornelius Agrippa, is in reality only an unknown progression; and time but a succession of numbers. Hence, futurity being a compound of chance and time, these are made to serve Occult calculations in order to find the result of an event, or the future of one's destiny. Said Pythagoras:

There is a mysterious connection between the Gods and numbers, on which the science of arithmancy is based. The soul is a world that is self-moving; the soul contains in itself, and is, the quaternary, the tetraktys [the perfect cube].

There are lucky and unlucky, or beneficent and maleficent numbers. Thus while the ternary - the first of the odd numbers (the one being the perfect and standing by itself in Occultism) - is the divine figure or the triangle; the duad was disgraced by the Pythagoreans from the first. It represented Matter, the passive and evil principle - the number of Maya, illusion.

While the number one symbolized harmony, order or the good principle (the one God expressed in Latin by Solus, from which the word Sol, the Sun, the symbol of the Deity), number two expressed a contrary idea. The science of good and evil began with it. All that is double, false, opposed to the only reality, was depicted by the binary. It also expressed the contrasts in Nature which are always double: night and day, light and darkness, cold and heat, dampness and dryness, health and sickness, error and truth, male and female, etc. . . . The Romans dedicated to Pluto the second month of the year, and the second day of that month to expiations in honour of the Manes. Hence the same rite established by the Latin Church, and faithfully copied. Pope John XIX, instituted in 1003 the Festival of the Dead, which had to be celebrated on the 2nd of November, the second month of autumn. [Extracted from Ragon, Maconnerie Occulte. p.427, note.]

On the other hand the triangle, a purely geometrical figure, had great honour shewn it by every nation, and for this reason:

In geometry a straight line cannot represent an absolutely perfect figure, any more than two straight lines. Three straight lines, on the other hand, produce by their junction a triangle, or the first absolutely perfect figure. Therefore, it symbolized from the first and to this day the Eternal - the first perfection. The word for deity in Latin, as in French, begins with D, in Greek the delta or triangle Δ, whose three sides symbolize the trinity, or the three kingdoms, or, again, divine nature.

In the middle is the Hebrew Yod, the initial of Jehovah [see Eliphas Levi's Dogme et Rituel, i. 154], the animating spirit or fire, the generating principle represented by the letter G, the initial of "God" in the northern languages, whose philosophical significance is generation. [Summarised from Ragon, ibid., p.428, note.]

As stated correctly by the famous Mason Ragon, the Hindu Trimurti is personified in the world of ideas by Creation, Preservation and Destruction, or Brahma, Vishnu and Shiva; in the world of matter by Earth, Water and Fire, or the Sun, and symbolised by the Lotus, a flower that lives by earth, water, and the sun. [Ragon mentions the curious fact that the first four numbers in German are named after the elements.

"Ein, or one, means the air, the element which, ever in motion, penetrates matter throughout, and whose continual ebb and tide is the universal vehicle of life. "

Zwei, two, is derived from the old German Zweig, signifying germ, fecundity; it stands for earth the fecund mother of all. "

Drei, three is the trienos of the Greeks, standing for water, whence the Sea-gods, Tritons: and trident, the emblem of Neptune - the water, or sea, in general being called Amphitrite (surrounding water). "

Vier, four, a number meaning in Belgiam fire . . . It is in the quaternary that the first solid figure is found, the universal symbol of immortality, the Pyramid, 'whose first syllable means fire.' Lysis and Timaeus of Loeris claimed that there was not a thing one could name that had not the quaternary for its root. . . The ingenious and mystical idea which led to the veneration of the ternary and the triangle was applied to number four and its figure: it was said to express a living being, I, the vehicle of the triangle 4, vehicle of God, or man carrying in him the divine principle."

Finally, "the Ancients represented the world by the number five. Diodorus explains it by saying that the number represents earth, fire, water, air and ether or spiritus. Hence, the origin of Pente (five) and of Pan (the God) meaning in Greek all." (Compare Ragon. op. cit., pp. 428-430.) It is left with the Hindu Occultists to explain the relation this Sanskrit word Pancha (five) has to the elements, the Greek Pente having for its root the Sanskrit term.] The Lotus, sacred to Isis had the same significance in Egypt, whereas in the Christian symbol, the Lotus, not being found in either Judaea or Europe, was replaced by the water-lily.

THE UNIVERSAL LANGUAGE -

In every Greek and Latin Church, in all the pictures of the Annunciation, the Archangel Gabriel is depicted with this trinitarian symbol in his hand standing before Mary, while above the chief altar or under the dome, the Eye of the Eternal is painted within a triangle, made to replace the Hebrew Yod or God.

Truly, says Ragon, there was a time when numbers and alphabetical characters meant something more than they do now - the images of a mere insignificant sound.

Their mission was nobler then. Each of them represented by its form a complete sense, which, besides the meaning of the word, had a double [The system of the so-called Senzar characters is still more wonderful and difficult, since each letter is made to yield several meanings, a sign placed at the commencement showing the true meaning.] interpretation adapted to a dual doctrine. Thus when the sages desired to write something to be understood only by the savants, they confabulated a story, a dream, or some other fictitious subject with personal names of men and localities, that revealed by their lettered characters the true meaning of the author by that narrative. Such were all their religious creations. [Ragon, Op, cit., p.431, note.]

Every appellation and term had its raison d'être. The name of a plant or mineral denoted its nature to the Initiate at the first glance. The essence of everything was easily perceived by him once that it was figured by such characters. The Chinese characters have preserved much of this graphic and pictorial character to this day, though the secret of the full system is lost. Nevertheless, even now, there are those among that nation who can write a long narrative, a volume, on one page; and the symbols that are explained historically, allegorically and astronomically, have survived until now.

Moreover, there exists a universal language among the Initiates, which an Adept, and even a disciple, of any nation may understand by reading it in his own language. We Europeans, on the contrary, possess only one graphic sign common to all, & (and); there is a language richer in metaphysical terms than any on earth, whose every word is expressed by like common signs. The Litera Pythagorae, so called, the Greek Y (the English capital Y) if traced alone in a message, was as explicit as a whole page filled with sentences, for it stood as a symbol for a number of things - for white and black Magic, for instance. [The Y exoterically signifies only the two paths of virtue of vice, and stands also for the numeral 150 and with a dash over the letter Y for 150.000.] Suppose one man enquired of another: To what School of Magic does so and so belong? And the answer came back with the letter traced with the right branch thicker than the left, then it meant "to right hand or divine Magic;" but if the letter was traced in the usual way, with the left branch thicker than the right, then it meant the reverse, the right or left branch being the whole biography of a man. In Asia, especially in the Devanâgarî characters, every letter had several secret meanings.

Interpretations of the hidden sense of such apocalyptic writings are found in the keys given in the Kabalah, and they are among its more secret lore. St. Hieronymus assures us that they were known to the School of the Prophets and taught therein, which is very likely. Molitor, the learned Hebraist, in his work on tradition says that:

The two and twenty letters of the Hebrew alphabet were regarded as an emanation, or the visible expression of the divine forces inherent in the ineffable name.

These letters find their equivalent in, and are replaced by numbers, in the same way as in the other systems. For instance, the twelfth and the sixth letter of the alphabet yield eighteen in a name; the other letter of that name added being always exchanged for that figure which corresponds to the alphabetical letter; then all those figures are subjected to an algebraical process which transforms them again into letters; after which the latter yield to the enquirer "the most hidden secrets of divine Permanency (eternity in its immutability) in the Futurity."

SECTION XI

THE HEXAGON WITH THE CENTRAL POINT, OR THE SEVENTH KEY

Arguing the virtue in names (Baalshem), Molitor thinks it impossible to deny that the Kabalah - its present abuses notwithstanding - has some very profound and scientific basis to stand upon. And if it is claimed, he argues, that before the Name of Jesus every other Name must bend, why should not the Tetragrammaton have the same power? [Tradition, chap, on "Numbers."]

This is good sense and logic. For if Pythagoras viewed the hexagon formed of two crossed triangles as the symbol of creation, and the Egyptians, as that of the union of fire and water (or of generation), the Essenes saw in it the seal of Solomon, the Jews the Shield of David, the Hindus the sign of Vishnu (to this day); and if even in Russia and Poland the double triangle is regarded as a powerful talisman - then so widespread a use argues that there is something in it. It stands to reason, indeed, that such an ancient and universally revered symbol should not be merely laid aside to be laughed at by those who know nothing of its virtues or real Occult significance. To begin with, even the known sign is merely a substitute for the one used by the Initiates. In a Tântrika work in the British Museum, a terrible curse is called down upon the head of him who shall ever divulge to the profane the real Occult hexagon known as the "Sign of

Vishnu," "Solomon's Seal," etc.

The great power of the hexagon - with its central mystic sign the T, or the Svastika, a septenary - is well explained in the seventh key of Things Concealed, for it says

The seventh key is the hieroglyph of the sacred septenary, of royalty, of the priesthood [the Initiate], of triumph and true result by struggle. It is magic power in all its force, the true "Holy Kingdom." In the Hermetic Philosophy it is the quintessence resulting from the union of the two forces of the great Magic Agent [Akâsha, Astral Light.] . . . It is equally Jakin and Boaz bound by the will of the Adept and overcome by his omnipotence.

The force of this key is absolute in Magic. All religions have consecrated this sign in their rites.

We can only glance hurriedly at present at the long series of antediluvian works in their postdiluvian and fragmentary, often disfigured, form. Although all of these are the inheritance from the Fourth Race - now lying buried in the unfathomed depths of the ocean - still they are not to be rejected. As we have shown, there was but one Science at the dawn of mankind, and it was entirely divine. If humanity on reaching its adult period has abused it - especially the last Sub-Races of the Fourth Root-Race - it has been the fault and sin of the practitioners who desecrated the divine knowledge, not of those who remained true to its pristine dogmas. It is not because the modern Roman Catholic Church, faithful to her traditional intolerance, is now pleased to see in the Occultist, and even in the innocent Spiritualist and Masons, the descendants of "the Kischuph, the Hamite, the Kasdim, the Cephene, the Ophite and the Khartumim" - all these being "the followers of Satan," that they are such indeed. The State or National Religion of every country has ever and at all times very easily disposed of rival schools by professing to believe they were dangerous heresies - the old Roman Catholic State Religion as much as the modern one.

The anathema, however, has not made the public any the wiser in the Mysteries of the Occult Sciences. In some respects the world is all the better for such ignorance. The secrets of nature generally cut both ways, and in the hands of the undeserving they are more than likely to become murderous. Who in our modern day knows anything of the real significance of, and the powers contained in, certain characters and signs - talismans - whether for beneficent or evil purposes? Fragments of the Runes and the writing of the Kischuph, found scattered in old mediaeval libraries; copies from the Ephesian and Milesian letters or characters; the thrice famous Book of Thoth, and the terrible treatises (still preserved) of Targes, the Chaldaean, and his disciple Tarchon, the Etruscan - who flourished long before the Trojan War - are so many names and appellations void of sense (though met with in classical literature) for the educated modern scholar. Who, in the nineteenth century, believes in the art, described in such treatises as those of Targes, of evoking and directing thunderbolts?

OCCULT WEAPONS -

Yet the same is described in the Brâhmanical literature, and Targes copied his "thunderbolts" from the Astra, [This is a kind of magical bow and arrow calculated to destroy in one moment whole armies; it is mentioned in the Ramayana, the Puranas and elsewhere.] those terrible engines of destruction known to the Mahabharatan Aryans. A whole arsenal of dynamite bombs would pale before this art - if it ever becomes understood by the Westerns. It is from an old fragment that was translated to him, that the late Lord Bulwer Lytton got his idea of Vril. It is a lucky thing, indeed, that, in the face of the virtues and philanthropy that grace our age of iniquitous wars, of anarchists and dynamiters, the secrets contained in the books discovered in Numa's tomb should have been burnt. But the science of Circe and Medea is not lost. One can discover it in the apparent gibberish of the Tantrika Sutras, the Kuku-ma of the Bhutani and the Sikhim Dugpas and "Red-caps" of Tibet, and even in the sorcery of the Nilgiri Mula Kurumbas. Very luckily few outside the high practioners of the Left Path and of the Adepts of the Right - in whose hands the weird secrets of the real meaning are safe - understand the "black" evocations. Otherwise the Western as much as the Eastern Dugpas might make short work of their enemies. The name of the latter is legion, for the direct descendants of the antediluvian sorcerers hate all those who are not with them, arguing that, therefore, they are against them.

As for the "Little Albert" - though even this small half-esoteric volume has become a literary relic - and the "Great Albert" or the "Red Dragon," together with the numberless old copies still in existence, the sorry remains of the mythical Mother Shiptons and the Merlins - we mean the false ones

- all these are vulgarised imitations of the original works of the same names. Thus the "Petite Albert" is the disfigured imitation of the great work written in Latin by Bishop Adalbert, an Occultist of the eighth century, sentenced by the second Roman Concilium. His work was reprinted several centuries later and named Alberti Parvi Lucii Libellus de Mirabilibus Naturae Arcanis. The severities of the Roman Church have ever been spasmodic. While one learns of this condemnation, which placed the Church, as will be shown, in relation to the Seven Archangels, the Virtues or Thrones of God, in the most embarrassing position for long centuries, it remains a wonder indeed, to find that the Jesuits have not destroyed the archives, with all their countless chronicles and annals, of the History of France and those of the Spanish Escurial, along with them. Both history and the chronicles of the former speak at length of the priceless talisman received by Charles the Great from a Pope. It was a little volume on Magic - or Sorcery, rather - all full of kabalistic figures, signs mysterious sentences and invocations to the stars and planets. These were talismans against the enemies of the King (les ennemis de Charlemagne), which talismans, the chronicler tells us, proved of great help, as "every one of them [the enemies] died a violent death." The small volume, Enchiridinum Leonis Papie, has disappeared and is very luckily out of print. Again the Alphabet of Thoth can be dimly traced in the modern Tarot which can be had at almost every bookseller's in Paris. As for its being understood or utilised, the many fortune-tellers in Paris, who make a professional living by it, are sad specimens of failures of attempts at reading, let alone correctly interpreting the symbolism of the Tarot without a preliminary philosophical study of the Science. The real Tarot, in its complete symbology, can be found only in the Babylonian cylinders, that any one can inspect and study in the British Museum and elsewhere. Any one can see these Chaldaean, antediluvian rhombs, or revolving cylinders, covered with sacred signs; but the secrets of these divining "wheels," or, as de Mirville calls them, "the rotating globes of Hecate," have to be left untold for some time to come. Meanwhile there are the "turning-tables" of the modern medium for the babes, and the Kabalah for the strong. This may afford some consolation.

People are very apt to use terms which they do not understand, and to pass judgments on prima facie evidence. The difference between White and Black Magic is very difficult to realise fully, as both have to be judged by their motive, upon which their ultimate though not their immediate effects depend, even though these may not come for years. Between the "right and the left hand [Magic] there is but a cobweb thread," says an Eastern proverb. Let us abide by its wisdom and wait till we have learned more.

We shall have to return at greater length to the relation of the Kabalah to Gupta Vidya, and to deal further with esoteric and numerical systems, but we must first follow the line of Adepts in post Christian times.

SECTION XII

THE DUTY OF THE TRUE OCCULTIST TOWARD RELIGIONS

HAVING disposed of pre-Christian Initiates and their Mysteries - though more has to be said about the latter - a few words must be given to the earliest post-Christian Adepts, irrespective of their personal belief and doctrines, or their subsequent places in History, whether sacred or profane. Our task is to analyse this adeptship with its abnormal thaumaturgical, or, as now called, psychological powers; to give each of such Adepts his due, by considering, firstly, what are the historical records about them that have reached us at this late day and secondly, to examine the laws of probability with regard to the said powers.

And at the outset the writer must be allowed a few words in justification of what has to be said. It would be most unfair to see in these pages, any defiance to, or disrespect for, the Christian religion - least of all, a desire to wound anyone's feelings. The Theosophist believes in neither Divine nor Satanic miracles. At such a distance of time he can only obtain prima facie evidence and judge of it by the results claimed. There is neither Saint nor Sorcerer, Prophet nor Soothsayer for him; only Adepts, or proficients in the production of feats of a phenomenal character, to be judged by their words and deeds. The only distinction he is now able to trace depends on the results achieved - on the evidence whether they were beneficent or maleficent in their character as affecting those for or against whom the powers of the Adept were used. With the division so arbitrarily made between proficients in "miraculous" doings of this or that Religion by their respective followers and advocates, the Occultist cannot and must not be concerned. The Christian whose Religion commands him to regard Peter and Paul as Saints, and divinely inspired and glorified Apostles, and to view Simon and Apollonius as Wizards and Necromancers, helped by, and serving the ends of, supposed Evil Powers - is quite justified in thus doing if he be a sincere orthodox Christian. But so also is the Occultist justified, if he would serve truth and only truth, in rejecting such a one-sided view. The student of Occultism must belong to no special creed or sect, yet he is bound to show outward respect to every creed and faith, if he would become an Adept of the Good Law. He must not be bound by the prejudged and sectarian opinions of anyone, and he has to form his own opinions and to come to his own conclusions in accordance with the rules of evidence furnished to him by the Science to which he is devoted. Thus, if the Occultist is, by way of illustration, a Buddhist, then, while regarding Gautama Buddha as the grandest of all the Adepts that lived, and the incarnation of unselfish love, boundless charity, and moral goodness, he will regard in the same light Jesus - proclaiming Him another such incarnation of every divine virtue. He will reverence the memory of the great Martyr, even while refusing to recognise in Him the incarnation on earth of the One Supreme Deity, and the "Very God of Gods" in Heaven. He will cherish the ideal man for his personal virtues, not for the claims made on his behalf by fanatical dreamers of the early ages, or by a shrewd calculating Church and Theology. He will even believe in most of the "assorted miracles," only explaining them in accordance with the rules of his own Science and by his psychic discernment. Refusing them the term "miracle" - in the theological sense of an event "contrary to the established laws of nature' - he will nevertheless view them as a deviation from the laws known (so far) to Science, quite another thing. Moreover the Occultist will, on the prima facie evidence of the Gospels - whether proven or not - class most of such works as beneficent, divine Magic, though he will be justified in regarding such events as casting out devils into a herd of swine [Matthew, viii. 30-34.] as allegorical, and as pernicious to true faith in their dead-letter sense. This is the view a genuine, impartial Occultist would take. And in this respect even the fanatical Mussulmans who regard Jesus of Nazareth as a great Prophet, and show respect to Him, are giving a wholesome lesson in charity to Christians, who teach and accept that "religious tolerance is impious and absurd," [Dogmatic Theology, iii. 345.] and who will never refer to the prophet of Islam by any other term but that of a "false prophet."

CHRISTIAN AND NON-CHRISTIAN ADEPTS –

It is on the principles of Occultism, then, that Peter and Simon, Paul and Apollonius, will now be examined.

These four Adepts are chosen to appear in these pages with good reason. They are the first in post-Christian Adeptship - as recorded in profane and sacred writings - to strike the key-note of "miracles," that is of psychic and physical phenomena. It is only theological bigotry and intolerance that could so maliciously and arbitrarily separate the two harmonious parts into two distinct manifestations of Divine and Satanic Magic, into "godly" and "ungodly" works.

SECTION XIII

POST-CHRISTIAN ADEPTS AND THEIR DOC-TRINES

WHAT does the world at large know of Peter and Simon, for example? Profane history has no record of these two, while that which the so-called sacred literature tells us of them is scattered about, contained in a few sentences in the Acts. As to the Apocrypha, their very name forbids critics to trust to them for information. The Occultists, however claim that, one-sided and prejudiced as they may be, the apocryphal Gospels contain far more historically true events and facts than does the New Testament, the Acts included. The former are crude tradition, the latter [the official Gospels] are an elaborately made up legend. The sacredness of the New Testament is a question of private belief and of blind faith, and while one is bound to respect the private opinion of one's neighbour, no one is forced to share it.

Who was Simon Magus, and what is known of him? One learns in the Acts simply that on account of his remarkable magical Arts he was called "the Great Power of God." Philip is said to have baptised this Samaritan; and subsequently he is accused of having offered money to Peter and John to teach him the power of working true "miracles," false ones, it is asserted, being of the Devil [viii. 9, 10.] This is all, if we omit the words of abuse freely used against him for working "miracles" of the latter kind. Origen mentions him as having visited Rome during the reign of Nero, [Adv. Celsum.] and Mosheim places him along the open enemies of Christianity; [Eccles. Hist., i. 140.] but Occult tradition accuses him of nothing worse than refusing to recognise "Simeon" as Vicegerent of God, whether that "Simeon" was Peter or anyone else being still left an open question with the critics.

UNFAIR CRITICISM –

That which Irenaeus [Contra Haereses, 1. xxiii. 1-4.] and Epiphanius [Comtra Haereses, ii, 1-6.] say of Simon Magus - namely, that he represented himself as the incarnated trinity; that in Samaria he was the Father, in Judaea the Son, and had given himself out to the Gentiles as the Holy Spirit - is simply backbiting. Times and events change; human nature remains the same and unaltered under every sky and in every age. The charge is the result and product of the traditional and now classical odium theologicum. No Occultists - all of whom have experienced personally, more or less, the effects of theological rancour - will ever believe such things merely on the word of an Irenaeus, if, indeed, he ever wrote the words himself. Further on it is narrated of Simon that he took about with him a woman whom he introduced as Helen of Troy, who had passed through a hundred reincarnations, and who, still earlier, in the beginning of aeons, was Sophia, Divine Wisdom, an emanation of his own (Simon's) Eternal Mind, when he (Simon) was the "Father"; and finally that by her he had "begotten the Archangels and Angels, by whom this world was created," etc.

Now we all know to what a degree of transformation

and luxuriant growth any bare statement can be subjected and forced, after passing through only half a dozen hands. Moreover, all these claims may be explained and even shown to be true at bottom, Simon Magus was a Kabalist and a Mystic, who, like so many other reformers, endeavoured to found a new Religion based on the fundamental teachings of the Secret Doctrine, yet without divulging more than necessary of its mysteries. Why then should not Simon, a Mystic, deeply imbued with the fact of serial incarnations (we may leave out the number "one hundred," as a very probable exaggeration of his disciples), speak of any one whom he knew psychically as an incarnation of some heroine of that name, and in the way he did - if he ever did so? Do we not find in our own century some ladies and gentlemen, not charlatans but intellectual persons highly honoured in society, whose inner conviction assures them that they were - one Queen Cleopatra, another one Alexander the Great, a third Joan of Arc, and who or what not? This is a matter of inner conviction, and is based on more or less familiarity with Occultism and belief in the modern theory of reincarnation. The latter differs from the one genuine doctrine of old, as will be shown, but there is no rule without its exception.

As to the Magus being "one with God the Father, God the Son, and God the Holy Ghost," this again is quite reasonable, if we admit that a Mystic and Seer has a right to use allegorical language; and in this case, moreover, it is quite justified by the doctrine of Universal Unity taught in Esoteric Philosophy. Every Occultist will say the same, on (to him) scientific and logical grounds, in full accordance with the doctrine he professes. Not a Vedantin but says the same thing daily: he is, of course Brahman, and he is Parabrahman, once that he rejects the individuality of his personal spirit, and recognizes the Divine Ray which dwells in his Higher Self as only a reflection of the Universal Spirit. This is the echo in all times and ages of the primitive doctrine of Emanations. The first Emanation from the Unknown is the "Father,[Op cit., ii.337.] the second the "Son," and all and everything proceeds from the One, or that Divine Spirit which is "unknowable. Hence, the assertion that by her (Sophia, or Minerva, the Divine Wisdom) he (Simon), when yet in the bosom of the Father, himself the Father (or the first collective Emanation), begot the Archangels - the "Son" - who were the creators of this world.

The Roman Catholics themselves, driven to the wall by the irrefutable arguments of their opponents - the learned Philologists and Symbologists who pick to shreds Church dogmas and their authorities, and point out the plurality of the Elohim in the Bible - admit today that the first "creation" of God, the Tsaba, or Archangels, must have participated in the creation of the universe. Might not we suppose:

Although "God alone created the heaven and the earth" . . .that however unconnected they [the angels] may have been with the primordial ex nihilo creation, they may have received a mission to achieve, to continue, and to sustain it?[Op cit., ii.337.]

exclaims De Mirville, in answer to Renan, Lacour, Maury and the tutti quanti of the French Institute. With certain alterations it is precisely this which is claimed by the Secret

Doctrine. In truth there is not a single doctrine preached by the many Reformers of the first and the subsequent centuries of our era, that did not base its initial teachings on this universal cosmogony. Consult Mosheim and see what he has to say of the many "heresies" he describes. Cerinthus, the Jew,

Taught that the Creator of this world . . . the Sovereign God of the Jewish people, was a Being . . . who derived his birth from the Supreme God; that this Being, moreover ,

Fell by degrees from his native virtue and primitive dignity.

THE TWO ETERNAL PRINCIPLES –

Basildes, Carpocrates and Valentinus, the Egyptian Gnostics of the second century, held the same ideas with a few variations. Basilides preached seven Aeons (Hosts or Archangels), who issued from the substance of the Supreme. Two of them, Power and Wisdom, begot the heavenly hierarchy of the first class and dignity; this emanated a second; the latter a third, and so on; each subsequent evolution being of a nature less exalted than the precedent, and each creating for itself a Heaven as a dwelling, the nature of each of these respective Heavens decreasing in splendour and purity as it approached nearer to the earth. Thus the number of these Dwellings amounted to 365; and over all presided the Supreme Unknown called Abraxas, a name which in the Greek method of numeration yields the number 365, which in its mystic and numerical meaning contains the number 355, or the man value [Ten is the perfect number of the Supreme God among the "manifested" deities, for number "I"is the symbol of the Universal Unit, or male principle in Nature, and a number "0" the feminine symbol Chaos, the Deep, the two forming thus the symbol of Androgyne nature as well as the full value of the solar year, which was also the value of Jehovah and Enoch. Ten, with Pythagoras, was the symbol of the Universe; also of Enos, the Son of Seth, or the "Son of Man" who stands as the symbol of the solar year of 365 days, and whose years are therefore given as 365 also. In the Egyptian Symbology Abraxas was the Sun, the "Lord of the Heavens." The Circle is the symbol of the one Unmanifesting Principle, the plane of whose figure is infinitude eternally, and this is crossed by a diameter only during Manvantaras.] This was a Gnostic Mystery based upon that of primitive Evolution, which ended with "man."

Saturnilus of Antioch promulgated the same doctrine slightly modified. He taught two eternal principles, Good and Evil, which are simply Spirit and Matter. The seven Angels who preside over the seven Planets are the Builders of our Universe - a purely Eastern doctrine, as Saturnilus was an Asiatic Gnostic. These Angels are the natural Guardians of the seven Regions of our Planetary System, one of the most powerful among these seven creating Angels of the third order being "Saturn," the presiding genius of the Planet, and the God of the Hebrew people: namely, Jehovah, who was venerated among the Jews, and to whom they dedicated the seventh day or Sabbath, Saturday - "Saturn's day" among the Scandinavians and also among the Hindus.

Marcion, who also held the doctrine of the two opposed

principles of Good and Evil, asserted that there was a third Deity between the two - one of a "mixed nature" - the God of the Jews, the Creator (with his Host) of the lower, or our, World. Though ever at war with the Evil Principle, this intermediate Being was nevertheless also opposed to the Good Principle, whose place and title he coveted.

Thus Simon was only the son of his time, a religious Reformer like so many others, and an Adept among the Kabalists. The Church, to which a belief in his actual existence and great powers is a necessity - in order the better to set off the "miracle" performed by Peter and his triumph over Simon - extols unstintingly his wonderful magic feats. On the other hand, Scepticism, represented by scholars and learned critics, tries to make away with him altogether. Thus, after denying the very existence of Simon, they have finally thought fit to merge his individuality entirely in that of Paul. The anonymous author of Supernatural Religion assiduously endeavoured to prove that by Simon Magus we must understand the Apostle Paul, whose Epistles were secretly as well as openly calumniated and opposed by Peter, and charged with containing "dysnoetic learning." Indeed this seems more than probable when we think of the two Apostles and contrast their characters.

The Apostle of the Gentiles was brave, outspoken, sincere, and very learned; the Apostle of Circumcision, cowardly, cautious, insincere, and very ignorant. That Paul had been, partially at least, if not completely, initiated into the theurgic mysteries, admits of little doubt. His language, the phraseology so peculiar to the Greek philosophers, certain expressions used only by the Initiates, are so many sure earmarks to that supposition. Our suspicion has been strengthened by an able article entitled "Paul and Plato," by Dr. A. Wilder, in which the author puts forward one remarkable and, for us, very precious observation. In the Epistles to the Corinthians, he shows Paul abounding with "expressions suggested by the initiations of Sabazius and Eleusis, and the lectures of the (Greek) philosophers. He (Paul) designates himself as idiotes - a person unskilful in the Word, but not in the gnosis or philosophical learning. 'We speak wisdom among the perfect or initiated,' he writes, even the hidden wisdom, 'not the wisdom of this world, nor of the Archons of this world, but divine wisdom in a mystery, secret - which none of the Archons of this world knew.'"[I. Cor.,ii. 6-8.]

What else can the Apostle mean by those unequivocal words, but that he himself, as belonging to the Mystae (Initiated), spoke of things shown and explained only in the Mysteries? The "divine wisdom in a mystery which none of the Archons of this world knew," has evidently some direct reference to the Basileus of the Eleusinian Initiation who did know. The Basileus belonged to the staff of the great Hierophant, and was an Archon of Athens, and as such was one of the chief Mystae, belonging to the interior Mysteries, to which a very select and small number obtained an entrance. [Compare Taylor's Eleusinian and Bacchic Mysteries.] The magistrates supervising the Eleusinia were called Archons. [Isis Unveiled., ii. 89.]

We will deal, however, first with Simon the Magician.

SECTION XIV

SIMON AND HIS BIOGRAPHER HIPPOLYTUS

A S shown in our earlier volumes, Simon was a pupil of the Tanaim of Samaria, and the reputation he left behind him, together with the title of "the Great Power of God," testify in favour of the ability and learning of his Masters. But the Tanaim were Kabalists of the same secret school as John of the Apocalypse, whose careful aim it was to conceal as much as possible the real meaning of the names in the Mosiac Books.

Still the calumnies so jealously disseminated against Simon Magus by the unknown authors and compilers of the Acts and other writings, could not cripple the truth to such an extent as to conceal the fact that no Christian could rival him in thaumaturgic deeds. The story told about his falling during an aerial flight, breaking both his legs and then committing suicide, is ridiculous. Posterity has heard but one side of the story. Were the disciples of Simon to have a chance, we might perhaps find that it was Peter who broke his legs. But as against this hypothesis we know that this Apostle was too prudent ever to venture himself in Rome. On the confession of several ecclesiastical writers, no Apostle ever performed such "supernatural wonders," but of course pious people will say this only the more proves that it was the Devil who worked through Simon. He was accused of blasphemy against the Holy Ghost, only because he introduced as the "Holy Spiritus" the Men's (Intelligence) or "the Mother of all." But we find the same expression used in the Book of Enoch, in which, in contradistinction to the "Son of Man," he speaks of the "Son of the Woman." In the Codex of the Nazarenes, and in the Zohar, as well as in the Books of Hermes, the same expression is used; and even in the apocryphal Evangelium of the Hebrews we read that Jesus admitted the female sex of the Holy Ghost by using the expression "My Mother, the Holy Pneuma."

After long ages of denial, however, the actual existence of Simon Magus has been finally demonstrated, whether he was Saul, Paul or Simon. A manuscript speaking of him under the last name has been discovered in Greece and has put a stop to any further speculation.

In his Histoire des Trois Premiers Siecles de L'Eglise, [Op. cit., ii. 395.] M. de Pressensé gives his opinion on this additional relic of early Christianity. Owing to the numerous myths with which the history of Simon abounds - he says - many Theologians (among Protestants, he ought to have added) have concluded that it was no better than a clever tissue of legends. But he adds:

It contains positive facts, it seems, now warranted by the unanimous testimony of the Fathers of the Church and the narrative of Hippolytus recently discovered. [Quoted by De Mirville. Op cit., vi. 41 and 42.]

This MS. is very far from being complimentary to the alleged founder of Western Gnosticism. While recognizing great powers in Simon, it brands him as a priest of Satan

- which is quite enough to show that it was written by a Christian. It also shows that, like another servant, "of the Evil One" - as Manes is called by the Church - Simon was a baptised Christian; but that both, being too well versed in the mysteries of true primitive Christianity, were persecuted for it. The secret of such persecution was then, as it is now, quite transparent to those who study the question impartially. Seeking to preserve his independence, Simon could not submit to the leadership or authority of any of the Apostles, least of all to that of either Peter or John, the fanatical author of the Apocalypse. Hence charges of heresy followed by "anathema maranatha." The persecutions by the Church were never directed against Magic, when it was orthodox; for the new Theurgy, established and regulated by the Fathers, now known to Christendom as "grace" and "miracles," was, and is still, when it does happen, only Magic - whether conscious or unconscious. Such phenomena as have passed to posterity under the name of "divine miracles" were produced though powers acquired by great purity of life and ecstacy. Prayer and contemplation added to asceticism are the best means of discipline in order to become a Theurgist, where there is no regular initiation. For intense prayer for the accomplishment of some object is only intense will and desire, resulting in unconscious Magic. In our own day George Muller of Bristol has proved it. But "divine miracles" are produced by the same causes that generate effects of Sorcery.

UNEVEN BALANCES –
The whole difference rests on the good or evil effects

aimed at, and on the actor who produces them. The thunders of the Church were directed only against those who dissented from the formulae and attributed to themselves the production of certain marvellous effects, instead of fathering them on a personal God; and thus while those Adepts in Magic Arts who acted under her direct instructions and auspices were proclaimed to posterity and history as saints and friends of God, all others were hooted out of the Church and sentenced to eternal calumny and curses from their day to this. Dogma and authority have ever been the curse of humanity, the great extinguishers of light and truth. [Mr. St.George Lane-Fox has admirably expressed the idea in his eloquent appeal to the many rival schools and societies in India. "I feel sure," he said, " that the prime motive, however dimly perceived, by which you, as the promoters of these movements, were actuated, was a revolt against the tyrannical and almost universal establishment throughout all existing social and so-called religious institutions of a usurped authority in some external form supplanting and obscuring the only real and ultimate authority, the indwelling spirit of truth revealed to each individual soul, true conscience in fact, that supreme source of all human wisdom and power which elevates man above the level of the brute." (To the Members of the Aryan Samâj, the Theosophical Society, Brahmo and Hindu Samaj and other Religious and Progressive Societies in India.)]

It was perhaps the recognition of a germ of that which, later on, in the then nascent Church, grew into the virus of insatiate power and ambition, culminating finally in the dogma of infallibility, that forced Simon, and so many others, to break away from her at her very birth. Sects and dissensions began with the first century. While Paul rebukes Peter to his face, John slanders under the veil of vision the Nicolaitans, and makes Jesus declare that he hates them. [Revelation, ii.6.] Therefore we pay little attention to the accusations against Simon in the MS. found in Greece.

It is entitled Philosophumena. Its author, regarded as Saint Hippolytus by the Greek Church, is referred to as an "unknown heretic" by the Papists, only because he speaks in it "very slanderously" of Pope Callistus, also a Saint. Nevertheless, Greeks and Latins agree in declaring the Philosophumena to be an extraordinary and very erudite work. Its antiquity and genuineness have been vouched for by the best authorities of Tubingen.

Whoever the author may have been, he expresses himself about Simon in this wise:

Simon, a man well versed in magic arts, deceived many persons partly by the art of Thrasymedes,[This "art" is not common jugglery, as some define it now: it's a kind of psychological jugglery, if jugglery at all, where fascination and glamour are used as means of producing illusions. It is hypnotism on a large scale.] and partly with the help of demons.[The author asserts in this his Christian persuasion.] . . . He determined to pass himself off as a god. . . Aided by his wicked arts, he turned to profit not only the teachings of Moses, but those of the poets . . . His disciples use to this day his charms. Thanks to incantations, to philtres, to their attractive caresses [Magnetic passes, evidently, followed by a trance and sleep.] and what they call "sleeps," they send demons to influence all those whom they would fascinate. With this object they employ what they call "familiar demons." ["Elementals" used by the highest Adept to do mechanical, not intellectual work, as a physicist uses gases and other compounds.]

Further on the MS. reads:

The Magus (Simon) made those who wished to enquire of the demon, write what their question was on a leaf of parchment; this, folded in four, was thrown into a burning brazier, in order that the smoke should reveal the contents of the writing to the Spirit (demon) (Philos., IV. IV.) Incense was thrown by handfuls on the blazing coals, the Magus adding, on pieces of papyrus, the Hebrew names of the Spirits he was addressing, and the flame devoured all. Very soon the divine Spirit seemed to overwhelm the Magician, who uttered unintelligible invocations, and plunged in such a state he answered every question - phantasmal apparitions being often raised over the flaming brazier (ibid., iii.); at other times fire descended from heaven upon objects previously pointed out by the Magician (ibid.); or again the deity evoked, crossing the room, would trace fiery orbs in its flight. (ibid., ix.). [Quoted from De Mirville. op.cit.,vi.43.]

So far the above statements agree with those of Anastasius the Sinaïte:

People saw Simon causing statues to walk; precipitating himself into the flames without being burnt; metamorphosing his body into that of various animals [lycanthropy]; raising at banquets phantoms and spectres; causing the furniture in the rooms to move about, by invisible spirits. He gave out that he was escorted by a number of shades to whom he gave the name of "souls of the dead." Finally, he used to fly in the air . . . (Anast., Patrol, Grecque, vol. lxxxix., col. 523, quaest. xx.).[Ibid.,vi.45.]

Suetonius says in his Nero,

In those days an Icarus fell at his first ascent near Nero's box and covered it with his blood. [Ibid., p.46.]

This sentence, referring evidently to some unfortunate acrobat who missed his footing and tumbled, is brought forward as a proof that it was Simon who fell.[Amédée Fleury. Rapports de St.Paul avec Sénèque. ii. 100. The whole of this is summarised from De Mirville.]

STONES AS "EVIDENCES." –

But the latter's name is surely too famous, if one must credit the Church Fathers, for the historian to have mentioned him simply as "an Icarus." The writer is quite aware that there exists in Rome a locality names Simonium, near the Church of SS. Cosmas and Daimanus (Via Sacra), and the ruins of the ancient temple of Romulus, where the broken pieces of a stone, on which it is alleged the two knees of the Apostle Peter were impressed in thanksgiving after his supposed victory over Simon, are shown to this day. But what does this exhibition amount to? For the broken fragments of one stone, the Buddhists of Ceylon show a whole rock on Adam's Peak with another imprint upon it. A crag stands upon its platform, a terrace of which supports a huge boulder, and on the boulder rests for nearly three thousand years the sacred footprint of a foot five feet long. Why not credit the legend of the latter, if we have to accept that of St.Peter? "Prince of Apostles," or "Prince of Reformers," or even the "First-born of Satan," as Simon is called, all are entitled to legends and fictions. One may be allowed to discriminate, however.

That Simon could fly, i.e., raise himself in the air for a few minutes, is no impossibility. Modern mediums have performed the same feat supported by a force that Spiritualists persist in calling "spirits." But if Simon did so, it was with the help of a self-acquired blind power that heeds little the prayers and commands of rival Adepts, let alone Saints. The fact is that logic is against the supposed fall of Simon at the prayer of Peter. For had he been defeated publicly by the Apostle, his disciples would have abandoned him after such an evident sign of inferiority, and would have become orthodox Christians. But we find even the author of Philosophumena, just such a Christian, showing otherwise. Simon had lost so little credit with his pupils and the masses, that he went on daily preaching in the Roman Campania after his supposed fall from the clouds "far above the Capitolium," in which fall he broke his legs only! Such a lucky fall is in itself sufficiently miraculous, one would say.

SECTION XV

ST. PAUL THE REAL FOUNDER OF PRESENT CHRISTIANITY

We may repeat with the author of Phallicism:

We are all for construction - even for Christian, although of course philosophical construction. We have nothing to do with reality, in man's limited, mechanical, scientific sense, or with realism. We have undertaken to show that mysticism is the very life and soul of religion; [But we can never agree with the author "that rites and ritual and formal worship and prayers are of absolute necessity of things," for the external can develop and grow and receive worship only at the expense of, and to the detriment of, the internal, the only real and true.] . . . that the Bible is only misread and misrepresented when rejected as advancing supposed fabulous and contradictory things; that Moses did not make mistakes, but spoke to the "children of men" in the only way in which children in their nonage can be addressed; that the world is indeed, a very different place from that which it is assumed to be; that what is derided as superstition is the only true and the only scientific knowledge, and moreover that modern knowledge and modern science are to a great extent not only superstition, but superstition of a very destructive and deadly kind.[H. Jennings, op. cit., pp.37.38.]

All this is perfectly true and correct. But it is also true

that the New Testament, the Acts and the Epistles - however much the historical figure of Jesus may be true - all are symbolical and allegorical sayings, and that "it was not Jesus but Paul who was the real founder of Christianity;" [See Isis Unveiled, ii.574.] but it was not the official Church Christianity, at any rate. "The disciples were called Christians first in Antioch," the Acts of the Apostles tell us, [xi. 26.] and they were not so called before, nor for a long time after, but simply Nazarenes.

This view is found in more than one writer of the present and the past centuries. But, hitherto, it has always been laid aside as an unproven hypothesis, a blasphemous assumption; though, as the author of Paul, the Founder of Christianity [Art, by Dr. A. Wilder, in Evolution.] truly says:

ABROGATION OF LAW BY INITIATES -

Such men as Irenaeus, Epiphanius and Eusebius have transmitted to posterity a reputation for such untruth and dishonest practices that the heart sickens at the story of the crimes of that period.

The more so, since the whole Christian scheme rests upon their sayings. But we find now another corroboration, and this time on the perfect reading of biblical glyphs. In The Source of Measures we find the following:

It must be borne in mind that our present Christianity is Pauline, not Jesus. Jesus, in his life, was a Jew, conforming to the law; even more, He says: "The scribes and pharisees sit in Moses' seat; whatsoever therefore they command you to do, that observe and do." And again: "I did not come to destroy but to fulfil the law," Therefore, he was under the law to the day of his death, and could not, while in life, abrogate one jot or title of it. He was circumcised and commanded circumcision. But Paul said of circumcision that it availed nothing, and he (Paul) abrogated the law. Saul and Paul - that is, Saul, under the law, and Paul, freed from the obligations of the law - were in one man, but parallelisms in the flesh, of Jesus the man under the law as observing it, who thus died in Chrestos and arose, freed from its obligations, in the spirit world as Christos, or the triumphant Christ. It was the Christ who was freed, but Christ was the Spirit. Saul in the flesh was the function of, and parallel of Chrestos. Paul in the flesh was the function and parallel of Jesus become Christ in the spirit, as an early reality to answer to and act for the apotheosis; and so armed with all authority in the flesh to abrogate human law. [Op. cit.,p.262.]

The real reason why Paul is shown as "abrogating the law" can be found only in India, where to this day the most ancient customs and privileges are preserved in all their purity, notwithstanding the abuse levelled at the same. There is only one class of persons who can disregard the law of Brâhmanical institutions, caste included, with impunity, and that is the perfect "Svâmis," the Yogis - who have reached, or are supposed to have reached, the first step towards the Jivanmukta state - or the full Initiates. And Paul was undeniably an Initiate. We will quote a passage or two from Iris Unveiled, for we can say now nothing better than what was said then:

Take Paul, read the little of original that is left of him in the writings attributed to this brave, honest, sincere man, and see whether anyone can find a word therein to show that Paul meant by the word Christ anything more than the abstract ideal of the personal divinity indwelling in man. For Paul, Christ is not a person, but an embodied idea. " If any man is in Christ he is a new creation," he is reborn, as after initiation, for the Lord is spirit - the spirit of man. Paul was the only one of the apostles who had understood the secret ideas underlying the teachings of Jesus, although he had never met him.

But Paul himself was not infallible or perfect.

Bent upon inaugurating a new and broad reform, one embracing the whole of humanity, he sincerely set his own doctrines far above the wisdom of the ages, above the ancient Mysteries and final revelation to the Epoptae.

Another proof that Paul belonged to the circle of the "Initiates" lies in the following fact. The apostle had his head shorn at Cenchreae, where Lucius (Apuleius) was initiated, because "he had a vow." The Nazars - or set apart - as we see in the Jewish Scriptures, had to cut their hair, which they wore long, and which "no razor touched" at any other time, and sacrifice it on the altar of initiation. And the Nazars were a class of Chaldaean Theurgists or Initiates.

It is shown in Isis Unveiled that Jesus belonged to this class.

Paul declares that: "According to the grace of God which is given unto me, as a wise master-builder, I have laid the foundation." (1. Corinth., iii. 10.)

The expression, master-builder, used only once in the

whole Bible, and by Paul, may be considered as a whole revelation. In the Mysteries, the third part of the sacred rites was called Epoteia, or revelation, reception into the secrets. In substance it means the highest stage of clairvoyance - the diviner; . . . but the real significance of the word is "overseeing," from "σπτομαι-" I see myself." In Sanskrit the root âp had the same meaning originally, though now it is understood as meaning "to obtain." [In its most extensive meaning, the Sanskrit word has the same literal sense as the Greek term: both imply "revelation," by no human agent, but through the "receiving of the sacred drink." In India the initiated receive the "Soma," sacred drink, which helped to liberate his soul from the body: and in the Eleusinian Mysteries it was the sacred drink offered at the Epopteia. The Grecian Mysteries are wholly derived from the Brahmanical Vaidic rites, and the latter from the Ante-Vaidic religious Mysteries - primitive Wisdom Philosophy.]

The word epopteia is compound from 'επι' "upon," and "σπτομαι-" "to look," or an overseer, an inspector - also used for a master-builder. The title of master-mason, in Freemasonry, is derived from this, in the sense used in the Mysteries. Therefore, when Paul entitles himself a "master-builder," he is using a word pre-eminently kabalistic, theurgic, and masonic, and one which no other apostle uses. He thus declares himself an adept, having the right to initiate others.

If we search in this direction, with those sure guides, the Grecian Mysteries and the Kabalah, before us, it will be easy to find the secret reason why Paul was so persecuted and hated by Peter, John, and James. The author of the

Revelation was a Jewish Kabalist, pur sang, with all the hatred inherited by him from his forefathers toward the Pagan Mysteries. [It is needless to state that the Gospel according to John was not written by John, but by a Platonist or a Gnostic belonging to the Neoplatonic school.] His jealousy during the life of Jesus extended even to Peter; and it is but after the death of their common master that we see the two apostles - the former of whom wore the Mitre and the Petaloon of the Jewish Rabbis - preach so zealously the rite of circumcision.

PAUL CHANGED TO SIMON –

In the eyes of Peter, Paul, who had humiliated him, and whom he felt so much his superior in "Greek learning" and philosophy, must have naturally appeared as a magician, a man polluted with the "Gnosis," with the "wisdom" of the Greek Mysteries - hence, perhaps, "Simon the Magician" as a comparison, not a nickname. [Ibid.,loc. cit. The fact that Peter persecuted the "Apostle of the Gentiles" under that name, does not necessarily imply that there was no Simon Magus individually distinct from Paul. It may have become a generic name of abuse. Theodoret and Chrysostom, the earliest and most prolific commentators on the Gnosticism of those days, seem actually to make of Simon a rival of Paul and to state that between them passed frequent messages. The former, as a diligent propagandist of what Paul terms the "antithesis of the Gnosis" (I Epistle to Timothy), must have been a sore thorn in the side of the apostle. There are sufficient proofs of the actual existence of Simon Magus.]

SECTION XVI

PETER A JEWISH KABALIST, NOT AN INITIATE

As to Peter, biblical criticism has shown that in all probability he had no more to do with the foundation of the Latin Church at Rome than to furnish the pretext, so readily seized upon by the cunning Irenaeus, of endowing the Church with a new name for the Apostle - Petra or Kiffa - a name which, by an easy play upon words, could be readily connected to Petroma. The Petroma was a pair of stone tablets used by the Hierophants at the Initiations, during the final Mystery. In this lies concealed the secret of the Vatican claim to the seat of Peter. As already quoted in Isis Unveiled, ii.92:

In the Oriental countries the designation Peter (in Phoenician and Chaldaic an interpreter), appears to have been the title of this personage. [Taylor's Eleusinian and Bacchic Mysteries, Wilder's ed., p. x.]

So far, and as the "interpreters" of Neo-Christianism, the Popes have most undeniably the right to call themselves successors to the title of Peter, but hardly the successors to, least of all the interpreters of, the doctrines of Jesus, the Christ; for there is the Oriental Church, older and far purer than the Roman hierarchy, which, having ever faithfully held to the primitive teachings of the Apostles, is known historically to have refused to follow the Latin seceders from the original Apostolic Church, though, curiously enough, she is still referred to by her Roman sister as the "Schismatic" Church. It is useless to repeat the reasons for the statements above made, as they may all be found in Isis Unveiled, [ii.91-94.] where the words, Peter, Patar, and Pitar, are explained, and the origin of the "Seat of Pitah" is shown. The reader will find upon referring to the above pages that an inscription was found on the coffin of Queen Mentuhept of the Eleventh Dynasty (2250 B.C. according to Bunsen), which in its turn was shown to have been transcribed from the Seventeenth Chapter of the Book of the Dead, dating certainly not later than 4500 B.C. or 496 years before the World's Creation, in the Genesiacal chronology.

THE SEAT OF PETER –

Nevertheless, Baron Bunsen shows the group of the hieroglyphics given (Peter-ref-su, the "Mystery Word") and the sacred formulary mixed up with a whole series of glosses and various interpretations on a monument 4,000 years old.

This is identical with saying that the record (the true interpretation) was at that time no longer intelligible . . . We beg our readers to understand that a sacred text, a hymn, containing the words of a departed spirit, existed in such a state, about 4.000 years ago, as to be all but unintelligible to royal scribes. [Bunsen, Egypt's Place in History. v.90.]

"Unintelligible" to the non-initiated - this is certain; and it is so proved by the confused and contradictory glosses. Yet there can be no doubt that it was - for it still is - a mystery word. The Baron further explains:

It appears to me that our PTR is literally the old Aramaic

and Hebrew "Patar," which occurs in the history of Joseph as the specific word for interpreting, whence also Pitrum is the term for interpretation of a text, a dream.

This word, PTR, was partially interpreted owing to another word similarly written in another group of hieroglyphics, on a stele, the glyph used for it being an opened eye, interpreted by De Rougé [Stele, p.44.] as "to appear," and by Bunsen as "illuminator," which is more correct. However, it may be, the word Patar, or Peter, would locate both master and disciple in the circle of initiation, and connect them with the Secret Doctrine; while in the "Seat of Peter" we can hardly help seeing a connection with Petroma, the double set of stone tablets used by the Hierophant at the Supreme Initiation during the final Mystery, as already stated, also with the Pitha-sthâna (seat, or the place of a seat), a term used in the Mysteries of the Tantriks in India, in which the limbs of the Satî are scattered and then united again, as those of Osiris by Isis. [See Dowson's Hindu Classical Dict., sub voc., "Pitha-sthânam."] Pitha is a Sanskrit word, and is also used to designate the seat of the initiating Lama.

Whether all the above terms are due simply to "coincidences" or otherwise is left to the decision of our learned Symbologists and Philologists. We state facts - and nothing more. Many other writers, far more learned and entitled to be heard than the author has ever claimed to be, have sufficiently demonstrated that Peter never had anything to do with the foundation of the Latin Church; that his supposed name Petra, or Kiffa, also the whole story of his Apostleship at Rome, are simply a play on the term, which meant in every country, in one or another form, the Hierophant or interpreter of the Mysteries; and that finally, far from dying a martyr at Rome, where he had probably never been, he died at a good old age at Babylon. In Sepher Tolaoth Jeshu, a Hebrew manuscript of great antiquity - evidently an original and very precious document, if one may judge from the care the Jews took to hide it from the Christians - Simon (Peter) is referred to as "a faithful servant of God," who passed his life in austerities and meditation, a Kabalist and a Nazarene who lived at Babylon "at the top of a tower, composed hymns, preached charity," and died there.

SECTION XVII

APPOLLONIUS OF TYANA

IT is said in Isis Unveiled that the greatest teachers of divinity agree that nearly all ancient books were written symbolically and in a language intelligible only to the Initiated. The biographical sketch of Apollonius of Tyana affords an example. As every Kabalist knows, it embraces the whole of the Hermetic Philosophy, being a counterpart in many respects of the traditions left us of King Solomon. It reads like a fairy story, but, as in the case of the latter, sometimes facts and historical events are presented to the world under the colours of fiction.

The journey to India represents in its every stage, though of course allegorically, the trials of a Neophyte, giving at the same time a geographical and topographical idea of a certain country as it is even now, if one knows where to look for it. The long discourses of Apollonius with the Brâhmans, their sage advice, and the dialogues with the Corinthian Menippus would, if interpreted, give the Esoteric Catechism. His visit to the empire of the wise men, his interview with their king Hiarchas, the oracle of Amphiaraus, explain symbolically many of the secret dogmas of Hermes - in the generic sense of the name - and of Occultism. Wonderful is this to relate, and were not the statement supported by numerous calculations already made, and the secret already half revealed, the writer would never have dared to say it. The travels of the great Magus are correctly, though allegorically described - that is to say, all that is related to Damis had actually taken place - but the narrative is based upon the Zodiacal signs. As transliterated by Damis under the guidance of Appollonius and translated by Philostratus, it is a marvel indeed. At the conclusion of what may now be related of the wonderful Adept of Tyana our meaning will become clearer. Suffice it to say for the present that the dialogues spoken of would disclose, if correctly understood, some of the most important secrets of Nature. Eliphas Levi points out the great resemblance which exists between King Hiarchus and the fabulous Hiram, from whom Solomon procured the cedars of Lebanon and the gold of Ophir. But he keeps silent as to another resemblance of which, as a learned Kabalist, he could not be ignorant. Moreover, according to his invariable custom, he mystifies the reader more than he teaches him, divulging nothing and leading him off the right track.

Like most of the historical heroes of hoary antiquity, whose lives and works strongly differ from those of commonplace humanity, Apollonius is to this day a riddle, which has, so far, found no Oedipus. His existence is surrounded with such a veil of mystery that he is often mistaken for a myth. But according to every law of logic and reason, it is quite clear that Apollonius should never be regarded in such a light. If the Tyanean Theurgist may be put down as a fabulous character, then history has no right to her Caesars and Alexanders. It is quite true that this Sage, who stands unrivalled in his thaumaturgical powers to this day - on evidence historically attested - came into the arena of public life no one seems to know whence, and disappeared from it, no one seems to know whither. But the reasons for this are evident. Every means was used - especially during the fourth and fifth centuries of our era - to sweep from people's minds the remembrance of this great and holy man. The circulation of his biographies, which were many and enthusiastic, was prevented by the Christians, and for a very good reason, as we shall see. The diary of Damis survived most miraculously, and remained alone to tell the tale. But it must not be forgotten that Justin Martyr often speaks of Apollonius, and the character and truthfulness of this good man are unimpeachable, the more in that he had good reason to feel bewildered. Nor can it be denied that there is hardly a Church Father of the first six centuries that left Apollonius unnoticed. Only, according to invariable Christian customs of charity, their pens were dipped as usual in the blackest ink of odium theologicum, intolerance and one-sidedness. St. Jerome (Hieronymus) gives at length the story of St. John's alleged contest with the Sage of Tyana - a competition of "miracles" - in which, of course, the truthful saint [See Preface to St. Matthew's Gospel. Baronius , i.752, quoted in De Mirville, VI, 63. Jerome is the Father who having found the authentic and original Evangel (the Hebrew text), by Matthew the Apostle-publican, in the library of Caesarea, "written by the hand of Matthew" (Hieronymus: De Viris, Illus. Chap. III) - as he himself admits - set it down as heretical, and substituted for it his own Greek text. And it is also he who perverted the text in the Book of Job to enforce belief in the resurrection in flesh (see Isis Unveiled. Vol. II, pp. 181 and 182, et seq.) quoting in support the most learned authorities.] describes in glowing colours the defeat of Apollonius, and seeks corroboration in St. John's Apocrypha proclaimed doubtful even by the Church. [De Mirville gives the following thrilling account of the "contest." "John, pressed, as St. Jerome tells us, by all the churches of Asia to proclaim more solemnly [in the face of the miracles of Apollonius] the divinity of Jesus Christ, after a long prayer with his disciples on the Mount of Patmos and being in ecstasy by the divine Spirit, made heard amid thunder and lightning his famous In Principio erat Verbum. When that sublime extasis, that caused him to be named the 'Son of Thunder,' had passed, Apollonius was compelled to retire and to disappear. Such was his defeat, less bloody but as hard as that of Simon, the Magician. ("The Magician Theurgist." VI 63.) For our part we have never heard of extasis producing thunder and lightning and we are at a loss to understand the meaning.]

THE MYSTERIOUS TEACHER

Therefore it is that nobody can say where or when Apollonius was born, and everyone is equally ignorant of the date at which, and of the place where he died. Some think he was eighty or ninety years old at the time of his death, others that he was one hundred or even one hundred and seventeen. But, whether he ended his days at Ephesus in the year 96 A.D., as some say, or whether the event took place at Lindus in the temple of Pallas-Athene, or whether again he disappeared from the temple of Dictynna, or whether, as others maintain, he did not die at all, but when a hundred years old renewed his life by Magic, and went on working for the benefit of humanity, no one can tell. The Secret Doctrine alone have noted his birth and subsequent career. But then - "Who hath believed in that report?"

All that history knows is that Apollonius was the enthusiastic founder of a new school of contemplation. Perhaps less metaphorical and more practical than Jesus, he nevertheless inculcated the same quintessence of spirituality, the same high moral truths. He is accused of having confined them to the higher classes of society instead of doing what Buddha and Jesus did, instead of preaching them to the poor and the afflicted. Of his reasons for acting in such an exclusive way it is impossible to judge at so late a date. But Karmic law seems to be mixed up with it. Born, as we are told, among the aristocracy, it is very likely that he desired to finish the work undone in this particular direction by his predecessor, and sought to offer "peace on earth and good will" to all men, and not alone to the outcast and the criminal. Therefore he associated with the kings and mighty ones of the age. Nevertheless, the three "miracle-workers" exhibited striking similarity of purpose. Like Jesus and like Buddha, Apollonius was the uncompromising enemy of all outward show of piety, all display of useless religious ceremonies, bigotry and hypocrisy. That his "miracles" were more wonderful, more varied, and far better attested in History than any others, it is also true. Materialism denies; but evidence, and the affirmations of even the Church herself, however much he is branded by her, show this to be the fact. [This is the old, old story. Who of us, Theosophists, but knows by bitter personal experiences what clerical hatred, malice and persecution can do in this direction; to what an extent of falsehood, calumny and cruelty these feelings can go, even in our modern day, and what exemplars of Christ like charity His alleged and self-constituted servants have shown themselves to be!]

The calumnies set afloat against Apollonius were as numerous as they were false. So late as eighteen centuries after his death he was defamed by Bishop Douglas in his work against miracles. In this the Right Reverend bishop crushed himself against historical facts. For it is not in the miracles, but in the identity of ideas and doctrines preached that we have to look for a similarity between Buddha, Jesus and Apollonius. If we study the question with a dispassionate mind, we shall soon perceive that the ethics of Gautama, Plato, Apollonius, Jesus, Ammonius Sakkas, and his disciples, were all based on the same mystic philosophy - that all worshipped one divine ideal, whether they considered it as the "Father" of humanity, who lives in man, as man lives in Him, or as the Incomprehensible Creative Principle. All led God-like lives. Ammonius, speaking of his philosophy, taught that their school dated from the days of Hermes, who brought this wisdom from India. It was the same mystical contemplation throughout as that of the Yogin: the communion of the Brahman with his own luminous Self - the "Atman." [Isis Unveiled, ii. 342.]

The groundwork of the Eclectic School is thus shown to be identical with the doctrines of the Yogis - the Hindu Mystics; it is proved that it has a common origin, from the same source as the earlier Buddhism of Gautama and of his Arhats.

The Ineffable Name in the search for which so many Kabalists - unacquainted with any Oriental or even European Adepts - vainly consume their knowledge and lives, dwells latent in the heart of every man. This mirific name which, according to the most ancient oracles, "rushes into the infinite worlds,αφοιτητω οτροφαλιγαι ," can be obtained in a twofold way: by regular initiation, and through the "small voice" which Elijah heard in the cave of Horeb, the mount of God. And "when Elijah heard it he wrapped his face in his mantle and stood in the entering of the cave. And behold there came the voice."

When Apollonius of Tyana desired to hear the "small voice," he used to wrap himself up entirely in a mantle of fine wool, on which he placed both his feet, after having performed certain magnetic passes, and pronounced not the "name" but an invocation well known to every adept. Then he drew the mantle over his head and face, and his translucid or astral spirit was free. On ordinary occasions he no more wore wool than the priests of the temples. The possession of the secret combination of the "name" gave the Hierophant supreme power over every being, human or otherwise, inferior to himself in soul-strength. [Loc. cit., ii, 343, 344.]

APOLLONIUS CANNOT BE DESTROYED

To whatever school he belonged, this fact is certain, that Apollonius of Tyana left an imperishable name behind him. Hundreds of works were written upon this wonderful man; historians have seriously discussed him; pretentious fools, unable to come to any conclusion about the Sage, have tried to deny his very existence. As to the Church, although she execrates his memory, she has ever tried to present him in the light of a historical character. Her policy now seems to be to direct the impression left by him into another channel - a well known and a very old stratagem. The Jesuits, for instance, while admitting his "miracles," have set going a double current of thought, and they have succeeded, as they succeed in all they undertake. Apollonius is represented by one party as an obedient "medium of Satan," surrounding his theurgical powers by a most wonderful and dazzling light; while the other party professes to regard the whole matter as a clever romance, written with a predetermined object in view.

In his voluminous Memoirs of Satan, the Marquis de Mirville, in the course of his pleading for the recognition of the enemy of God as the producer of spiritual phenomena, devotes a whole chapter to this great Adept. The following translation of passages in his book unveils the whole plot. The reader is asked to bear in mind that the Marquis wrote every one of his works under the auspices and authorisation of the Holy See of Rome.

It would be to leave the first century incomplete and to offer an insult to the memory of St. John, to pass over in silence the name of one who had the honour of being his special antagonist, as Simon was that of St. Peter, Elymas that of Paul, etc. In the first years of the Christian era, . . . there appeared at Tyana in Cappadocia one of those men of whom the Pythagorean School was so very lavish. As great a traveller as was his master, initiated in all the secret doctrines of India, Egypt and Chaldaea, endowed, therefore, with all the theurgic powers of the ancient Magi, he bewildered, each in its turn, all the countries which he visited, and which all - we are obliged to admit - seem to have blessed his memory. We could not doubt this fact without repudiating real historical records. The details of his life are transmitted to us by a historian of the fourth century (Philostratus), himself the translator of a diary that recorded day by day the life of the philosopher, written by Damis, his disciple and intimate friend. [Pneumatologie, vi. 62.]

De Mirville admits the possibility of some exaggerations in both recorder and translator; but he "does not believe they hold a very wide space in the narrative." Therefore, he regrets to find the Abbe Freppel "in his eloquent Essays, [Les Apologistes Chrétiens au Second Siècle. p.106.] calling the diary of Damis a romance." Why?

[Because] the orator bases his opinion on the prefect similitude, calculated as he imagines, of that legend with the life of the Saviour. But in studying the subject more profoundly, he [Abbe Freppel] can convince himself that neither Apollonius nor Damis, nor again Philostratus ever claimed a greater honour than a likeness to St. John. This programme was in itself sufficiently fascinating, and the travesty as sufficiently scandalous; for owing to magic arts Apollonius had succeeded in counterbalancing, in appearance, several of the miracles at Ephesus [produced by St. John], etc. [Pneumatologie, vi. 62.]

The anguis in herba has shown its head. It is the perfect, the wonderful similitude of the life of Apollonius with that of the Saviour that places the Church between Scylla and Charybdis. To deny the life and the "miracles" of the former, would amount to denying the trustworthiness of the same Apostles and patristic writers on whose evidence is built the life of Jesus himself. To father the Adept's beneficent deeds, his raisings of the dead, acts of charity, healing powers, etc., on the " old enemy" would be rather dangerous at this time. Hence the stratagem to confuse the ideas of

those who rely upon authorities and criticisms. The Church is far more clear-sighted than any of our great historians. The Church knows that to deny the existence of that Adept would lead her to denying the Emperor Vespasian and his Historians, the Emperors Alexander Severus and Aurelianus and their Historians, and finally to deny Jesus and every evidence about Him, thus preparing the way to her flock for finally denying herself. It becomes interesting to learn what she says in this emergency, through her chosen speaker, De Mirville. It is as follows:

What is there so new and so impossible in the narrative of Damis concerning their voyages to the countries of the Chaldees and the Gymnosophists? - he asks. Try to recall, before denying, what were in those days those countries of marvels par excellence, as also the testimony of such men as Pythagoras, Empedocles and Democritus, who ought to be allowed to have known what they were writing about. With what have we finally to reproach Apollonius? Is it for having made, as the Oracles did, a series of prophecies and predictions wonderfully verified? No: because, better studied now, we know what they are. [Many are they who do not know: hence, they do not believe in them.] The Oracles have now become to us, what they were to every one during the past century, from Van Dale to Fontenelle.

DE MIRVILLE ON APOLLONIUS

Is it for having been endowed with second sight, and having had visions at a distance? [Just so. Apollonius, during a lecture he was delivering at Ephesus before an audience of many thousands, perceived the murder of the Emperor Domitian in Rome and notified it at the very moment it was taking place, to the whole town: and Swedenborg, in the same manner, saw from Gothenburg the great fire at Stockholm and told it to his friends, no telegraph being in use in those days.] No; for such phenomena are at the present day endemical in half Europe. Is it for having boasted of his knowledge of every existing language under the sun, without having ever learned one of them? But who can be ignorant of the fact that this is the best criterion [No criterion at all. The Hindu Saddhus and Adepts acquire the gift by the holiness of their lives. The Yoga-Vidya teaches it, and no "spirits" are required.] of the presence and assistance of a spirit of whatever nature it may be? Or is it for having believed in transmigration (reincarnation)? It is still believed in (by millions) in our day. No one has any idea of the number of the men of Science who long for the re-establishment of the Druidical Religion and of the Mysteries of Pythagoras. Or is it for having exorcised the demons and the plague? The Egyptians, the Etruscans and all the Roman Pontiffs had done so long before. [As to the Pontiffs, the matter is rather doubtful.] For having conversed with the dead? We do the same today, or believe we do so - which is all the same. For having believed in the Empuses? Where is the Demonologist that does not know that the Empuse is the "south demon" referred to in David's Psalms, and dreaded then as it is feared even now in all Northern Europe? [But this alone is no reason why people should believe in this class of spirits. There are better authorities for such belief.] For having made himself invisible at will? It is one of the achievements of mesmerism. For having appeared after his (supposed) death to the Emperor Aurelian above the city walls of Tyana, and for having compelled him thereby to raise the siege of that town? Such was the mission of every hero beyond the tomb, and the reason of the worship vowed to the Manes. [De Mirville's aim is to show that all such apparitions of the Manes or disembodied Spirits are the work of the Devil. "Satan's simulacra."] For having descended into the famous den of Trophonius, and taken from it an old book preserved for years after by the Emperor Adrian in his Antium library? The trustworthy and sober Pausanias had descended into the same den before Apollonius, and came back no less a believer. For having disappeared at his death? Yes, like Romulus, like Votan, like Lycurgus, like Pythagoras, [He might have added: like the great Shankaracharya, Tsong-Kha-Pa, and so many other real Adepts - even his own Master, Jesus: for this is indeed a criterion of true Adeptship, though "to disappear" one need not fly up in the clouds.] always under the most mysterious circumstances, ever attended by apparitions, revelations, etc. Let us stop here and repeat once more: had the life of Apollonius been simple romance, he would never have attained such a celebrity during his lifetime or created such a numerous sect, one so enthusiastic after his death.

And, so to add to this, had all this been a romance, never would a Caracalla have raised a haroon to his memory, [See Dion Cassius. XXVII XVIII, 2] or Alexander Severus have placed his bust between those of two Demi-Gods and of the true God, [Lampridlius, Adrian, xxxix. 2.] or an Empress have corresponded with him. Hardly rested from the hardships of the siege at Jerusalem, Titus would not have hastened to write to Apollonius a letter, asking to meet him at Argos and adding that his father and himself (Titus) owed all to him, the great Apollonius, and that, therefore, his first thought was for their benefactor. Nor would the Emperor Aurelian have built a temple and a shrine to that great Sage, to thank him for his apparition and communication at Tyana. That posthumous conversation, as all knew, saved the city, inasmuch as Aurelian had in consequence raised the siege. Furthermore, had it been a romance, History would not have had Vopiscus, [The passage runs as follows: "Aurelian had determined to destroy Tyana, and the town owed its salvation only to a miracle of Apollonius; this man so famous and wise, this great friend of the Gods, appeared suddenly before the Emperor, as he was returning to his tent, in his own figure and form, and said to him in the Pannonian language: 'Aurelian, if thou wouldst conquer, abandon these evil designs against my fellow-citizens: if thou wouldst command, abstain from shedding innocent blood; and if thou wouldst live, abstain from injustice.' Aurelian, familiar with the face of Apollonius, whose portraits he had seen in many temples, struck with wonder, immediately vowed to him (Apollonius) statue, portrait and temple, and returned completely to ideas of mercy." And then Vopiscus adds: "If I have believed more and more in the virtues of the majestic Apollonius, it is because, after gathering my information from the most serious men, I have found all these facts corroborated in the Books of the Ulpian Library." (See Flavius Vopiscus, Aurelianus). Vopiscus wrote in 250 and consequently preceded Philostratus by a century.] one of the most trustworthy Pagan Historians, to certify to it. Finally, Apollonius would not have been the object of the admiration of such a noble character as Epictetus, and even of several of the Fathers of the Church; Jerome for instance, in his better moments, writing thus of Apollonius:

This travelling philosopher found something to learn wherever he went; and profiting everywhere thus improved with every day. [Ep. ad Paulinum.]

Apollonius No Fiction

As to his prodigies, without wishing to fathom them, Jerome most undeniably admits them as such; which he would assuredly never have done, had he not been compelled to do so by facts. To end the subject, had Apollonius been a simple hero of a romance, dramatised in the fourth century, the Ephesians would not, in their enthusiastic gratitude, have raised to him a golden statue for all the benefits he had conferred upon them. [The above is mostly summarised from De Mirville. loc cit., pp. 66-69]

SECTION XVIII

FACTS UNDERLYING ADEPT BIOGRAPHIES

THE tree is known by its fruits; the nature of the Adept by his words and deeds. These words of charity and mercy, the noble advice put into the mouth of Apollonius (or of his sidereal phantom), as given by Vopiscus, show the Occultists who Apollonius was. Why then call him the "Medium of Satan" seventeen centuries later? There must be a reason, and a very potent reason, to justify and explain the secret of such a strong animus of the Church against one of the noblest men of his age. There is a reason for it, and we give it in the words of the author of the Key to the Hebrew-Egyptian Mystery in the Source of Measures, and of Professor Seyffarth. The latter analyses and explains the salient dates in the life of Jesus, and thus throws light on the conclusions of the former. We quote both, blending the two.

According to solar months (of thirty days, one of the calendars in use among the Hebrews) all remarkable events of the Old Testament happened on the days of the equinoxes and the solstices; for instance, the foundations and dedications of the temples and alters [and consecration of the tabernacle]. On the same cardinal days, the most remarkable events of the New Testament happened; for instance, the annunciation, the birth, the resurrection of Christ, and the birth of John the Baptist. And thus we learn that all remarkable epochs of the New Testament were typically sanctified a long time before by the Old Testament, beginning at the day succeeding the end of the Creation, which was the day of the vernal equinox. During the crucifixion, on the 14th day of Nisan, Dionysius Areopagita saw, in Ethopia, an eclipse of the sun, and he said, "Now the Lord (Jehovah) is suffering something." Then Christ arose from the dead on the 22d March, 17 Nisan, Sunday, the day of the vernal equinox (Seyf., quoting Philo de Septen) - that is, on Easter, or on the day when the sun gives new life to the earth. The words of John the Baptist "He must increase, but I must decrease," serve to prove, as is affirmed by the fathers of the church, that John was born on the longest day of the year, and Christ, who was six months younger, on the shortest, 22d June and 22d December, the solstices.

JESUS AND APOLLONIUS-

This only goes to show that, as to another phase, John and Jesus were but epitomisers of the history of the same sun, under differences of aspect or condition; and one condition following another, of necessity, the statement, Luke, ix. 7, was not only not an empty one, but it was true, that which "was said of some, that (in Jesus) John was risen from the dead." (And this consideration serves to explain why it has been that the Life of Apollonius of Tyana, by Philostratus, has been so persistently kept back from translation and from popular reading. Those who have studied it in the original have been forced to the comment that either the Life of Apollonius has been taken from the New Testament, or that the New Testament narratives have been taken from the Life of Apollonius, because of the manifest sameness of the means of construction of the narratives. The explanation is simple enough, when it is considered that the names of Jesus Hebrew ש׳‎, and Apollonius, or Apollo, are alike names of the sun in the heavens; and necessarily the history of the one, as to his travels through the signs, with the personifications of his sufferings, triumphs and miracles, could be but the history of the other, where there was a widespread, common method of describing those travels by personification.) It seems also that, for long afterward, all this was known to rest upon an astronomical basis; for the secular church, so to speak, was founded by Constantine, and the objective condition of the worship established was that part of his decree, in which it was affirmed that the venerable day of the sun should be the day set apart for the worship of Jesus Christ, as Sun-day. There is something weird and startling in some other facts about this matter. The prophet Daniel (true prophet, as says Graetz). [A "true prophet" because an Initiate, one perfectly versed in Occult astronomy.] by use of the pyramid numbers, or astrological numbers, foretold the cutting off of the Meshiac, as it happened (which would go to show the accuracy of his astronomical knowledge, if there was an eclipse of the sun at that time). . . . Now, however, the temple was destroyed in the year 71, in the month Virgo, and 71 is the Dove number, as shown, or 71X5 = 355, and with the fish, a Jehovah number.

"Is it possible," queries, further on the author, thus answering the intimate thought of every Christian and

Occultist who reads and studies his work:

Is it possible that the events of humanity do run co-ordinately with these number forms? If so, while Jesus Christ, as an astronomical figure, was true to all that has been advanced, and more, possibly. He may, as a man, have filled up, under the numbers, answers in the sea of life to predestined type. The personality of Jesus does not appear to have been destroyed, because, as a condition, he was answering to astronomical forms and relations. The Arabian says, "Your destiny is written in the stars." [Key to Hebrew-Egyptian Mystery. p. 259 et seq. Astronomy and physiology are the bodies, astrology and psychology their informing souls: the former being studied by the eye of sensual perception, the latter by the inner or "soul-eye": and both are exact sciences.]

Nor is the "personality" of Apollonius "destroyed," for the same reason. The case of Jesus covers the ground for the same possibility in the cases of all Adepts and Avataras - such as Buddha, Shankaracharya, Krishna, etc. - all of these as great and as historical for their respective followers and in their countries, as Jesus of Nazareth is now for Christians and in this land.

But there is something more in the old literature of the early centuries. Iamblichus wrote a biography of the great Pythagoras.

The latter so closely resembles the life of Jesus that it may be taken for a travesty. Diogenes Laërtius and Plutarch relate the history of Plato according to a similar style. [New Platonism and Alchemy. p.12.]

Why then wonder at the doubts that assail every scholar who studies all these lives? The Church herself knew all these doubts in her early stages; and though only one of her Popes has been known publicly and openly as a Pagan, how many more were there who were too ambitious to reveal the truth?

This "mystery," for mystery indeed it is to those who, not being Initiates, fail to find the key of the perfect similitude between the lives of Pythagoras, Buddha, Apollonius, etc, - is only a natural result for those who know that all these great characters were Initiates of the same school. For them there is neither "travesty" nor "copy" of one from the other; for them they are all "originals," only painted to represent one and the same subject: the mystic, and at the same time the public, life of the Initiates sent into the world to save portions of humanity, if they could not save the whole bulk. Hence, the same programme for all. The assumed "immaculate origin" for each, referring to their "mystic birth" during the Mystery of Initiation, and accepted literally by the multitudes, encouraged in this by the better informed but ambitious clergy. Thus, the mother of each one of them was declared a virgin, conceiving her son directly by the Holy Spirit of God; and the Sons, in consequence, were the "Sons of God," though in truth, none of them was any more entitled to such recognition than were the rest of his brother Initiates, for they were all - so far as their mystic lives were concerned - only "the epitomisers of the history of the same Sun," which epitome is another mystery within the Mystery. The biographies of the external personalities bearing the names of such heroes have nothing to do with, and are quite independent of the private lives of the heroes, being only the mystic records of their public and, parallel therewith, of their inner lives, in their characters as Neophytes and Initiates.

BIOGRAPHIES OF INITIATES-

Hence, the manifest sameness of the means of construction of their respective biographies. From the beginning of Humanity the Cross, or Man, with his arms stretched out horizontally, typifying his kosmic origin, was connected with his psychic nature and with the struggles which lead to Initiation. But, if it is once shown that (a) every true Adept had, and still has, to pass through the seven and the twelve trials of Initiation, symbolised by the twelve labours of Hercules; (b) that the day of his real birth is regarded as that day when he is born into the world spiritually, his very age being counted from the hour of his second birth, which makes of him a "twice-born," a Dvija or Initiate, on which day he is indeed born of a God and from an immaculate Mother; and (c) that the trials of all these personages are made to correspond with the Esoteric significance of initiatory rites - all of which corresponded to the twelve zodiacal signs - then every one will see the meaning of the travels of all those heroes through the signs of the Sun in Heaven; and that they are in each individual case a personification of the "sufferings, triumphs and miracles" of an Adept, before and after his Initiation. When to the world at large all this is explained, then also the mystery of all those lives, so closely resembling each other that the history of one seems to be the history of the other, and vice versa, will, like everything else, become plain.

Take an instance. The legends - for they are all legends for exoteric purposes, whatever may be the denials in one case - of the lives of Krishna, Hercules, Pythagoras, Buddha, Jesus, Apollonius, Chaitanya. On the worldly plane, their biographies, if written by one outside the circle, would differ greatly from what we read of them in the narratives that are preserved of their mystic lives. Nevertheless, however much masked and hidden from the profane gaze, the chief features of such lives will all be found there in common. Each of those characters is represented as a divinely begotten Soter (Saviour), a title bestowed on deities, great kings and heroes; everyone of them, whether at their birth or afterwards, is searched for, and threatened with death (yet never killed) by an opposing power (the world of Matter and Illusion), whether it be called a king Kansa, king Herod, or king Mara (the Evil Power). They are all tempted, persecuted and finally said to have been murdered at the end of the rite of Initiation, i.e. in their physical personalities, of which they are supposed to have been rid for ever after spiritual "resurrection" or "birth." And having thus come to an end by this supposed violent death, they all descend to the Nether World, the Pit or Hell - the Kingdom of Temptation, Lust and Matter, therefore of Darkness, whence returning, having overcome the "Chrest-condition," they are glorified and become "Gods."

It is not in the course of their everyday life, then, that the great similarity is to be sought, but in their inner state and in the most important events of their career as religious teachers.

All this is connected with, and built upon, an astronomical basis, which serves, at the same time, as a foundation for the representation of the degrees and trials of Initiation: descent into the Kingdom of Darkness and Matter, for the last time, to emerge therefrom as "Suns of Righteousness," is the most important of these and, therefore, is found in the history of all the Soters - from Orpheus and Hercules, down to Krishna and Christ.

Says Euripides:

Heracles, who has gone from the chambers of earth,

Leaving the nether home of Pluto. [Heracles 807]

And Virgil writes:

At Thee the Stygian lakes trembled; Thee the janitor of Orcus

Feared . . . Thee not even Typhon frightened . . .

Hail, true son of Jove, glory added to the Gods. [Aeneid, viii., 274, ff.]

Orpheus seeks, in the kingdom of Pluto, Eurydice, his lost Soul; Krishna goes down into the infernal regions and rescues therefrom his six brothers, he being the seventh Principle; a transparent allegory of his becoming a "perfect Initiate," the whole of the six Principles merging into the seventh. Jesus is made to descend into the kingdom of Satan to save the soul of Adam, or the symbol of material physical humanity.

Have any of our learned Orientalists ever thought of

searching for the origin of this allegory, for the parent "Seed" of that "Tree of Life" which bears such verdant boughs since it was first planted on earth by the hand of its "Builders"? We fear not. Yet it is found, as is now shown, even in the exoteric, distorted interpretations of the Vedas - of the Rig Veda, the oldest, the most trustworthy of all the four - this root and seed of all future Initiate-Saviours being called in it the Visvakarmâ, the "Father" Principle, "beyond the comprehension of mortals;" in the second stage Sûrya, the "Son," who offers Himself as a sacrifice to Himself; in the third, the Initiate, who sacrifices His physical to His Spiritual Self.

SIMILARITY OF LEGENDS-

It is in Visvakarmâ, the "omnificent" who becomes (mystically) Vikkartana, the "sun shorn of his beams," who suffers for his too ardent nature, and then becomes glorified (by purification), that the keynote of the Initiation into the greatest Mystery of Nature was struck. Hence the secret of the wonderful "similarity."

All this is allegorical and mystical, and yet perfectly comprehensible and plain to any student of Eastern Occultism, even superficially acquainted with the Mysteries of Initiation. In our objective Universe of Matter and false appearances the Sun is the most fitting emblem of the life-giving, beneficent Deity. In the subjective, boundless World of Spirit and Reality the bright luminary has another and a mystical significance, which cannot be fully given to the public. The so-called "idolatrous" Parsis and Hindus are certainly nearer the truth in their religious reverence for the Sun, than the cold, ever-analysing, and as ever-mistaken, public is prepared to believe, at present. The Theosophists, who will be alone able to take in the meaning, may be told that the Sun is the external manifestation of the Seventh Principle of our Planetary System, while the Moon is its Fourth Principle, shining in the borrowed robes of her master, saturated with and reflecting every passionate impulse and evil desire of her grossly material body, Earth. The whole cycle of Adeptship and Initiation and all its mysteries are connected with, and subservient to, these two and the Seven Planets. Spiritual clairvoyance is derived from the Sun; all psychic states, diseases, and even lunacy, proceed from the Moon.

According even to the data of History - her conclusions being remarkably erroneous while her premises are mostly correct - there is an extraordinary agreement between the "legends" of every Founder of a Religion (and also between the rites and dogmas of all) and the names and course of constellations headed by the Sun. It does not follow, however, because of this, that both Founders and their Religions should be, the one myths, and the other superstitions. They are, one and all, the different versions of the same natural primeval Mystery, on which the Wisdom-Religion was based, and the development of its Adepts subsequently framed

And now once more we have to beg the reader not to lend an ear to the charge - against Theosophy in general and the writer in particular - of disrespect toward one of the greatest and noblest characters in the History of Adeptship

- Jesus of Nazareth - nor even of hatred to the Church. The expression of truth and fact can hardly be regarded, with any approximation to justice, as blasphemy or hatred. The whole question hangs upon the solution of that one point: Was Jesus as "Son of God" and "Saviour" of Mankind, unique in the World's annals? Was His case - among so many similar claims - the only exceptional and unprecedented one; His birth the sole supernaturally immaculate; and were others as maintained by the Church, but blasphemous Satanic copies and plagiarisms by anticipation? Or was He only the "son of his deeds," a pre-eminently holy man, and a reformer, one of many, who paid with His life for the presumption of endeavouring, in the face of ignorance and despotic power, to enlighten mankind and make its burden lighter by His Ethics and Philosophy? The first necessitates a blind, all-resisting faith; the latter is suggested to every one by reason and logic. Moreover, had the Church always believed as she does now - or rather, as she pretends she does, in order to be thus justified in directing her anathema against those who disagree with her - or has she passed through the same throes of doubt, nay, of secret denial and belief, suppressed only by the force of ambition and love of power?

The question must be answered in the affirmative as to the second alternative. It is an irrefutable conclusion, and a natural inference based on facts known from historical records. Leaving for the present untouched the lives of many Popes and Saints that loudly belied their claims to infallibility and holiness, let the reader turn to Ecclesiastical History, the records of the growth and progress of the Christian Church (not of Christianity), and he will find the answer on those pages. Says a writer:

The Church has known too well the suggestions of freethought created by enquiry, as also all those doubts that provoke her anger today; and the "sacred truths" she would promulgate have been in turn admitted and repudiated, transformed and altered, amplified and curtailed, by the dignitaries of the Church hierarchy, even as regards the most fundamental dogmas.

Where is that God or Hero whose origin, biography, and genealogy were more hazy, or more difficult to define and finally agree upon than those of Jesus? How was the now irrevocable dogma with regard to His true nature settled at last? By His mother, according to the Evangelists, He was a man - a simple mortal man; by His Father He is God! But how? Is He then man or God, or is He both at the same time? asks the perplexed writer. Truly the propositions offered on this point of the doctrine have caused floods of ink and blood to be shed, in turn, on poor Humanity, and still the doubts are not at rest. In this as in everything else , the wise Church Councils have contradicted themselves and changed their minds a number of times.

NATURE OF CHRIST-

Let us recapitulate and throw a glance at the texts offered for our inspection. This is History.

The Bishop Paul of Samosata denied the divinity of Christ at the first Council of Antioch; at the very origin and birth of theological Christianity, He was called "Son of God" merely on account of His holiness and good deeds. His blood was corruptible in the Sacrament of the Eucharist.

At the Council of Nicaea, held A.D. 325, Arius came out with his premisses, which nearly broke asunder the Catholic Union.

Seventeen bishops defended the doctrines of Arius, who was exiled for them. Nevertheless, thirty years after, A.D. 355, at the Council of Milan, three hundred bishops signed a letter of adherence to the Arian views, notwithstanding that ten years earlier, A.D. 345, at a new Council of Antioch, the Eusebians had proclaimed that Jesus Christ was the Son of God and One with His Father.

At the Council of Sirmium, A.D. 357, the "Son" had become no longer consubstantial. The Anomaeans, who denied that consubstantiality, and the Arians were triumphant. A year later, at the second Council of Ancyra, it was decreed that the "Son was not consubstantial but only similar to the Father in his substance." Pope Liberius ratified the decision. During several centuries the Council fought and quarrelled, supporting the most contradictory and opposite views, the fruit of their laborious travail being the Holy Trinity, which, Minerva-like, issued forth from the theological brain, armed with all the thunders of the Church. The new mystery was ushered into the world amid some terrible strifes, in which murder and other crimes had a high hand. At the Council of Saragossa, A.D. 380, it was proclaimed that the Father, Son and Holy Spirit are one and the same Person, Christ's human nature being merely an "illusion" - an echo of the Avatâric Hindu doctrine. "Once upon this slippery path the

Fathers had to slide down ad absurdum - which they did not fail of doing." How deny human nature in him who was born of a woman? The only wise remark made during one of the Councils of Constantinople came from Eutyches, who was bold enough to say: "May God preserve me from reasoning on the nature of my God" - for which he was excommunicated by Pope Flavius.

At the Council of Ephesus, A.D. 449, Eutyches had his revenge. As Eusibius, the veracious Bishop of Caesarea, was forcing him into the admission of two distinct natures in Jesus Christ, the Council rebelled against him and it was proposed that Eusebius should be burned alive. The bishops arose like one man, and with fists clenched, foaming with rage, demanded that Eusebius should be torn into halves, and be dealt by as he would deal with Jesus, whose nature he divided. Eutyches was re-established in his power and office, Eusebius and Flavius deposed. Then the two parties attacked each other most violently and fought. St. Flavius was so ill-treated by Bishop Diodorus, who assaulted and kicked him, that he died a few days from the injuries inflicted.

Every incongruity was courted in these Councils, and the result is the present living paradoxes called Church dogmas. For instance, at the first Council of Ancyra, A.D. 314, it was asked, "In baptising a woman with child, is the unborn baby also baptised by the fact?" The Council answered in the negative; because as was alleged, "the person thus receiving baptism must be a consenting party, which is impossible to the child in the mother's womb." Thus then unconsciousness is a canonical obstacle to baptism, and thus no child baptised nowadays is baptised at all in fact. And then what becomes of the tens of thousands of starving heathen babies baptised by the missionaries during famines, and otherwise surreptitiously "saved" by the too zealous Padres? Follow one after another the debates and decisions of the numberless Councils, and behold on what a jumble of contradictions the present infallible and Apostolic Church is built!

And now we can see how greatly paradoxical, when taken literally, is the assertion in Genesis: "God created man in his own image." Besides the glaring fact that it is not the Adam of dust (of Chapter ii.) who is thus made in the divine image, but the Divine Androgyne (of Chapter i.), or Adam Kadmon, one can see for oneself that God - the God of the Christians at any rate - was created by man in his own image, amid the kicks, blows and murders of the early Councils.

A curious fact, one that throws a flood of light on the claim that Jesus was an Initiate and a martyred Adept, is given in the work, (already so often referred to) which may be called "a mathematical revelation" - The Source of Measures.

Attention is called to the part of the 46th verse of the 27th Chapter of Matthew, as follows: "Eli, Eli, Lama Sabachthani? - that is to say, My God, my God, why hast thou forsaken me?" Of course, our versions are taken from the original Greek manuscripts (the reason why we have no original Hebrew manuscripts concerning these occurrences being because the enigmas in Hebrew would betray themselves on comparison with the sources of their derivation, the Old Testament).

A SERIOUS MISTRANSLATION

The Greek manuscripts, without exception, give these words as -

Ηλι Ηλι λαμα .σαβαχθανι

They are Hebrew words, rendered into the Greek, and in Hebrew are as follows:

אֵלִי אֵלִי לְמָה שְׁבַקְתֵּנִי׃

The scripture of these words says, "that is to say, My God, my God, why hast thou forsaken me?" as their proper translation. Here then are the words beyond all dispute; and beyond all question, such is the interpretation given of them by Scripture. Now the words will not bear this interpretation, and it is a false rendering. The true meaning is just the opposite of the one given, and is -

My God, My God, how thou dost glorify me!

But even more, for while lama is why, or how, as a verbal it connected the idea of to dazzle, or adverbially, it could run "how dazzlingly," and so on. To the unwary reader this interpretation is enforced, and made to answer, as it were, to the fulfilment of a prophetic utterance, by a marginal reference to the first verse of the twenty-second Psalm, which reads:

"My God, my God, why hast thou forsaken me?"

The Hebrew of this verse for these words is -

אֵלִי אֵלִי לְמָה עֲזַבְתָּנִי׃

as to which the reference is correct, and the interpretation sound and good, but with an utterly different word. The words are -   Eli, Eli, lamah azabvtha-ni?

No wit of man, however scholarly, can save this passage from falseness of rendering on its face; and as so, it becomes a most terrible blow upon the proper first-face sacredness of the recital. [App., vii., p.301.]

For ten years or more, sat the revisers (?) of the Bible, a most imposing and solemn array of the learned of the land, the greatest Hebrew and Greek scholars of England, purporting to correct the mistakes and blunders, the sins of omission and of commission of their less learned predecessors, the translators of the Bible. Are we going to be told that none of them saw the glaring difference between the Hebrew words in Psalm xxii., Azabbvtha-ni , and sabachthani in Matthew; that they were not aware of the deliberate falsification?

For "falsification" it was. And if we are asked the reason why the early Church Fathers resorted to it, the answer is plain: Because the Sacramental words belonged in their true rendering to Pagan temple rites. They were pronounced after the terrible trials of Initiation, and were still fresh in the memory of some of the "Fathers" when the Gospel of Matthew was edited into the Greek language. Because, finally, many of the Hierophants of the Mysteries, and many more of the Initiates were still living in those days, and the sentence rendered in its true words would class Jesus directly with the simple Initiates. The words "My God, my Sun, thou hast poured thy radiance upon me?" were the final words that concluded the thanksgiving prayer of the Initiate, "the Son and the glorified Elect of the Sun." In Egypt we find to this day carvings and paintings that represent the rite. The candidate is between two divine sponsors; one "Osiris-Sun" with the head of a hawk, representing life, the other Mercury - the ibis-headed, psychopompic genius, who guides the Souls after death to their new abode, Hades - standing for the death of the physical body, figuratively. Both are shown pouring the "stream of life," the water of purification, on the head of the Initiate, the two streams of which, interlacing, form a cross. The better to conceal the truth, this basso-relievo has also been explained as a "Pagan presentment of a Christian truth." The Chevalier des Mousseaux calls this Mercury:

The assessor of Osiris-Sol, as St. Michael is the assessor, Ferouer, of the Word.

The monogram of Chrestos and the Labarum, the standard of Constantine - who, by the by, died a Pagan and was never baptised - is a symbol derived from the above rite and also denotes "life and death." Long before the sign of the Cross was adopted as a Christian symbol, it was employed as a secret sign of recognition among Neophytes and Adepts. Says Eliphas Levi:

The sign of the cross adopted by the Christians does not belong exclusively to them. It is kabalistic, and represents the oppositions and quaternary equilibrium of the elements. We see by the occult verse of the Pater, to which we have called attention in another work, that there were originally two ways of making it, or, at least, two very different formulas to express its meaning; one reserved for priests and initiates; the other given to neophyte and the profane. [Dogme et

Rituel de la Haute Magie, ii, 88.]

One can understand now why the Gospel of Matthew, the Evangel of the Ebionites, has been for ever excluded in its Hebrew form from the world's curious grace.

Jerome found the authentic and original Evangel written in Hebrew, by Matthew the Publican, at the library collected at Caesarea by the martyr Pamphilius, "I received permission from the Nazaraeans, who at Beroea of Syria used this (gospel to translate it, " he writes toward the end of the fourth century. [(Hieronymus, Des Viris Illust., III) "It is remarkable that, while all Church Fathers say that Matthew wrote in Hebrew, the whole of them use the Greek text as the genuine apostolic writing, without mentioning what relation the Hebrew Matthew has to our Greek one! It had many peculiar additions which are wanting in our (Greek) Evangel" (Olshausen, Nachweis der Echtheit der Sammtlichen Schriften des Neuen Test., p.32; Dunlap, Sod, the Son of Man, p. 44.)]

SECRET DOCTRINE OF JESUS

"In the Evangel which the Nazarenes and Ebionites use," said Jerome, "which recently I translated from Hebrew into Greek, and which is called by most persons the genuine gospel of Matthew," etc. [Comment to Matthew (XII, 13) Book 11. Jerome adds that it was written in the Chaldaic language, but with Hebrew letters.]

That the apostles had received a "secret doctrine" from Jesus, who confessed it in an unguarded moment. Writing to the Bishops Chromatius and Heliodorus, he complains that "a difficult work is enjoined, since this (translation) has been commanded me by your Felicities, which St Matthew himself, the Apostle and Evangelist, did not wish to be openly written. For if this had not been secret he (Matthew) would have added to the Evangel that what he gave forth was his ; but he made up this book sealed up in the Hebrew characters, which he put forth even in such way that the book, written in Hebrew letters and by the hand of himself, might be possessed by the men most religious ; who also, in the course of time, received it from those who preceded them. But this very book they never gave to any one to be transcribed, and its text they related some one way and another." ["St. Jerome." v.445: Dunlap, Sod, the Son of Man, p. 46.] And he adds further on the same page: "And it happened that this book, having been published by a disciple of Manichaeus, named Seleucus, who also wrote falsely The Acts of the Apostles, exhibited matter not for edification, but for destruction; and that this (book) was approved in a synod which the ears of the Church properly refused to listen to." [This accounts also for the rejection of the works of Justin Martyr, who used only this "Gospel according to the Hebrews," as also did most probably Tatian, his disciple. At what a later period the divinity of Christ was fully established we can judge by the mere fact that even in the fourth century Eusebius did not denounce this book as spurious, but only classed it with such as the Apocalypse of John: and Credner (Zur Gesch. des Kan, p. 129) shows Nicephorus inserting it, together with the Revelation, in his Stichometry, among the Antilegomena. The Ebionites, the genuine primitive Christians, rejecting the rest of the Apostolic writings, make use only of this Gospel (Adv Hev., i. 26) and the Ebionites, as Epiphanius declares, firmly believed, with the Nazarenes, that Jesus was but a man, "of the seed of a man."]

Jerome admits, himself, that the book which he authenticates as being written "by the hand of Matthew," was nevertheless a book which, notwithstanding that he translated it twice, was nearly unintelligible to him, for it was arcane. Nevertheless, Jerome coolly sets down every commentary upon it but his own as heretical. More than that, Jerome knew that this Gospel was the only original one, yet he becomes more zealous than ever in his persecution of the "Heretics." Why? Because to accept it was equivalent to reading the death sentence of the established Church. The Gospel according to the Hebrews was well known to have been the only one accepted for four centuries by the Jewish Christians, the Nazarenes and the Ebionites. And neither of the latter accepted the divinity of Christ. [Isis Unveiled. II, 182-3.]

The Ebionites were the first, the earliest Christians, whose representative was the Gnostic author of the Clementine Homilies, and as the author of Supernatural Religion shows, 8 [Op. cit., II, 5] Ebionitic Gnosticism had once been the purest form of Christianity. They were the pupils and followers of the early Nazarenes - the kabalistic Gnostics. They believed in the Aeons, as the Cerinthians did, and that "the world was put together by Angels" (Dhyan Chohans), as Epiphanius complains (Contra Ebionitas) : "Ebion had the opinion of the Nazarenes, the form of Cerinthians." "They decided that Christ was of the seed of a man," he laments. [See also Isis Unveiled, ii. 180, to end of chapter.] Thus again:

The badge of Dan-Scorpio is death-life, in the symbol .as crossbones and skull ☠ , . . or life-death . . . the standard of Constantine, the Roman Emperor. Abel has been shown to be Jesus, and Cain-Vulcain, or Mars, pierced him. Constantine was the Roman Emperor, whose warlike god was Mars, and a Roman soldier pierced Jesus on the cross . . . .

But the piercing of Abel was the consummation of his marriage with Cain, and this was proper under the form of Mars Generator; hence the double glyph, one of Mars-Generator [Osiris-Sun] and Mars-Destroyer [Mercury the God of Death in the Egyptian basso-relievo] in one; significant, again, of the primal idea of the living cosmos, or of birth and death, as necessary to the continuation of the stream of life. [Source of Measure, p.299. This "stream of life" being emblematised in the Philloc basso-relievo just mentioned, by the water poured in the shape of a Cross on the initiated candidate by Osiris - Life and the Sun - and Mercury - Death. It was the finale of the rite of Initiation after the seven and the twelve tortures in the Crypts of Egypt were passed through successfully.]

To quote once more from Isis Unveiled:

A Latin cross of a perfect Christian shape was found hewn upon the granite slabs of the Adytum of the Serapeum; and the monks did not fail to claim that the cross had been hallowed by the Pagans in a "spirit of prophecy." At least, Sozomen, with an air of triumph, records the fact. [Another untrustworthy, untruthful and ignorant writer, an ecclesiastical historian of the fifth century. His alleged history of the strife between the Pagans, Neoplatonists, and the Christians of Alexandria and Constantinople, which extends from the year 324 to 439, dedicated by him to Theodosius, the younger, is full of deliberate falsifications.] But archaeology and symbolism, those tireless and implacable enemies of clerical false pretences, have found in the hieroglyphics of the legend running round the design at least a partial interpretation of its meaning.

According to King and other numismatists and archaeologists, the cross was placed there as the symbol of eternal life.

THE CROSS AND CRUCIFIX

Such a Tau, or Egyptian cross, was used in the Bacchic and Eleusinian Mysteries. Symbol of the dual generative power, it was laid upon the breast of the Initiate, after his "new birth" was accomplished, and the Mystae had returned from their baptism in the sea. It was a mystic sign that his spiritual birth had regenerated and united his astral soul with his divine spirit, and that he was ready to ascend in spirit to the blessed abodes of light and glory - the Eleusinia. The Tau was a magic talisman at the same time as a religious emblem. It was adopted by the Christians through the Gnostics and Kabalists, who used it largely, as their numerous gems testify. These in turn had the Tau (or handled cross) from the Egyptians, and the Latin Cross from the Buddhist missionaries, who brought it from India (where it can be found even now) two or three centuries B.C. The Assyrians, Egyptians, ancient Americans, Hindus and Romans had it in various, but very slight modifications of shape. Till very late in the middle ages, it was considered a potent spell against epilepsy and demoniacal possession, and the "signet of the living God" brought down in St. John's vision by the angel ascending from the east to "seal the servants of our God in the foreheads," was but the same mystic Tau - the Egyptian Cross. In the painted glass of St. Denis (France) this angel is represented as stamping this sign on the forehead of the elect; the legend reads, SIGNUM TAY. In King's Gnostics, the author reminds us that "this mark is commonly borne by St. Anthony, an Egyptian recluse." [Gems of the Orthodox Christians. Vol. 1., p.135.] What the real meaning of the Tau was, is explained to us by the Christian St. John, the Egyptian Hermes, and the Hindu Brahmans. It is but too evident that, with the Apostle at least, it meant the "Ineffable Name," as he calls this "signet of the living God" a few chapters further on [Revelation, XIV, 1] "Father's name written in their foreheads."

The Brahmâtmâ the chief of the Hindu Initiates, had on his headgear two keys, symbol of the revealed mystery of life and death, placed cross-like; and in some Buddhist pagodas of Tartary and Mongolia, the entrance of a chamber within the temple, generally containing the staircase which leads to the inner dagoba. [A Dagoba is a small temple of globular form, in which are preserved the relics of Gautama.] and the porticos of some Prachidas [Prachidas are buildings of all sizes and forms, like our mausoleums, and are sacred to votive offerings to the dead.] are ornamented with a cross formed of two fishes, as found on some of the zodiacs of the Buddhists. We should not wonder at all at learning that the sacred device in the tombs in the catacombs at Rome, the "Vesica Piscis," was derived from the said Buddhist zodiacal sign. How general must have been that geometrical figure in the world-symbols, may be inferred from the fact that there is a Masonic tradition that Solomon's temple was built on three foundations, forming the "triple Tau" or three crosses.

In its mystical sense, the Egyptian cross owes its origin, as an emblem, to the realisation by the earliest philosophy of an androgynous dualism of every manifestation in nature, which proceeds from the abstract ideal of a likewise androgynous deity, while the Christian emblem is simply due to chance. Had the Mosaic law prevailed, Jesus should have been lapidated. [The Talmudistic records claim that, after having been hanged, he was lapidated and buried under the water at the junction of two streams. Mishna Sanhedrin, Vol. V1., p.4: Talmud, of Babylon, same article, 43a, 67a.] The crucifix was an instrument of torture, and utterly common among Romans as it was unknown among Semitic nations. It was called the "Tree of Infamy." It is but later that it was adopted as a Christian symbol; but during the first two decades the apostles looked upon it with horror.[Coptic Legends of the Crucifixion. MSS. XI]. It is certainly not the Christian Cross that John had in mind when speaking of the "signet of the living God," but the mystic Tau - the Tetragrammaton, or mighty name, which, on the most ancient Kabalistic talismans, was represented by the four Hebrew letters composing the Holy Word.

The famous Lady Ellenborough, known among the Arabs of Damascus, and in the desert, after her last marriage, as Hanoum Medjouye, had a talisman in her possession, presented to her by a Druse from Mount Lebanon. It was recognised by a certain sign on its left corner as belonging to that class of gems which is known in Palestine as a "Messianic" amulet, of the second or third century B.C. It is a green stone of a pentagonal form; at the bottom is engraved a fish, higher, Solomon's Seal; [We are at a loss to understand why King, in his Gnostic Gems, represents Solomon's Seal as a five-pointed star, whereas it is six-pointed, and is the signet of Vishnu in India.] and still higher, the four Chaldaic letters - Jod, He, Vau, He, IAHO, which form the name of the Deity. These are arranged in quite an unusual way, running from below upward, in reversed order, and forming the Egyptian Tau. Around these there is a legend which, as the gem is not our property, we are not at liberty to give. The Tau, in its mystical sense, as well as the Crux ansata, is the Tree of Life.

It is well known that the earliest Christian emblems - before it was ever attempted to represent the bodily appearance of Jesus - were the Lamb, the Good Shepherd, and The Fish. The origin of the latter emblem, which has so puzzled the archaeologists, thus becomes comprehensible. The whole secret lies in the easily ascertained fact that, while in the Kabalah the King Messiah is called "Interpreter," or Revealer of the Mystery, and shown to be the fifth emanation, in the Talmud - for reasons we will now explain - the Messiah is very often designated as "DAG," or the Fish. This is an inheritance from the Chaldees, and relates - as the very name indicates - to the Babylonian Dagon, the man-fish, who was the instructor and interpreter of the people, to whom he appeared. Abarbanel explains the name, by stating that the sign of his (Messiah's) coming is the conjuction of Saturn and Jupiter in the sign Pisces. [King (Gnostics) gives the figure of a Christian symbol, very common during the middle ages of three fishes, interlaced into a triangle, and having the FIVE letters (a most sacred Pythagorean number) IXΘYX engraved on it. The number five relates to the same kabalistic computation.] Therefore, as the Christians were intent upon identifying their Christos with the Messiah of the Old Testament, they adopted it so readily as to forget that its true origin might be traced still further back than the Babylonian Dagon. How eagerly and closely the ideal of Jesus was united, by the early Christians, with every imaginable kabalistic and pagan tenet, may be inferred from the language of Clemens, of Alexandria, addressed to his co-religionists.

THE STORY OF JESUS

When they were debating upon the choice of the most appropriate symbol to remind them of Jesus, Clemens advised them in the following words. Let the engraving upon the gem of your ring be either a dove or a ship running before the wind (the Argha), or a fish." Was the good father, when writing this sentence, labouring under the recollection of Joshua, son of Nun (called Jesus in the Greek and Slavonian versions); or had he forgotten the real interpretation of these pagan symbols? [Op. cit.,II 253-256.]

And now, with the help of all these passages scattered

hither and thither in Isis and other works of this kind, the reader will see and judge for himself which of the two explanations - the Christian or that of the Occultist - is the nearer to truth. If Jesus were not an Initiate, why should all these allegorical incidents of his life be given? Why should such extreme trouble be taken, so much time wasted trying to make the above: (a) answer and dovetail with purposely picked out sentences in the Old Testament, to show them as prophecies; and (b) to preserve in them the initiatory symbols, the emblems so pregnant with Occult meaning and all of these belonging to Pagan mystic Philosophy? The author of the Source of Measures gives out that mystical intent; but only once now and again, in its one-sided, numerical and kabalistic meaning, without paying any attention to, or having concern with, the primeval and more spiritual origin, and he deals with it only so far as it related to the Old Testament. He attributes the purposed change in the sentence "Eli, Eli, lama sabachthani" to the principle already mentioned of the crossed bones and skull in the Labarum.

As an emblem of death, being placed over the door of life and signifying birth, or of the intercontainment of two opposite principles in one, just as, mystically, the Saviour was held to be man-woman. [Op. cit., 301. All this connects Jesus with great Initiates and solar heroes: all this is purely Pagan, under a newly-evolved variation, the Christian scheme.].

The author's idea is to show the mystic blending by the Gospel writers of Jehovah, Cain, Abel, etc., with Jesus (in accordance with Jewish kabalistic numeration); the better he succeeds, the more clearly he shows that it was a forced blending, and that we have not a record of the real events of the life of Jesus, narrated by eyewitnesses or the Apostles. The narrative is all based on the signs of the Zodiac:

Each a double sign or male-female [in ancient astrological Magic] - viz.: it was Taurus-Eve, and Scorpio was Mars-Lupa, or Mars with the female wolf [in relation to Romulus]. So, as these signs were opposites of each other, yet met in the centre, they were connected; and so in fact it was, and in a double sense, the conception of the year was in Taurus, as the conception of Eve by Mars, her opposite, in Scorpio. The birth would be at the winter solstice, or Christmas. On the contrary, by conception in Scorpio - viz., of Lupa by Taurus - birth would be in Leo. Scorpio was Chrestos in humiliation, while Leo was Christos in triumph. While Taurus-Eve fulfilled astronomical functions, Mars-Lupa fulfilled spiritual ones by type. [Op. cit.,296.]

The author bases all this on Egyptian correlations and meanings of Gods and Goddesses, but ignores the Aryan, which are far earlier.

Mooth or Mouth, was the Egyptian cognomen of Venus, (Eve, mother of all living) [as Vach, mother of all living, a permutation of Aditi, as Eve was one of Sephira] or the moon. Plutarch (Isis, 374) hands it down that Isis was sometimes called Muth, which word means mother . . . (Issa, אשה woman). (Isis, p.372). Isis, he says is that part of Nature, which, as feminine, contains in herself, as (nutrix) nurse, all things to be born. . . "Certainly the moon, " speaking astronomically, "chiefly exercises this function in Taurus, Venus being the house (in opposition to Mars, generator, in

Scorpio), because the sign is luna, hypsoma. Since. . . Isis Metheur differs from Isis Muth and that in the vocable Muth the notion of bringing forth may be concealed and since fructification must take place, Sol being joined with Luna in Libra, it is not improbable that Muth first indeed signifies Venus in Libra; hence Luna in Libra. (Beiträge zur Kenntniss, pars 11, S. 9, under Muth.) [Pp. 294. 295.]

Then Fuerst, under Bohu, is quoted to show

The double play upon the word Muth by help of which the real intent is produced in the occult way . . . sin, death, and woman are one in the glyph, and correlatively connected with intercourse and death. [P.295.]

All this is applied by the author only to the exoteric and Jewish euhemerised symbols, whereas they were meant, first of all, to conceal cosmogonical mysteries, and then, those of anthropological evolution with reference to the Seven Races, already evoluted and to come, and especially as regards the last branch races of the third Root-Race. However, the word void [primeval Chaos] is shown to be taken for Eve-Venus-Naamah, agreeably with Fuerst's definition; for as he says:

In this primitive signification [of void] was בהו (bohu) taken in the Biblical cosmogony, and used in establishing the dogma יש מאין [Jes(us) m'aven, Jes-us from nothing] respecting creation. (Which shows the writers of the New Testament considerably skilled in the Kabalah and Occult Sciences, and corroborates still more our assertion.) Hence Aquila translates ουδεν vulg. vacua (hence vacca, cow) [hence also the horns of Isis - Nature, Earth, and the Moon -

taken from Vàch, the Hindu "Mother of all that lives," identified with Viràj and called in Atharvaveda the daughter of Kàma, the first desires: "That daughter of thine, O kàma, is called the cow, she whom Sages name Vach-Viraj," who was milked by Brihaspati, the Rishi, which is another mystery] Onkelos and Samarit קיד׳

THE PRIMITIVE WOMAN-

The Phoenician cosmogony has connected Bohu בוהו βaavBaav into a personified expression denoting the primitive substance, and as a deity, the mother of races of the Gods [which is Aditi and Vach]. The Aramean name בוהתא , בוהתא , בוהתא , βαφος, Buto, for the mother of the gods, which passed over to the Gnostics, Babylonians and Egyptians, is identical then with Môt (מות ., our Muth) properly, (βωθoriiginated in Phoenician from an interchange of b with m. [Pp. 295. 296]

Rather, one would say, go to the origin. The mystic euhemerisation of Wisdom and Intelligence, operating in the work of cosmic evolution, or Buddhi under the names of Brahma, Purusha, etc., as male power, and Aditi-Vàch, etc., as female, whence Sarasvati, Goddess of Wisdom, who became under the veils of Esoteric concealment, Butos, Bythos - Depth, the grossly material, personal female, called Eve, the "primitive woman" of Irenaeus, and the world springing out of Nothing.

The workings out of this glyph of 4th Genesis help to the comprehension of the division of one character into the forms of two persons; as Adam and Eve, Cain and Abel, Abram

and Isaac, Jacob and Esau, and so on [all male and female]
. . . Now, as linking together several great salient points in
the Biblical structure: (1) as to the Old and New Testament;
with also (2) as to the Roman Empire; (3) as to confirming
the meaning and uses of symbols; and (4) as to confirming
the entire explanation and reading of the glyphs; as (5)
recognizing and laying down the base of the great pyramid as
the foundation square of the Bible construction; (6) as well as
the new Roman adoption under Constantine - the following
given: [Had we known the learned author before his book
was printed, he might have been perchance prevailed upon
to add a seventh link from which all others, far preceding
those enumerated in point of time, and surpassing them in
universally philosophical meaning, have been derived, aye,
even to the great pyramid, whose foundation square was,
in its turn, the great Aryan Mysteries.]

Cain has been shown to be . . . the 360 circle of the Zodiac,
the perfect and exact standard, b a squared division; hence
his name of Melchizadik . . . [The geometrical and numerical
demonstrations here follow.] It has been repeatedly stated
that the object of the Great Pyramid construction was to
measure the heavens and the earth . . . (the objective spheres
as evoluting from the subjective, purely spiritual Kosmos,
we beg leave to add); therefore, its measuring containment
would indicate all the substance of measure of the heaven
and the earth, or agreeably to ancient recognition, Earth, Air,
Water and Fire.[We would say cosmic Matter, Spirit, Chaos,
and Divine Light, for the Egyptians idea was identical in this
with the Aryan. However, the author is right with regard to

the Occult Symbology of the Jews. They were a remarkably matter of fact, unspiritual people at all times, yet even with them "Ruach" was Divine Spirit, not "air."] (The base side of this pyramid was diameter to a circumference in feet of 2400. The characteristic of this is 24 feet, or 6 X 4 = 24, or this very Cain-Adam square.) Now, by the restoration of the encampment of the Israelites, as initiated by Moses, by the great scholar, Father Athanasius Kircher, the Jesuit priest, the above is precisely by Biblical record and traditionary sources, the method of laying off this encampment. The four interior squares were devoted to (1) Moses and Aaron; (2) Kohath; (3) Gershom; and (4) Merari - the last three being the head of the Levites. The attributes of these squares were the primal attributes of Adam-Mars and were concreted of the elements, Earth, Air, Fire, Water, or ⌐ = Iam = Water, ⌐ . Nour = Fire, = Rouach = Air, and = Iabeshah = Earth. The initial letters of these words are INRI. [The words translated as Iesus Nazarenus Rex Iudaeorum - "Jesus, King of the Jews."] This square of INRI is the Adam square, which was extended from, as a foundation, into four others of 145 X 2 = 288, to the side of the large square of 288 X 4 = 115 -2, = the whole circumference. But this square is the display of also circular elements and 115-2 can denote this. Put INRI into a circle, or read it as the lett the square, as to its value of 1521, and we have which reads 115-2 of this fact.

But as seen Cain denotes this as, or in, the 115 of his name: which 115 was the very complement to make up the

360 day year, to agree with the balances of the standard circle, which were Cain. The corner squares of the larger square are, A = Leo, and B = Dan Scorpio; and it is seen that Cain pierces Abel at the intersection of the equinoctial with the solstice cross lines, referred to from Dan-Scorpio on the celestial circle. But Dan-Scorpio borders on Libra, the scales, whose sign is ⬄ (which sign is that of the ancient pillow on which the back of the head to the ears[Mr Ralston Skinner shows that the symbol ⸓ the crossed bones and skull, has the letter P Koph, the half of the head behind the ears.] rested, the pillow of Jacob), and is represented for one symbol as XPS · · Also the badge of Dan-Scorpio is death-life, in the symbol ⸓ Now the cross is the emblem of the origin of measures, in the Jehovah form of a straight line ONE of a denomination of 20612, the perfect circumference; hence Cain was this as Jehovah, for the text says that he was Jehovah. But the attachment of a man to this cross was that of 113: 355 to 6561: 5153 X 4 = 20612, as shown. Now, over the head of Jesus crucified was placed the inscription, of which the initial letters of the words have always been retained as symbolic, and handed down and used as a monogram of Jesus Chrestos - viz., INRI or Jesus Nazarenus Rex Judaeorum; but they are located on the Cross, or the cubed form of the circular origin of measures which measure the substance of Earth, Air, Fire and Water, or INRI = 1152, as shown. Here is the man on the cross, or 113; 355 combined with 6561: 5153 X 4 = 20612. These are the pyramid-base numbers as coming from 113: 355 as the Hebrew source; whence the Adam-square, which is the pyramid base, and

the centre one to the larger square of the encampment. Bend INRI into a circle, and we have 1152, or the circumference of the latter. But Jesus dying (or Abel married) made use of the very words needed to set forth all. He says, Eli, Eli, Lama Sabachthani . . . Read them by their power values, in circular form, as produced from the Adam form as shown, and we have . אֵלִ . = 113, אֵלִ = 113, or 113-311: לְמָה = 345, or Moses in the Cain-Adam pyramid circle: שַׁבְּתָ = 710, equals Dove, or Jonah and 710 divided by 2 = 355, or 355 -553: and finally, as determinative of all ִנ or ni......... where נ = nun, fish = 565, and ִ = 1 or 10; together 565 ִ . = יהוה or the Christ value.

KABALISTIC READING OF GOSPELS-

[All of the above] throws light on the transfiguration scene on the mount. There were present there Peter and James and John with Jesus; or מ lami, James, Water; פטר , Peter, Earth יוחנן , John, Spirit, Air, and ישׁע , Jesus, Fire, Life - together INRI. But behold Eli and Moses met them there, or . אֵל and משׁה or Eli and Lamah, or 113 and 345. And this shows that the scene of transfiguration was connected with the one above set forth. [Pp. 296 -302 . By these numbers, explains the author. "Eli is 113 (by placing the word in a circle): amah being 345, is by change of letters to suit the same value משׁה (in a circle) or Moses, while Sabachth is John or the dove, or Holy Spirit, because (in a circle) it is 710 (or 355 X 2). The termination ni, as meni or 5651, becomes Jehovah.]

This kabalistical reading of the Gospel narratives - hitherto supposed to record the most important, the most mystically awful, yet most real events of the life of Jesus - must fall with terrible weight upon some Christians. Every honest trusting believer who has shed tears of reverential emotion over the events of the short period of the public life of Jesus of Nazareth, has to choose one of the two ways opening before him after reading the aforesaid: either his faith has to render him quite impervious to any light coming from human reasoning and evident fact; or he must confess that he has lost his Saviour. The One whom he had hitherto considered as the unique incarnation on this earth of the One Living God in heaven, fades into thin air, on the authority of the properly read and correctly interpreted Bible itself. Moreover, since on the authority of Jerome himself and his accepted and authentic confession, the book written by the hand of Matthew "exhibits matter not for edification but for destruction" (of Church and human Christianity, and only that) what truth can be expected from his famous Vulgate? Human mysteries, concocted by generations of Church Fathers bent upon evolving a religion of their own invention, are seen instead of a divine Revelation; and that this was so is corroborated by a prelate of the Latin Church. Saint Gregory Nazianzen wrote to his friend and confidant, St. Jerome:

Nothing can impose better on a people than verbiage; the less they understand the more they admire . . . Our fathers and doctors have often said, not what they thought, but that to which circumstances and necessity forced them.

Which then of the two - clergy, or the Occultists and

Theosophists - are the more blasphemous and dangerous? Is it those who would impose upon the world's acceptance a Saviour of their own fashioning, a God with human shortcomings, and who therefore is certainly not a perfect divine Being; or those others who say: Jesus of Nazareth was in Initiate, a holy, grand and noble character, but withal human, though truly "a Son of God"?

If Humanity is to accept a so-called supernatural Religion, how far more logical to the Occultist and the Psychologist seems the transparent allegory given of Jesus by the Gnostics. They, as Occultists, and with Initiates for their Chiefs, differed only in their renderings of the story and in their symbols, and not at all in substance. What say the Ophites, the Nazarenes, and other "heretics"? Sophia, "the Celestial Virgin," is prevailed upon to send Christos, her emanation, to the help of perishing humanity, from whom Ilda-Baoth (the Jehovah of the Jews) and his six Sons of Matter (the lower terrestrial Angels) are shutting out the divine light. Therefore, Christos, the perfect, [The Western personification of that power, which the Hindus call the Vija, the "one seed," or Maha Vishnu - a power, not the God - or that mysterious Principle that contains in itself the Seed of Avatârism.]

Uniting himself with Sophia [divine wisdom] descended through the seven planetary regions, assuming in each an analogous form . . . [and] entered into the man Jesus at the moment of his baptism in the Jordan. From this time forth Jesus began to work miracles; before that he had been entirely ignorant of his own mission.

Ilda-Baoth, discovering that Christos was bringing to an end his kingdom of Matter, stirred up the Jews, his own people, against Him, and Jesus was put to death. When Jesus was on the Cross Christos and Sophia left His body, and returned to Their own sphere. The material body of Jesus was abandoned to the earth, but He Himself, the Inner Man, was clothed with a body made up of aether. [Arise into Nervi from this decrepit body into which thou hast been sent. Ascend into thy former abode, O blessed Avatâr!"]

Thenceforth he consisted merely of soul and spirit . . . During his sojourn upon earth of eighteen months after he had risen, he received from Sophia that perfect knowledge, that true Gnosis, which he communicated to the small portion of the Apostles who were capable of receiving the same. [The Gnostics and their Remains. King. pp.100, 101.]

The above is transparently Eastern and Hindu; it is the Esoteric Doctrine pure and simple, save for the names and the allegory. It is, more or less, the history of every Adept who obtains Initiation.

UNIVERSAL TEACHINGS-

The Baptism in the Jordan is the Rite of Initiation, the final purification, whether in sacred pagoda, tank, river, or temple lake in Egypt or Mexico. The perfect Christos and Sophia - divine Wisdom and Intelligence - enter the Initiate at the moment of the mystic rite, by transference from Guru to Chela, and leave the physical body, at the moment of the death of the latter, to re-enter the Nirmânakâya, or the astral Ego of the Adept.

The spirit of Buddha [collectively] overshadows the Bodhisattvas of his Church says the Buddhist Ritual of Aryasangha.

Says the Gnostic teaching:

When he [the spirit of Christos] shall have collected all the Spiritual, all the Light [that exists in matter], out of Ildabaoth's empire, Redemption is accomplished and the end of the world arrived. [Loc. Cit.]

Say the Buddhists;

When Buddha [the Spirit of the Church] hears the hour strike, he will send Maitreya Buddha - after whom the old world will be destroyed.

That which is said of Basilides by King may be applied as truthfully to every innovator, so called, whether of a Buddhist or of a Christian Church. In the eyes of Clemens Alexandrinus, he says, the Gnostics taught very little that was blameable in their mystical transcendental views.

In his eyes the latter (Basilides), was not a heretic, that is an innovator upon the accepted doctrines of the Catholic Church, but only a theosophic speculator who sought to express old truths by new formulae. [Op. cit.,p. 258.]

There was a Secret Doctrine preached by Jesus; and "secrecy" in those days meant Secrets, or Mysteries of Initiation, all of which have been either rejected or disfigured by the Church. In the Clementine Homilics we read:

And Peter said: "We remember that our Lord and Teacher, commanding us, said 'Guard the mysteries for me and the sons of my house.'" Wherefore also he explained to His disciples privately the Mysteries of the Kingdom of the

Heavens.[Homilies XIX. XX,I]

SECTION XIX

ST. CYPRIAN OF ANTIOCH

THE Aeons (Stellar Spirits) - emanated from the Unknown of the Gnostics, and identical with the Dhyan Chohans of the Esoteric Doctrine - and their Pleroma, having been transformed into Archangels and the "Spirits of the Presence" by the Greek and Latin Churches, the prototypes have lost caste. The Pleroma[The Pleroma constituted the synthesis or entirety of all the spiritual entities. St. Paul still used the name in his Epistles.] was now called the "Heavenly Host," and therefore the old name had to become identified with Satan and his "Host." Might is right in every age, and History is full of contrasts. Manes has been called the "Paraclete" [The "Comforter," second Messiah, intercessor. "A term applied to the Holy Ghost." Manes was the disciple of Terebinthus, an Egyptian Philosopher, who, according to the Christian Socrates (1.i., cited by Tillemont, iv. 584). "while invoking one day the demons of the air, fell from the roof of his house and was killed."] by his followers. He was an Occultist, but passed to posterity, owing to the kind exertions of the Church, as a Sorcerer, so a match had to be found for him by way of contrast. We recognise this match in St. Cyprianus of Antioch, a self-confessed if not a real "Black Magician," it seems, whom the Church - as a reward for his contrition and humility - subsequently raised to the high rank of Saint and Bishop.

What history knows of him is not much, and it is mostly based on his own confession, the truthfulness of which is warranted, we are told, by St. Gregory, the Empress Eudoxia, Photius and the Holy Church. This curious document was ferreted out by the Marquis de Mirville, [Cy.Op. cit.,vi, 169-183.] in the Vatican, and by him translated into French for the first time, as he assures the reader. We beg his permission to retranslate a few pages, not for the sake of the penitent Sorcerer, but for that of some students of Occultism, who will thus have an opportunity of comparing the methods of ancient Magic (or as the Church calls it, Demonism) with those of modern Theurgy and Occultism.

MAGIC IN ANTIOCH-

The scenes described took place at Antioch about the middle of the third century, 252 A.D., says the translator. This Confession was written by the penitent Sorcerer after his conversion; therefore, we are not surprised to find how much room he gives in his lamentations to reviling his Initiator "Satan," or the "Serpent Dragon," as he calls him. There are other and more modern instances of the same trait in human nature. Converted Hindus, Parsis and other "heathen" of India are apt to denounce their forefathers' religions at every opportunity. Thus runs the Confession:

O all of you who reject the real mysteries of Christ, see my tears! . . .You who wallow in your demoniacal practices, learn by my sad example all the vanity of their [the demons'] baits . . . I am that Cyprianus, who, vowed to Apollo from his infancy, was early initiated into all the arts of the dragon. ["The great serpent placed to watch the temple," comments de Mirville. "How often have we repeated that it was no symbol, no personification but really a serpent occupied by a god!" - he exclaims; and we answer that at Cairo in a Mussulman, not a heathen temple, we have seen, as thousands of other visitors have also seen, a huge serpent that lived there for centuries, we were told, and was held in great respect. Was it also "occupied by a God," or possessed, in other words?] Even before the age of seven I had already been introduced into the temple of Mithra: three years later, my parents taking me to Athens to be received as citizen, I was permitted likewise to penetrate the mysteries of Ceres lamenting her daughter,[The Mysteries of Demeter, or the "afflicted mother".] and I also became the guardian of the Dragon in the Temple of Pallas.

Ascending after that to the summit of Mount Olympus, the Seat of the Gods, as it is called, there too I was initiated into the sense, and the real meaning of their [the Gods'] speeches and their clamorous manifestations (strepituum). It is there that I was made to see in imagination (phantasia) [or mayâ] those trees and all those herbs that operate such prodigies with the help of demons; . . . and I saw their dances, their warfares, their snares, illusions and promiscuities. I heard their singing. [By the satyrs.] I saw finally, for forty consecutive days, the phalanx of the Gods and Goddesses, sending from Olympus, as though they were Kings, spirits to represent them on earth and act in their name among all the nations. [This looks rather suspicious and seems interpolated. De Mirville tries to have what he says of Satan and his Court sending their imps on earth to tempt humanity and masquerade at seances corroborated by the ex-sorcerer.]

At that time I lived entirely on fruit, eaten only after sunset, the virtues of which were explained to me by the seven priests of the sacrifices. [This does not look like sinful food. It is the diet of Chelas to this day.]

When I was fifteen my parents desired that I should be made acquainted, not only with all the natural laws in connection with the generation and corruption of bodies on earth, in the air and in the seas, but also with all the other forces grafted ["Grafted" is the correct expression. "The seven Builders graft the divine and the beneficent forces on to the gross material nature of the vegetable and mineral kingdoms every Second Round - says the Catechism of Lanoos.] (insitas) on these by the Prince of the World in order to counteract their primal and divine constitution. [Only the Prince of the World is not Satan, as the translator would make us believe, but the collective Host of the Planetary. This is a little theological backbiting.] At twenty I went to Memphis, where, penetrating into the Sanctuaries, I was taught to discern all that pertains to the communications of demons [Daimones or Spirits] with terrestrial matters, their aversion for certain places, they sympathy and attraction for others, their expulsion from certain planets, certain objects and laws, their persistence in preferring darkness and their resistance to light. [Here the Elemental and Elementary Spirits are evidently meant.] There I learned the number of the fallen Princes, [The reader has already learned the truth about them in the course of the present work.] that which takes place in human souls and the bodies they enter into communication with.

I learnt the analogy that exists between earthquakes and the rains, between the motion of the earth [Pity the penitent Saint had not imparted his knowledge of the rotation of the earth and heliocentric system earlier to his Church. That might have saved more than one human life - that of Bruno for one.] and the motion of the seas; I saw the spirits of the Giants plunged in subterranean darkness and seemingly supporting the earth like a man carrying a burden on is shoulders. [Chelas in their trials of initiation, also see in trances artificially generated for them, the vision of the Earth supported by an elephant on the top of a tortoise standing on nothing - and this, to teach them to discern the true from the false.].

When thirty I travelled to Chaldaea to study there the true power of the air, placed by some in the fire and by the more learned in light [Akâsha]. I was taught to see that the planets were in their variety as dissimilar as the plants on earth, and the stars were like armies ranged in battle order. I knew the Chaldaean division of Ether into 365 parts, [Relating to the days of the year, also to 7X7 divisions of the earth's sublunary sphere, divided into seven upper and seven lower spheres with their respective Planetary Hosts or "armies."] and I perceived that everyone of the demons who divide it among themselves [Daimon is not "demon," as translated by De Mirville, but Spirit.] was endowed with that material force that permitted him to execute the orders of the Prince and guide all the movements therein [in the Ether]. [All this is to corroborate his dogmatic assertions that Pater Aether or Jupiter is Satan! and that pestilential diseases, cataclysms, and even thunderstorms that prove disastrous, come from the Satanic Host dwelling in Ether - a good warning to the men of Science!] They [the Chaldees] explained to me how those Princes had become participants in the Council of Darkness, ever in opposition to the Council of Light.

I got acquainted with the Mediatores [surely not mediums as De Mirville explains!] [The translator replaces the word Mediators by mediums, excusing himself in a footnote by saying that Cyprian must have meant modern mediums!] and upon seeing the covenants they were mutually bound by, I was struck with wonder upon learning the nature of their oaths and observances.[Cypriannus simply meant to hint at the rites and mysteries of Initiation, and the pledge of secrecy and oaths that bound the Initiates together. His translator, however, has made a Witches Sabbath of it instead.]

SORCERER BECOME SAINT

Believe me, I saw the Devil; believe me I have embraced him ["Twelve centuries later, in full renaissance and reform, the world saw Luther do the same [embrace the Devil he means?] - according to his own confession and in the same conditions," explains De Mirville in a footnote, showing thereby the brotherly love that binds Christians. Now Cyprianus meant by the Devil (if the word is really in the original text) his Initiator and Hierophant. No Saint - even a penitent Sorcerer - would be so silly as to speak of his (the Devil's) rising from his seat to see him to the door, were it otherwise.] [like the witches at the Sabbath (?)] when I was yet young, and he saluted me by the title of the new Jambres, declaring me worthy of my ministry (initiation). He promised me continual help during life and a principality after death. [Every Adept has a "principality after his death."] Having become in great honour (an Adept) under his tuition, he placed under my orders a phalanx of demons, and when I bid him goodbye, "Courage, good success, excellent Cyprian," he exclaimed, rising up from his seat to see me to the door, plunging thereby those present into a profound admiration. [Which shows that it was the Hierophant and his disciples. Cyprianus shows himself as grateful as most of the other converts (the modern included) to his Teachers and Instructors.

Having bidden farewell to his Chaldaean Initiator, the future Sorcerer and Saint went to Antioch. His tale of "iniquity" and subsequent repentance is long but we will make it short. He became "an accomplished Magician," surrounded by a host of disciples and "candidates to the perilous and sacrilegious art." He shows himself distributing love-philtres and dealing in deathly charms "to rid young wives of old husbands, and to ruin Christian virgins." Unfortunately Cyprianus was not above love himself. He fell in love with the beautiful Justine, a converted maiden, after having vainly tried to make her share the passion one named Aglaides, a profligate, had for her. His "demons failed" he tells us, and he got disgusted with them. This disgust brings on a quarrel between him and his Hierophant, whom he insists on indentifying with the Demon; and the dispute is followed by a tournament between the latter and some Christian converts, in which the "Evil One" is, of course, worsted. The Sorcerer is finally baptised and gets rid of his enemy. Having laid at the feet of Anthimes, Bishop of Antioch, all his books on Magic, he became a Saint in company with the beautiful Justine, who had converted him; both suffered martyrdom under the Emperor Diocletian; and both are buried side by side in Rome, in the Basilica of St. John Lateran, near the Baptistery.

SECTION XX

THE EASTERN GUPTA VIDYA & THE KABALAH

WE now return to the consideration of the essential identity between the Eastern Gupta Vidya and the Kabalah as a system, while we must also show the dissimilarity in their philosophical interpretations since the Middle Ages.

It must be confessed that the views of the Kabalists - meaning by the word those students of Occultism who study the Jewish Kabalah and who know little, if anything, of any other Esoteric literature or of its teachings - are as varied in their synthetic conclusions upon the nature of the mysteries taught even in the Zohar alone, and are as wide of the true mark, as are the dicta upon it of exact Science itself. Like the mediaeval Rosicrucian and the Alchemist - like the Abbot Trithemius, John Reuchlin, Agrippa, Paracelsus, Robert Fludd, Philalethes, etc. - by whom they swear, the continental Occultists see in the Jewish Kabalah alone the universal well of wisdom; they find in it the secret lore of nearly all the mysteries of Nature - metaphysical and divine - some of them including herein, as did Reuchlin, those of the Christian Bible. For them the Zohar is an Esoteric Thesaurus of all the mysteries of the Christian Gospel; and the Sephyr Yetsirah is the light that shines in every darkness, and the container of the keys to open every secret in Nature. Whether many of our modern followers of the mediaeval Kabalists have an idea of the real meaning of the symbology of their chosen Masters is another question. Most of them have probably never given even a passing thought to the fact that the Esoteric language used by the Alchemists was their own, and that it was given out as a blind, necessitated by the dangers of the epoch they lived in, and not as the Mystery-language, used by the Pagan Initiates, which the Alchemists had retranslated and re-veiled once more.

A MYSTERY WITHIN A MYSTERY-

And now the situation stands thus: as the old Alchemists have not left a key to their writings, the latter have become a mystery within an older mystery. The Kabalah is interpreted and checked only by the light which mediaeval Mystics have thrown upon it, and they, in their forced Christology, had to put a theological dogmatic mask on every ancient teaching, the result being that each Mystic among our modern European and American Kabalists interprets the old symbols in his own way, and each refers his opponents to the Rosicrucian and the Alchemist of three and four hundred years ago. Mystic Christian dogma is the central maelstrom that engulfs every old Pagan symbol, and Christianity - Anti-Gnostic Christianity, the modern retort that has replaced the alembic of the Alchemists - has distilled out of all recognition the Kabalah, i.e., the Hebrew Zohar and other rabbinical mystic works. And now it has come to this: The student interested in the Secret Sciences has to believe that the whole cycle of the symbolical "Ancient of Days," every hair of the mighty beard of Macroprosopos, refers only to the history of the earthly career of Jesus of Nazareth! And we are told that the Kabalah "was first taught to a select company of angels" by Jehovah himself - who, out of modesty, one must think, made himself only the third Sephiroth in it, and a female one into the bargain. So many Kabalists, so many explanations. Some believe - perchance with more reason than the rest - that the substance of the Kabalah is the basis upon which masonry is built, since modern Masonry is undeniable the dim and hazy reflection of primeval Occult Masonry, of the teaching of those divine Masons who established the Mysteries of the prehistoric and prediluvian Temples of Initiation, raised by truly superhuman Builders. Others declare that the tenets expounded in the Zohar relate merely to mysteries terrestrial and profane, having no more concern with metaphysical speculations - such as the soul, or the post-mortem life of man - than have the Mosaic books. Others, again - and these are the real, genuine Kabalists, who had their instructions from initiated Jewish Rabbis - affirm that if the two most learned Kabalists of the mediaeval period, John Reuchlin and Paracelsus, differed in their religious professions - the former being the Father of the Reformation and the latter a Roman Catholic, at least in appearance - the Zohar cannot contain much of Christian dogma or tenet, one way or the other. In other words, they maintain that the numerical language of the Kabalistic works teaches universal truths - and not any one Religion in particular. Those who make this statement are perfectly right in saying that the Mystery-language used in the Zohar and in other Kabalistic literature was once, in a time of unfathomable antiquity, the universal language of

Humanity. But they become entirely wrong if to this fact they add the untenable theory that this language was invented by, or was the original property of, the Hebrews, from whom all the other nations borrowed it.

They are wrong, because, although the Zohar (.(זהר ZHR)) , The Book of Splendour of Rabbi Simeon Ben Iochai, did indeed originate with him - his son, Rabbi Eleazar, helped by his secretary, Rabbi Abba, compiling the Kabalistic teachings of his deceased father into a work called the Zohar - those teachings were not Rabbi Simeon's, as the Gupta Vidya shows. They are as old as the Jewish nation itself. , and far older. In short, the writings which pass at present under the title of the Zohar of Rabbi Simeon are about as original as were the Egyptian synchronistic Tables after being handled by Eusebius, or as St. Paul's Epistles after their revision and correction by the "Holy Church." [This is proved if we take but a single recorded instance. J. Picus de Mirandola, finding that there was more Christianity than Judaism in the Kabalah, and discovering in it the doctrines of the Trinity, the Incarnation, the Divinity of Jesus, etc., wound up his proofs of this with a challenge to the world at large from Rome. As Ginsburg shows: "In 1486, when only twenty-four years old, he [Pieus] published nine hundred [Kabalistic] theses, which were placarded in Rome, and undertook to defend them in the presence of all European scholars whom he invited to the Eternal City, promising to defray their travelling expenses.]

Let us throw a rapid retrospective glance at the history and the tribulations of that very same Zohar, as we know of them from trustworthy tradition and documents. We need not stop to discuss whether it was written in the first century B.C. , or in the first century A.D. Suffice it for us to know that there was at all times a Kabalistic literature among the Jews; that though historically it can be traced only from the time of the Captivity, yet from the Pentateuch down to the Talmud the documents of that literature were ever written in a kind of Mystery-language, were, in fact, a series of a symbolical records which the Jews had copied from the Egyptian and the Chaldaean Sanctuaries, only adapting them to their own national history - if history it can be called. Now that which we claim - and it is not denied even by the most prejudiced Kabalist, is that although Kabalistic lore had passed orally through long ages down to the latest Pre-Christian Tanaim, and although David and Solomon may have been great Adepts in it, as is claimed, yet no one dared to write it down till the days of Simeon Ben Iochai.

AUTHORSHIP OF THE ZOHAR-

In short, the lore found in Kabalistic literature was never recorded in writing before the first century of the modern era.

This brings the critic to the following reflection: While in India we find the Vedas and the Brahmanical literature written down and edited ages before the Christian era - the Orientalists themselves being obliged to concede a couple of millenniums of antiquity to the older manuscripts; while the most important allegories in Genesis are found recorded on Babylonian tiles centuries B.C.; while the Egyptian sarcophagi yearly yield proofs of the origin of the doctrines borrowed and copied by the Jews; yet the Monotheism of the Jews is exalted and thrown into the teeth of all the Pagan nations, and the so-called Christian Revelation is placed above all others, like the sun above a row of street gas lamps. Yet it is perfectly well known, having been ascertained beyond doubt or cavil, that no manuscript, whether Kabalistic, Talmudistic, or Christian, which has reached our present generation, is of earlier date than the first centuries of our era, whereas this can certainly never be said of the Egyptian papyri or the Chaldaean tiles, or even of some Eastern writings.

But let us limit our present research to the Kabalah, and chiefly to the Zohar - called also the Midrash. This book, whose teachings were edited for the first time between 70 and 110 A.D., is known to have been lost, and its contents to have been scattered throughout a number of minor manuscripts, until the thirteenth century. The idea that it was the composition of Moses de Leon of Valladolid, in Spain, who passed it off as a pseudograph of Simeon Ben Iochai, is ridiculous, and was well disposed of by Munk - though he does point to more than one modern interpolation in the Zohar. At the same time it is more than certain that the present Book of Zohar was written by Moses de Leon, and, owing to joint editorship, is more Christian in its colouring than is many a genuine Christian volume. Munk gives the reason why, saying that it appears evident that the author made use of ancient documents, and among these of certain Midraschim, or collections of traditions and Biblical expositions, which we do not now possess.

As a proof, also, that the knowledge of the Esoteric

system taught in the Zohar came to the Jews very late indeed - at any rate, that they had so far forgotten it that the innovations and additions made by de Leon provoked no criticism, but were thankfully received - Munk quotes from Tholuck, a Jewish authority, the following information: Haya Gaon, who died in 1038, is to our knowledge the first author who developed (and perfected) the theory of the Sephiroth, and he gave them names which we find again among the Kabalistic names used by Dr. Jellinek. Moses Ben Schem-Tob de Leon, who held intimate intercourse with the Syrian and Chaldaean Christian learned scribes was enabled through the latter to acquire a knowledge of some of the Gnostic writings. [This account is summarised from Isaac Myer's Qabbalah, p.10 et seq.]

Again, the Sepher Jetzirah (Book of Creation) - though attributed to Abraham and though very archaic as to its contents - is first mentioned in the eleventh century by Jehuda Ho Levi (Chazari). And these two, the Zohar and Jetzirah, are the storehouse of all the subsequent Kabalistic works. Now let us see how far the Hebrew sacred canon itself is to be trusted.

The word "Kabalah" comes from the root "to receive," and has a meaning identical with the Sanskrit "Smriti" ("received by tradition") - a system of oral teaching, passing from one generation of priests to another, as was the case with the Brahmanical books before they were embodied in manuscript. The Kabalistic tenets came to the Jews from the Chaldaeans; and if Moses knew the primitive and universal language of the Initiates, as did every Egyptian priest, and was thus acquainted with the numerical system on which it was based, he may have - and we say he has - written Genesis and other "scrolls." The five books that now pass current under his name, the Pentateuch, are not withal the original Mosaic Records. [There is not in the decalogue one idea that is not the counterpart, or the paraphrase, of the dogmas and ethics among the Egyptians long before the time of Moses and Aaron. (The Mosaic Law a transcript from the Egyptian Sources: vide Geometry in Religion, 1890)] Nor were they written in the old Hebrew square letters, nor even in the Samaritan characters, for both alphabets belong to a date later than that of Moses, and Hebrew - as it is now known - did not exist in the days of the great lawgiver, either as a language or as an alphabet.

As no statements contained in the records of the Secret Doctrine of the East are regarded as of any value by the world in general, and since to be understood by and convince the reader one has to quote names familiar to him, and use arguments and proofs out of documents which are accessible to all, the following facts may perhaps demonstrate that our assertions are not merely based on the teachings of Occult Records.

CHALDAIC AND HEBREW

(1) The great Orientalist and scholar, Klaproth, denied positively the antiquity of the so-called Hebrew alphabet, on the ground that the square Hebrew characters in which the Biblical manuscripts are written, and which we use in printing,

were probably derived from the Palmyrene writing, or some other Semitic alphabet, so that the Hebrew Bible is written merely in the Chaldaic phonographs of Hebrew words.

The late Dr. Kenealy pertinently remarked that the Jews and Christians rely on

A phonograph of a dead and almost unknown language, as abstruse as the cuneiform letters on the mountains of Assyria, [Book of God. Kenealy, p.383. The reference to Klaproth is also from this page.]

(2) The attempts made to carry back the square Hebrew character to the time of Esdras (B.C. 458) have all failed.

(3) It is asserted that the Jews took their alphabet from the Babylonians during their captivity. But there are scholars who do not carry the now-known Hebrew square letters beyond the late period of the fourth century, A.D. [See Asiat. Jour., N.S. vii., p.275, quoted by Kenealy.]

The Hebrew Bible is precisely as if Homer were printed, not in Greek, but in English letters; or as if Shakespeare's works were phonographed in Burmese. [Book of God, loc. cit.]

(4) Those who maintain that the ancient Hebrew is the same as the Syraic or Chaldaic have to see what is said in Jeremiah, wherein the Lord is made to threaten the house of Israel with bringing against it the mighty and ancient nation of the Chaldaeans:

A nation whose language thou knowest not, neither understandest what they say. [Op.cit., v.15.]

This is quoted by Bishop Walton [Prolegomena.iii, 13, quoted by Kenealy. p.385.] against the assumption of the identity of Chaldaic and Hebrew, and ought to settle the question.

(5) The real Hebrew of Moses was lost after the seventy years' captivity, when the Israelites brought back Chaldaic with them and grafted it on their own language, the fusion resulting in a dialectical variety of Chaldaic, the Hebrew tincturing it very slightly and ceasing from that time to be a spoken language.[See Book of God. p.385. Care should be taken, " says Butler (quoted by Kenealy. p489), " to distinguish between the Pentateuch in the Hebrew language but in the letters of the Samaritan alphabet, and the version of the Pentateuch in the Samaritan language. One of the most important differences between the Samaritan and the Hebrew text respects the duration of the period between the deluge and the birth of Abraham. The Samaritan text makes it longer by some centuries than the Hebrew text; and the Septuagint makes it longer by some centuries than the Samaritan." It is observable that in the authentic translation of the Latin Vulgate, the Roman Church follows the computation expressed in the Hebrew text; and in her Martyrology follows that of the Seventy, both texts being inspired, as she claims.]

As to our statement that the present Old Testament does not contain the original Books of Moses, this is proven by the facts that:

(1) The Samaritans repudiated the Jewish canonical books and their "Law of Moses." They will have neither the Psalms of David, nor the Prophets, nor the Talmud and Mishna: nothing but the real Books of Moses, and in quite a different edition. [See Rev. Joseph Wolff's Journal. p. 200.] The Books of Moses and of Joshua are disfigured out of recognition by the Talmudists, they say,

(2) The "black Jews" of Cochin, Southern India - who know nothing of the Babylonian Captivity or of the ten "lost tribes" (the latter a pure invention of the Rabbis), proving that these Jews must have come to India before the year 600 B.C. - have their Books of Moses which they will show to no one. And these Books of Laws differ greatly from the present scrolls. Nor are they written in the square Hebrew characters (semi-Chaldaic and semi-Palmyrean) but in the archaic letters, as we were assured by one of them - letters entirely unknown to all but themselves and a few Samaritans.

(3) The Karaim Jews of the Crimea - who call themselves the descendants of the true children of Israel, i.e. of the Sadducees - reject the Torah and the Pentateuch of the Synagogue, reject the Sabbath of the Jews (keeping Friday), will have neither the Books of the Prophets nor the Psalms - nothing but their own Books of Moses and what they call his one and real Law.

This makes it plain that the Kabalah of the Jews is but the distorted echo of the Secret Doctrine of the Chaldaeans, and that the real Kabalah is found only in the Chaldaean Book of Numbers now in the possession of some Persian Sufis. Every nation in antiquity had its traditions based on those of the Aryan Secret Doctrine; and each nation points to this day to a Sage of its own race who had received the primordial revelation from, and had recorded it under the orders of, a more or less divine Being. Thus it was with the Jews, as with all others. They had received their Occult Cosmogony and Laws from their Initiate, Moses, and they have now entirely mutilated them.

Adi is the generic name in our Doctrine of all the first men, i.e.., the first speaking races, in each of the seven zones - hence probably "Ad-am."

THE FIRST MEN

And such first men, in every nation, are credited with having been taught the divine mysteries of creation. Thus, the Sabaeans (according to a tradition preserved in the Sufi works) say that when the "Third First Man" left the country adjacent to India for Babel, a tree [A tree is symbolically a book - as "pillar" is another synonym of the same.] was given to him, then another and a third tree, whose leaves recorded the history of all the races; the "Third First Man" meant one who belonged to the Third Root-Race, and yet the Sabaeans call him Adam. The Arabs of Upper Egypt, and the Mohammedans generally have recorded a tradition that the Angel Azaz-el brings a message from the Wisdom-Word of God to Adam whenever he is reborn; this the Sufis explain by adding that this book is given to every Seli-Allah ("the chosen one of God") for his wise men. The story narrated by the Kabalists - namely, that the book given to Adam before his Fall (a book full of mysteries and signs and events which either had been, were, or were to be) was taken away by the Angel Raziel after Adam's Fall, but again restored to him lest men might lose its wisdom and instruction; that this book was delivered by Adam to Seth, who passed it to Enoch, and the latter to Abraham, and so on in succession to the most wise of every generation - relates to all nations, and not to the Jews alone. For Berosus narrates in his turn that Xisuthrus compiled a book, writing it at the command of his deity, which book was buried in Zipara [The wife of Moses, one of the seven daughters of a Midian priest, is called Zipora. It was Jethro, the priest of Midian, who initiated Moses, Zipora, one of the seven daughters, being simply one of the seven Occult powers that the Hierophant was and is supposed to pass to the initiated novice.] or Sippara, the City of the Sun, in Ba-bel-on-ya, and was dug up long afterwards and deposited in the temple of Belos; it is from this book that Berosus took his history of the antediluvian dynasties of Gods and Heroes. Aelian (in Nimrod) speaks of a Hawk (emblem of the Sun), who in the days of the beginnings brought to the Egyptians a book containing the wisdom of their religion. The Sam-Sam of the Sabaeans is also a Kabalah, as is the Arabic Zem-Zem (Well of Wisdom). [See for these details the Book of God, pp. 244, 250]

We are told by a very learned Kabalist that Seyffarth assets that the old Egyptian tongue was only old Hebrew, or a Semitic dialect; and he proves this, our correspondent thinks, by sending him "some 500 words in common" in the two languages. This proves very little to our mind. It only shows that the two nations lived together for centuries, and that before adopting the Chaldaean for their phonetic tongue the Jews had adopted the old Coptic or Egyptian. The Israelitish Scriptures drew their hidden wisdom from the primeval Wisdom-Religion that was the source of other Scriptures, only it was sadly degraded by being applied to things and mysteries of this Earth, instead of to those in the higher and ever-present, though invisible, spheres. Their national history, if they can claim any autonomy before their return from the Babylonian captivity, cannot be carried back one day earlier than the time of Moses. The language of Abraham - if Zeruan (Saturn, the emblem of time - the "Sar," "Saros," a "cycle") can be said to have any language - was not Hebrew, but Chaldaic, perhaps Arabic, and still more likely some old Indian dialect. This is shown by numerous proofs, some of which we give here; and unless, indeed, to please the tenacious and stubborn believers in Bible chronology, we cripple the years of our globe to the Procrustean bed of 7,000 years, it becomes self-evident that the Hebrew cannot be called an old language, merely because Adam is supposed to have used it in the Garden of Eden. Bunsen says in Egypt's Place in Universal History that in the

Chaldean tribe immediately connected with Abraham, we find reminiscences of dates disfigured and misunderstood as genealogies of single men, or figures of epochs. The Abrahamic recollections go back at least three millennia beyond the grandfather of Jacob [Op. cit. V. 85.]

The Bible of the Jews has ever been an Esoteric Book in its hidden meaning, but this meaning has not remained one and the same throughout since the days of Moses. It is useless, considering the limited space we can give to this subject, to attempt anything like the detailed history of the vicissitudes of the so-called Pentateuch, and besides, the history is too well known to need lengthy disquisitions. Whatever was, or was not, the Mosaic Book of Creation - from Genesis down to the Prophets - the Pentateuch of today is not the same. It is sufficient to read the criticisms of Erasmus, and even of Sir Isaac Newton, to see clearly that the Hebrew Scriptures had been tampered with and re-modelled, had been lost and rewritten, a dozen times before the days of Ezra. This Ezra himself may yet one day turn out to have been Azara; the Chaldaean priest of the Fire and Sun-God, a renegade who through his desire of becoming a ruler, and in order to create an Ethnarchy, restored that old lost Jewish Books in his own way.

MANY EVENTS NOT HISTORICAL-

It was an easy thing for one versed in the secret system of Esoteric numerals, or Symbology, to put together events from the stray books that had been preserved by various tribes, and make of them an apparently harmonious narrative of creation and of the evolution of the Judaean race. But in its hidden meaning, from Genesis to the last word of Deuteronomy, the Pentateuch is the symbolical narrative of the sexes, and is an apotheosos of Phallicism, under astronomical and physiological personations. [As is fully shown in the Source of Measures and other works.] Its co-ordination, however, is only apparent; and the human hand appears at every moment, is found everywhere in the "Book of God." Hence the Kings of Edom discuss in Genesis before any king had reigned in Israel; Moses records his own death, and Aaron dies twice and is buried in two different places, to say nothing of other trifles. For the Kabalist they are trifles, for he knows that all these events are not history, but are simply the cloak designed to envelope and hide various physiological peculiarities; but for the sincere Christian, who accepts all these "dark sayings" in good faith, it matters a good deal. Solomon may very well be regarded as a myth [Surely even Masons would never claim the actual existence of Solomon? As Kenealy shows, he is not noticed by Herodotus, nor by Plato, nor by any writer of standing. It is most extraordinary, he says, "that the Jewish nation, over whom but a few years before the mighty Solomon had reigned in all his glory, with a magnificence scarcely equalled by the greatest monarchs, spending nearly eight thousand millions of gold on a temple, was overlooked by the historian Herodotus, writing of Egypt on the one hand, and of Babylon on the other - visiting both places, and of course passing almost necessarily within a few miles of the splendid capital of the national Jerusalem? How can this be accounted for? " he asks (p.457). Nay, not only are there no proofs of the twelve tribes of Israel having ever existed, but Herodotus, the most accurate of historians, who was in Assyria when Ezra flourished, never mentions the Israelites at all: and Herodotus was born in 484 B.C. How is this?] by the Masons, as they lose nothing by it, for all their secrets are Kabalistic and allegorical - for those few, at any rate, who understand them. For the Christian, however, to give up Solomon, the son of David - from whom Jesus is made to descend - involves a real loss. But how even the Kabalists can claim great antiquity for the Hebrew texts of the old Biblical scrolls now possessed by the scholars is not made at all apparent. For it is certainly a fact of history, based on the confessions of the Jews themselves, and of Christians likewise, that:

The Scriptures having perished in the captivity of Nabuchodonozar, Esdras, the Levite, the priest, in the times of Artaxerxes, king of the Persians, having become inspired, in the exercise of prophecy restored again the whole of the ancient Scriptures. [Clement, Stromateis. XXII.]

One must have a strong belief in "Esdras," and especially in his good faith, to accept the now-existing copies as genuine Mosaic Books; for:

Assuming that the copies, or rather phonographs which had been made by Hilkiah and Esdras, and the various anonymous editors, were really true and genuine, they must have been wholly exterminated by Antiochus; and the versions of the Old Testament which now subsist must have been made by Judas, or by some unknown compilers, probably from the Greek of the Seventy, long after the appearance and death of Jesus. [Book of God. p.408.]

The Bible, therefore, as it is now (the Hebrew texts, that is), depends for its accuracy on the genuineness of the Septuagint; this, we are again told, was written miraculously by the Seventy, in Greek, and the original copy having been lost since that time, our texts are retranslated back into Hebrew from that language. But in this vicious circle of proofs we once more have to rely upon the good faith of two Jews - Josephus and Philo Judaeus of Alexandria - these two Historians being the only witnesses that the Septuagint was written under the circumstances narrated. And yet it is just these circumstances that are very little calculated to inspire one with confidence. For what does Josephus tell us? He says that Ptolemy Philadelphus, desiring to read the Hebrew Law in Greek, wrote to Eleazar, the high-priest of the Jews, begging him to send him six men from each of the twelve tribes, who should make a translation for him. Then follows a truly miraculous story, vouchsafed by Aristeas, of these seventy-two men from the twelve tribes of Israel, who, shut up in an island, compiled their translation in exactly seventy-two days, etc.

All this is very edifying, and one might have had very little reason to doubt the story, had not the "ten lost tribes" been made to play their part in it. How could these tribes, lost between 700 and 900 B.C., each send six men some centuries later, to satisfy the whim of Ptolemy, and to disappear once more immediately afterwards from the horizon? A miracle, verily.

We are expected, nevertheless, to regard such documents as the Septuagint as containing direct divine revelation: Documents originally written in a tongue about which nobody now knows anything; written by authors that are practically mythical, and at dates as to which no one is able even to make a defensible surmise; documents of the original copies of which there does not now remain a shred.

THE REAL HEBREW CHARACTERS LOST −

Yet people will persist in talking of the ancient Hebrew, as if there were any man left in the world who knows one word of it. So little, indeed was Hebrew known that both the Septuagint and the New Testament had to be written in a heathen language (the Greek), and no better reasons for it given than what Hutchinson says, namely, that the Holy Ghost chose to write the New Testament in Greek.

The Hebrew language is considered to be very old, and yet there exists no trace of it anywhere on the old monuments, not even in Chaldaea. Among the great number of inscriptions of various kinds found in the ruins of that country:

One in the Hebrew Chaldee letter and language has never been found; nor has a single authentic medal or gem in this newfangled character been ever discovered, which could carry it even to the days of Jesus. [Book of God. p.453.]

The original Book of Daniel is written in a dialect which is a mixture of Hebrew and Aramaic; it is not even in Chaldaic, with the exception of a few verses interpolated later on. According to Sir. W. Jones and other Orientalists, the oldest discoverable languages of Persia are the Chaldaic and Sanskrit, and there is no trace of the "Hebrew" in these. It would be very surprising if there were, since the Hebrew known to the Philologists does not date earlier than 500 B.C., and its characters belong to a far later period still. Thus, while the real Hebrew characters, if not altogether lost are nevertheless so hopelessly transformed -

A mere inspection of the alphabet showing that it has been shaped and made regular, in doing which the characteristic marks of some of the letters have been retrenched in order to make them more square and uniform - [Asiatic Journal, VII., p.275, quoted by Kenealy.]

That no one but an initiated Rabbi of Samaria or a "Jain" could read them, the new system of the masoretic points has made them a sphinx-riddle for all. Punctuation is now to be found everywhere in all the later manuscripts, and by means of it anything can be made of a text; a Hebrew scholar can put on the texts any interpretation he likes. Two instances given by Kenealy will suffice:

In Genesis,x1ix. 21, we read:

Naphtali is a hind let loose; he giveth goodly words.

By only a slight alternation of the points Bochart changes this into:

Napthali is a spreading tree, shooting forth beautiful branches.

So again, in Psalms (xxix.9), instead of:
The voice of the Lord maketh the hind to calve, and discovereth the forests;
Bishop Lowth gives:

The voice of the Lord striketh the oak, and discovereth the forests.

The same word in Hebrew signifies "God" and "nothing," etc. [Book of God. p.385.]

With regard to the claim made by some Kabalists that there was in antiquity one knowledge and one language, this claim is also our own, and it is very just. Only it must be added, to make the thing clear, that this knowledge and language have both been esoteric every since the submersion of the Atlanteans. The Tower of Babel myth relates to that enforced secrecy. Men falling into sin were regarded as no longer trustworthy for the reception of such knowledge, and, from being universal, it became limited to the few. Thus, the "one-lip" - or the Mystery-language - being gradually denied to subsequent generations, all the nations became severally restricted to their own national tongue; and forgetting the primeval Wisdom-language, they stated that the Lord - one of the chief Lords or Hierophants of the Mysteries of the Java Aleim - had confounded the languages of all the earth, so that the sinners could understand one another's speech no longer. But Initiates remained in every land and nation, and the Israelites, like all others, had their learned Adepts. One of the keys to this Universal Knowledge is a pure geometrical and numerical system, the alphabet of every great nation having a numerical value for every letter, [Speaking of the hidden meaning of the Sanskrit words, Mr. T. Subba Row, in his able article on "The Twelve Signs of the Zodiac." gives some advice as to the way in which one should proceed to find out "the deep significance of ancient Sanskrit nomenclature in the old Aryan myths. 1. Find out the synonyms of the word used which have other meanings. 2. Find out the numerical value of the letters composing of the word according to the methods of the ancient Tântrik works [Tântrika Shastra - works on Incantation and Magic]. 3. Examine the ancient myths or allegories if there are any, which have any special connection with the word in question. 4. Permute the different syllables composing the word and examine the new combinations that will thus be formed and their meanings." etc. But he does not give the principal rule. And no doubt he is quite right. The Tântrika Shâstras are as old as Magic itself. Have they also borrowed their Esotericism from the Hebrews?] and, moreover, a system of permutation of syllables and synonyms which is carried to perfection in the Indian Occult methods, and which the Hebrew certainly has not. This one system, containing the elements of Geometry and Numeration, was used by the Jews for the purpose of concealing their Esoteric creed under the mask of a popular and national monotheistic Religion. The last who knew the system to perfection were the learned and "atheistical" Sadducees, the greatest enemies of the pretensions of the Pharisees and of their confused notions brought from Babylon.

HEBREW ESOTERICISM NOT PRIMITIVE-

Yes, the Sadducees, the Illusionists, who maintained that the Soul, the Angels, and all similar Beings, were illusions because they were temporary - thus showing themselves at one with Eastern Esotericism. And since they rejected every book and Scripture, with the exception of the Law of Moses, it seems that the latter must have been very different from what it is now. [Their founder, Sadoc, was the pupil, through Antigonus Saccho, of Simon the Just. They had their own secret Book of the Law ever since the foundation of their sect (about 400 B.C.) and this volume was unknown to the masses. At the same time of the Separation the Samaritans recognized only the Book of the Law of Moses and the Book of Joshua, and their Pentateuch is far older, and is different from the Septuagint. In 168 B.C. Jerusalem had its temple plundered, and its Sacred Books - namely, the Bible made up by Ezra and finished by Judas Maccabeus - were lost (see Burder's Josephus, vol. ii. pp. 331-335): after which the Massorah completed the work of destruction (even of Ezra's once-more adjusted Bible) begun by the change into square from horned letters. Therefore the later Pentateuch accepted by the Pharisees was rejected and laughed at by the Sadducees. They are generally called atheists; yet, since those learned men, who made no secret of their freethought, furnished from among their number the most eminent of the Jewish high-priests, this seems impossible. How could the Pharisees and the other two believing and pious sects allow notorious atheists to be selected for such posts? The answer is difficult to find for bigotry and for believers in a personal, anthropomorphic God but very easy for those who accept facts. The Sadducees were called atheists because they believed as the initiated Moses believed, thus differing very widely from the latter made-up Jewish legislator and hero of Mount Sinai.]

The whole of the foregoing is written with an eye to our Kabalists. Great scholars as some of them undoubtedly are, they are nevertheless wrong to hang the harps of their faith on the willows of Talmudic growth - on the Hebrew scrolls, whether in square or pointed characters, now in our public libraries, museums, or even in the collections of

Paleographers. There do not remain half-a-dozen copies from the true Mosaic Hebrew scrolls in the whole world. And those who are in possession of these - as we indicated a few pages back - would not part with them, or even allow them to be examined, on any consideration whatever. How then can any Kabalist claim priority for Hebrew Esotericism, and say, as does one of our correspondents, that "the Hebrew has come down from a far remoter antiquity than any of them [whether Egyptian or even Sanskrit!], and that it was the source, or nearer to the old original source, than any of them"? [The measurements of the Great Pyramid being those of the temple of Solomon, of the Ark of the Covenant, etc., according to Piazzi Smythe and the author of the Source of Measures, and the Pyramid of Gizeh being shown on astronomical calculations to have been built 4950 B.C., and Moses having written his books - for the sake of argument - not even half that time before our era, how can this be? Surely if any one borrowed from the other, it is not the Pharaohs from Moses. Even philology shows not only the Egyptian, but even the Mongolian, older than the Hebrew.]

As our correspondent says: "It becomes more convincing to me every day that in a far past time there was a mighty civilization with enormous learning, which had a common language over the earth, as to which its essence can be recovered from the fragments which now exist."

Aye, there existed indeed a mighty civilization, and a still mightier secret learning and knowledge, the entire scope of which can never be discovered by Geometry and the Kabalah alone: for there are seven keys to the large entrance-door, and not one, nor even two, keys can ever open it sufficiently to allow more than glimpses of what lies within.

Every scholar must be aware that there are two distinct styles - two schools, so to speak - plainly traceable in the Hebrew Scriptures: the Elohistic and the Jehovistic. The portions belonging to these respectively are so blended together, so completely mixed up by later hands, that often all external characteristics are lost. Yet it is also known that the two schools were antagonistic; that the one taught esoteric, the other exoteric, or theological doctrines; that the one, the Elohists, were Seers (Roch), whereas the other, the Jehovists, were prophets (Nabhi) [This alone shows how the Books of Moses were tampered with. In Samuel (ix.9), it is said: "He that is now a prophet [Nabhi] was beforetime called a Seer [Roch]." Now since before Samuel, the word "Roch" is met nowhere in the Pentateuch, but its place is always taken by that of "Nabhi," this proves clearly that the Mosaic text has been replaced by that of the later Levites. (See for fuller details Jewish Antiquities, by the Rev. D. Jennings. D.D.)] and that the latter - who later became Rabbis - were generally only nominally prophets by virtue of their official position, as the Pope is called the infallible and inspired vicegerent of God. That, again, the Elohists meant by "Elohim" "forces," identifying their Deity, as in the Secret Doctrine, with Nature; while the Jehovists made of Jehovah a personal God externally, and used the term simply as a phallic symbol - a number of them secretly disbelieving even in metaphysical, abstract Nature, and synthesizing all on the terrestrial scale. Finally, the Elohists made of man the divine incarnate image of the Elohim, emanated first in all Creation; and the Jehovists show him as the last, the crowning glory of the animal creation, instead of his being the head of all the sensible beings on earth. (This is reversed by some Kabalists, but the reversion is due to the designedly-produced confusion in the texts, especially in the first four chapters of Genesis.)

Take the Zohar and find in it the description relating to Ain-Suph, the Western or Semitic Parabrahman. What passages have come so nearly up to the Vedantic ideal as the following:

The creation [the evolved Universe] is the garment of that which has no name, the garment woven from the Deity's own substance. [Zohar. i.2a.]

The Concealed of all the Concealed-   Between that which is Ain or "nothing," and the Heavenly Man, there is an Impersonal First Cause, however, of which it is said:

Before It gave any shape to this world, before It produced any form, It was alone, without form or similitude to anything else. Who, can comprehend It, how It was before the creation, since It was formless? Hence it is forbidden to represent It by any form, similitude, or even by Its sacred name, by a single letter or a single point. [Zohar, 42b.]

The sentence that follows, however, is an evident later interpolation; for it draws attention to a complete contradiction:

And to this the words (Deut. iv. 15), refer - "Ye saw no manner of similitude on the day the Lord spake unto you."

But this reference to Chapter iv. of Deuteronomy, when in Chapter v, God is mentioned as speaking "face to face" with the people, is very clumsy.

Not one of the names given to Jehovah in the Bible has any reference whatever to either Ain-Suph or the Impersonal First-Cause (which is the Logos) of the Kabalâh; but they all refer to the Emanations.

It says;

For although to reveal itself to us, the concealed of all the concealed sent forth the Ten Emanations [Sephiroth] called the Form of God, Form of the Heavenly Man, yet since even this luminous form was too dazzling for our vision, it had to assume another form, or had to put on another garment, which is the Universe. The Universe, therefore, or the visible world, is a farther expansion of the Divine Substance, and is called in the Kabalah "The Garment of God." [Zohar, i.2a. See Dr. Ch. Ginsburg's essay on The Cabbalah, its Doctrines, Developments and Literature.]

This is the doctrine of all the Hindu Puranas, especially that of the Vishnu Purâna. Vishnu pervades the Universe and is that Universe; Brahmâ enters the Mundane Egg, and issues from it as the Universe; Brahmâ even dies with it and there remains only Brahman , the impersonal, the eternal, the unborn, and the unqualifiable. The Ain-Suph of the Chaldeans and later of the Jews is assuredly a copy of the Vaidic Deity; while the "Heavenly Adam," the Macrocosm which unites in itself the totality of beings and is the Esse of the visible Universe, finds his original in the Puranic Brahmâ. In Sod,"the Secret of the Law," one recognizes the expressions used in the oldest fragments of the Gupta Vidyâ, the Secret Knowledge. And it is not venturing too much to say that even a Rabbi quite familiar with his own special Rabbinical Hebrew would only comprehend its secrets thoroughly if he added to his learning a serious knowledge of the Hindu philosophies. Let us turn to Stanza I. of the Book of Dzyan for an example.

The Zohar premises, as does the Secret Doctrine, a universal, eternal Essence, passive - because absolute - in all that men call attributes. The pregenetic or pre-cosmical Triad is a pure metaphysical abstraction. The notion of a triple hypostasis in one Unknown Divine Essence is as old as speech and thought. Hiranyagarbha, Hari, and Shankara - the Creator, the Preserver, and the Destroyer - are the three manifested attributes of it, appearing and disappearing with Kosmos; the visible Triangle, so to speak, on the plane of the ever-invisible Circle. This is the primeval root-thought of thinking Humanity; the Pythagorean Triangle emanation from the ever-concealed Monad, or the Central Point.

Plato speaks of it and Plotinus calls it an ancient doctrine, on which Cudworth remarks that:

Since Orpheus, Pythagoras, and Plato, who all of them asserted a Trinity of divine hypostases, unquestionably derived their doctrine from the Egyptians, it may be reasonably suspected that the Egyptians did the like before them. [Cudworth, I. iii. quoted by Wilson. Vishnu Purana, i. 14, note.]

The Egyptians certainly derived their Trinity from the Indians. Wilson justly observes:

As, however, the Grecian accounts and those of the Egyptians are much more perplexed and unsatisfactory than those of the Hindus, it is most probable that we find amongst them the doctrine in its most original, as well as most methodical and significant form. [Vishnu Purana. I, 14]

This, then, is the meaning:

"Darkness alone filled the Boundless All, for Father, Mother and Son were once more One." [Stanza i. 4.]

Space was, and is ever, as it is between the Manvantara. The Universe in its pre-kosmic state was once more homogeneous and one - outside its aspects. This was a Kabalistic, and is now a Christian teaching.

As is constantly shown in the Zohar, the Infinite Unity, or Ain-Suph, is ever placed outside human thought and appreciation; and in Sepher Jetzirah we see the Spirit of God - the Logos, not the Deity itself -

One is the Spirit of the Living God . . Who liveth forever. Voice, Spirit, [of the spirit], and Word: this is the Holy Spirit, [Mishna, i. 9.]

Three-in-one and Four –

and the Quaternary. From this Cube emanates the whole Kosmos.

Says the Secret Doctrine:

"It is called to life. The mystic Cube in which rests the Creative Idea, the manifesting Mantra [or articulate speech - Vâch] and the holy Pûrusha [both radiations of prima material] exist in the Eternity in the Divine Substance in their latent state.

- during Pralaya.

And in the Sepher Jetzirah, when the Three-in-One are

to be called into being - by the manifestation of Shekinah, the first effulgency or radiation in the manifesting Kosmos - the "Spirit of God," or Number One, [In its manifested state it becomes Ten, the Universe. In the Chaldaean Kabalah it is sexless. In the Jewish, Shekinah is female, and the early Christians and Gnostics regarded the Holy Ghost, as a female potency. In the Book of Numbers "Shekina" is made to drop the final "h" that makes it a female potency. Nârâyana, the Mover on the Waters, is also sexless: but it is our firm belief that Shekinah and Daiviprakriti, the "Light of the Logos," are one and the same thing philosophically.] fructifies and awakens the dual Potency, Number Two, Air, and Number Three, Water; in these "are darkness and emptiness, slime and dung" - which is Chaos, the Tohu-Vah-Bohu. The Air and Water emanate Number Four, Ether or Fire, the Son. This is the Kabalistic Quaternary. This Fourth Number, which in the manifested Kosmos is the One, or the Creative God, is with the Hindus the "Ancient," Sanat, the Prajâpati of the Vedas and the Brahmâ of the Brâhmans - the heavenly Androgyne, as he becomes the male only after separating himself into two bodies, Vâch and Virâj. With the Kabalists, he is at first the Jah-Havah, only later becoming Jehovah, like Virâj, his prototype; after separating himself as Adam-Kadmon into Adam and Eve in the formless, and into Cain-Abel in the semi-objective world, he became finally the Jah-Havah, or man and woman, in Enoch, the son of Seth.

For, the true meaning of the compound name of Jehovah - of which, unvoweled, you can make almost anything - is: men and women, or humanity composed of its two sexes. From the first chapter to the end of the fourth chapter of Genesis every name is a permutation of another name, and every personage is at the same time somebody else. A Kabalist traces Jehovah from the Adam of earth to Seth, the third son - or rather race - of Adam. [The Elohim create the Adam of dust, and in him Jehovah-Binah separates himself into Eve, after which the male portion of God becomes the Serpent, tempts himself in Eve, then creates himself in her as Cain, passes into Seth, and scatters from Enoch, the Son of Man, or Humanity, as Jodheva.] Thus Seth is Jehovah male; and Enos, being a permutation of Cain and Abel, is Jehovah male and female, or our mankind. The Hindu Brahmâ-Virâj, Virâj-Manu, and Manu-Vaivasvata, with his daughter and wife, Vâch, present the greatest analogy with these personages - for anyone who will take the trouble of studying the subject in both the Bible and the Purânas. It is said of Brahma that he created himself as Manu, and that he was born of, and was identical with, his original self, while he constituted the female portion Shâta-rupa" (hundred-formed) In this Hindu Eve, "the mother of all living beings," Brahmâ created Virâj, who is himself, but on a lower scale, as Cain is Jehovah on an inferior scale: both are the first males of the Third Race. The same idea is illustrated in the Hebrew name of God (הוה) Read from right to left "Jod" (י) is the father. "He" (ה) the mother, "Vau" (ו) the son, and "He" (ה), repeated at the end of the word, is generation, the act of birth, materiality. This is surely a sufficient reason why the God of the Jews and Christians should be personal, as much as the male

Brahma, Vishnu, or Shiva of the orthodox, exoteric Hindu.

Thus the term of Jhvh alone - now accepted as the name of "One living [male] God" - will yield, if seriously studied, not only the whole mystery of Being (in the Biblical sense,) but also that of the Occult Theogony, from the highest divine Being, the third in order, down to man. As shown by the best Hebraists:

The verbal ו ו ו ו or Hâyâh, or E-y-e, means to be, to exist, while ו ו ו ו or Chayah or H-y-e, means to live, as motion of existence.[The Source of Measures. p.5]

Hence Eve stands as the evolution and the never-ceasing "becoming" of Nature. Now if we take the almost untranslatable Sanskrit word Sat, which means the quintessence of absolute immutable Being, or Be-ness - as it has been rendered by an able Hindu Occultist - we shall find no equivalent for it in any language; but it may be regarded as most closely resembling "Ain," or "En-Suph," Boundless Being. Then the term Hâyâh, "to be," as passive, changeless, yet manifested existence may perhaps be rendered by the Sanskrit Jivatma, universal life or soul, in its secondary or cosmic meaning; while "Châyâh," "to live," as "motion of existence," is simply Prâna, the ever-changing life in its objective sense. It is at the head of this third category that the Occultist finds Jehovah - the Mother, Binah, and the Father, Arelim.

THE SEPTENARY SEPHIRA-

This is made plain in the Zohar, when the emanation and evolution of the Sephiroth are explained: First, Ain-Suph, then

Shekinah, the Garment or Veil of Infinite Light, then Sephira or the Kadmon, and, thus making the fourth, the spiritual Substance sent forth from the Infinite Light. This Sephira is called the Crown, Kether, and has besides, six other names - in all seven. These names are: 1. Kether; 2. the Aged; 3. the Primordial Point; 4. the White Head; 5. the Long Face; 6. the Inscrutable Height; and 7. Ehejeh ("I am".) [This identifies Sephira, the third potency, with Jehovah the Lord, who says to Moses out of the burning bush: "(Here) I am." (Exodus, iii.4). At this time the "Lord" has not yet become Jehovah. It was not the one male God who spoke, but the Elohim manifested, or the Sephiroth in their manifested collectivity of seven, contained in the triple Sephira.] This Septenary Sephira is said to contain in itself the nine Sephiroth. But before showing how she brought them forth, let us read an explanation about the Sephiroth in the Talmud, which gives it as an archaic tradition, or Kabalah.

There are three groups (or orders) of Sephiroth: 1. The Sephiroth called "divine attributes" (the Triad in the Holy Quaternary); 2. the sidereal (personal) Sephiroth; 3. the metaphysical Sephiroth, or a periphrasis of Jehovah, who are the first three Sephiroth (Kether, Chokmah and Binah), the rest of the seven being the personal "Seven Spirits of the Presence" (also of the planets, therefore). Speaking of these, the angels are meant, though not because they are seven, but because they represent the seven Sephiroth which contain in them the universality of the Angels.

This shows (a) that, when the first four Sephiroth are separated, as a Triad-Quaternary - Sephira being its synthesis - there remain only seven Sephiroth, as there are seven Rishis; these become ten when the Quaternary, or the first divine Cube, is scattered into units; and (b) that while Jehovah might have been viewed as the Deity, if he be included in the three divine groups or orders of the Sephiroth, the collective Elohim, or the quaternary indivisible Kether, once that he becomes a male God, he is not more than one of the Builders of the lower group - a Jewish Brahmâ. [The Brahmans were wise in their generation when they gradually, for no other reason than this, abandoned Brahmâ, and paid less attention to him individually than to any other deity. As an abstract synthesis they worshipped him collectively and in every God, each of which represents him. As Brâhma, the male, he is far lower than Shiva, the Lingam, who personates universal generation, or Vishnu, the preserver - both Shiva and Vishnu being the regenerators of life after destruction. The Christians might do worse than follow their example, and worship God in Spirit, and not in the male Creator.] A demonstration is now attempted.

The first Sephira, containing the other nine, brought them forth in this order: (2) Hokmah (Chokmah, or Wisdom), a masculine active potency represented among the divine names as Jah; and, as a permutation or an evolution into lower forms in this instance - becoming the Auphanim (or the Wheels - cosmic rotation of matter) among the army, or the angelic hosts. From this Chokmah emanated a feminine passive potency called (3) Intelligence, Binah, whose divine name is Jehovah, and whose angelic name, among the Builders and Hosts, is Arelim. [A plural word, signifying a collective host generically: literally, the "strong lion."] It is from the union of these two potencies, male and female (or Chokmah and Binah) that emanated all the other Sephiroth, the seven orders of the Builders. Now if we call Jehovah by his divine name, then he becomes at best and forthwith "a female passive" potency in Chaos. And if we view him as a male God, he is no more than one of many, an Angel, Arelim. But straining the analysis to its highest point, and if his male name Jah, that of Wisdom, be allowed to him, still he is not the "Highest and the one Living God;" for he is contained with many others within Sephira, and Sephira herself is a third Potency in Occultism, though regarded as the first in the exoteric Kabalah - and is one, moreover, of lesser importance than the Vaidic Aditi, or the Primordial Water of Space, which becomes after many a permutation of the Astral Light of the Kabalist.

Thus the Kabalah, as we have it now, is shown to be of the greatest importance in explaining the allegories and "dark sayings" of the Bible. As an Esoteric work upon the mysteries of creation, however, it is almost worthless as it is now disfigured, unless checked by the Chaldaean Book of Numbers or by the tenets of the Easter Secret Science, or Esoteric Wisdom. The Western nations have neither the original Kabalah, nor yet the Mosaic Bible.

Finally, it is demonstrated by internal as well as by external evidence, on the testimony of the best European Hebraists, and the confessions of the learned Jewish Rabbis themselves, that "an ancient document forms the essential basis of the Bible, which received very considerable insertions and supplements;" and that "the Pentateuch arose out of the primitive or older document by means of a supplementary one." Therefore in the absence of the Book of Numbers,, [The writer possesses only a few extracts, some dozen pages in all, verbatim quotations from that priceless work, of which but two or three copies, perhaps, are still extant.] the Kabalists of the West are only entitled to come to definite conclusions, when they have at hand some data at least from that "ancient document" - data now found scattered throughout Egyptian papyri, Assyrian tiles, and the traditions preserved by the descendants of the disciples of the last Nazars. Instead of that, most of them accept as their authorities and infallible guides Fabre d'Olivet - who was a man of immense erudition and of speculative mind, but neither a Kabalist nor an Occultist, either Western or Eastern - and the Mason Ragon, the greatest of the "Widow's sons," who was even less of an Orientalist than d'Olivet, for Sanskrit learning was almost unknown in the days of both these eminent scholars.

SECTION XXI

HEBREW ALLEGORIES

How can any Kabalist, acquainted with the foregoing, deduce his conclusions with regard to the true Esoteric beliefs of the primitive Jews, from only that which he now finds in the Jewish scrolls? How can any scholar - even though one of the keys to the universal language be now positively discovered, the true key to the numerical reading of a pure geometrical system - give out anything as his final conclusion? Modern Kabalistic speculation is on a par now with modern "speculative Masonry;" for as the latter tries vainly to link itself with the ancient - or rather the archaic - Masonry;" of the Temples, failing to make the link because all its claims have been shown to be inaccurate from an archaeological standpoint, so fares it also with Kabalistic speculation. As no mystery of Nature worth running after can be revealed to humanity by settling whether Hiram Abif was a living Sidonian Builder, or a solar myth, so no fresh information will be added to Occult Lore by the details of the exoteric privileges conferred on the Collegia Fabrorum by Numa Pompilius. Rather must the symbols used in it be studies in the Aryan light, since all the Symbolism of the ancient Initiations came to the West with the light of the Eastern Sun. Nevertheless, we find the most learned Masons and Symboligists declaring that all these weird symbols and glyphs, that run back to a common origin of immense antiquity, were nothing more than a display of cunning natural phallicism, or emblems of primitive typology. How much nearer the truth is the author of The Source of Measures, who declares that the elements of human and numerical construction in the Bible do not shut out the spiritual elements in it, albeit so few now understand them. The words we quote are as suggestive as they are true:

How desperately blinding becomes a superstitious use, through ignorance, of such emblems when they are made to possess the power of bloodshed and torture, through orders of propaganda of any species of religious cultus.

THE HEBREW BIBLE DOES NOT EXIST

When one thinks of the horrors of a Moloch, or Baal, or Dagon worship; of the correlated blood deluges under the Cross baptized in gore by Constantine, at the initiative of he secular Church; . . . when one thinks of all this and then that the cause of all has been simply ignorance of the real radical reading of the Moloch, and Baal, and Dagon, and the Cross and the Tphillin, all running back to a common origin, and after all being nothing more than a display of pure and natural mathematics, . . . one is apt to feel like cursing ignorance, and to lose confidence in what are called intuitions of religion; one is apt to wish for a return of the day when all the world was of one lip and of one knowledge . . .. But while these elements [of the construction of the pyramid] are rational and scientific, ... let no man consider that with this discovery comes a cutting off of the spirituality [Aye: but that spirituality can never be discovered, far less proved, unless we turn to the Aryan Scriptures and Symbology. For the Jews it was lost, save for the Sadducees, from the day that the "chosen people" reached the Promised Land, the national Karma preventing Moses from reaching it.] of the Bible intention, or of man's relation to this spiritual foundation. Does one wish to build a house? No house was ever actually built with tangible material until first the architectural design of building had been accomplished, no matter whether the structure was palace or hovel. So with these elements and numbers. They are not of man, nor are they of his invention. They have been revealed to him to the extent of his ability to realize a system, which is the creative system of the eternal God. . . . But spiritually, to man the value of this matter is that he can actually in contemplation, bridge over all material construction of the cosmos, and pass into the very thought and mind of God, to the extent of recognizing this system of design for cosmic creation - yea, even before the words went forth: " Let there be." [Op.cit., pp. 317-319]

But true as above words may be, when coming from one who has rediscovered, more completely than anyone else has done during the past centuries, one of the keys to the universal Mystery Language, it is impossible for an Eastern Occultist to agree with the conclusion of the able author of The Source of Measures. He "has set out to find the truth," and yet he still believes that:

The best and most authentic vehicle of communication from [the creative] God to man . . . is to be found in the Hebrew Bible.

To this we must and shall demur, giving our reasons for

it in a few words. The "Hebrew Bible" exists no more, as has been shown in the foregoing pages, and the garbled accounts, the falsified and pale copies we have of the real Mosaic Bible of the Initiates, warrant the making of no such sweeping assertion and claim. All that the scholar can fairly claim is that the Jewish Bible, as now extant - in its latest and final interpretation, and according to the newly-discovered key - may give a partial presentment of the truths it contained before it was mangled. But how can he tell what the Pentateuch contained before it has been recomposed by Esdras; then corrupted still more by the ambitious Rabbis in later times, and otherwise remodelled and interfered with? Leaving aside the opinion of the declared enemies of the Jewish Scripture, one may quote simply what their most devoted followers say.

Two of these are Horne and Prideaux. The avowels of the former will be sufficient to show how much now remains of the original Mosaic books, unless indeed we accept his sublimely blind faith in the inspiration and editorship of the Holy Ghost. He writes that when a Hebrew scribe found a writing of any author he was entitled, if he thought fit, being "conscious of the aid of the Holy Spirit," to do exactly as he pleased with it - to cut it up, or copy it, or use as much of it as he deemed right, and so to incorporate it with his own manuscript. Dr. Kenealy aptly remarks of Horne, that it is almost impossible to get any admission from him.

That makes against his church, so remarkably guarded is he [Horne] in his phraseology and so wonderfully discreet in the use of words that his language, like a diplomatic letter, perpetually suggests to the mind ideas other than those which he really means; I defy any unlearned person to read his chapter on "Hebrew characters" and to derive any knowledge from it whatever on the subject on which he professes to treat. [The Book of God. pp. 388, 389]

And yet this same Horne writes:

We are persuaded that the things to which reference is made proceeded from the original writers or compilers of the books [Old Testament]. Sometimes they took other writings, annals, genealogies, and such like, with which they incorporated additional matter, or which they put together with greater or less condensation. The Old Testament authors used the sources they employed (that is, the writing of other people) with freedom and independence. Conscious of the aid of the Divine Spirit, they adapted their own productions, or the productions of others, to the wants of the times. But in these respects they cannot be said to have corrupted the text of Scriptures. They made the text.

But of what did they make it? Why, of the writings of other persons, justly observes Kenealy:

And this is Horne's notion of what the Old Testament is - a cento from the writings of unknown persons collected and put together by those who, he says, were divinely inspired. No infidel that I know of has ever made so damaging a charge as this against the authenticity of the Old Testament. [See Horne's Introduction (10th edition), vol. ii. p.33. as quoted by Dr. Kenealy. p.389.]

SOME HEBREWS WERE INITIATES-

This is quite sufficient, we think, to show that no key to the universal language-system can ever open the mysteries of Creation in a work in which, whether through design or carelessness, nearly every sentence has been made to apply to the latest outcome of religious views - to Phallicism, and to nothing else. There are a sufficient number of stray bits in the Elohistic portions of the Bible to warrant the inference that the Hebrews who wrote it were Initiates; hence the mathematical coordinations and the perfect harmony between the measures of the Great Pyramid and the numerals of the Biblical glyphs. But surely if one borrowed from the other, it cannot be the architects of the Pyramid who borrowed from Solomon's Temple, if only because the former exists to this day as a stupendous living monument of Esoteric records, while the famous temple has never existed outside of the far later Hebrew scrolls. [The author says that Parker's quadrature is "that identical measure which was used anciently as the perfect measure, by the Egyptians, in the construction of the Great Pyramid, which was built to monument it and its uses." and that "from it the sacred cubit-value was derived, which was the cubit-value used in the construction of the Temple of Solomon, the Ark of Noah, and the Ark of the Covenant" (p.22). This is a grand discovery, no doubt, but it only shows that the Jews profited well by their captivity in Egypt, and that Moses was a great Initiate.] Hence there is a great distance between the admission that some Hebrew Bible must be the best standard, as being the highest representative of the archaic Esoteric System.

Nowhere does the Bible say, moreover, that the Hebrew is the language of God; of this boast, at any rate, the authors are not guilty. Perhaps because in the days when the Bible was last edited the claim would have been too preposterous - hence dangerous. The compilers of the Old Testament, as it exists in the Hebrew canon, knew well that the language of the Initiates in the days of Moses was identical with that of the Egyptian Hierophants; and that none of the dialects that had sprung from the old Syriac and the pure old Arabic of Yarab - the father and progenitor of the primitive Arabians, long before the time of Abraham, in whose days the ancient Arabic had already become vitiated - that none of those languages was the one sacerdotal universal tongue. Nevertheless all of them included a number of words which could be traced to common roots. And to do this is the business of modern Philology, though to this day, with all the respect due to the labours of the eminent Philologists of Oxford and Berlin, that Science seems to be hopelessly floundering in the Cimmerian darkness of mere hypothesis.

Ahrens, when speaking of the letters as arranged in the Hebrew sacred scrolls, and remaking that they were musical notes, had probably never studied Aryan Hindu music. In the Sanskrit language letters are continually arranged in the sacred Ollas so that they may become musical notes. For the whole Sanskrit alphabet and the Vedas, from the first word to the last, are musical notations reduced to writing; the two are inseparable.[See Theosophist. 1879. art. "Hindu Music," p.47.] As Homer distinguished between the "language of

Gods" and the "language of men." [The Sanskrit letters are far more numerous than the poor twenty-two letters of the Hebrew alphabet. They are all musical, and they are read - or rather chanted - according to a system given in very old Tântrika works, and are called Devanâgari, the speech, or language, of the Gods. And since each letter answers to a numeral, the Sanskrit affords a far larger scope for expression, and it must necessarily be far more perfect than the Hebrew, which followed the same system but could apply it only in a very limited way. If either of these two languages were taught to humanity by the Gods, surely it would more likely be the Sanskrit, the perfect form of the most perfect language on earth, than the Hebrew, the roughest and the poorest. For once anyone believes in a language of divine origin, he can hardly believe at the same time that Angels or Gods or any divine Messengers have had to develop it from a rough monosyllable form into a perfect one, as we see in terrestrial linguistic evolution.] so did the Hindus. The Devanagari, the Sanskrit characters, are the "speech of the Gods," and Sanskrit is the divine language.

It is argued in defence of the present version of the Mosaic Books that the mode of language adopted was an "accommodation" to the ignorance of the Jewish people. But the said "mode of language" drags down the "sacred text" of Esdras and his colleagues to the level of the most unspiritual and gross phallic religions. This plea confirms the suspicions entertained by some Christian Mystics and many philosophical critics, that;

(a) Divine Power as an Absolute Unity had never anything

more to do with the Biblical Jehovah and the "Lord God" than with any other Sephiroth or number. The Ain-Suph of the Kabalah of Moses is as independent of any relation with the created Gods as is Parabrahman Itself.

(b) The teachings veiled in the Old Testament under allegorical expressions are all copied from the Magical Texts of Babylonia, by Esdras and others, while the earlier Mosaic Text had its source in Egypt.

A few instances known to almost all Symbologists of note, and especially to the French Egyptologists, may help to prove the statement. Furthermore, no ancient Hebrew Philosopher, Philo no more than the Sadducees, claimed, as do now the ignorant Christians, that the events in the Bible should be taken literally. Philo says most explicitly:

The verbal statements are fabulous [in the Book of Law]: it is in the allegory that we shall find the truth.

THE SEVEN CREATIVE GODS-

Let us give a few instances, beginning with the latest narrative, the Hebrew, and thus if possible trace the allegories to their origin.

1. Whence the Creation in six days, the seventh day as day of rest, the seven Elohim, [In the first chapter of Genesis the word "God" represents the Elohim - Gods in the plural, not one God. This is a cunning and dishonest translation. For the whole Kabalah explains sufficiently that the Alhim (Elohim) are seven: each, creates one of the seven

things enumerated in the first chapter, and these answer allegorically to the seven creations. To make this clear, count the verses in which it is said "And God saw that it was good," and you will find that this is said seven times - in verses 4, 10, 12, 18, 21, 25, and 31. And though the compilers cunningly represent the creation of man as occurring on the sixth day, yet, having made man "male and female in the image of God," the Seven Elohim repeat the sacramental sentence. "It was good, " for the seventh time, thus making of man the seventh creation, and showing the origin of this bit of cosmogony to be in the Hindu creations. The Elohim are, of course, the seven Egyptian Khnûmû, the "assistant-architects": the seven Amshaspends of the Zoroastrians: the Seven Spirits subordinate to Ildabaoth of the Nazareans; the seven Prajâpati of the Hindus, etc.] and the division of space into heaven and earth, in the first chapter of Genesis?

The division of the vault above from the Abyss, or Chaos, below is one of the first acts of creation or rather of evolution, in every cosmogony. Hermes in Pymander speaks of a heaven seen in seven circles with seven Gods in them. We examine the Assyrian tiles and find the same on them - the seven creative Gods busy each in his own sphere. The cuneiform legends narrate how Bel prepared the seven mansions of the Gods; how heaven was separated from the earth. In the Brahmanical allegory everything is septenary, from the seven zones, or envelopes, of the Mundane Egg down to the seven continents, islands, seas, etc. The six days of the week and the seventh, the Sabbath, are based primarily on the seven creations of the Hindu Brahma, the seventh being that of man; and secondarily on the number of generation. It is pre-eminently and most conspicuously phallic. In the Babylonian system the seventh day, or period, was that in which man and the animals were created.

2. The Elohim make a woman out of Adam's rib. [Gen., ii.21, 22.] This process is found in the Magical Texts translated by G. Smith.

The seven Spirits bring forth the woman from the loins of the man, explains Mr. Sayce in his Hibbert Lectures. [Op.cit., p.395, note.]

The mystery of the woman who was made from the man is repeated in every national religion, and in Scriptures far antedating the Jewish. You find it in the Avestan fragments, in the Egyptian Book of the Dead, and finally in Brahmâ, the male, separating from himself, as a female self, Vâch, in whom he creates Virâj.

3. The two Adams of the first and second chapters in Genesis originated from garbled exoteric accounts coming from the Chaldaeans and the Egyptian Gnostics, revised later from the Persian traditions, most of which are old Aryan allegories. As Adam Kadmon is the seventh creation, [The seventh esoterically, exoterically the sixth.] so the Adam of dust is the eighth; and in the Purânas one finds an eighth, the Anugraha creation, and the Egyptian Gnostics had it. Irenaeus, complaining of the heretics says of the Gnostics:

Sometimes they will have him [man] to have been made on the sixth day, and sometimes on the eighth. [Contra

Hereses. 1. xviii.2.]

The author of The Hebrew and Other Creations writes:

These two creations of man on the sixth day and on the eighth were those of the Adamic, or fleshly man, and of the spiritual man, who were known to Paul and the Gnostics as the first and second Adam, the man of earth and the man of Heaven. Irenaeus also says they insisted that Moses began with the Ogdoad of the Seven Powers and their mother, Sophia (the old Kefa of Egypt, who is the Living Word at Ombos). Op. cit, by Gerald Massey. p.19]

Sophia is also Aditi with her seven sons.

One might go on enumerating and tracing the Jewish "revelations" ad infinitum to their original sources, were it not that the task is superfluous, since so much is already done in that direction by others - and done thoroughly well, as in the case of Gerald Massey, who has sifted the subject to the very bottom. Hundreds of volumes, treatises, and pamphlets are being written yearly in defence of the "divine-inspiration" claim for the Bible; but symbolical and archaeological research is coming to the rescue of truth and fact - therefore of the Esoteric Doctrine - upsetting every argument based on faith and breaking it as an idol with feet of clay. A curious and learned book, The Approaching End of the Age, by H. Gratton Guinness, professes to solve the mysteries of the Bible chronology and to prove thereby God's direct revelation to man. Among other things its author thinks that:

It is impossible to deny that a septiform chronology was divinely appointed in the elaborate ritual of Judaism.

SEVEN KEYS TO ALL ALLEGORIES-

This statement is innocently accepted and firmly believed in by thousands and tens of thousands, only because they are ignorant of the Bibles of other nations. Two pages from a small pamphlet, a lecture by Mr. Gerald Massey, [Op cit., p.278] so upset the arguments and proofs of the enthusiastic Mr. Grattan Guinness, spread over 760 pages of small print, as to prevent them from ever raising their heads any more. Mr. Massey treats of the Fall, and says:

Here, as before, the genesis does not begin at the beginning. There was an earlier Fall than that of the Primal Pair. In this the number of those who failed and fell was seven. We meet with those seven in Egypt - eight with the mother - where they are called the "Children of Inertness," who were cast out from Am-Smen, the Paradise of the Eight; also in a Babylonian legend of Creation, as the Seven Brethren, who were Seven Kings, like the Seven Kings in the Book of Revelation; and the Seven Non-Sentient Powers, who became the Seven Rebel Angels that made war in heaven. The Seven Kronidae, described as the Seven Watchers, who in the beginning were formed in the interior of heaven. The heaven, like a vault, they extended or hollowed out; that which was not visible they raised, and that which had no exit they opened; their work of creation being exactly identical with that of the Elohim in the Book of Genesis. These are the Seven elemental Powers of space, who were continued as Seven Timekeepers. It is said of them: "In watching was their office, but among the stars of heaven their watch they kept not," and their failure was the Fall. In the Book of Enoch the same Seven Watchers in heaven are stars which transgressed the commandment of God before their time arrived, for they came not in their proper season, therefore was he offended with them, and bound them until the period of the consummation of their crimes, at the end of the secret, or great year of the World, i.e., the Period of Precession, when there was to be restoration and rebeginning. The Seven deposed constellations are seen by Enoch, looking like seven great blazing mountains overthrown - the seven mountains in Revelation, on which the Scarlet Lady sits.[The Hebrew and other Creations; with a reply to Prof. A.H. Sayce, p.19.]

There are seven keys to this, as to every other allegory, whether in the Bible or in pagan religions. While Mr. Massey has hit upon the key in the mysteries of cosmogony, John Bentley in his Hindu Astronomy claims that the Fall of the Angels, or War in Heaven, as given by the Hindus, is but a figure of the calculations of time-periods, and goes on to show that among the Western nations the same war, with like results, took the form of the war of the Titans.

In short, he makes it astronomical. So does the author of The Source of Measures:

The celestial sphere with the earth, was divided into twelve compartments [astronomically], and these compartments were esteemed as sexed, the lords or husbands being respectively the planets presiding over them. This being the settled scheme, want of proper correction would bring it to pass, after a time, that error and confusion would ensue by the compartments coming under the lordship of the wrong planets. Instead of lawful wedlock, there would be illegal intercourse, as between the planets, "sons of Elohim." and these compartments, "daughters of H-Adam," or the earth-man: and in fact the fourth verse of sixth Genesis will bear this interpretation for the usual one, viz., "In the same days, or periods, there were untimely births in the earth; and also behind that, when the sons of Elohim came to the daughters of H-Adam, they begat to them the offspring of harlotry," etc., astronomically indicating this confusion. [Op. cit., p.243.]

Do any of these learned explanations explain anything except a possible ingenious allegory, and a personification of the celestial bodies, by the ancient Mythologists and Priests? Carried to their last word they would undeniably explain much, and would thus furnish one of the right seven keys, fitting a great many of the Biblical puzzles yet opening none naturally and entirely, instead of being scientific and cunning master-keys. But they prove one thing - that neither the septiform chronology nor the septiform theogony and evolution of all things is of divine origin in the Bible. For let us see the sources at which the Bible sipped its divine inspiration with regard to the sacred number seven. Says Mr. Massey in the same lecture:

The Book of Genesis tells us nothing about the nature of these Elohim, erroneously rendered "God," who are creators of the Hebrew beginning, and who are themselves preextant and seated when the theatre opens and the curtain ascends. It says that in the beginning the Elohim created the heaven and the earth. In thousands of books the Elohim have been discussed, but . . . with no conclusive result . . . The Elohim are Seven in number, whether as nature-powers, gods of constellations, or planetary gods, . . . as the Pitris and Patriarchs, Manus and Fathers of earlier times. The Gnostics, however, and the Jewish Kabalah preserve an account of the Elohim of Genesis by which we are able to identify them with other forms of the seven primordial powers . . . Their names are Ildabaoth , Jehovah (or Jao), Sabaoth, Adonai, Eloeus, Orfus, and astanphaeus. Ildabaoth signifies the Lord God of the fathers, that is the fathers who preceded the Father; and thus the seven are identical with the seven Pitris or Fathers of India (Irenaeus, B.L., xxx., 5). Moreover, the Hebrew Elohim were preextant by name and nature as Phoenician divinities or powers. Sanchoniathon mentions them by name, and describes them as Auxiliaris of Kronos or Time. In this phase, then, the Elohim are timekeepers in heaven! In the Phoenician mythology the Elohim are the Seven sons of Sydik [Melchizedek], identical with the Seven Kabiri, who in Egypt are the Seven sons of Ptah, and the Seven Spirits of Ra in The Book of the Dead; . . . in America with the seven Hohgates, . . . in Assyria with the seven Lumazi . . .

GERALD MASSEY ON THE SEVEN CREATORS-

They are always seven in number . . . who Kab - that is, turn round, together, whence the "Kab-iri." . . . They are also the Ili or Gods, in Assyrian, who were seven in number! . . . They were first born of the Mother in Space, [When they are the Anupâdakas (Parentless) of the Secret Doctrine. See Stanzas, i.9, Vol.i. 56.] and then the Seven

Companions passed into the sphere of time as auxiliaries of Kronus, or Sons of the Male Parent. As Damascius says in his Primitive Principles, the Magi consider that space and time were the source of all; and from being powers of the air the gods were promoted to become timekeepers for men. Seven constellations were assigned to them .. . .As the seven turned round in the ark of the sphere they were designated the Seven Sailors' Companions, Rishis, or Elohim. The first "Seven Stars" are not planetary. They are the leading stars of seven constellations which turned round with the Great Bear in describing the circle of the year. [These originated with the Aryans, who placed therein their "bright-crested" (Chitra-Shikhandan) Seven Rishis. But all this is far more Occult than appears on the surface.] These the Assyrians called the seven Lumazi, or leaders of the flocks of stars, designated sheep. On the Hebrew line of descent or development, these Elohim are identified for us by the Kabalists and Gnostics, who retained the hidden wisdom or gnosis, the clue of which is absolutely essential to any proper understanding of mythology or theology. . . . There were two constellations with seven stars each. We call them the Two Bears. But the seven stars of the Lesser Bear were once considered to be the seven heads of the Polar Dragon, which we meet with - as the beast with seven heads - in the Akkadian Hymns and in Revelation. The mythical dragon originated in the crocodile, which is the dragon of Egypt. . . . Now in one particular cult, the Sut-Typhonian, the first god was Sevekh [the sevenfold], who wears the crocodile's head, as well as the Serpent, and who is the Dragon or whose constellation was the Dragon. .

. . In Egypt the Great Bear was the constellation of Typhon, or Kepha, the old genetrix, called the Mother of Revolutions; and the Dragon with seven heads was assigned to her son, Sevekh-Kronus, or Saturn, called the Dragon of Life. That is, the typical dragon or serpent with seven heads was female at first, and then the type was continued, as male in her son Sevekh, the Sevenfold Serpent, in Ea the Sevenfold, ... Iao Chnubis, and others. We find these two in The Book of Revelation. One is the Scarlet Lady, the mother of mystery, the great harlot, who sat on a scarlet-coloured beast with seven heads, which is the Red Dragon of the Pole. She held in her hand the unclean things of her fornication. That means the emblems of the male and female, imaged by the Egyptians at the Polar Centre, the very uterus of creation, as was indicated by the Thigh constellation, called the Khepsh of Typhon, the old Dragon, in the northern birthplace of Time in heaven. The two revolved about the pole of heaven, or the Tree, as it was called, which was figured at the centre of the starry motion. In The Book of Enoch these two constellations are identified as Leviathan and Behemoth-Bekhmut, or the Dragon and Hippopotamus=Great Bear, and they are the primal pair that were first created in the Garden of Eden. So that the Egyptian first mother, Kefa [or Kepha] whose name signifies "mystery," was the original of the Hebrew Chavah, our Eve; and therefore Adam is one with Sevekh the sevenfold one, the solar dragon in whom the powers of light and darkness were combined, and the sevenfold nature was shown in the seven rays worn by the Gnostic Iao-Chnubis, god of the number seven, who is Sevekh by name and a form of the first father as head of the Seven. [Op.cit., pp. 19-22]

All this gives the key to the astronomical prototype of the allegory in Genesis, but it furnishes no other key to the mystery involved in the sevenfold glyph. The able Egyptologist shows also that Adam himself according to Rabbinical and Gnostic tradition, was the chief of the Seven who fell from Heaven, and he connects these with the Patriarchs, thus agreeing with the Esoteric Teaching. For by mystic permutation and the mystery of primeval rebirths and adjustment, the Seven Rishis are in reality identical with the seven Prajâpatis, the fathers and creators of mankind, and also with the Kumâras, the first sons of Brahmâ, who refused to procreate and multiply. This apparent contradiction is explained by the sevenfold nature - make it fourfold on metaphysical principles and it will come to the same thing - of the celestial men, the Dhyan Chohans. This nature is made to divide and separate; and while the higher principles (Atma-Buddhi) of the "Creators of Men" are said to be the Spirits of the seven constellations, their middle and lower principles are connected with the earth and are shown.

Without desire or passion, inspired with holy wisdom, estranged from the Universe and undesirous of progeny, [Vishnu Purana, Wilson's Translation, I, 101. The period of these Kumaras is Pre-Adamic. i.e. before the separation of the sexes, and before humanity had received the creative, or sacred, fire of Prometheus.] remaining Kaumâric (virgin and undefiled): therefore it is said they refuse to create. For this they are cursed and sentenced to be born and reborn "Adams," as the Semites would say.

Meanwhile let me quote a few lines more from Mr. G. Massey's lecture, the fruit of his long researches in Egyptology and other ancient lore, as it shows that the septenary division was at one time a universal doctrine:

Adam as the father among the Seven is identical with the Egyptians Atum, . . . whose other name of Adon is identical with the Hebrew Adonai. In this way the second Creation in Genesis reflects and continues the later creation in the mythos which explains it. The Fall of Adam to the lower world led to his being humanised on earth, by which process the celestial was turned into the mortal, and this, which belongs to the astronomical allegory, got literalised as the Fall of Man, or descent of the soul into matter, and the conversion of the angelic into an earthly being . . . .

THE FATHER AND MOTHER-

It is found in the [Babylonian] texts, when Ea, the first father, is said to "grant forgiveness to the conspiring gods," for whose "redemption did he create mankind." (Sayce; Hib. Lec.,p. 140) . . . The Elohim, then, are the Egyptian, Akkadian, Hebrew, and Phoenician form of the universal Seven Powers, who are Seven in Egypt, Seven in Akkad, Babylon, Persia, India, Britain, and Seven among the Gnostics and Kabalists. They were the Seven fathers who preceded the Father in Heaven, because they were earlier than the individualised fatherhood on earth . . .

When the Elohim said: "Let us make man in our image, after our likeness." there were seven of them who represented the seven elements, powers, or souls that went to the making of the human being who came into existence before the Creator was represented anthropomorphically, or could have conferred the human likeness on the Adamic man. It was in the sevenfold image of the Elohim that was first created, with his seven elements, principles, or souls, [The Secret Doctrine says that this was the second creation, nor the first, and that it took place during the Third Race, when men separated, i.e., began to be born as distinct men and women. See Vol. ii. of this work, Stanzas and Commentaries.] and therefore he could not have been formed in the image of the one God. The seven Gnostic Elohim tried to make a man in their own image, but could not for lack of virile power. [This is a Western mangling of the Indian doctrine of the Kumaras.] Thus their creation in earth and heaven was a failure . . . because they themselves were lacking in the soul of the fatherhood! When the Gnostic Ildabaoth, [He was regarded by several Gnostic sects as one with Jehovah. See Isis Unveiled, vol ii., p.184.] chief of the Seven, cried: "I am the father and God," his mother Sophia [Achamoth] replied: "Do not tell lies, Ildabaoth, for the first man (Anthropos, son of Anthropos [Or "man, son of man." The Church found in this a prophecy and a confession of Christ, the "Son of Man!"]) is above thee." That is, man who had now been created in the image of the fatherhood was superior to the gods who were derived from the Mother-Parent alone! [See Stanza ii., Secret Doctrine. ii.16.] For, as it had been first on earth, so was it afterwards in heaven [the Secret Doctrine reaches the reverse]; and thus the primary gods were held to be soulless like the earliest races of men . . . . The Gnostics taught that the Spirits of Wickedness, the inferior Seven, derived their origin from the great Mother alone, who produced without the fatherhood! It was in the image, then, of the sevenfold Elohim that the seven races were formed which we sometimes hear of as the Pre-Adamite races of men, because they were earlier than the fatherhood, which was individualised only in the second Hebrew Creation. [See Stanza ii.,5, Secret Doctrine. ii.16]

This shows sufficiently how the echo of the Secret Doctrine - of the Third and Fourth Races of men, made complete by the incarnation in humanity of the Manasa Putra, Sons of Intelligence or Wisdom - reached every corner of the globe. The Jews, however, although they borrowed of the older nations the groundwork on which to build their revelation, never had more than three keys out of the seven in their mind, while composing their national allegories - the astronomical, or numerical (metrology) and above all the purely anthropological, or rather physiological key. This resulted in the most phallic religion of all, and has now passed, part and parcel, into Christian theology, as is proved by the lengthy quotations made from a lecture of an able Egyptologist, who can make naught of it save astronomical myths and phallicism, as is implied by his explanations of "fatherhood" in the allegories.

SECTION XXII

THE "ZOHAR" ON CREATION AND THE ELOHIM

THE opening sentence in Genesis, as every Hebrew scholar knows, is:

Now there are two well-known ways of rendering this line, as any other Hebrew writing: one exoteric, as read by the orthodox Bible interpreters (Christian), and the other Kabalistic, the latter, moreover, being divided into the Rabbinical and the purely Kabalistic or Occult method. As in Sanskrit writing, the words are not separated in the Hebrew, but are made to run together - especially in the old systems. For instance, the above, divided, would read: "B'rashith bara Elohim eth hashamayim v'eth h'areths;" and it can be made to read thus: "B'rash ithbara Elohim ethhashamayim v'eth'arets," thus changing the meaning entirely. The latter means, "In the beginning God made the heavens and the earth," whereas the former, precluding the idea of any beginning, would simply read that "out of the ever-existing Essence [divine] [or out of the womb - also head - thereof] the dual [or androgyne] Force [Gods] shaped the double heaven;" the upper and the lower heaven being generally explained as heaven and earth. The latter word means Esoterically the "Vehicle," as it gives the idea of an empty globe, within which the manifestation of the world takes place. Now, according to the rules of Occult symbolical reading as established in the old Sepher Jetzirah (in the

Chaldaean Book of Numbers) [The Sepher Jetzirah now known is but a portion of the original one incorporated in the Chaldean Book of Numbers. The fragment now in possession of the Western Kabalists is one greatly tampered with by the Rabbis of the Middle Ages, as its masoretic points show. The "Masorah" scheme is a modern blind, dating after our era and perfected in Tiberias. (See Isis Unveiled. vol. ii. pp. 430-431.)] the initial fourteen letters (or "B'rasitb' raalaim") are in themselves quite sufficient to explain the theory of "creation" without any further explanation or qualification. Every letter of them is a sentence; and, placed side by side with the hieroglyphic or pictorial initial version of "creation" in the Book of Dzyan, the origin of the Phoenician and Jewish letters would soon be found out. A whole volume of explanations would give no more to the student of primitive Occult Symbology than this: the head of a bull within a circle, a straight horizontal line, a circle or sphere, then another one with three dots in it, a triangle, then the Svastika (or Jaina cross); after these come an equilateral triangle within a circle, seven small bulls' heads standing in three rows, one over the other; a black round dot (an opening), and then seven lines, meaning Chaos or Water (feminine).

Anyone acquainted with the symbolical and numerical value of the Hebrew letters will see at a glance that this glyph and the letters of "B'rasitb' raalaim" are identical in meaning. "Beth" is "abode" or "region;" "Resh," a "circle" of "head;" "Aleph," "bull" (the symbol of generative or creative power); [In the oldest symbolism - that used in the Egyptian hieroglyphics - when the bull's head only is found it means the Deity, the Perfect Circle, with the procreative power latent in it. When the whole bull is represented, a solar God, a personal deity is meant, for it is then the symbol of the acting generative power.] "Shin," a "tooth" (300 exoterically - a trident or three in one in its Occult meaning); "Jodh," the perfect unity or "one" ; [It took three Root-Races to degrade the symbol of the One Abstract Unity manifested in Nature as a Ray emanating from infinity (the Circle) into a phallic symbol of generation, as it was even in the Kabalah. This degradation began with the Fourth Race, and had its raison d'etre in Polytheism, as the latter was invented to screen the One Universal Deity from profanation. The Christians may plead ignorance of its meaning as an excuse for its acceptance. But why sing never-ceasing laudations to the Mosaic Jews who repudiated all the other Gods, preserved the most phallic, and then most impudently proclaimed themselves Monotheists? Jesus ever steadily ignored Jehovah. He went against the Mosaic commandments. He recognized his Heavenly Father alone, and prohibited public worship.] "Tau," the "root" or "foundation" (the same as the cross with the Egyptians and Aryans): again, "Beth," "Resh," and "Aleph." Then "Aleph," or seven bulls for the seven Alaim: an ox-goad, "Lamedh," active procreation; "He," the "opening" or "matrix:" "Yodh," the organ of procreation; and "Mem," "water" or "chaos," the female Power near the male that precedes it.

The most satisfactory and scientific exoteric rendering of the opening sentence of Genesis - on which was hung in blind faith the whole Christian religion, synthesized by its fundamental dogmas - is undeniably the one given in the Appendix to The Source of Measures by Mr. Ralston Skinner. He gives, and we must admit in the ablest, clearest, and most scientific way, the numerical reading of this first sentence and chapter in Genesis.

Angels as Builders- By the means of number 31, or the word "El" (1 for Aleph" and 30 for "Lamedh"), and other numerical Bible symbols, compared with the measures used in the great pyramid of Egypt, he shows the perfect identity between its measurements - inches, cubits, and plan - and the numerical values of the Garden of Eden, Adam and Eve, and the Patriarchs. In short, the author shows that the pyramid contains in itself architecturally the whole of Genesis, and discloses the astronomical, and even the physiological, secrets in its symbols and glyphs; yet he will not admit, it would seem, the psycho-cosmical and spiritual mysteries involved in these. Nor does the author apparently see that the root of all this has to be sought in the archaic legends and the Pantheon of India. [Is it everything to have found out that the celestial circle of 360 degrees is determined by "the full word-form of Elohim," and that this yields, when the word is placed in a circle, "3'1415, or the relation of circumference to a diameter of one." This is only its astronomical or mathematical aspect. To know the full septenary significance of the "Primordial Circle," the pyramid and the Kabalistic Bible must be read in the light of the figure on which the temples of India are built. The mathematical squaring of the circle is only the terrestrial résumé of the problem. The Jews were content with the six days of activity and the seventh of rest. The progenitors of mankind solved the greatest problem of the Universe with their seven Rays or Rishis.] Failing this, whither does his great and admirable labour lead him? Not further than to find out that Adam, the earth, and Moses of Jehovah "are the same" - or to the a-b-c of comparative Occult Symbology - and that the days in Genesis being "circles" "displayed by the Hebrews as squares," the result of the sixth-day's labour culminates in the fructifying principle. Thus the Bible is made to yield Phallicism, and that alone.

Nor - read in this light, and as its Hebrew texts are interpreted by Western scholars - can it ever yield anything higher or more sublime than such phallic elements, the root and the corner-stone of its dead-letter meaning. Anthropomorphism and Revelation dig the impassable chasm between the material world and the ultimate spiritual truths. That creation is not thus described in the Esoteric Doctrine is easily shown. The Roman Catholics give a reading far more approaching the true Esoteric meaning than that of the Protestant. For several of their saints and doctors admit that the formation of heaven and earth of the celestial bodies, etc., belongs to the work of the "Seven Angels of the Presence." St. Denys calls the "Builders" "the coöperators of God," and St. Augustine goes even farther, and credits the Angels with the possession of the divine thought, the prototype, as he says, of everything created.[Genesis begins with the third stage of "creation," skipping the preliminary two.] And, finally, St. Thomas Aquinas has a long dissertation upon this topic, calling God the primary, and the Angels the secondary, cause of all visible effects. In this, with some dogmatic differences of form, the "Angelic Doctor" approaches very nearly the Gnostic ideas. Basilides speaks of the lowest order of Angels as the Builders of our material world, and Saturnilus held, as did the Sabaeans, that the Seven Angels who preside over the planets are the real creators of the world; the Kabalist-monk, Trithemius, in his De Secundis Deis, taught the same.

The eternal Kosmos, the Macrocosm, is divided in the Secret Doctrine, like man, the Microcosm, into three Principles and four Vehicles, [The three root-principles are, exoterically: Man, Soul, and Spirit (meaning by "man" the intelligent personality), and esoterically: Life, Soul, and Spirit: the four vehicles are Body, Astral double, Animal (or human) Soul, and Divine Soul (Sthula-Sharira, Linga-Sharira, Kâma-rûpa, and Buddhi, the vehicle of Atma or Spirit). Or, to make it still clearer: (1) the seventh Principle has for its vehicle the Sixth (Buddhi): (2) the vehicle of Manas is Kâma-rûpa; (3) that of Jiva or Prana (life) is the Linga-Sharira (the "double" of man: the Linga-Sharira proper can never leave the body till death; that which appears is an astral body, reflecting the physical body and serving as a vehicle for the human soul, or intelligence); and (4) the Body, the physical vehicle of all the above collectively. The Occultist recognizes the same order as existing for the cosmical totality, the psycho-cosmical Universe.] which in their collectivity are the seven Principles. In the Chaldaean of Jewish Kabalah, the Kosmos is divided into seven worlds: the Original, the Intelligible, the Celestial, the Elementary, the Lesser (Astral), the Infernal (Kâma-loka or Hades), and the Temporal (of man). In the

Chaldaean system it is in the Intelligible World, the second, that appear the "Seven Angels of the Presence," or the Sephiroth (the three higher ones being, in fact, one, and also the sum total of all). They are also the "Builders" of the Eastern Doctrine: and it is only in the third, the celestial world, that the seven planets and our solar system are built by the seven Planetary Angels, the planets becoming their visible bodies. Hence - as correctly stated - if the universe as a whole is formed out of the Eternal One Substance or Essence, it is not that everlasting Essence, the Absolute Deity, that builds it into shape; this is done by the first Rays, the Angels or Dhyân Chohans, that emanate from the One Element, which becoming periodically Light and Darkness, remains eternally, in its Root-Principle, the one unknown, yet existing Reality.

A learned Western Kabalist. Mr. S. L. MacGregor Mathers, whose reasoning and conclusions will be the more above suspicion since he is untrained in Eastern Philosophy and unacquainted with its Secret Teachings, writes on the first verse of Genesis in an unpublished essay:

Berashith Bara Elohim - "in the beginning the Elohim created!" Who are these Elohim of Genesis?

WHO ARE THE ELOHIM?

Va-Vivra Elohim Ath Ha-Adam Be-Tzalmo, Be-Tzelem Elohim Bara Otho. Zakhar Vingebah Bara Otham - "And the Elohim created the Adam in Their own Image, in the Image of the Elohim created They them, Male and Female created They them!" Who are they, the Elohim? The ordinary English translation of the Bible renders the word Elohim by "God:" it translates a plural noun by a singular one. The only excuse brought forward for this is the somewhat lame one that the word is certainly plural, but is not to be used in a plural sense: that it is "a plural denoting excellence." But this is only an assumption whose value may be justly gauged by Genesis i. 26, translated in the orthodox Biblical version thus: "And God [Elohim] said, 'Let us make man in our own image, after our likeness.'" Here is a distinct admission of the fact that "Elohim" is not a "plural of excellence," but a plural noun denoting more than one being. [St. Denys, the Areopagite, the supposed contemporary of St. Paul, his co-disciple, and first Bishop of St. Denis, near Paris, teaches that the bulk of the "work of creation" was performed by the "Seven Spirits of the Presence" - God's co-operators, owing to a participation of the divinity in them. (Hierarch., p.196) And St. Augustine also thinks that "things were rather created in the angelic minds than in Nature, that is to say, that the angels perceived and knew them (all things) in their thoughts before they could spring forth into actual existence." (Vid De Genesis ad Litteram p.11.) (Summarized from De Mirville. Vol.II., pp. 337-338.) Thus the early Christian Fathers, even a non-initiate like St-Augustine, ascribed the creation of the visible world to Angels, or Secondary Powers, while St. Denys not only specifies these as the "Seven Spirits of the Presence," but shows them owing their power to the informing divine energy - Fohat in the Secret Doctrine. But the egotistical darkness which caused the Western races to cling so desperately to the Geo-centric System, made them also neglect and despise all those fragments of the true Religion which would have deprived them and the little globe they took for the centre of the Universe of the signal honour of having been expressly "created" by the One, Secondless, Infinite God!]

What, then, is the proper translation of "Elohim," and to whom is it referable? "Elohim" is not only a plural, but a feminine plural! And yet the translators of the Bible have rendered it by a masculine singular! Elohim is the plural of the feminine noun El-h, for the final letter, -h, marks the gender. It, however, instead of forming the plural in -oth, takes the usual termination of the masculine plural, which is -im.

Although in the great majority of cases the nouns of both genders take the terminations appropriated to them respectively, there are yet many masculines which form the plural in -oth, as well as feminine which form it in -im while some nouns of each gender take alternately both. It must be observed, however, that the termination of the plural does not affect its gender, which remains the same as in the singular . . .

To find the real meaning of the symbolism involved in this word Elohim we must go to that key of Jewish Esoteric Doctrine, the little-known and less-understood Kabalah. There we shall find that this word represents two united masculine and feminine Potencies, co-equal and co-eternal, conjoined in everlasting union for the maintenance of the Universe - the great Father and Mother of Nature, into whom the Eternal One conforms himself before the Universe can subsist. For the teaching of the Kabalah is that before the Deity conformed himself thus - i.e., as male and female - the

Worlds of the Universe could not subsist; or in the words of Genesis, that "the earth was formless and void." Thus, then, is the conformation of the Elohim, the end of the Formless and the Void and the Darkness, for only after conformation can the Ruach Elohim - the "Spirit of the Elohim" - vibrate upon the countenance of the Waters. But this is a very small part of the information which the Initiate can derive from the Kabalah concerning this word Elohim.

Attention must here be called to the confusion - if not worse - which reigns in the Western interpretations of the Kabalah. The eternal One is said to conform himself into two: the Great Father and Mother of Nature. To begin with, it is a horribly anthropomorphic conception to apply terms implying sexual distinction to the earliest and first differentiations of the One. And it is even more erroneous to identify these first differentiations - the Purusha and Prakriti of Indian Philosophy - with the Elohim, the creative powers here spoken of; and to ascribe to these (to our intellects) unimaginable abstractions, the formation and construction of this visible world, full of pain, sin, and sorrow. In truth, the "creation by the Elohim" spoken of here is but a much later "creation," and the Elohim, far from being supreme, or even exalted powers in Nature, are only lower Angels. This was the teaching of the Gnostics, the most philosophical of all the early Christian Churches. They taught that the imperfections of the world were due to the imperfection of its Architects or Builders - the imperfect, and therefore inferior, Angels. The Hebrew Elohim correspond to the Prajâpati of the Hindus, and it is shown elsewhere from the Esoteric interpretation of the Purânas that the Prajâpati were the fashioners of man's material and astral form only: that they could not give him intelligence or reason, and therefore in symbolical language they "failed to create man." But, not to repeat what the reader can find elsewhere in this work, his attention needs only to be called to the fact that "creation" in this passage is not the Primary Creation, and that the Elohim are not "God," nor even the higher Planetary Spirits, but the Architects of this visible physical planet and of man's material body, or encasement.

A fundamental doctrine of the Kabalah is that the gradual development of the Deity from negative to positive Existence is symbolized by the gradual development of the Ten Numbers of the denary scale of numeration, from the Zero, through the Unity, into the plurality. This is the doctrine of the Sephiroth, or Emanations.

For the inward and concealed Negative Form concentrates a centre which is the primal Unity. But the Unity is one and indivisible: it can neither be increased by multiplication nor decreased by division, for $1 \times 1 = 1$, and no more; and 1 divided by1 = 1, and no less. And it is this changelessness of the Unity or Monad, which makes it a fitting type of the One and Changeless Deity. It answers thus to the Christian idea of God the Father, for as the Unity is the parent of the other numbers, so is the Deity the Father of All.

MONAD, DUAD, AND TRIAD-

The philosophical Eastern mind would never fall into the error which the connotation of these words implies. With them the "One and Changeless" - Parabrahman - the Absolute All and One, cannot be conceived as standing in any relation to things finite and conditioned, and hence they would never use such terms as these, which in their very essence imply such a relation. Do they, then, absolutely sever man from God? On the contrary. They feel a closer union than the Western mind has done in calling God the "Father of All," for they know that in his immortal essence man is himself the Changeless, Secondless One.

But we have just said that the Unity is one and changeless by either multiplication or division; how then is two, the Duad, formed? By reflection. For, unlike Zero, the Unity is partly definable - that is, in its positive aspect; and the definition creates an Eikon or Eidolon of itself which, together with itself, forms a Duad; and thus the number two is to a certain extent analogous to the Christian idea of the Son as the Second Person. And as the Monad vibrates, and recoils into the Darkness of the Primary Thought, so is the Duad left as its vice-gerent and representative, and thus co-equal and co-eternal with the Duad in the bosom of the Unity, yet, as it were, proceeding therefrom in the numerical conception of its sequence.

This explanation would seem to imply that Mr. Mathers is aware that this "creation" is not the truly divine or primary one, since the Monad - the first manifestation on our plane of objectivity - "recoils into the Darkness of the Primal Thought," i.e., into the subjectivity of the first divine Creation.

And this, again, also partly answers to the Christian idea of the Holy Ghost, and of the whole three forming a Trinity in unity. This also explains the fact in geometry of the three right lines being the smallest number which will make a plane rectilineal figure, while two can never enclose a space, being powerless and without effect till completed by the number Three. These three first numbers of the decimal scale the Qabalists call by the names of Kether, the Crown, Chokmah, Wisdom, and Binah, Understanding; and they furthermore associate with them these divine names: with the Unity, Eheich, "I exist;" with the Duad, Yah; and with the Triad, Elohim; they especially also call the Duad, Abba - the Father and the Triad, Aima - the Mother, whose eternal conjunction is symbolized in the word Elohim.

But what especially strikes the student of the Kabalah is the malicious persistency with which the translators of the Bible have jealously crowded out of sight and suppressed every reference to the feminine form of the Deity. They have, as we have just seen, translated the feminine plural "Elohim," by the masculine singular, "God." But they have done more than this: they have carefully hidden the fact that the word Ruach - the "Spirit" - is feminine, and that consequently the Holy Ghost of the New Testament is a feminine Potency. How many Christians are cognizant of the fact that in the account of the Incarnation in Luke (i.35) two divine Potencies are mentioned?

"The Holy Ghost shall come upon thee, and the Power of the Highest shall overshadow thee." The Holy Ghost (the feminine Potency) descends, and the Power of the Highest (the masculine Potency) is united therewith. "Therefore also that holy thing which shall be born of thee shall be called the Son of God" - of the Elohim namely, seeing that these two

Potencies descend.

In the Sepher Yetzirah, or Book of Formation, we read:

"One is She the Ruach Elohim Chum - (Spirit of the Living Elohim). . . . Voice, Spirit, and Word; and this is She, the Spirit of the Holy One." Here again we see the intimate connection which exists between the Holy Spirit and the Elohim. Furthermore, farther on in this same Book of Formation - which is be it remembered, one of the oldest of the Kabalistical Books, and whose authorship is ascribed to Abraham the Patriarch - we shall find the idea of a Feminine Trinity in the first place, from whom a masculine Trinity proceeds; or as it is said in the text: "Three Mothers whence proceed three Fathers." And yet this double Triad forms, as it were, but one complete Trinity. Again it is worthy of note that the Second and Third Sephiroth (Wisdom and Understanding) are both distinguished by feminine names, Chokmah and Binah, notwithstanding that to the former more particularly the masculine idea, and to the latter the feminine, are attributed, under the titles of Abba and Aima (or Father and Mother). This Aima (the Great Mother) is magnificently symbolized in the twelfth chapter of the Apocalypse, which is undoubtedly one of the most Kabalistical books in the Bible. In fact, without the Kabalistical keys its meaning is utterly unintelligible.

Now, in the Hebrew, as in the Greek, alphabet, there are no distinct numeral characters, and consequently each letter has a certain numerical value attached to it. From this circumstance results the important fact that every Hebrew word constitutes a number, and every number a word. This is referred to in the Revelations (xiii. 18) in mentioning the "number of the beast"! In the Kabalah words of equal numerical values are supposed to have a certain explanatory connection with each other. This forms the science of Gematria, which is the first division of the Literal Kabalah. Furthermore, each letter of the Hebrew alphabet had for the Initiates of the Kabalah a certain hieroglyphical value and meaning which, rightly applied, gave to each word the value of a mystical sentence; and this again was variable according to the relative positions of the letters with regard to each other. From these various Kabalistical points of view let us now examine this word Elohim. First then we can divide the word into the two words, which signify "The Feminine Divinity of the Waters;" compare with the Greek Aphrodite, "sprung from the foam of the sea."

THE CREATIVE GODS

Again it is divisive into the "Mighty One, Star of the Sea," or "the Mighty One breathing forth the Spirit upon the Waters." Also by combination of the letters we get "the Silent Power of Iah." And again, "My God, the Former of the Universe," for Mah is a secret Kabalistical name applied to the idea of Formation. Also we obtain "Who is my God." Furthermore "the Mother in Iah."

The total number is 1+30+5+10+40=86 "Violent heat," or "the Power of Fire." If we add together the three middle letters we obtain 45, and the first the last letter yield 41, making thus "the Mother of Formation." Lastly, we shall find the two divine names "El" and "Yah," together with the letter m, which signifies "Water," for Mem, the name of this letter, means "water."

If we divide it into its component letters and take them as hieroglyphical signs we shall have:

"Will perfected through Sacrifice progressing through successive Transformation by Inspiration."

The last few paragraphs of the above, in which the word "Elohim" is Kabalistically analysed, show conclusively enough that the Elohim are not one, nor two, nor even a trinity, but a Host - the army of the creative powers.

The Christian Church, in making of Jehovah - one of these very Elohim - the one Supreme God, has introduced hopeless confusion into the celestial hierarchy, in spite of the volumes written by Thomas Aquinas and his school on the subject. The only explanation to be found in all their treatises on the nature and essence of the numberless classes of celestial beings mentioned in the Bible - Archangels, Thrones, Seraphim, Cherubim, Messengers, etc. - is that "The angelic host is God's militia." They are "Gods the creatures," while he is "God the Creator," but of their true functions - of their actual place in the economy of Nature - not one word is said. They are

More brilliant than the flames, more rapid than the wind, and they live in love and harmony, mutually enlightening each other, feeding on bread and a mystic beverage - the communion wine and water? - surrounding as with a river of fire the throne of the Lamb, and veiling their faces with their wings. This throne of love and glory they leave only to carry to the stars, the earth, the kingdoms and all the sons of God, their brothers and pupils, in short, to all creatures like themselves the divine influence. . . . As to their number, it is that of the great army of Heaven (Sabaoth), more numerous than the stars . . . . Theology shows us these rational luminaries, each constituting a species, and containing in their natures such or another position of Nature covering immense space, though of a determined area; residing - incorporeal though they are - within circumscribed limits; . . . . more rapid than light or thunderbolt, disposing of all the elements of Nature, providing at will inexplicable mirages [illusions?], objective and subjective   in turn, speaking to men a language at one time articulate, at another purely spiritual. [De Mirville, ii. 295.]

We learn farther on in the same work that it is these Angels and their hosts who are referred to in the sentence of verse I, chapter ii. of Genesis: Igitur perfecti sunt coeli et terra et omnis ornatus eorum:" and that the Vulgate has peremptorily substituted for the Hebrew word "tsaba" ("host" that of "ornament;" Munck shows the mistake of substitution and the derivation of the compound title, "Tsabaoth-Elohim," from "tsaba." Moreover, Cornelius a Lapide, "the master of all Biblical commentators," says de Mirville, shows us that such was the real meaning. Those Angels are stars.

All this, however, teaches us very little as to the true functions of this celestial army, and nothing at all as to its place in evolution and its relation to the earth we live on. For an answer to the question. "Who are the true Creators?" we must go to the Esoteric Doctrine, since there only can the key be found which will render intelligible the Theogonies of the various world-religions.

There we find that the real creator of the Kosmos, as of all visible Nature - if not of all the invisible hosts of Spirits not yet drawn into the "Cycle of Necessity," or evolution - is "the Lord - the Gods," or the "Working Host," the "Army" collectively taken, the "One in many."

The One is infinite and unconditioned. It cannot create, for It can have to relation to the finite and conditioned. If everything we see, from the glorious suns and planets down to the blades of grass and the specks of dust, had been created by the Absolute Perfection and were the direct work of even the First Energy that proceeded from It, [To the Occultists and Chela the difference made between Energy and Emanation need not be explained. The Sanskrit word "Sakti" is untranslatable. It may be Energy, but it is one that proceeds through itself, not being due to the active or conscious will of the one that produces it. The "First-Born," or Logos, is not an Emanation, but an Energy inherent in and co-eternal with Parabrahman, the One. The Zohar speaks of emanations, but reserves the word for the seven Sephiroth emanated from the first three - which form one triad - Kether, Chokmah, and Binah. As for these three, it explains the difference by calling them "immanations," something inherent to and coeval with the subject postulated, or in other words," "Energies."

It is these "Auxiliaries," the Auphanim, the half human Prajâpatis, the Angels, the Architects under the leadership of the "Angel of the Great Council," with the rest of the Kosmos-Builders of other nations, that can alone explain the imperfection of the Universe. This imperfection is one of the arguments of the Secret Science in favour of the existence and activity of these "Powers." And who know better than the few philosophers of our civilised lands how near the truth Philo was in ascribing the origin of evil to the admixture of inferior potencies in the arrangement of matter, and even in the formation of man - a task entrusted to the divine Logos.] then every such thing would have been perfect, eternal, and unconditioned like its author.

GOD THE HOST-

The millions upon millions of imperfect works found in Nature testify loudly that they are the products of finite, conditioned beings - though the latter were and are Dhyân Chohans, Archangels, or whatever else they may be named. In short, these imperfect works are the unfinished production of evolution, under the guidance of the imperfect Gods. The Zohar gives us this assurance as well as the Secret Doctrine. It speaks of the auxiliaries of the "Ancient of Days," the "Sacred Aged," and calls them Auphanim, or the living Wheels of the celestial orbs, who participate in the work of the creation of the Universe.

Thus it is not the "Principle," One and Unconditioned, nor even Its reflection, that creates, but only the "Seven Gods" who fashion the Universe out of the eternal Matter, vivified into objective life by the reflection into it of the One Reality.

The Creator is they - "God the Host" - called in the Secret Doctrine the Dhyan Chohans; with the Hindus the Prajâpatis;

with the Western Kabalists the Sephiroth; and with the Buddhist the Devas - impersonal because blind forces. They are the Amshaspends with the Zoroastrians, and while with the Christian Mystic the "Creator" is the "Gods of the God," with the dogmatic Churchman he is the "God of the Gods," the "Lord of lords," etc.

"Jehovah" is only the God who is greater than all Gods in the eyes of Israel.

I know, that the lord [of Israel] is great and that our Lord is above all gods.[Psalms cxxxv. 5.]

And again:

For all the gods of the nations are idols, but the Lord made the heavens. [Psalms xcvi.5.]

The Egyptian Neteroo, translated by Champollion "the other Gods," are the Elohim of the Biblical writers, behind which stands concealed the One God, considered in the diversity of his powers. [Rather as Ormazd or Ahura-Mazda, Vit-nam-Ahmi, and all the unmanifested Logoi. Jehovah is the manifested Virâj, corresponding to Binah, the third Sephira in the Kabalah, a female Power which would find its prototype rather in the Prajâpati, than in Brahma, the Creator.] This One is not Parabrahman, but the Unmanifested Logos, the Demiurgos, the real Creator or Fashioner, that follows him, standing for the Demiurgi collectively taken. Further on the great Egyptologist adds:

We see Egypt concealing and hiding, so to say, the God of Gods behind the agents she surrounds him with ; she gives the precedence to her great gods before the one and sole Deity, so that the attributes of that God become their

property. Those great Gods proclaim themselves uncreate
. . . . Neith is 'that which is ," as Jehovah; [Neith is Aditi,
evidently.] Thoth is self-created [The Self-created Logos,
Narâyana, Purushottama, and others.] without having been
begotten, etc. Judaism annihilating these potencies before
the grandeur of its God, they cease to be simply Powers,
like Philo's Archangels, like the Sephiroth of the Kabalah,
like the Ogdoades of the Gnostics - they merge together
and become transformed into God himself. [Mère d'Apis.
pp. 32-35. Quoted by De Mirville.]

Jehovah is thus, as the Kabalah teaches, at best but the
"Heavenly Man," Adam Kadmon, used by the self-created
Spirit, the Logos, as a chariot, a vehicle in His descent
towards manifestation in the phenomenal world.

Such are the teachings of the Archaic Wisdom, nor can
they be repudiated even by the orthodox Christian, if he be
sincere and open-minded in the study of his own Scripture.
For if he reads St. Paul's Epistles carefully he will find that
the Secret Doctrine and the Kabalah are fully admitted by
the "Apostle of the Gentiles." The Gnosis which he appears
to condemn is no less for him than for Plato "the supreme
knowledge of the truth and of the One Being;" [See Republic.
I. vi.] for what St. Paul condemns is not the true, but only the
false, Gnosis and its abuses: otherwise how could he use the
language of a Platonist pur sang? The Ideas, types (Archai),
of the Greek Philosopher; the Intelligences of Pythagoras;
the Aeons or Emanations of the Pantheist; the Logos or
Word, Chief of these intelligences; the Sophia or Wisdom;
the Demiurgos, the Builder of the world under the direction

of the Father, the Unmanifested Logos, from which He emanates; Ain-Suph, the Unknown of the Infinite; the angelic Periods; the Seven Spirits who are the representatives of the Seven of all the older cosmogonies - are all to be found in his writings, recognized by the Church as canonical and divinely inspired. Therein, too, may be recognized the Depths of Ahriman, Rector of this our World, the "God of this World;" the Pleroma of the Intelligences; the Archontes of the air; the Principalities, the Kabalistic Metatron; and they can easily be identified again in the Roman Catholic writers when read in the original Greek and Latin texts, English translations giving but a very poor idea of the real contents of these.

SECTION XXIII

WHAT THE OCCULTISTS AND KABALISTS HAVE TO SAY

THE Zohar, an unfathomable store of hidden wisdom and mystery, is very often appealed to by Roman Catholic writers. A very learned Rabbi, now the Chevalier Drach, having been converted to Roman Catholicism, and being a great Hebraist, thought fit to step into the shoes of Picus de Mirando and John Reuchlin, and to assure his new co-religionists that the Zohar contained in it pretty nearly all the dogmas of Catholicism. It is not our province to show here how far he has succeeded or failed; only to bring one instance of his explanations and preface it with the following.

The Zohar, is already shown, is not a genuine production of the Hebrew mind. It is the repository and compendium of the oldest doctrine of the East transmitted orally at first, and then written down in independent treatises during the Captivity at Babylon, and finally brought together by Rabbi Simeon Ben Iochai, toward the beginning of the Christian era. As Mosaic cosmogony was born under a new form in Mesopotamian countries, so the Zohar was a vehicle in which were focussed rays from the light of Universal Wisdom. Whatever likenesses are found between it and the Christian teachings, the compilers of the Zohar never had Christ in their minds. Were it otherwise there would not be one single Jew of the Mosaic law left in the world by this time. Again, if one is to accept literally what the Zohar says, then any religion under the sun may find corroboration in its symbols and allegorical sayings; and this, simply because this work is the echo of the primitive truths, and every creed is founded on some of these; the Zohar being but a veil of the Secret Doctrine. This is so evident that we have only to point to the said ex-Rabbi, the Chevalier Drach, to prove the fact.

In Part III, fol. 87 (col. 346th) the Zohar treats of the Spirit guiding the Sun, its Rector, explaining that it is not the Sun itself that is meant thereby, but the Spirit "on, or under" the Sun. Drach is anxious to show that it was Christ who was meant by that "Sun," or the Solar Spirit therein. In his comment upon that passage which refers to the Solar Spirit as "that stone which the builders rejected," he asserts most positively that this

Sun-stone (pierre soleil) is identical with Christ, who was that stone, and that therefore the sun is undeniably (sans contredit) the second hypostasis of the Deity, [Harmonie entre l'Eglise et la Synagogue. t. 11., p.427 by the Chevalier Drach. See de Mirville.] or Christ.

If this be true, then the Vaidic or pre-Vaidic Aryans, Chaldaeans and Egyptians, like all Occultists past, present, and future, Jews included, have been Christians from all eternity. If this be not so, then modern Church Christianity is Paganism pure and simple exoterically, and transcendental and practical Magic or Occultism, Esoterically.

For this "stone" has a manifold significance, a dual existence, with gradations, a regular progression and retrogression. It is a "mystery" indeed.

The Occultists are quite ready to agree with St. Chrystostom, that the infidels - the profane, rather -

Being blinded by sun-light, thus lose sight of the true Sun in the contemplation of the false one.

But if that Saint, and along with him now the Hebraist Drach, chose to see in the Zohar and the Kabalistic Sun " the second hypostasis," this is no reason why all others should be blinded by them. The mystery of the Sun is the grandest perhaps, of all the innumerable mysteries of Occultism. A Gordian knot, truly, but one that cannot be severed with the double-edged sword of scholastic casuistry. It is a true deo dignus vindice nodus, and can be untied only by the Gods. The meaning of this is plain, and every Kabalist will understand it.

Contra solem ne loquaris was not said by Pythagoras with regard to the visible Sun. It was the "Sun of Initiation" that was meant, in its triple form - two of which are the "Day-Sun" and the "Night-Sun."

If behind the physical luminary there were no mystery that people sensed instinctively, why should every nation, from the primitive peoples down to the Parsis of today, have turned towards the Sun during prayers?

THE MYSTERY OF THE SUN-

The Solar Trinity is not Mazdean, but is universal, and is as old as man . All the temples in Antiquity were invariably made to face the Sun, their portals to open to the East. See the old temples of Memphis and Baalbec, the Pyramids of the

Old and of the New (?) Worlds, the Round Towers of Ireland, and the Serapeum of Egypt. The Initiates alone could give a philosophical explanation of this, and a reason for it - its mysticism notwithstanding - were only the world ready to receive it, which, alas! it is not. The last of the Solar Priests in Europe was the Imperial Initiate, Julian, now called the Apostate. [Julian died for the same crime as Socrates. Both divulged a portion of the solar mystery, the heliocentric system being only a part of what was given during Initiation - one consciously, the other unconsciously, the Greek Sage never having been initiated. It was not the real solar system that was preserved in such secrecy, but the mysteries connected with the Sun's constitution. Socrates was sentenced to death by earthly and worldly judges: Julian died a violent death because the hitherto protecting hand was withdrawn from him, and, no longer shielded by it, he was simply left to his destiny or Karma. For the student of Occultism there is a suggestive difference between the two kinds of death. Another memorable instance of the unconscious divulging of secrets pertain to mysteries is that of the poet, P. Ovidius Naso, who, like Socrates, had not been initiated. In his case, the Emperor Augustus, who was an Initiate, mercifully changed the penalty of death into banishment to Tomos on the Euxine. This sudden change from unbounded royal favour to banishment has been a fruitful scheme of speculation to classical scholars not initiated into the Mysteries. They have quoted Ovid's own lines to show that it was some great and heinous immorality of the Emperor of which Ovid had become unwillingly cognizant. The inexorable law of the death penalty always following upon the revelation of any portion of the Mysteries to the profane, was unknown to them. Instead of seeing the amiable and merciful act of the Emperor in its true light, they have made it an occasion for traducing his moral character. The poet's own words can be no evidence, because as he was not an Initiate, it could not be explained to him in what his offence consisted. There have been comparatively modern instances of poets unconsciously revealing in their verses so much of the hidden knowledge as to make even Initiates suppose them to be fellow-Initiates, and come to talk to them on the subject. This only shows that the sensitive poetic temperament is sometimes so far transported beyond the bounds of ordinary sense as to get glimpses into what has been impressed on the Astral Light. In the Light of Asia there are two passages that might make an Initiate of the first degree think that Mr. Edwin Arnold had been initiated himself in the Himalyan ashrams, but this is not so.] He tried to benefit the world by revealing at least a portion of the great mystery of the τρεπλασος and - he died. "There are three in one," he said of the Sun - the central Sun [A proof that Julian was acquainted with the heliocentric system.] being a precaution of Nature: the first is the universal cause of all, Sovereign Good and perfection; the Second Power is paramount Intelligence, having dominion over all reasonable beings, νοεροις;the third is the visible Sun. The pure energy of solar intelligence proceeds from the luminous seat occupied by our Sun in the centre of heaven, that pure energy being the Logos of our system; the "Mysterious Word Spirit produces all through the Sun, and never operates through any other medium," says Hermes Trismegistus. For it is in the Sun, more than in any other heavenly body that the [unknown] Power placed the seat of its habitation. Only neither Hermes Trismegistus nor Julian an initiated Occultist, nor any other, meant by this Unknown Cause Jehovah, or Jupiter. They referred to the cause that produced all the manifested "great Gods" or Demiurgi (the Hebrew God included) of our system. Nor was our visible, material Sun meant, for the latter was only the manifested symbol. Philolaus the Pythagorean, explains and completes Trismegistus by saying:

The Sun is a mirror of fire, the splendour of whose flames by their reflection in that mirror [the Sun] is poured upon us, and that splendour we call image.

It is evident that Philolaus referred to the central spiritual Sun, whose beams and effulgence are only mirrored by our central Star, the Sun. This is as clear to the Occultists as it was to the Pythagoreans. As for the profane of pagan antiquity, it was, of course, the physical Sun that was the "highest God" for them, as it seems - if Chevalier Drach's view be accepted - to have now virtually become for the modern Roman Catholics. If words mean anything, the statements made by the Chevalier Drach that "this sun is, undeniably, the second hypostasis of the Deity," imply what we say; as "this Sun" refers to the Kabalistic Sun, and "hypostasis" means substance or subsistence of the Godhead or Trinity - distinctly personal. As the author, being an ex-Rabbi, thoroughly versed in Hebrew, and in the mysteries of the Zohar, ought to know the value of words; and as, moreover, in writing this, he was bent upon reconciling "the seeming contradictions," as he puts it, between Judaism and Christianity - the fact becomes quite evident.

But all this pertains to questions and problems which will be solved naturally and in the course of the development of the doctrine. The Roman Catholic Church stands accused, not of worshipping under other names the Divine Beings worshipped by all nations in Antiquity, but of declaring idolatrous, not only the Pagans ancient and modern, but every Christian nation that has freed itself from the Roman yoke. The accusation brought against herself by more than one man of Science, of worshipping the stars like true Sabaeans of old, stands to this day uncontradicted, yet no star-worshipper has ever addressed his adoration to the material stars and planets, as will be shown before the last page of this work is written; none the less it is true that those Philosophers alone who studied Astrology and Magic knew that the last word of those sciences was to be sought in, and expected from, the Occult forces emanating from those constellations.

SECTION XXIV

MODERN KABALISTS IN SCIENCE AND OCCULT ASTRONOMY

THERE is a physical, an astral, and a super-astral Universe in the three chief divisions of the Kabalah; as there are terrestrial, super-terrestrial, and spiritual Beings. The "Seven Planetary Spirits" may be ridiculed by Scientists to their hearts' content, yet the need of intelligent ruling and guiding Forces in so much felt to this day that scientific men and specialists, who will not hear of Occultism or of ancient systems, find themselves obliged to generate in their inner consciousness some kind of semi-mystical system. Metcalf's "sun-force" theory, and that of Zaliwsky, a learned Pole, which made Electricity the Universal Force and placed its storehouse in the Sun, [La Gravitation par l'Electricité, p.7. quoted by De Mirville, iv. 156] were revivals of the Kabalistic teachings. Zaliwsky tried to prove that Electricity, producing "the most powerful, attractive, calorific, and luminous effects," was present in the physical constitution of the Sun and explained its peculiarities. This is very near the Occult teaching. It is only by admitting the gaseous nature of the Sun-reflector, and the powerful Magnetism and Electricity of the solar attraction and repulsion, that one can explain (a) the evident absence of any waste of power and luminosity in the Sun - inexplicable by the ordinary laws of combustion; and (b) the behaviour of the planets, so often contradicting every accepted rule of weight and gravity. And Zaliwsky makes this "solar electricity" "differ from anything known on earth."

Father Secchi may be suspected of having sought to introduce Forces of quite a new order and quite foreign to gravitation, which he had discovered in Space. [De Mirville. iv.157.] in order to reconcile Astronomy with theological Astronomy. But Nagy, a member of the Hungarian Academy of Sciences, was no clerical, and yet he develops a theory on the necessity of intelligent Forces whose complacency "would lent itself to all the whims of the comets." He suspects that:

Notwithstanding all the actual researches on the rapidity of light - that dazzling product of an unknown force . . . . which we see too frequently to understand – that light is motionless in reality.

[C. E. Love, the well-known railway builder and engineer in France, tired of blind forces, made all the (then) "imponderable agents" - now called "forces" - subordinates of Electricity, and declares the latter to be

an Intelligence - albeit molecular in nature and material. [Essai sur l'Identité des Agents Producteurs du Son, de la Lumiere, etc., p.15, ibid .]

In the author's opinion these Forces are atomistic agents, endowed with intelligence, spontaneous will, and motion, [Ibid.,p.218.] and he thus, like the Kabalists, makes the cousal Forces substantial, while the Forces that act on this plane are only the effects of the former, as with him matter is eternal, and the Gods also; [Summarised from Ibid., p.213. De Mirville, iv.158.] so is the Soul likewise, though it has inherent in itself a still higher Soul [Spirit], preëxistent, endowed with memory, and superior to Electric Force; the latter is subservient to the higher Souls, those superior Souls forcing it to act according to the eternal laws. The concept is rather hazy, but is evidently on the Occult lines. Moreover, the system proposed is entirely pantheistic, and is worked out in a purely scientific volume. Monotheists and Roman Catholics fall foul of it, of course; but one who believes in the Planetary Spirits and who endows Nature with living Intelligences, must always expect this.

In this connection, however, it is curious that after the moderns have so laughed at the ignorance of the ancients, who, knowing only of seven planets [yet having an ogdoad which did not include the earth!], invented therefore seven Spirits to fit in with the number, Babinet should have vindicated the "superstition" unconsciously to himself. In the Revue des Deux Mondes this eminent French Astronomer writes:

THE PLACE OF NEPTUNE -

The ogdoad of the Ancients included the earth [which is an error] i.e., eight or seven according to whether or not the earth was comprised in the number. [May. 1855. Ibid., p.139.]

De Mirville assures his readers that:

M. Babinet was telling me but a few days ago that we had in reality only eight big planets, including the earth, and so many small ones between Mars and Jupiter . . . .Herschell offering to call all those beyond the seven primary planets asteroids! [La Terre et notre Systieme solaire. De Mirville, iv. 139.]

There is a problem to be solved in this connection. How do Astronomers know that Neptune is a planet, or even that it is a body belonging to our system? Being found on the very confines of our Planetary World, so called, the latter was arbitrarily expanded to receive it; but what really mathematical and infallible proof have Astronomers that it is (a) a planet, and (b) one of our planets? None at all! It is as such an immeasurable distance from us, the apparent diameter of the sun being to Neptune but one-fortieth of the sun's apparent diameter to us, and it is so dim and hazy when seen through the best telescope that it looks like an astronomical romance to call it one of our planets. Neptune's heat and light are reduced to 1/900th part of the heat and light received by the earth. His motion and that of his satellites have always looked suspicious. They do not agree - in appearance at least - with those of the other planets. His system is retrograde, etc. But even the latter abnormal fact resulted only in the creation of new hypotheses by our Astronomers, who forthwith suggested a probable overturn of Neptune, his collision with another body, etc. Was Adams' and Leverrier's discovery so welcomed because Neptune was as necessary as was Ether to throw a new glory upon astronomical prevision, upon the certitude of modern scientific data and principally upon the power of mathematical analysis? It would so appear. A new planet that widens our planetary domain by more than four hundred million leagues is worthy of annexation. Yet, as in the case of terrestrial annexation, scientific authority may be proved "right" only because it has "might." Neptune's motion happens to be dimly perceived: Eureka! it is a planet! A mere motion, however, proves very little. It is now an ascertained fact in Astronomy that there are no absolutely fixed stars in Nature, [If, as Sir W. Herschel thought, the so-called fixed stars have resulted from, and owe their origin to nebular combustion, they cannot be fixed any more than is our sun, which was believed to be motionless and is now found to rotate around its axis every twenty-five days. As the fixed star nearest to the sun, however, is eight-thousand times farther away from him than is Neptune the illusions furnished by the telescopes must be also eight-thousand times as great. We will therefore leave the question at rest, repeating only what A. Maury said in his work (La Terre et l'Homme, published in 1858): "It is utterly impossible, so far, to decide anything concerning Neptune's constitution, analogy alone authorising us to ascribe to him a rotary motion like that of other planets." (De Mirville, iv. 140).] even though such stars should continue to exist in astronomical parlance, while they have passed from the scientific imagination. Occultism, however, has a strange theory of its own with regard to Neptune.

Occultism says that if several hypotheses resting on mere assumption - which have been accepted only because they have been taught by eminent men of learning - are taken away from the Science of Modern Astronomy, to which they serve as props, then even the presumably universal law of gravitation will be found to be contrary to the most ordinary truths of mechanics. And really one can hardly blame Christians - foremost of all the Roman Catholics - however scientific some of these may themselves be, for refusing to quarrel with their Church for the sake of scientific beliefs. Nor can we even blame them for accepting in the secresy of their hearts - as some of them do - the theological "Virtues" and "Archons" of Darkness, instead of all the blind forces offered them by Science.

Never can there be intervention of any sort in the marshalling and the regular precession of the celestial bodies! The law of gravitation is the law of laws; who ever witnessed a stone rising in the air against gravitation? The permanence of the universal law is shown in the behaviour of the sidereal worlds and globes eternally faithful to their primitive orbits; never wandering beyond their respective paths. Nor is there any intervention needed, as it could only be disastrous. Whether the first sidereal incipient rotation took place owing to an intercosmic chance, or to the spontaneous development of latent primordial forces; or again, whether that impulse was given once for all by God or Gods - it does not make the slightest difference. At this stage of cosmic evolution no intervention, superior or inferior, is admissible. Were any to take place, the universal clock-work would stop, and Kosmos would fall into pieces.

Such are stray sentences, pearls of wisdom, fallen from time to time from scientific lips, and now chosen at random to illustrate a query. We lift our diminished heads and look heavenward. Such seems to be the fact: worlds, suns, and stars, the shining myriads of the heavenly hosts, remind the Poet of an infinite, shoreless ocean, whereon move swiftly numberless squadrons of ships, millions upon millions of cruisers, large and small, crossing each other, whirling and gyrating in every direction; and Science teaches us, that though they be without rudder or compass or any beacon to guide them, they are nevertheless secure from collision - almost secure, at any rate, save in chance accidents - as the whole celestial machine is built upon and guided by an immutable, albeit blind, law, and by constant and accelerating force or forces.

SELF-GENERATION EX-NIHOLO?-

"Built upon" by whom? "By self-evolution," is the answer. Moreover, as dynamics teach that

A body in motion tends to continue in the same state of relative rest or motion unless acted upon by some external force,

this force has to be regarded as self-generated - even if not eternal, since this would amount to the recognition of perpetual motion - and so well self-calculated and self-adjusted as to last from the beginning to the end of Kosmos. But "self-generation" has still to generate from something, generation ex-nihilo being as contrary to reason as it is to Science. Thus we are placed once more between the horns of a dilemma: are we to believe in perpetual motion or in self-generation ex-nihilo? And if in neither, who or what is that something, which first produced that force or those forces?

There are such things in mechanics as superior levers, which give the impulse and act upon secondary or inferior levers. The former, however, need an impulse and occasional renovation, otherwise they would themselves very soon stop and fall back into their original status. What is the external force which puts and retains them in motion? Another dilemma!

As to the law of cosmical non-intervention, it could be justified only in one case, namely, if the celestial mechanism were perfect; but it is not. The so-called unalterable motions of celestial bodies alter and change incessantly; they are very often disturbed, and the wheels of even the sidereal locomotive itself occasionally jump off their invisible rails, as may be easily proved. Otherwise why should Laplace speak of the probable occurrence at some future time of an out-and-out reform in the arrangements of the planets; [Exposition du vrai System du Monde. p. 282.] or Lagrange maintain the gradual narrowing of the orbits; or our modern Astronomers, again, declare that the fuel in the sun is slowly disappearing? If the laws and forces which govern the behaviour of the celestial bodies are immutable, such modifications and wearing-out of substance or fuel, of force and fluids, would be impossible; yet they are not denied. Therefore one has to suppose that such modifications will have to rely upon the laws of forces, which will have to self-regenerate themselves once more on such occasions, thus producing an astral antinomy, and a kind of physical palinomy, since, as Laplace says, one would then see fluids disobeying themselves and reacting in a way contrary to all their attributes and properties.

Newton felt very uncomfortable about the moon. Her behaviour in progressively narrowing the circumference of her orbit around the earth made him nervous, lest it should end one day in our satellite falling upon the earth. The world, he confessed, needed repairing, and that very often. [See the passage quoted by Herschel in Natural Philosophy, p.

165. De Mirville. iv.165.] In this he was corroborated by Herschel. [l,oc. cit.] He speaks of real and quite considerable deviations, besides those which are only apparent, but gets some consolation from his conviction that somebody or something will probably see to things.

We may be answered that the personal beliefs of some pious Astronomers, however great they may be as scientific characters, are no proofs of the actual existence and presence in space of intelligent supramundane Beings, of either Gods or Angels. It is the behaviour of the stars and planets themselves that has to be analysed and inferences must be drawn therefrom. Renan asserts that nothing that we know of the sidereal bodies warrants the idea of the presence of any Intelligence, whether internal or external to them.

Let us see, says Reynaud, if this is a fact, or only one more empty scientific assumption.

The orbits traversed by the planets are far from being immutable. They are, on the contrary, subject to perpetual mutation in position, as in form. Elongations, contractions, and orbital widenings, oscillations from right to left, slackening and quickening of speed . . .. And all this on a plane which seems to vacillate. [Terre et Ciel. p.28. Ibid.]

As is very pertinently observed by des Mousseux:

Here is a path having little of the mathematical and mechanical precision claimed for it; for we know of no clock which, having gone slow for several minutes should catch up the right time of itself and without the turn of a key.

So much for blind law and force. As for the physical impossibility - a miracle indeed in the sight of Science - of a stone raised in the air against the law of gravitation, this is what Babinet - the deadliest enemy and opponent of the phenomena of levitation - (cited by Arago) says:

ARE THERE ANGELS IN STARS?-

Everyone knows the theory of bolides [meteors] and aerolithes . . . . In Connecticut an immense aerolith was seen [a mass of eighteen hundred feet in diameter], bombarding a whole American zone and returning to the spot [in mid-air] from which it had started. [Oeuvres d'Arago.vol.i., 219: quoted by De Mirville, iii. 462.]

Thus we find in both of the cases above cited - that of self-correcting planets and meteors of gigantic size flying back into the air - a "blind force" regulating and resisting the natural tendencies of "blind matter," and even occasionally repairing its mistakes and correcting its failures. This is far more miraculous and even "extravagant," one would say, than any "Angel-guided" Element.

Bold is he who laughs at the idea of Von Haller, who declares that:

The stars are perhaps an abode of glorious Spirits; as here Vice reigns, there is Virtue master. ["Die Sterne sind vielleicht ein Sitz Verklarter Geister;

Wie hier das Laster herrscht, ist dort die Tugend Meister.]

SECTION XXV

EASTERN AND WESTERN OCCULTISM

IN The Theosophist for March, 1886, [Op.cit.,p.411] in an answer to the "Solar Sphinx," a member of the London Lodge of the Theosophical Society wrote as follows:

We hold and believe that the revival of Occult Knowledge now in progress will some day demonstrate that the Western system represents ranges of perceptions which the Eastern - at least as expounded in the pages of The Theosophist—has yet to attain.[Whenever Occult doctrines were expounded in the pages of The Theosophist, care was taken each time to declare a subject incomplete when the whole could not be given in its fullness, and no writer has ever tried to mislead the reader. As to the Western "ranges of perception" concerning doctrines really Occult, the Eastern Occultists have been made acquainted with them for some time past. Thus they are enabled to assert with confidence that the West may be in possession of Hermetic philosophy as a speculative system of dialectics, the latter being used in the West admirably well, but it lacks entirely the knowledge of Occultism. The genuine Eastern Occultist keeps silent and unknown, never publishes what he knows, and rarely even speaks of it, as he knows too well the penalty of indiscretion.]

The writer is not the only person labouring under this erroneous impression. Greater Kabalists than he had said the same in the United States. This only proves that the knowledge possessed by Western Occultists of the true Philosophy, and the "ranges of perceptions" and thought of the Eastern doctrines, is very superficial. This assertion will be easily demonstrated by giving a few instances, instituting comparisons between the two interpretations of one and the same doctrine---the Hermetic Universal Doctrine. It is the more needed since, were we to neglect bringing forward such comparisons, our work would be left incomplete.

PRIMORDIAL MATTER-

We may take the late Éliphas Lévi, rightly referred to by another Western Mystic, Mr. Kenneth Mackenzie, as "one of the greatest representatives of modern Occult Philosophy," [See The Royal Masonic Cyclopaedia,art. "Sepher Jetzirah."] as presumably the best and most learned expounder of the Chaldaean Kabalah, and compare his teaching with that of Eastern Occultists. In his unpublished manuscripts and letters, lent to us by a Theosophist, who was for fifteen years his pupil, we had hoped to find that which he was unwilling to publish. What we do find, however, disappoints us greatly. We will take these teachings, then, as containing the essence of Western or Kabalistic Occultism, analyzing and comparing them with the Eastern interpretation as we go on.

Éliphas Lévi teaches correctly, though in language rather too rhapsodically rhetorical to be sufficiently clear to the beginner, that

Eternal life is Motion equilibrated by the alternate manifestations of force.

But why does he not add that this perpetual motion is

independent of the manifested Forces at work? He says:

Chaos is the Tohu-vah-bohu of perpetual motion and the sum total of primordial matter; and he fails to add that Matter is "primordial" only at the beginning of every new reconstruction of the Universe: matter in abscondito, as it is called by the Alchemists, is eternal, indestructible, without beginning or end. It is regarded by Eastern Occultists as the eternal Root of all, the Mûlaprakriti of the Vedântin, and the Svabhâvat of the Buddhist; the Divine Essence, in short, or Substance; the radiations from This are periodically aggregated into graduated forms, from pure Spirit to gross Matter; the Root, or Space, is in its abstract presence the Deity Itself, the Ineffable and Unknown One Cause.

Ain-Suph with him also is the Boundless, the infinite and One Unity, secondless and causeless as Parabrahman. Ain-Suph is the indivisible point, and therefore, as "being everywhere and nowhere," is the absolute All. It is also "Darkness" because it is absolute Light, and the Root of the seven fundamental Cosmic Principles. Yet Éliphas Lévi, by simply stating that "Darkness was upon the face of the Earth," fails to show (a) that "Darkness" in this sense is Deity Itself, and he is therefore withholding the only philosophical solution of this problem for the human mind; and (b) he allows the unwary student to believe that by "Earth" our own little globe—an atom in the Universe—is meant. In short, this teaching does not embrace the Occult Cosmogony, but deals simply with Occult Geology and the formation of our cosmic speck. This is further shown by his making a resume of the Sephirothal Tree in this wise:

God is harmony, the astronomy of Powers and Unity outside of the World.

This seems to suggest (a) that he teaches the existence of an extra-cosmic God, thus limiting and conditioning both the Kosmos and the divine Infinity and Omnipresence which cannot be extraneous to or outside of one single atom; and (b) that by skipping the whole of the pre-cosmic period—the manifested Kosmos here being meant —the very root of Occult teaching he explains only the Kabalistic meaning of the dead-letter of the Bible and Genesis, leaving its spirit and essence untouched. Surely the "ranges of perception" of the Western mind will not be greatly enlarged by such a limited teaching.

Having said a few words on Tohu-vah-bohu—the meaning of which Wordsworth rendered graphically as "higgledy-piggledy"—and having explained that this term denoted Cosmos, he teaches that:

Above the dark abyss [Chaos] were the Waters . . . . the earth [la terre!] was Tohu-vah-bohu, i.e., in confusion, and darkness covered the face of the Deep, and vehement Breath moved on the Waters when the Spirit exclaimed [?], "Let there be light," and there was light. Thus the earth [our globe, of course] was in a state of cataclysm; thick vapours veiled the immensity of the sky, the earth was covered with waters and a violent wind was agitating this dark ocean, when at a given moment the equilibrium revealed itself and light reappeared; the letters that compose the Hebrew word "Bereshith" (the first word of Genesis) are "Beth," the binary, the verb manifested by the act, a feminine letter;

then "Resch," the Verbum and Life, number 20, the disc multiplied by 2; and "Aleph," the spiritual principle, the Unit, a masculine letter.

Place these letters in a triangle and you have the absolute Unity, that without being included into numbers creates the number, the first manifestation, which is 2, and these two united by harmony resulting from the analogy of contraries [opposites], make I, only. This is why God is called Elohim (plural).

All this is very ingenious, but is very puzzling, besides being incorrect. For owing to the first sentence, "Above the dark abyss were the Waters," the French Kabalist leads the student away from the right track. This an Eastern Chela will see at a glance, and even one of the profane may see it. For if the Tohu-vah-bohu is "under" and the Waters are "above," then these two are quite distinct from each other, and this is not the case.

THE GREAT DEEP –

This statement is a very important one, inasmuch as it entirely changes the spirit and nature of Cosmogony, and brings it down to a level with exoteric Genesis—gerhaps it was so stated with an eye to this result. The Tohu-vah-bohu is the "Great Deep," and is identical with "the Waters of Chaos," or the primordial Darkness. By stating the fact otherwise it makes both "the Great Deep" and the "Waters"—which cannot be separated except in the phenomenal world --- limited as to space and conditioned as to their nature. Thus Éliphas in his desire to conceal the last word of Esoteric

Philosophy, fails—whether intentionally or otherwise does not matter—to point out the fundamental principle of the one true Occult Philosophy, namely, the unity and absolute homogeneity of the One Eternal Divine Element, and he makes of the Deity a male God. Then he says:

Above the Waters was the powerful Breath of the Elohim [the creative Dhyan Chohans]. Above the Breath appeared the Light, and above the Light the Word . . . that created it.

Now the fact is quite the reverse of this: it is the Primeval Light that creates the Word or Logos, Who in His turn creates physical light. To prove and illustrate what he says he gives the following figure:

Now any Eastern Occultist upon seeing this would not hesitate to pronounce it a "left hand" magic figure. It is entirely reversed, and it represents the third stage of religious thought, that current in Dvapara Yuga, when the one principle is already separated into male and female, and humanity is approaching the fall into materiality which brings the Kali Yuga. A student of Eastern Occultism would draw it thus:

For the Secret Doctrine teaches us that the reconstruction of the Universe takes place in this wise: At the periods of new generation, perpetual Motion becomes Breath; from the Breath comes forth primordial Light, through whose radiance manifest the Eternal Thought concealed in darkness, and this becomes the Word (Mantra). [In the exoteric sense, the Mantra (or that psychic faculty or power that conveys perception or thought) is the older portion of the Vedas, the second part of which is composed of the Brâhmanas. In Esoteric phraseology Mantra is the Word made flesh, or rendered objective, through divine magic.] It is That (the Mantra or Word) from which all This (the Universe) sprang into being.

Further on Éliphas Lévi says:

This [the concealed Deity] radiated a ray into the Eternal Essence [Waters of Space] and, fructifying thereby the primordial germ, the Essence expanded. [The secret meaning of the word "Brahmâ" is "expansion," "increase," or "growth."] giving birth to the Heavenly Man from whose mind were born all forms.

The Kabalah states very nearly the same. To learn what it really teaches one has to reverse the order in which Éliphas Lévi gives it, replacing the word "above by that of "in" as there cannot surely be any "above" or "under"" in the Absolute. This is what he says:

Above the waters the powerful breath of the Elohim; above the Breath the Light; above Light the Word, or the Speech that created it. We see here the spheres of evolution: the soul [?] driven from the dark centre (Darkness) toward the luminous circumference. At the bottom of the lowest circle is the Tohu-vah-bohu, or the chaos which precedes all manifestation [Naissances—generation]; then the region of Water; then Breath; then Light; and, lastly, the Word.

THE CHAOS OF GENESIS –

The construction of the above sentences shows that the learned Abbé had a decided tendency to anthropomorphize creation, even though the latter has to be shaped out of preëxisting material, as the Zohar shows plainly enough.

This is how the "great" Western Kabalist gets out of the difficulty: he keeps silent on the first stage of evolution and imagines a second Chaos. Thus he says:

The Tohu-vah-bohu is the Latin Limbus, or twilight of the morning and evening of life,[Why not give at once its theological meaning, as we find it in Webster? With the Roman Catholics it means simply "purgatory," the borderland between heaven and hell (Limbus patrum and

Limbus infantum), the one for all men, whether good, bad or indifferent: the other for the souls of unbaptized children! With the ancients it meant simply that which in Esoteric Buddhism is called the Kâma Loka, between Devachan and Avitchi.] It is in perpetual motion, [As Chaos, the eternal Element, not as the Kâma Loka surely?] it decomposes continually [A proof that by this word Éliphas Lévi means the lowest region of the terrestrial Akasha.] and the work of putrefaction accelerates, because the world is advancing towards regeneration [Evidently he is concerned only wiht our periodical world, or the terrestrial globe.] .The Tohu-vah-bohu of the Hebrews is not exactly the confusion of things called Chaos by the Greeks, and which is found described in the commencement of the Metamorphosis of Ovid; it is something greater and more profound; it is the foundation of religion, it is the philosophical affirmation of the immateriality of God.

Rather an affirmation of the materiality of a personal God. If a man has to seek his Deity in the Hades of the ancients— for the Tohu-vah bohu, or the Limbus of the Greeks, is the Hall of Hades —then one can wonder no longer at the accusations brought forward by the Church against the "witches" and sorcerers versed in Western Kabalism, that they adored the goat Mendes, or the devil personified by certain spooks and Elementals. But in face of the task Éliphas Lévi had set before himself—that of reconciling Jewish Magic with Roman ecclesiasticism—he could say nothing else.

Then he explains the first sentence in Genesis:

Let us put on one side the vulgar translation of the sacred

texts and see what is hidden in the first chapter of Genesis.

He then gives the Hebrew text quite correctly, but transliterates it:

Bereschith Bara Eloim uth aschamam ouatti aares ouares ayete Tohu-vah-bohu. . . . Ouimas Eloim rai avur ouiai aour.

And he then explains:

The first word, "Bereschith," signifies "genesis," a word equivalent to "nature." "The act of generation or production," we maintain; not "nature." He then continues:

The phase, then, is incorrectly translated in the Bible. It is not "in the beginning," for it should be at the stage of the generating force.[In the "reawakening" of the Forces would be more correct.] which would thus exclude every idea of the ex-nihilo . . . .as nothing cannot produce something. The word "Eloim" or "Elohim" signifies the generating Powers, and such is the Occult sense of the first verse . . . . "Bereschith" ("nature" or "genesis'), "Bara" ("created') "Eloim" ("the forces") "Athat-ashamaim" ("heavens") "ouath" and "oaris" ("the earth"); that is to say, "The generative potencies created indefinitely (eternally) [An action which is incessant in eternity cannot be called "creation;" it is evolution, and the eternally or ever—becoming of the Greek Philosopher and the Hindu Vedantin: it is the Sat and the one Beingness of Parmenides, or the Being identical with Thought. Now how can the Potencies be said to "create movement, once it is seen movement never had any beginning, but existed in the Eternity? Why not say that the reawakened Potencies transferred motion from the eternal to the temporal plane of being? Surely this is not Creation.] those forces that are the equilibrated opposites that we call heaven and earth, meaning the space and the bodies, the volatile and the fixed, the movement and the weight.

Now this, if it be correct, is too vague to be understood by any one ignorant of the Kabalistic teaching. Not only are his explanations unsatisfactory and misleading—in his published works they are still worse—but his Hebrew transliteration is entirely wrong; it precludes the student, who would compare it for himself with the equivalent symbols and numerals of the words and letters of the Hebrew alphabet, from finding anything of that he might have found were the words correctly spelt in the French transliteration.

Compared even with exoteric Hindu Cosmogony, the philosophy which Éliphas Lévi gives out as Kabalistic is simply mystical Roman Catholicism adapted to the Christian Kabalah. His Histoire de la Magie shows it plainly, and reveals also his object, which he does not even care to conceal. For, while stating with his Church, that

The Christian religion has imposed silence on the lying oracles of the Gentiles and put an end to the prestige of the false gods, [Histoire de la Magie. Int., p.1.]

he promises to prove in his work that the real Sanctum Regnum, the great Magic Art, is in that Star of Bethlehem which led the three Magi to adore the Savior of this World. He says:

We will prove that the study of the sacred Pentagram had to lead all the Magi to know the new name which should be raised above all names, and before which every being capable of worship has to bend his knees. [Histoire de la

Magic. Int., p.2.]

THE BIBLE OF HUMANITY –

This shows that Lévi's Kabalah is mystic Christianity, and not Occultism; for Occultism is universal and knows no difference between the "Saviours" (or great Avatâras) of the several old nations. Éliphas Lévi was not an exception in preaching Christianity under a disguise of Kabalism. He was undeniably "the greatest representative of modern Occult Philosophy," as it is studied in Roman Catholic countries generally, where it is fitted to the preconceptions of Christian students. But he never taught the real universal Kabalah, and least of all did he teach Eastern Occultism. Let the student compare the Eastern and Western teaching, and see whether the philosophy of the Upanishads" has yet to attain the ranges of perception" of this Western system. Everyone has the right to defend the system he prefers, but in doing this, there is no need to throw slurs upon the system of one's brother.

In view of the great resemblance between many of the fundamental "truths" of Christianity and the "myths" of Brâhmanism, there have been serious attempts made lately to prove that the Bhagavad Gita and most of the Brâhamanas and the Purânas are of a far later date than the Mosaic Books and even than the Gospels. But were it possible that an enforced success should be obtained in this direction, such argument cannot achieve its object, since the Rig Veda remains. Brought down to the most modern limits of the age assigned to it, its date cannot be made to overlap that of the Pentateuch, which is admittedly later.

The Orientalists know well that they cannot make away with the landmarks, followed by all subsequent religions, set up in that "Bible of Humanity" called the Rig Veda. It is there that at the very dawn of intellectual humanity were laid the foundation-stones of all the faiths and creeds, of every fane and church built from first to last; and they are still there. Universal "myths," personifications of Powers divine and cosmic, primary and secondary, and historical personages of all the now-existing as well as of extinct religions are to be found in the seven chief Deities and their 330,000,000 correlations of the Rig Veda, and those Seven, with the odd millions, are the Rays of the one boundless Unity.

But to THIS can never be offered profane worship. It can only be the "object of the most abstract meditation, which Hindus practice in order to obtain absorption in it." At the beginning of every "dawn" of "Creation," eternal Light—which is darkness—assumes the aspect of so-called Chaos" chaos to the human intellect; the eternal Root to the superhuman or spiritual sense.

"Osiris is a black God." These were the words pronounced at "low breath" at Initiation in Egypt, because Osiris Noumenon is darkness to the mortal. In this Chaos are formed the "Waters," Mother Isis, Aditi, etc. They are the "Waters of Life," in which primordial germs are created—or rather reawakened—by the primordial Light. It is Purushottama, or the Divine Spirit, which in its capacity of Nârâyna, the Mover on the Waters of Space, fructifies and infuses the Breath of life into that germ which becomes the "Golden Mundane Egg," in which the male Brahmâ is created; [The Vaishnavas, who regard Vishnu as the Supreme God and the fashioner of the Universe, claim that Brahmâ sprang from the navel of Vishnu, the "imperishable," or rather from the lotus that grew from it. But the word "navel" here means the Central point, the mathematical symbol of infinitude, or Parabrahman, the One and the Secondless.] and from this the first Prajapâti, the Lord of Beings, emerges, and becomes the progenitor of mankind. And though it is not he, but the Absolute, that is said to contain the Universe in Itself, yet it is the duty of the male Brahmâ to manifest it in a visible form. Hence he has to be connected with the procreation of species, and assumes, like Jehovah and other male Gods in subsequent anthropomorphism, a phallic symbol. At best every such male God, the "Father" of all, becomes the "Archetypal Man." Between him and the Infinite Deity stretches an abyss. In the theistic religions of personal Gods the latter are degraded from abstract Forces into physical potencies. The Water of Life—the "Deep" of Mother Nature—is viewed in its terrestrial aspect in anthropomorphic religions. Behold, how holy it has become by theological magic! It is held sacred and is deified now as of old in almost every religion. But if Christians use it as a means of spiritual purification in baptism and prayer; if Hindus pay reverence to their sacred streams, tanks and rivers; if Pârsi, Mahommedan and Christian alike believe in its efficacy, surely that element must have some great and Occult significance. In Occultism it stands for the Fifth Principle of Kosmos, in the lower septenary: for the whole visible Universe was built by Water, say the Kabalists who know the difference between the two waters —the "Waters of Life" and those of Salvation—so confused together in dogmatic religions. The "King-Preacher" says of himself:

I, the Preacher, was king over Israel in Jerusalem, and I gave my heart to seek and search out by wisdom concerning all things that are done under heaven. [Ecclesiastes. i. 12. 13.]

Speaking of the great work and glory of the Elohim [It is probably needless to say here what everyone knows. The translation of the Protestant Bible is not a word for word rendering of the earlier Greek and Latin Bibles: the sense is very often disfigured, and "God" is put where "Jahve" and "Elohim" stand.]—unified into the "Lord God" in the English Bible, whose garment, he tells us, is light and heaven the curtain—he refers to the builder

CHAOS IS THEOS OR KOSMOS -

Who layeth the beams of his chambers in the waters,[Psalms. civ. 2.3.] that is, the divine Host of the Sephiroth, who have constructed the Universe out of the Deep, the Waters of Chaos. Moses and Thales were right in saying that only earth and water can bring forth a living Soul, water being on this plane the principle of all things. Moses was an Initiate, Thales a Philosopher - i.e., a Scientist, for the words were synonymous in his day.

The secret meaning of this is that water and earth stand in the Mosaic Books for the prima materia and the creative (feminine) Principle on our plane. In Egypt Osiris was Fire, and Isis was the Earth or its synonym Water; the two opposing elements—just because of their opposite properties—

being necessary to each other for a common object; that of procreation. The earth needs solar heat and rain to make her throw out her germs. But these procreative properties of Fire and Water, or Spirit and Matter, are symbols but of physical generation. While the Jewish Kabalists symbolized these elements only in their application to manifested things, and reverenced them as the emblems for the production of terrestrial life, the Eastern Philosophy noticed them only as an illusive emanation from their spiritual prototypes, and no unclean or unholy thought marred its Esoteric religious symbology.

Chaos, as shown elsewhere, is Theos, which becomes Kosmos: it is Space, the container of everything in the Universe. As Occult Teachings assert, it is called by the Chaldaeans, Egyptians, and every other nation Tohu-vah-bohu, or Chaos, Confusion, because Space is the great storehouse of Creation, whence proceed not forms alone, but also ideas, which could receive their expression only through the Logos, the Word, Verbum, or Sound.

The numbers 1, 2, 3, 4 are the successive emanations from Mother [Space] as she forms running downward her garment, spreading it upon the seven steps of Creation.[To avoid misunderstanding of the word "creation" so often used by us, the remarks of the author of Through the Gates of Gold may be quoted owing to their clearness and simplicity. "The words 'to create' are often understood by the ordinary mind to convey the idea of evolving something out of nothing. This is clearly not its meaning. We are mentally obliged to provide our Creator with chaos from which to produce the worlds. The tiller of the soil, who is the typical producer of social life, must have his material: his earth, his sky, rain and sun, and the seeds to place within the earth. Out of nothing he can produce nothing. Out of a void nature cannot arise: there is that material beyond, behind, or within, from which she is shaped by our desire for a Universe." (P.72)] The roller returns upon itself, as one end joins the other in infinitude, and the numbers 4, 3, and 2 are displayed, as it is the only side of the veil that we can perceive, the first number being lost in its inaccessible solitude.

. . . .Father, which is Boundless Time, generates Mother, which is infinite Space, in Eternity; and Mother generates Father in Manvantaras, which are divisions of durations, that Day when that world becomes one ocean. Then the Mother becomes Nârâ [Waters —the Great Deep] for Nara [the Supreme Spirit] to rest—or move—upon, when, it is said, that 1, 2, 3, 4 descend and abide in the world of the unseen, while the 4, 3, 2, become the limits in the visible world to deal with the manifestations of Father [Time]. [Commentary on Stanza ix. on Cycles.]

This relates to the Mahâyugas which in figures become 432, and with the addition of noughts, 4,320.000.

Now it is surpassingly strange, if it be a mere coincidence, that the numerical value of Tohu-vah-bohu, or "Chaos" in the Bible—which Chaos, of course, is the "Mother" Deep, or the Waters of Space—should yield the same figures. For this is what is found in a Kabalist manuscript:

It is said of the Heavens and the Earth in the second verse of Genesis that they were "Chaos and Confusion"—

that is, they were "Tohu-vah-bohu;" "and darkness was upon the face of the deep." i.e., "the perfect material out of which construction was to be made lacked organization." The order of the digits of these words as they stand—i.e., [Or, read from right to left, the letters and their corresponding numerals stand thus: "t," 4: "h." 5: "bh," 2: "v," 6: "v" 6: "h," 5: " "v" or "w," 6: which yields "thuvbhu," 4566256, or "Tohu-vah-bohu."] the letters rendered by their numerical value—is 6,526,654 and 2,386. By art speech these are key-working numbers loosely shuffled together, the germs and keys of construction, but to be recognized, one by one, as used and required. They follow symmetrically in the work as immediately following the first sentence of grand enunciation: "In Rash developed itself Gods, the heavens and the earth."

Multiply the numbers of the letters of "Tohu-vah-bohu" together continuously from right to left, placing the consecutive single products as we go, and we will have the following series of values, viz., (a) 30, 60, 360, 2,160, 10,800, 43,200, or as by the characterizing digits; 3, 6, 36, 216, 108, and 432; (b) 20, 120, 720 , 1,440, 7,200, or 2, 12, 72, 144, 72, 432, the series closing in 432, one of the most famous numbers of antiquity, and which, though obscured, crops out in the chronology up to the Flood. [Mr. Ralston Skinner's MSS.]

ONE HUNDRED AND EIGHT -

This shows that the Hebrew usage of play upon the numbers must have come to the Jews from India. As we have seen, the final series yields, besides many another combination, the figures 108 and 1008—the number of the names of Vishnu, whence the 108 grains of the Yogi's rosary—and close with 432, the truly "famous" number in Indian and Chaldaean antiquity, appearing in the cycle of 4,320,000 years in the former, and in the 432,000 years, the duration of the Chaldaean divine dynasties.

SECTION XXVI

THE IDOLS AND THE TERAPHIM

THE meaning of the "fairy-tale" told by the Chaldaean Qû-Tâmy is easily understood. His modus operandi with the "idol of the moon" was that of all the Semites , before Terah, Abraham's father made images—the Teraphim, called after him—or the "chosen people" of Israel ceased divining by them. These teraphim were just as much "idols" as in any pagan image or statue. [That the teraphim was a statue, and no small article either, is shown in Samuel xix., where Michal takes a teraphim ("image," as it is translated) and puts it in bed to represent David, her husband, who ran away from Saul (see verse 13, et seq.) It was thus of the size and shape of a human figure—a statue or real idol.] The injunction "Thou shalt not bow to a graven image," or teraphim, must have either come at a later date, or have been disregarded, since the bowing-down to and the divining by the teraphim seems to have been so orthodox and general that the "Lord" actually threatens the Israelites, through Hosea, to deprive them of their teraphim.

For the children of Israel shall abide many days without a king, . . . without a sacrifice, and without an image.

Matzebah, or statue, or pillar, is explained in the Bible to mean "without an ephod and without teraphim." [Op.cit., iii..4.]

Father Kircher supports very strongly the idea that the statue of the Egyptian Serapis was identical in every way with those of the seraphim, or teraphim, in the temple of Solomon. Says Louis de Dieu:

They were, perhaps, images of angels, or statues dedicated to the angels, the presence of one of these spirits being thus attracted into a teraphim and answering the inquirers [consultants]; and even in this hypothesis the word "teraphim" would become the equivalent of "seraphim" by changing the "t" into "s" in the manner of the Syrians. [Louis de Dieu, Genesis, XXI. 19. See de Mirville, iii.257.]

DIVINING BY TERAPHIM –

What says the Septuagint? The teraphim are translated successively by ειδωλα—forms in someone's likeness; eidolon, an "astral body;" γλυπτα —the sculptured; κενοταφια—sculptures in the sense of containing something hidden, or receptacles; φηλους.—manifestations;αληφειας. truths or realities;μορφωματα. or φωτισμοις.—luminous, shining likenesses. The latter expression shows plainly what the teraphim were. The Vulgate translates the term by "annuntientes," the "messengers who announce," and it thus becomes certain that the teraphim were the oracles. They were the animated statues, the Gods who revealed themselves to the masses through the Initiated Priests and Adepts in the Egyptian, Chaldaean, Greek, and other temples.

As to the way of divining, or learning one's fate, and of being instructed by the teraphim, ["The teraphim of Abram's father, Terah, the 'maker of images,' were the Kabeiri Gods, and we see them worshipped by Micah, by the Danites, and others. (Judges, xvii., xviii, etc) Teraphim were identical with seraphim, and these were serpent images, the origin of which is in the Sanskrit 'Sarpa' (the 'serpent') a symbol sacred to all the deities as a symbol of immortality. Kiyun, or the God Kivan, worshipped by the Hebrews in the wilderness, is Shiva, the Hindu Saturn. (The Zendic 'h' is 's' in India; thus, 'Hapta' is 'Sapta:' 'Hindu' is 'Sindhaya.' (A. Wilder). "The "s" continually softens to "h" from Greece to Calcutta, from the Caucasus to Egypt,' says Dunlap. Therefore the letters 'k' 'h,' and 's' are interchangeable. The Greek story shows that Dardanus, the Arcadian, having received them as a dowry, carried them to Samothrace, and thence to Troy: and they were worshipped long before the days of glory of Tyre or Sidon, though the former had been built 2760 B.C. From where did Dardanus derive them?" Isis Unveiled. 1. 570.] it is explained quite plainly by Maimonides and Seldenus. The former says:

The worshippers of the teraphim claimed that the light of the principal stars [planets], penetrating into and filling the carved statue through and through, the angelic virtue [of the regents, or animating principle in the planets] conversed with them, teaching them many most useful arts and sciences. [Maimon. More Nevochim, III. xxx.]

In his turn Seldenus explains the same, adding that the teraphim [Those dedicated to the sun were made in gold, and those to the moon in silver.] were built and fashioned in accordance with the position of their respective planets, each of the teraphim being consecrated to a special "star-angel," those that the Greeks called stoichae, as also according to figures located in the sky and called the "tutelary Gods":

Those who traced out the στοιχεια. were called στοιχειωματικοι.[or the diviners by the planets] and the στοιχεια.[De Diis Syriis, Teraph, 11. Syat. p.31.]

Ammianus Marcellinus states that the ancient divinations were always accomplished with the help of the "spirits" of the elements (spiritus elementorum), or as they were called in Greek ηνενματα των οτοιχειων. Now the latter are not the "spirits" of the stars (planets), nor are they divine Beings; they are simply the creatures inhabiting their respective elements, called by the Kabalists elementary spirits, and by the Theosophists elementals. [Those that the Kabalists call elementary spirits are sylphs, gnomes, undines and salamanders, nature-spirits, in short. The spirits of the angels formed a distinct class.] Father Kircher, the Jesuit, tells the reader:

Every god had such instruments of divination to speak through. Each had his speciality.

Serapis gave instruction on agriculture; Anubis taught sciences; Horus advised upon psychic and spiritual matters; Isis was consulted on the rising of the Nile, and so on. [OEdipus. ii. 444].

This historical fact, furnished by one of the ablest and most erudite among the Jesuits, is unfortunate for the prestige of the "Lord God of Israel" with regard to his claims to priority and to his being the one living God. Jehovah, on the admission of the Old Testament itself, conversed with his elect in no other way, and this places him on a par with every other Pagan God, even of the inferior classes. In Judges, xvii., we read of Micah having an ephod and a teraphim fabricated, and consecrating them to Jehovah (see the Septuagint and the Vulgate); these objects were made by a founder from the two hundred shekels of silver given to him by his mother. True, King James' "Holy Bible" explains this little bit of idolatry by saying:

In those days there was no king in Israel, but every man did that which was right in his own eyes.

Yet the act must have been orthodox, since Micah, after hiring a priest, a diviner, for his ephod and teraphim, declares: "Now know I that the Lord will do me good." And if Micah's act—who

Had an house of Gods, and made an ephod and teraphim and consecrated one of his sons

to their service, as also to that of the "graven image" dedicated "unto the Lord" by his mother—now seems prejudicial, it was not so in those days of one religion and one lip. How can the Latin Church blame the act, since Kircher, one of her best writers, calls the teraphim "the holy instruments of primitive revelations;" since Genesis shows us Rebecca going " to enquire of the Lord," [Op. cit., xxv.22 et seq.] and the Lord answering her (certainly through his teraphim), and delivering to her several prophecies?

JEHOVAH AND TERAPHIM –

And if this be not sufficient, there is Saul, who deplores the silence of the ephod, [The ephod was a linen garment worn by the high priest, but as the thummim was attached to it the entire paraphernalia of divination was often comprised in that single word, ephod. See I Sam., xxviii. 6, and xxx. 7. 8.] and David who consults the thummim, and receives oral advice from the Lord as to the best way of killing his enemies.

The thumim and urim, however—the object in our days of so much conjecture and speculation —was not an invention of the Jews, nor had it originated with them, despite the minute instruction given about it by Jehovah to Moses. For the priest-hierophant of the Egyptian temples wore a breastplate of precious stones, in every way similar to that of the high priest of the Israelites.

The high-priests of Egypt wore suspended on their necks an image of saphire, called Truth, the manifestation of truth becoming evident in it.

Seldenus is not the only Christian writer who assimilates the Jewish to the Pagan teraphim, and expressed a conviction that the former had borrowed them from the Egyptians. Moreover, we are told by Döllinger, a preeminently Roman Catholic writer:

The teraphim were used and remained in many Jewish families to the days of Josiah. [Paganism and Judaism, iv. I 97].

As to the personal opinion of Döllinger, a papist, and of Seldenus, a Protestant—both of whom trace Jehovah in the teraphim of the Jews and "evil spirits" in those of the Pagans—it is the usual one-sided judgment of odium theologicum and sectarianism. Seldenus is right, however, in arguing that in the days of old, all such modes of communication had been primarily established for purposes of divine and angelic communications only. But

The holy Spirit [spirits, rather] spake [not] to the children of Israel [alone] by urim and thummim, while the tabernacle remained, as Dr. A. Cruden would have people believe. Nor had the Jews alone need of a "tabernacle" for such a kind of theophanic, or divine communication; for no Bath-Kol (or "Daughter of the divine Voice"), called thummim, could be heard whether by Jew, Pagan, or Christian, were there not a fit tabernacle for it. The "tabernacle" was simply the archaic telephone of those days of Magic when Occult powers were acquired by Initiation, just as they are now. The nineteenth century has replaced with an electric telephone the "tabernacle" of specified metals, wood, and special arrangements, and has natural mediums instead of high priests and hierophants. Why should people wonder, then, that instead of reaching Planetary Spirits and Gods, believers should now communicate with no greater beings than elementals and animated shells - the demons of Porphyry? Who these were, he tells us candidly in his work On the Good and Bad Demons:

They whose ambition is to be taken for Gods, and whose leader demands to be recognized as the Supreme God.

Mmost decidedly—and it is not the Theosophists who will ever deny the fact—there are good as well as bad spirits, beneficent and malevolent "Gods" in all ages. The whole trouble was, and still is, to know which is which. And this, we maintain, the Christian Church knows no more than her profane flock. If anything proves this, it is, most decidedly, the numberless theological blunders made in this direction. It is idle to call the Gods of the heathen "devils," and then to copy their symbols in such a servile manner, enforcing the distinction between the good and the bad with no weightier proof than that they are respectively Christian and Pagan. The planets—the elements of the Zodiac—have not figured only at Heliopolis as the twelve stones called the "mysteries of the elements" (elementorum arcana). On the authority of many an orthodox Christian writer they were found also in Solomon's temple, and may be seen to this day in several old Italian churches, and even in Notre Dame of Paris.

One would really say that the warning in Clement's Stromateis has been given in vain, though he is supposed to quote words pronounced by St. Peter. He says:

Do not adore God as the Jews do, who think they are the only ones to know Deity and fail to perceive that, instead of God, they are worshipping angels, the lunar months, and the moon. [Op cit.,I. vi. 5.]

Who after reading the above can fail to feel surprise that, notwithstanding such understanding of the Jewish mistake, the Christians are still worshipping the Jewish Jehovah, the Spirit who spoke through his teraphim! That this is so, and that Jehovah was simply the "tutelary genius," or spirit, of the people of Israel - only one of the pneuma ton stoicheion (or "great spirits of the elements"), not even a high "Planetary"— is demonstrated on the authority of St. Paul and of Clemens Alexandrinus, if the words they use have any meaning.

IDOL OF THE MOON –

With the latter, the word στοιχεια signifies not only elements, but also

Generative cosmological principles, and notably the signs [or constellations] of the Zodiac, of the months, days, the sun and the moon. [Discourse to the Gentiles, p. l46.]

The expression is used by Aristotle in the same sense. He says, των αστρων στοιχεια.[De Gener., III. iv.] while Diogenes Laertius calls δωδεκα στοιχεια. the twelve signs of the Zodiac. [See Cosmos, by Ménage, I., vi., p 101.] Now having the positive evidence of Ammianus Marcellinus to the effect that

Ancient divination was always accompanied with the help of the spirits of the elements,

or the same πνεαματα των στοιχειων., and seeing in the Bible numerous passages that (a) the Israelites, including Saul and David, resorted to the same divination, and used the same means; and (b) that it was their "Lord"—namely, Jehovah—who answered them, what else can we believe Jehovah to be than a "spiritus elementorum"?

Hence one sees no great difference between the "idol of the moon"—the Chaldaean teraphim through which spoke Saturn—and the idol or urim and thummim, the organ of Jehovah. Occult rites, scientific at the beginning—and forming the most solemn and sacred of sciences—have fallen through the degeneration of mankind into Sorcery, now called "superstition." As Diogenes explains in his History:

The Kaldhi, having made long observations on the planets and knowing better than anyone else the meaning of their motions and their influences, predict to people their futurity. They regard their doctrine of the five great orbs—which they call interpreters, and we, planets—as the most important. And though they allege that it is the sun that furnishes them with most of the predictions for great forthcoming events, yet they worship more particularly Saturn. Such predictions made to a number of kings, especially to Alexander, Antigonus, Seleucus, Nicanor, etc., . . . have been so marvellously realised that people were struck with admiration. [Op Cit., I .ii.]

It follows from the above that the declaration made by Qû-tâmy, the Chaldean Adept—to the effect that all that he means to impart in his work to the profane had been told by Saturn to the moon, by the latter to her idol, and by that idol, or teraphim, to himself, the scribe—no more implied idolatry than did the practice of the same method by King David. One fails to perceive in it, therefore, either an apocrypha or a "fairy-tale." The above-named Chaldaean Initiate lived at a period far anterior to that ascribed to Moses, in whose day the Sacred Science of the sanctuary was still in a flourishing condition. It began to decline only when such scoffers as Lucian had been admitted, and the pearls of the Occult Science had been too often thrown to the hungry dogs of criticism and ignorance.

SECTION XXVII

EGYPTIAN MAGIC

FEW of our students of Occultism have had the opportunity of examining Egyptian papyri—those living, or rather re-arisen witnesses that Magic, good and bad, was practised many thousands of years back into the night of time. The use of the papyrus prevailed up to the eighth century of our era, when it was given up, and its fabrication fell into disuse. The most curious of the exhumed documents were immediately purchased and taken away from the country. Yet there are a number of beautifully-preserved papyri at Bulak, Cairo, though the greater number have never been yet properly read. ["The characters employed on those parchments," writes De Mirville, " are sometimes hieroglyphics, placed perpendicularly, a kind of lineary tachygraphy (abridged characters), where the image is often reduced to a single stroke; at other times placed in horizontal lines; then the hieratic or sacred writing, going from right to left as in all Semitic languages; lastly, the characters of the country, used for official documents, mostly contracts, etc., but which since the Ptolemies has been also adopted for the monuments." [v.81. 80. A copy of the Harris papyrus, translated by Chabas-Papyrus Magique - may be studied at the British Museum.]

Others—those that have been carried away and may be found in the museums and public libraries of Europe—have fared no better. In the days of the Vicomte de Rougé, some twenty-five years ago, only a few of them "were two-thirds deciphered;" and among those some most interesting legends, inserted parenthetically and for purposes of explaining royal expenses, are in the Register of the Sacred Accounts.

This may be verified in the so-called "Harris" and Anastasi collections, and in some papyri recently exhumed; one of these gives an account of a whole series of magic feats performed before the Pharaohs Ramses II and III. A curious document, the first-mentioned, truly. It is a papyrus of the fifteenth century B.C., written during the reign of Ramses V., the last king of the eighteenth dynasty, and is the work of the scribe Thoutmes, who notes down some of the events with regard to defaulters occurring on the twelfth and thirteenth days of the month of Paophs. The document shows that in those days of "miracles" in Egypt the taxpayers were not found among the living alone, but every mummy was included. All and everything was taxed; and the Khou of the mummy, in default, was punished "by the priest-exorciser, who deprived it of the liberty of action." Now what was the Khou? Simply the astral body, or the aerial simulacrum of the corpse or the mummy—that which in China is called the Hauen, and in India the Bhût.

Upon reading this papyrus today, an Orientalist is pretty sure to fling it aside in disgust, attributing the whole affair to the crass superstition of the ancients. Truly phenomenal and inexplicable must have been the dullness and credulity of that otherwise highly philosophical and civilized nation if it could carry on for so many consecutive ages, for thousands of years, such a system of mutual deception! A system whereby the people were deceived by the priests, the priests by their King-Hierophants, and the latter themselves were cheated by the ghosts, which were, in their turn, but "the fruits of hallucination." The whole of antiquity, from Menes to Cleopatra, from Manu to Vikramaditya, from Orpheus down to the last Roman augur, were hysterical, we are told. This must have been so, if the whole were not a system of fraud. Life and death were guided by, and were under the sway of, sacred "conjuring." For there is hardly a papyrus, though it be a simple document of purchase and sale, a deed belonging to daily transactions of the most ordinary kind, and that has not Magic, white or black, mixed up in it. It looks as though the sacred scribes of the Nile had purposely, and in a prophetic spirit of race-hatred, carried out the (to them) most unprofitable task of deceiving and puzzling the generations of a future white race of unbelievers yet unborn! Anyhow, the papyri are full of Magic, as are likewise the stelae. We learn, moreover, that the papyrus was not merely a smooth-surfaced parchment, a fabric made of

Ligneous matter from a shrub, the pellicles of which superposed one over the other formed a kind of writing paper; but that the shrub itself, the implements and tools for fabricating the parchment etc., were all previously subjected to a process of magical preparation—according to the ordinance of the Gods, who had taught that art, as they had all others, to their Priest-Hierophants.

There are, however, some modern Orientalists who seem to have an inkling of the true nature of such things, and especially of the analogy and the relations that exist between the Magic of old and our modern-day phenomena.

EVIDENCE OF PAPYRI -

Chabas is one of these, for he indulges, in his translation of the "Harris" papyrus, in the following reflections:

Without having recourse to the imposing ceremonies of the wand of Hermes, or to the obscure formulae of an unfathomable mysticism, a mesmeriser in our own day will, by means of a few passes, disturb the organic faculties of a subject, inculcate the knowledge of a foreign language, transport him to a far-distant country, or into secret places, make him guess the thoughts of those absent, read in closed letters, etc. . . . The antre of the modern sybil is a modest-looking room, the tripod has made room for a small round table, a hat, a plate, a piece of furniture of the most vulgar kind; only the latter is even superior to the oracle of antiquity [how does M. Chabas know?], inasmuch as the latter only spoke, [And what of the "Mene, mene, tekel, upharsin," the words that "the fingers of a man's hand," whose body and arm remained invisible, wrote on the walls of Belshazzar's palace? (Daniel. v.) What of the writings of Simon the Magician, and the magic characters on the walls and in the air of the crypts of Initiation, without mentioning the tables of stone on which the finger of God wrote the commandments? Between the writing of one God and other Gods the difference, if any, lies only in their respective natures; and if the tree is to be known by its fruits, then preference would have to be given always to the Pagan Gods. It is the immortal "To be or not to be." Either all of them are - or at any rate, may be - true, or all are surely pious frauds and the result of credulity.] while the oracle of our day writes its answers. At the command of the medium the spirits of the dead descend to make the furniture creak, and the authors of bygone centuries deliver to us works written by them beyond the grave. Human credulity has no narrower limits today than it had at the dawn of historical times . . . . As teratology is an essential part of general physiology now, so the pretended Occult Sciences occupy in the annals of humanity a place which is not without its importance, and deserve for more than one reason the attention of the philosopher and the historian. [Papyrus Magique. p.186.]

Selecting the two Champollions, Lenormand, Bunsen, Victomte de Rougé, and several other Egyptologists to serve as our witnesses, let us see what they say of Egyptian Magic and Sorcery. They may get out of the difficulty by accounting for each "superstitious belief" and practice by attributing them to a chronic psychological and physiological derangement, and to collective hysteria, if they like; still facts are there, staring us in the face, from the hundreds of these mysterious papyri, exhumed after a rest of four, five, and more thousands of years, with their magical containments and evidence of antediluvian Magic.

A small library, found in Thebes, has furnished fragments of every kind of ancient literature, many of which are dated, and several of which have thus been assigned to the accepted age of Moses. Books or manuscripts on ethics, history, religion and medicine, calendars and registers, poems and novels—everything—may be had in that precious collection; and old legends - traditions of long forgotten ages (please to remark this: legends recorded during the Mosaic period)—are already referred to therein as belonging to an immense antiquity, to the period of the dynasties of Gods and Giants. Their chief contents, however, are formulae of exorcisms against black Magic, and funeral rituals: true breviaries, or the vade mecum of every pilgrim-traveller in eternity. These funeral texts are generally written in hieratic characters. At the head of the papyrus is invariably placed a series of scenes, showing the defunct appearing before a host of Deities successively, who have to examine him. Then comes the judgement of the Soul, while the third act begins with the launching of that Soul into the divine light. Such papyri are often forty feet long. [See Maspero's Guide to the Bulah Museum, among others.]

The following is extracted from general descriptions. It will show how the moderns understand and interpret Egyptian (and other) Symbology.

The papyrus of the priest Nevo-loo (or Nevolen), at the Louvre, may be selected for one case. First of all there is the bark carrying the coffin, a black chest containing the defunct's mummy. His mother, Ammenbem-Heb, and his sister, Hooissanoob, are near; at the head and feet of the corpse stand Nephtys and Isis clothed in red, and near them a priest of Osiris clad in his panther's skin, his censer in his right hand, and four assistants carrying the mummy's intestines. The coffin is received by the God Anubis (of the jackal's head), from the hands of female weepers. Then the Soul rises from its mummy and the Khou (astral body) of the defunct. The former begins its worship of the four genii of the East, of the sacred birds, and of Ammon as a ram. Brought into the "Palace of Truth," the defunct is before his judges. While the Soul, a scarabaeus, stands in the presence of Osiris, his astral Khou is at the door. Much laughter is provoked in the West by the invocations to various Deities, presiding over each of the limbs of the mummy, and of the living human body. Only judge: in the papyrus of the mummy Petamenoph "the anatomy becomes theographical," "astrology is applied to physiology," or rather "to the anatomy of the human body, the heart and the soul." The defunct's "hair belongs to the Nile, his eyes to Venus (Isis), his ears to Macedo, the guardian of the tropics; his nose to Anubis, his left temple to the Spirit dwelling in the sun . . . .What a series of intolerable absurdities and ignoble prayers . . . . to Osiris, imploring him to give the defunct in the other world, geese, eggs, pork, etc." [De Mirville (from whom much of the preceding is taken). v 8l, 85]

SYMBOLS AND THEIR READING –

It might have been prudent, perhaps, to have waited to ascertain whether all these terms of "geese, eggs, and pork" had not some other Occult meaning. The Indian Yogi who, in an exoteric work, is invited to drink a certain intoxicating liquor till he loses his senses, was also regarded as a drunkard representing his sect and class, until it was found that the Esoteric sense of that "spirit" was quite different; that it meant divine light, and stood for the ambrosia of Secret Wisdom.

The symbols of the dove and the lamb which abound

now in Eastern and Western Christian Churches may also be exhumed long ages hence, and speculated upon as objects of present-day worship. And then some "Occidentalist," in the forthcoming ages of high Asiatic civilization and learning, may write karmically upon the same as follows: "The ignorant and superstitious Gnostics and Agnostics of the sects of 'Pope' and 'Calvin' (the two monster Gods of the Dynamite-Christian period) adored a pigeon and a sheep!" There will be portable hand-fetishes in all and every age for the satisfaction and reverence of the rabble, and the Gods of one race will always be degraded into devils by the next one. The cycles revolve within the depths of Lethe, and Karma shall reach Europe as it has Asia and her religions.

Nevertheless, This grand and dignified language [in the Book of the Dead], these pictures full of majesty, this orthodoxy of the whole evidently proving a very precise doctrine concerning the immortality of the soul and its personal survival, as shown by De Rougé and Abbe Van Drival, have charmed some Orientalists. The psychostasy (or judgment of the Soul) is certainly a whole poem to him who can read it correctly and interpret the images therein. In that picture we see Osiris, the horned, with his sceptre hooked at the end —the original of the pastoral bishop's crook or crosier—the Soul hovering above, encouraged by Tmei, daughter of the Sun of Righteousness and Goddess of Mercy and Justice; Horus and Anubis, weighing the deeds of the soul. One of these papyri shows the Soul found guilty of gluttony sentenced to be re-born on earth as a hog; forthwith comes the learned conclusion of an Orientalist,

"This is an indisputable proof of belief in metempsychosis, of transmigration into animals," etc.

Perchance the Occult law of Karma might explain the sentence otherwise. It may, for all our Orientalists know, refer to the physiological vice in store for the Soul when re-incarnated—a vice that will lead that personality into a thousand and one scrapes and misadventures.

Tortures to begin with, then metempsychosis during 3,000 years as a hawk, an angel a lotus-flower, a heron, a stork, a swallow, a serpent, and a crocodile: one sees that the consolation of such a progress was far from being satisfactory.

Argues De Mirville, in his work on the Satanic character of the Gods of Egypt. [See De Mirville. v. 84, 85.] Again, a simple suggestion may throw on this a great light. Are the Orientalists quite sure they have read correctly the "metempsychosis during 3,000 years"? The Occult Doctrine teaches that Karma waits at the threshold of Devachan (the Amenti of the Egyptians) for 3,000 years; that then the eternal Ego is reincarnated de novo, to be punished in its new temporary personality for sins committed in the preceding birth, and the suffering for which in one shape or another, will atone for past misdeeds. And the hawk, the lotus-flower, the heron, serpent, or bird —every object in Nature, in short—had its symbolical and manifold meaning in ancient religious emblems. The man who all his life acted hypocritically and passed for a good man, but had been in sober reality watching like a bird of prey his chance to pounce upon his fellow creatures, and had deprived them of their property, will be sentenced by Karma to bear the punishment for hypocrisy and covetousness in a future life. What will it be? Since every human unit has ultimately to progress in its evolution, and since that "man" will be reborn at some future time as a good, sincere, well-meaning man, his sentence to be re-incarnated as a hawk may simply mean that he will be regarded metaphorically as such. That, notwithstanding his real, good, intrinsic qualities, he will, perhaps during a long life, be unjustly and falsely charged with and suspected of greed and hypocrisy and of secret exactions, all of which will make him suffer more than he can bear. The law of retribution can never err, and yet how many such innocent victims of false appearance and human malice do we not meet in this world of incessant illusion, of mistakes and deliberate wickedness. We see them every day, and they may be found within the personal experience of each of us.

REBIRTH AND TRANSMIGRATION –

What Orientalist can say with any degree of assurance that he has understood the religions of old? The metaphorical language of the priests has never been more than superficially revealed, and the hieroglyphics have been very poorly mastered to this day. [One sees this difficulty arise even with a perfectly known language like Sanskrit, the meaning of which is far easier to comprehend than the hieratic writings of Egypt. Everyone knows how hopelessly the Sanskritists are often puzzled over the real meaning and how they fail in rendering the meaning correctly in their respective translations, in which one Orientalist contradicts the other.

What says Isis Unveiled on this question of Egyptian rebirth and transmigration, and does it clash with anything that we say now?

It will be observed that this philosophy of cycles, which was allegorized by the Egyptian Hierophants in the "cycle of necessity," explains at the same time the allegory of the "Fall of Man," According to the Arabian descriptions, each of the seven chambers of the pyramids—those grandest of all cosmic symbols—was known by the name of a planet. The peculiar architecture of the pyramids shows in itself the drift of the metaphysical thought of their builders. The apex is lost in the clear blue sky of the land of the Pharaohs, and typifies the primordial point lost in the unseen Universe from whence started the first race of the spiritual prototypes of man. Each mummy from the moment that it was embalmed lost its physical individuality in one sense: it symbolised the human race. Placed in such a way as was best calculated to aid the exit of the "Soul," the latter had to pass through the seven planetary chambers before it made its exit through the symbolical apex. Each chamber typified, at the same time, one of the seven spheres [of our Chain] and one of the seven higher types of physico-spiritual humanity alleged to be above our own. Every 3000 years the soul, representative of its race, had to return to its primal point of departure before it underwent another evolution into a more perfected spiritual and physical transformation. We must go deep indeed into the abstruse metaphysics of Oriental mysticism before we can realise fully the infinitude of the subjects that were embraced at one sweep by the majestic thought of its exponents. [Op. cit.,i. 297.]

This is all Magic when once the details are given; and it relates at the same time to the evolution of our seven Root-Races, each with the characteristics of its special guardian or "God," and his Planet. The astral body of each Initiate, after death, had to reenact in its funeral mystery the drama of the birth and death of each Race—the past and the future—and pass through the seven "planetary chambers," which as said above, typified also the seven spheres of our Chain.

The mystic doctrine of Eastern Occultism teaches that "The Spiritual Ego [not the astral Khou] has to revisit, before it incarnates into a new body, the scenes it left at its last disincarnation. It has to see for itself and take cognizance of all the effects produced by the causes [the Nidânas] generated by its actions in a previous life; that, seeing, it should recognize the justice of the decree, and help the law of Retribution [Karma] instead of impeding it. [Book II., Commentary.]

The translations by Vicomte de Rougé of several Egyptian papyri, imperfect as they may be, give us one advantage: they show undeniably the presence in them of white, divine Magic, as well as of Sorcery, and the practice of both throughout all the dynasties. The Book of the Dead, far older than Genesis [Bunsen and Champollion so declare, and Dr. Carpenter says that the Book of the Dead, sculptured on the oldest monuments, with "the very phrases we find in the New Testament in connection with the Day of Judgment . . . was engraved probably 2,000 years before the time of

Christ." (See Isis Unveiled, i. 518.)] or any other book of the Old Testament, shows it in every line. It is full of incessant prayers and exorcisms against the Black Art. Therein Osiris is the conquerer of the "aerial demons." The worshipper implores his help against Matat, "from whose eye proceeds the invisible arrow." This "invisible arrow" that proceeds from the eye of the Sorcerer (whether living or dead) and that "circulates throughout the world," is the evil eye—cosmic in its origin, terrestrial in its effects on the microcosmical plane. It is not the Latin Christians whom it behoves to view this as a superstition. Their Church indulges in the same belief, and had even a prayer against the "arrow circulating in darkness."

The most interesting of all those documents, however, is the "Harris" papyrus, called in France "le papyrus magique de Chabas," as it was first translated by the latter. It is a manuscript written in hieratic characters, translated, commented upon, and published in 1860 by M. Chabas, but purchased at Thebes in 1855 by Mr. Harris. Its age is given at between twenty-eight and thirty centuries. We quote a few extracts from these translations:

Calendar of lucky and unlucky days . . . He who makes a bull work on the 20th of the month of Pharmuths will surely die; he who on the 24th day of the same month pronounces the name of Seth aloud will see trouble reigning in his house from that day; . . . . he who on the 5th day of Patchous leaves his house falls sick and dies.

Exclaims the translator, whose cultured instincts are revolted:

If one had not these words under our eyes, one could never

believe in such servitude at the epoch of the Ramessides. [De Mirville, v.88. Just such a calendar and horoscope interdictions exist in India in our day, as well as in China and all the Buddhist countries.]

The Egyptian Khous –

We belong to the nineteenth century of the Christian era, and are therefore at the height of civilization, and under the benign sway and enlightening influence of the Christian Church, instead of being subject to Pagan Gods of old. Nevertheless we personally know dozens, and have heard of hundreds, of educated, highly-intellectual persons who would as soon think of committing suicide as of starting on any business on a Friday, of dining at a table where thirteen sit down, or of beginning a long journey on a Monday. Napoleon the Great became pale when he saw three candles lit on a table. Moreover, we may gladly concur with De Mirville in this, at any rate, that such "superstitions" are "the outcome of observation and experience." If the former had never agreed with facts, the authority of the Calendar, he thinks, would not have lasted for a week. But to resume:

Genethliacal influences: The child born on the 5th day of Paophi will be killed by a bull; on the 27th by a serpent. Born on the 4th of the month of Athyr, he will succumb to blows.

This is a question of horoscopic predictions; judiciary astrology is firmly believed in in our own age, and has been proven to be scientifically possible by Kepler.

Of the Khous two kinds were distinguished: first, the justified Khous, i.e., those who had been absolved from sin by Osiris when they were brought before his tribunal; these lived a second life. Secondly, here were the guilty Khous, "the Khous dead a second time;" these were the damned. Second death did not annihilate them, but they were doomed to wander about and to torture people. Their existence had phases analogous to those of the living man, a bond so intimate between the dead and the living that one sees how the observation of religious funeral rites and exorcisms and prayers (or rather magic incantations) should have become necessary. [See De Mirville. iii.65]. Says one prayer:

Do not permit that the venom should master his limbs [of the defunct], . . .that he should be penetrated by any male dead, or any female dead; or that the shadow of any spirit should haunt him (or her)."

M. Chabas adds:

These Khous were beings of that kind to which human beings belong after their death; they were exorcised in the name of the god Chons . . . .The Manes then could enter the bodies of the living, haunt and obsess the formulae and talismans, and especially statues or divine figures were used against such formidable invasions. [Ibid. p.168]. They were combatted by the help of the divine power, the god   Chons being famed for such deliverances. The Khou, in obeying the order of the god, none the less preserved the precious faculty inherent in him of accommodating himself in any other body at will.

The most frequent formula of exorcism is as follows. It is very suggestive;

Men, gods, elect, dead spirits, amous, negroes, menti-u, do not look at this soul to show cruelty toward it.

This is addressed to all who were acquainted with Magic.

"Amulets and mystic names." This chapter is called "very mysterious," and contains invocations to Penhakahakaherher and Uranaokarsankrobite, and other such easy names. Says Chabas:

We have proofs that mystic names similar to these were in common use during the stay of the Israelites in Egypt.

And we may add that, whether got from the Egyptians or the Hebrews, these are sorcery names. The student can consult the works of Éliphas Lévi, such as his Grimoire des Sorciers. In these exorcisms Osiris is called Mamuram-Kahab, and is implored to prevent the twice-dead Khou from attacking the justified Khou and his next of kin, since the accursed (astral spook)

Can take any form he likes and penetrate at will into any locality or body.

In studying Egyptian papyri, one begins to find that the subjects of the Pharaohs were not very much inclined to the Spiritism or Spiritualism of their day. They dreaded the "blessed spirit" of the dead more than a Roman Catholic dreads the devil!

But how uncalled-for and unjust is the charge against the Gods of Egypt that they are these "devils," and against the priests of exercising their magic powers with the help of "the fallen angels," may be seen in more than one papyrus. For one often finds in them records of Sorcerers sentenced to the death penalty, as though they had been living under the protection of the holy Christian Inquisition. Here is one case during the reign of Ramses III, quoted by De Mirville from Chabas.

The first page begins with these words: "From the place where I am to the people of my country." There is reason to suppose, as one will see, that the person who wrote this, in the first personal pronoun, is a magistrate making a report, and attesting it before men, after an accustomed formula, for here is the main part of this accusation: "This Hai, a bad man, was an overseer [or perhaps keeper] of sheep: he said: "Can I have a book that will give me great power?' . . . . And a book was given him with the formulae of Ramses-Meri-Amen, the great God, his royal master; and he succeeded in getting a divine power enabling him to fascinate men.

OBSESSION IN EGYPT -

He also succeeded in building a place and in finding a very deep place, and produced men of Menh [magical homunculi?] and . . . love-writings . . stealing them from the Khen [the occult library of the palace] by the hand of the stonemason Atirma, . . . by forcing one of the supervisors to go aside, and acting magically on the others. Then he sought to read futurity by them and succeeded. All the horrors and abominations he had conceived in his heart, he did them really, he practised them all, and other great crimes as well, such as the horror [?] of all the Gods and Goddesses. Likewise let the prescriptions great [severe?] unto death be done unto him, such as the divine words order to be done to him." The accusation does not stop there, it specifies the crimes. The first line speaks of a hand paralysed by means of the men of Menh, to whom it is simply said, "Let such an effect be produced," and it is produced. Then come the great abominations, such as deserve death. . . . The judges who had examined him (the culprit) reported saying, "Let him die according to the order of Pharaoh, and according to what is written in the lines of the divine language."

M. Chabas remarks:

Documents of this kind abound, but the task of analysing them all cannot be attempted with the limited means we possess. [Maimonides in his Treatise on Idolatry says, speaking of Jewish teraphim: "They talked with men." To this day Christian Sorcerers in Italy, and negro Voodoos at New Orleans fabricate small wax figures in the likeness of their victims, and transpierce them with needles, the wound, as on the teraphim or Menh, being repercussed on the living, often killing them. Mysterious deaths are still many, and not all are traced to the guilty hand.

Then there is an inscription taken in the temple of Khous, the God who had power over the elementaries, at Thebes. It was presented by M. Prisse d'Avenue to the Imperial—now National —Library of Paris, and was translated first by Mr. S. Birch. There is in it a whole romance of Magic. It dates from the day of Ramses XII. [The Ramses of Lepsius, who reigned some 1300 years before our era.] of the twentieth dynasty; it is from the rendering of Mr. de Rougé as quoted by De Mirville, that we now translate it.

This monument tells us that one of the Ramses of the twentieth dynasty, while collecting at Naharain the tributes paid to Egypt by the Asiatic nations, fell in love with a daughter of the chief of Bakhten, one of his tributaries, married her and, bringing her to Egypt with him, raised her to the dignity of Queen, under the royal name of Ranefrou. Soon afterwards the chief of Bakhten dispatched a messenger to Ramses, praying the assistance of Egyptian science for Bent-Rosh, a young sister of the queen, attacked with illness in all her limbs.

The messenger asked expressly that a "wise-man" (an Initiate - Reh-Het) should be sent. The king gave orders that all the hierogrammatists of the palace and the guardians of the secret books of the Khen should be sent for, and choosing from among them the royal scribe Thoth-em-Hebi, an intelligent man, well versed in writing, charged him to examine the sickness. Arrived at Bakhten, Thoth-em-Hebi found that Bent-Rosh was possessed by a Khou (Em-seh-'eru ker h'ou), but declared himself too weak to engage in a struggle with him. [One may judge how trustworthy are the translations of such Egyptian documents when the sentence is rendered in three different ways by three Egyptologists. Rougé says: "He found her in a state to fall under the power of spirits," or, "with her limbs quite stiff." (?) another version: and Chabas translates: "And the Scribe found the Khou too wicked." Between her being in possession of an evil Khou and "with her limbs quite stiff." there is a difference.]

Eleven years elapsed, and the young girl's state did not improve. The chief of Bakhten again sent his messenger, and on his formal demand Khons-peiri-Seklerem-Zam, one of the divine forms of Chons - God the Son of the Theban Trinity - was dispatched to Bakhten. . . .

The God [incarnate] having saluted (besa) the patient,

she felt immediately relieved, and the Khou who was in her manifested forthwith with his intention of obeying the orders of the God. "O great God, who forces: the phantom to vanish," said the Khou, "I am thy slave and I will return whence I came!" [De Mirville, v.247, 248].

Evidently Khons-peiri-Seklerem-Zam was a real Hierophant of the class named the "Sons of God," since he is said to be one of the forms of the God Khons; which means either that he was considered as an incarnation of that God—an Avatâra—or that he was a full Initiate. The same text shows that the temple to which he belonged was one of those to which a School of Magic was attached. There was a Khen in it, or that portion of the temple which was inaccessible to all but the highest priest, the library or depository of sacred works, to the study and care of which special priests were appointed (those whom all the Pharaohs consulted in cases of great importance), and wherein they communicated with the Gods and obtained advice from them. Does not Lucian tell his readers in his description of the temple of Hierapolis, of "Gods who manifest their presence independently?" [Some translators would have Lucian speak of the inhabitants of the city, but they fail to show that this view is maintainable.] And further on that he once travelled with a priest from Memphis, who told him he had passed twenty-three years in the subterranean crypts of his temple, receiving instructions on Magic from the Goddess Isis herself. Again we read that it was by Mercury himself that the great Sesostris (Ramses II.) was instructed in the Sacred Sciences. On which Jablonsky remarks that we have here the reason why Amun (Ammon)—whence he thinks our "Amen" is derived—was the real evocation to the light. [De Mirville, v. 256,,257.]

In the Papyrus Anastasi, which teems with various formulae for the evocation of Gods, and with exorcisms against Khous and the elementary demons, the seventh paragraph shows plainly the difference made between the real Gods, the Planetary Angels, and those shells of mortals which are left behind in Kama-loka, as though to tempt mankind and to puzzle it the more hopelessly in its vain search after the truth, outside the Occult Sciences and the veil of Initiation.

TWO RITUALS OF MAGIC -

This seventh verse says with regard to such divine evocation or theomantic consultations:

One must invoke that divine and great name [How can De Mirville see Satan in the Egyptian God of the great divine Name, when he himself admits that nothing was greater than the name of the oracle of Dodona, as it was that of the God of the Jews, IAO, or Jehovah? That oracle had been brought by the Pelasgians to Dodona more then fourteen centuries B.C. and left with the forefathers of the Hellenes, and its history is well-known and may be read in Herodotus. Jupiter, who loved the fair nymph of the ocean. Dodona, had ordered Pelasgus to carry his cult to Thessaly. The name of the God of that oracle at the temple of Dodona was Zeus Pelasgicos, the Zeuspater (God the Father), or as De Mirville explains: "It was the name par excellence, the name that the

Jews held as the ineffable, the unpronounceable Name—in short, Jaoh-pater, i.e., 'he who was, who is, and who will be,' otherwise the Eternal." And the author admits that Maury is right "in discovering in the name of the Vaidic Indra the Biblical Jehovah," and does not even attempt to deny the etymological connection between the two names - "the great and the lost name with the sun and the thunder-bolts." Strange confessions, and still stranger contradictions.] only in cases of absolute necessity, and when one feels absolutely pure and irreproachable.

Not so in the formula of black Magic. Reuvens, speaking of the two rituals of Magic of the Anastasi collection, remarks that they

Undeniably form the most instructive commentary upon the Egyptian Mysteries attributed to Jamblichus, and the best pendant to that classical work, for understanding the thaumaturgy of the philosophical sects, thaumaturgy based on ancient Egyptian religion. According to Jamblichus, thaumaturgy was exercised by the ministry of secondary genii. [Reuvens" Letter to Letronne on the 75th number of the Papyri Anastasi." See De Mirville, v.255.]

Reuvens closes with a remark which is very suggestive and is very important to the Occultists who defend the antiquity and genuineness of their documents, for he says:

All that he [Jamblichus] gives out as theology we find as history in our papyri.

But then how deny the authenticity, the credibility, and, beyond all, the trustworthiness of those classical writers, who all wrote about Magic and its Mysteries in a most worshipful spirit of admiration and reverence? Listen to Pindarus, who exclaims:

Happy he who descends into the grave thus initiated, for he knows the end of his life and the kingdom [The Eleusinian Fields.] given by Jupiter. [Fragments. ix.]

Or to Cicero:

Initiation not only teaches us to feel happy in this life, but also to die with better hope. [De Legibus. 11. iv.]

Plato, Pausanias, Strabo, Diodorus and dozens of others bring their evidence as to the great boon of Initiation; all the great as well as the partially-initiated Adepts, share the enthusiasm of Cicero.

Does not Plutarch, thinking of what he had learned in his initiation, console himself for the loss of his wife? Had he not obtained the certitude at the Mysteries of Bacchus that "the soul [spirit] remains incorruptible, and that there is a hereafter"? . . . Aristophanes went even further: "All those who participated in the Myseries," he says, "led an innocent, calm, and holy life; they died looking for the light of the Eleusinian Fields [Devachan], while the rest could never expect anything but eternal darkness [ignorance?].

. . .And when one thinks about the importance attached by the States to the principle and the correct celebration of the Mysteries, to the stipulations made in their treaties for the security of their celebration, one sees to what degree those Mysteries had so long occupied their first and their last thought.

It was the greatest among public as well as private preoccupations, and this is only natural, since according to Döllinger, "the Eleusinian Mysteries were viewed as the efflorescence of all the Greek religion, as the purest essence of all its conceptions. [Judaism and Paganism. i. 184.]

Not only conspirators were refused admittance therein, but those who had not denounced them; traitors, perjurers, debauchees, [Frag of Styg., ap. Stob.] . . .so that Porphyry could say that: "Our soul has to be at the moment of death as it was during the Mysteries. i.e., exempt from any blemishes, passion, envy, hatred, or anger." [De Special. Legi.]

Truly,

Magic was considered a Divine Science which led to a participation in the attributes of the Divinity itself. [De Mirville. v. 278, 279.]

Herodotus, Thales, Parmenides, Empedocles, Orpheus, Pythagoras, all went, each in his day, in search of the wisdom of Egypt's great Hierophants, in the hope of solving the problems of the universe.

Says Philo:

The Mysteries were known to unveil the secret operations of Nature. [Isis Unveiled. i.25] The prodigies accomplished by the priests of theurgic magic are so well authenticated and the evidence—if human testimony is worth anything at all—is so overwhelming that, rather than confess that the pagan theurgists far outrivalled the Christians in miracles, Sir David Brewster conceded to the former the greatest proficiency in physics and everything that pertains to natural philosophy. Science finds herself in a very disagreeable dilemma . . . .

MAGICAL STATUES

"Magic," says Psellus, "formed the last part of the sacerdotal science. It investigated the nature, power, and quality of everything sublunary: of the elements and their parts, of animals, of various plants and their fruits, of stones and herbs. In short, it explored the essence and power of everything. From hence, therefore, it produced its effects. And it formed statues [magnetized] which procure health, and made all various figures and things [talismans], which could equally become the instruments of disease as well as of health. Often, too, celestial fire is made to appear through magic, and then statues laugh and lamps are spontaneously enkindled. [Isis Unveiled. I. 282. 283.]

This assertion of Psellus that Magic "made statues which procure health," is now proven to the world to be no dream, no vain boast of a hallucinated Theurgist. As Reuvens says, it becomes "history." For it is found in the Papyrus Magique of Harris and on the votive stele just mentioned. Both Chabas and De Rougé state that:

On the eighteenth line of this very mutilated monument is found the formula with regard to the acquiescence of the God (Chons) who made his consent known by a motion he imparted to his statue. [De Mirville. v.248]

There was even a dispute over it between the two Orientalists. While M. de Rougé wanted to translate the word "Han" by "favour" or "grace," M. Chabas insisted that "Han" meant a "movement" or "a sign" made by the statue.

Excesses of power, abuse of knowledge and personal ambition very often led selfish and unscrupulous Initiates to black Magic, just as the same causes led to precisely the same thing among Christian popes and cardinals; and it was black Magic that led finally to the abolition of the Mysteries, and not Christianity, as is often erroneously thought. Read Mommsen's Roman History, vol. i., and you will find that it was the Pagans themselves who put an end to the desecration of the Divine Science. As early as 560 B.C. the Romans had discovered an Occult association, a school of black Magic of the most revolting kind; it celebrated mysteries brought from Etruria, and very soon the moral pestilence had spread all over Italy.

More than seven thousand Initiates were prosecuted, and most of them were sentenced to death . . .

Later on, Titus-Livius shows us another three thousand Initiates sentenced during a single year for the crime of poisoning. [De Mirville. v. 281.]

And yet black Magic is derided and denied!

Paulthier may or may not be too enthusiastic in saying that India appears to him as the grand and primitive hearth of human thought, that has ended by embracing the whole ancient world,

but he was right in his idea. That primitive thought led to Occult knowledge, which is our Fifth Race is reflected from the earliest days of the Egyptian Pharaohs down to our modern times. Hardly a hieratic papyrus is exhumed with the tightly swathed-up mummies of kings and high priests that does not contain some interesting information for the modern students of Occultism.

All that is, of course, derided Magic, the outcome of primitive knowledge and of revelation, though it was practised in such ungodly ways by the Atlantean Sorceres that it has since become necessary for the subsequent Race to draw a thick veil over the practices which were used to obtain so-called magical effects on the psychic and on the physical planes. In the letter no one in our century will believe the statements, with the exception of the Roman Catholics, and these will give the acts a satanic origin. Nevertheless, Magic is so mixed up with the history of the world, that if the latter is ever to be written it has to rely upon the discoveries of Archaeology, Egyptology, and hieratic writings and inscriptions; if it insists that they must be free from that "superstition of the ages" it will never see the light. One can well imagine the embarrassing position in which serious Egyptologists, Assyriologists, savants and academicians find themselves. Forced to translate and interpret the old papyri and the archaic inscriptions on stelae and Babylonian cylinders, they find themselves compelled from first to last to face the distasteful, and to them repulsive, subject of Magic, with its incantations and paraphernalia. Here they find sober and grave narratives from the pens of learned scribes, made up under the direct supervision of Chaldaean or Egyptian Hierophants, the most learned among the Philosophers of antiquity. These statements were written at the solemn hour of the death and burial of Pharaohs, High Priests, and other mighty ones of the land of Chemi; their purpose was the introduction of the newly-born, Osirified Soul before the awful tribunal of the "Great Judge" in the region of Amenti—there where a lie was said to outweigh the greatest crimes. Were the Scribes and Hierophants, Pharaohs, and King—Priests all fools or frauds to have either believed in, or tried to make others believe in, such "cock-and-bull stories" as are found in the most respectable papyri? Yet there is no help for it.

ROMANCES - BUT TRUE -

Corroborated by Plato and Herodotus, by Manetho and Syncellus, as by all the greatest and most trustworthy authors and philosophers who wrote upon the subject, those papyri note down—as seriously as they note any history, or any fact well known and accepted as to need no commentary—whole royal dynasties of Manes, to wit, of shadows and phantoms (astral bodies), and such feats of magic skill and such Occult phenomena, that the most credulous Occultist of our own times would hesitate to believe them to be true.

The orientalists have found a plank of salvation, while yet publishing and delivering the papyri to the criticism of literary Sadducees: they generally call them "romances of the days of Pharaoh So-and-So." The idea is ingenious, if not absolutely fair.

SECTION XXVIII

THE ORIGIN OF THE MYSTERIES

ALL that is explained in the preceding Sections and a hundredfold more was taught in the Mysteries from time immemorial. If the first appearance of those institutions is a matter of historical tradition with regard to some of the later nations, their origin must certainly be assigned to the time of the Fourth Root Race. The Mysteries were imparted to the elect of that Race when the average Atlantean had begun to fall too deeply into sin to be trusted with the secrets of Nature. Their establishment is attributed in the Secret Works to the King-Initiates of the divine dynasties, when the "Sons of God" had gradually allowed their country to become Kookarmades (land of vice).

The antiquity of the Mysteries may be inferred from the history of the worship of Hercules in Egypt. This Hercules, according to what the priests told Herodotus, was not Grecian, for he says:

Of the Grecian Hercules I could not in no part of Egypt procure any knowledge: . . . the name was never borrowed by Egypt from Greece . . . . Hercules, ... as they [the priests] affirm is one of the twelve (great Gods,) who were reproduced from the earlier eight Gods 17,000 years before the year of Amasis.

Hercules is of Indian origin, and—his Biblical chronology put aside—Colonel Tod was quite right in his suggestion that he was Balarâma or Baladeva. Now one must read the Purânas with the Esoteric key in one's hand in order to find out how on almost every page they corroborate the Secret Doctrine. The ancient classical writers so well understood this truth that they unanimously attributed to Asia the origin of Hercules.

A section of the Mahâbhârata is devoted to the history of the Hercûla, of which race was Vyasa. . . . Diodorus has the same legend with some variety.

An Instant in Heaven –

He says: "Hercules was born amongst the Indians and, like the Greeks, they furnish him with a club and lion's hide." Both [Krishna and Baladeva] are (lords) of the race (cûla) of Heri (Heri-cul-es) of which the Greeks might have made the compound Hercules.[Tod's Rajasthañ,i.28.]

The Occult Doctrine explains that Hercules was the last incarnation of one of the seven "Lords of the Flame," as Krishna's brother, Baladeva. That his incarnations occurred during the Third, Fourth, and Fifth Root-Races, and that his worship was brought into Egypt from Lanka and India by the later immigrants. That he was borrowed by the Greeks from the Egyptians is certain, the more so as the Greeks place his birth at Thebes, and only his twelve labours at Argos. Now we find in the Vishnu Purâna a complete corroboration of the statement made in the Secret Teachings, of which Purânic allegory the following is a short summary:

Raivata, a grandson of Sharyâti, Manu's fourth son, finding no man worthy of his lovely daughter, repaired with her to Brahmâ's region to consult the God in this emergency.

Upon his arrival Hâ Hâ Hâhû, and other Gandharvas were singing before the throne, and Raivata, waiting till they had done, imagined that but one Muhûrta (instant) had passed, whereas long ages had elapsed. When they had finished Raivata prostrated himself and explained his perplexity. Then Brahmâ asked him whom he wished for a son-in-law, and upon hearing a few personages named, the Father of the World smiled and said: "Of those whom you have named the third and fourth generation [Root-Races] no longer survive, for many successions of ages [Chatur-Yuga, or the four Yuga cycles] have passed away while you were listening to our songsters. Now on earth the twenty-eighth great age of the present Manu is nearly finished and the Kali period is at hand. You must therefore bestow this virgin-gem upon some other husband. For you are now alone."

Then the Râja Raivata is told to proceed to Kushasthaî, his ancient capital, which was now Dvârakâ, and where reigned in his stead a portion of the divine being (Vishnu) in the person of Baladeva, the brother of Krishna, regarded as the seventh incarnation of Vishnu whenever Krishna is taken as a full divinity.

"Being thus instructed by the Lotus-born [Brahmâ], Raivata returned with his daughter to earth, where he found the race of men dwindled in stature [see what is said in the Stanzas and Commentaries of the races of mankind gradually decreasing in stature]; . . . reduced in vigour, and enfeebled in intellect. Repairing to the city of Kushasthalî, he found it much altered," "Krishna had reclaimed from the sea a portion of the country," which means in plain language that the continents had all been changed meanwhile—and "had renovated the city"—or rather built a new one, Dvârakâ; for one reads in the Bhagavad Purâna [Op. cit., ix. iii. 28.] that Kushasthalî was founded and built by Raivata within the sea; and subsequent discoveries showed that it was the same, or on the same spot, as Dvârakâ. Therefore it was on an island before. The allegory in Vishnu Purâna shows King Raivata giving his daughter to "the wielder of the ploughshare"–or rather "the plough-bannered"–Baladeva, who "beholding the damsel of excessively lofty height, ... shortened her with the end of his ploughshare, and she became his wife." [Vishnu Purâna. iv. i. Wilson's translation, iii. 248-254.]

This is a plain allusion to the Third and Fourth Races—to the Atlantean giants and the successive incarnations of the "Sons of the Flame" and other orders of Dhyân Chohans in the heroes and kings of mankind, down to the Kali Yuga, or Black Age, the beginning of which is within historical times. Another coincidence: Thebes is the city of a hundred gates, and Dvârakâ is so called from its many gateways or doors, from the word "Dvâra," "gateway." Both Hercules and Baladeva are of a passionate, hot temper, and both are renowned for the fairness of their white skins. There is not the slightest doubt that Hercules is Baladeva in Greek dress. Arrian notices the great similarity between the Theban and the Hindu Hercules, the latter being worshipped by the Suraseni who built Methorea, or Mathûrâ, Krishna's birthplace. The same writer places Sandracottus (Chandragupta, the grandfather of King Asoka, of the clan of Morya) in the direct line of the descendants of Baladeva.

There were no Mysteries in the beginning, we are taught. Knowledge (Vidyâ) was common property, and it reigned universally throughout the Golden Age (Satya Yuga). As says the Commentary:

Men had not created evil yet in those days of bliss and purity, for they were of God-like more than of human nature.

But when mankind, rapidly increasing in numbers, increased also in variety of idiosyncrasies of body and mind, then incarnated Spirit showed its weakness. Natural exaggerations, and along with these superstitions, arose in the less cultured and healthy minds.

GROWTH OF POPULAR BELIEFS -

Selfishness was born out of desires and passions hitherto unknown, and but too often knowledge and power were abused, until finally it became necessary to limit the number of those who knew. Thus arose Initiation.

Every separate nation now arranged for itself a religious system, according to its enlightenment and spiritual wants. Worship of mere form being discarded by the wise men, these confined true knowledge to the very few. The need of veiling truth to protect it from desecration becoming more apparent with every generation, a thin veil was used at first, which had to be gradually thickened according to the spread of personality and selfishness, and this led to the Mysteries. They came to be established in every country and among every people, while to avoid strife and misunderstanding exoteric beliefs were allowed to grow up in the minds of the profane masses. Inoffensive and innocent in their incipient stage—like a historical event arranged in the form of a fairy tale, adapted for and comprehensible to the child's mind—in those distant ages such beliefs could be allowed to grow and make the popular faith without any danger to the more philosophical and abstruse truths taught in the sanctuaries. Logical and scientific observation of the phenomena in Nature, which alone leads man to the knowledge of eternal truths—provided he approaches the threshold of observation unbiassed by preconception and sees with his spiritual eye before he looks at things from their physical aspect—does not lie within the province of the masses. The marvels of the One Spirit of Truth, the ever-concealed and inaccessible Deity, can be unravelled and assimilated only through Its manifestations by the secondary "Gods," Its acting powers. While the One and Universal Cause has to remain forever in abscondito, Its manifold action may be traced through the effects in Nature. The latter alone being comprehensible and manifest to average mankind, the Powers causing those effects were allowed to grow in the imagination of the populace. Ages later in the Fifth, the Aryan, Race some unscrupulous priests began to take advantage of the too-easy beliefs of the people in every country, and finally raised those secondary Powers to the rank of God and Gods, thus succeeding in isolating them altogether from the One Universal Cause of all causes. [There were no Brâhmans as a hereditary caste in days of old. In those long-departed ages a man became a Brâhman through personal merit and Initiation. Gradually, however, despotism crept in, and the son of a Brâhman was created a Brâhman by right of protection first, then by that of heredity. The rights of blood replaced those of real merit, and thus arose the body of Brâhmans which was soon changed into a powerful caste.]

Henceforward the knowledge of the primeval truths remained entirely in the hands of the Initiates.

The Mysteries had their weak points and their defects, as every institution welded with the human element must necessarily have. Yet Voltaire has characterised their benefits in a few words:

In the chaos of popular superstitions there existed an institution which has ever prevented man from falling into absolute brutality: it was that of the Mysteries.

Verily, as Ragon puts it of Masonry;

Its temple has Time for duration, the Universe for space . . . ."Let us divide that we may rule," have said the crafty; "Let us unite to resist," have said the first Masons.[Des Initiations Anciennes et Modernes. "The mysteries," says Ragon, "were the gift of India." In this he is mistaken, for the Âryan race had brought the mysteries of Initiation from Atlantis. Nevertheless he is right in saying that the mysteries preceded all civilisations, and that by polishing the mind and morals of the peoples they served as a base for all the laws—civil, political, and religious.]

Or rather, the Initiates whom the Masons have never ceased to claim as their primitive and direct Masters. The first and fundamental principle of moral strength and power is association and solidarity of thought and purpose. "The Sons of Will and Yoga" united in the beginning to resist the terrible and ever-growing iniquities of the left-hand Adepts, the Atlanteans. This led to the foundation of still more Secret Schools, temples of learning, and of Mysteries inaccessible to all except after the most terrible trials and probations.

Anything that might be said of the earliest Adepts and their divine Masters would be regarded as fiction. It is necessary, therefore, if we would know something of the primitive Initiates to judge of the tree by its fruits; to examine the bearing and the work of their successors in the Fifth Race as reflected in the works of the classic writers and the great philosophers. How were Initiation and the Initiates regarded during some 2,000 years by the Greek and Roman writers? Cicero informs his readers in very clear terms. He says:

An Initiate must practise all the virtues in his power: justice, fidelity, liberality, modesty, temperance; these virtues cause men to forget the talents that he may lack. [De Off.,i.e. 33.]

Ragon says"

When the Egyptian priests said: "All for the people, nothing through the people," they were right: in an ignorant nation truth must be revealed only to trustworthy persons . . . .We have seen in our days, "all through the people, nothing for the people," a false and dangerous system. The real axiom ought to be: "All for the people and with the people." [Des Initiations, p22.]

A TRUE PRIESTHOOD -

But in order to achieve this reform the masses have to pass through a dual transformation: (a) to become divorced from every element of exoteric superstition and priestcraft, and (b) to become educated men, free from every danger of being enslaved whether by a man or an idea.

This, in view of the preceding may seem paradoxical. The Initiates were "priests," we may be told—at any rate, all the Hindu, Egyptian, Chaldaean, Greek, Phoenician, and other Hierophants and Adepts were priests in the temples, and it was they who invented their respective exoteric creeds. To this the answer is possible: "The cowl does not make the friar." If one may believe tradition and the unanimous opinion of ancient writers, added to the examples we have in the "priests" of India, the most conservative nation in the world, it becomes quite certain that the Egyptian priests were no more priests in the sense we give to the word than are the temple Brâhmans. They could never be regarded as such if we take as our standard the European clergy. Laurens observes very correctly that:

The priests of Egypt were not, strictly speaking, ministers of religion. The word "priest," which translation has been badly interpreted, had an acceptation very different from the one that is applied to it among us. In the language of antiquity, and especially in the sense of the initiation of the priests of ancient Egypt, the word "priest" is synonymous with that of "philosopher." . . . . The institution of the Egyptian priests seems to have been really a confederation of sages gathered to study the art of ruling men, to centre the domain of truth, modulate its propagation, and arrest its too dangerous dispersion.[Essais Historiques sur la Franc-Maçonnerie, pp. 142. 143.]

The Egyptian Priests, like the Brâhmans of old, held the reins of the governing powers, a system that descended to them by direct inheritance from the Initiates of the great Atlantis. The pure cult of Nature in the earliest patriarchal days—the word "patriarch" applying in its first original sense to the Progenitors of the human race, [The word "patriarch" is composed of the Greek word "Patria" ("family." "tribe," or "nation") and "Archos" (a "chief", the paternal principle. The Jewish Patriarchs who were pastors, passed their name to the Christian Patriarchs, yet they were no priests, but were simply the heads of their tribes, like the Indian Rishis.] the Fathers, Chiefs, and Instructors of primitive men—became the heirloom of those   alone who could discern the noumenon beneath the phenomenon. Later, the Initiates transmitted their knowledge to the human kings, as their divine Masters had passed it to their forefathers. It was their prerogative and duty to reveal the secrets of Nature that were useful to mankind—the hidden virtues of plants, the art of healing the sick, and of bringing about brotherly love and mutual help among mankind. No Initiate was one if he could not heal—aye, recall to life from apparent death (coma) those who, too long neglected, would have indeed died during their lethargy. [There is no need to observe here that the resurrection of a really dead body is an impossibility in Nature.] Those who showed such powers were forthwith set above the crowds, and were regarded as Kings and Initiates . Gautama Buddha was a King-Initiate, a healer, and recalled to life those who were in the hands of death. Jesus and Apollonius were healers, and were both addressed as

Kings by their followers. Had they failed to raise those who were to all intents and purposes the dead, none of their names would have passed down to posterity; for this was the first and crucial test, the certain sign that the Adept had upon Him the invisible hand of a primordial divine Master, or was an incarnation of one of the "Gods."

The later royal privilege descended to our Fifth Race kings through the kings of Egypt. The latter were all initiated into the mysteries of medicine, and they healed the sick, even when, owing to the terrible trials and labours of final Initiation, they were unable to become full Hierophants. They were healers by privilege and by tradition, and were assisted in the healing art by the Hierophants of the temples, when they themselves were ignorant of Occult curative Science. So also in far later historical times we find Pyrrhus curing the sick by simply touching them with his foot; Vespasian and Hadrian needed only to pronounce a few words taught to them by their Hierophants, in order to restore sight to the blind and health to the cripple. From that time onward history has recorded cases of the same privilege conferred on the emperors and kings of almost every nation. [The kings of Hungary claimed that they could cure the jaundice; the Dukes of Burgandy were credited with preserving people from the plague; the kings of Spain delivered those possessed by the devil. The prerogative of curing the king's evil was given to the kings of France, in reward for the virtues of good King Robert. Francis the First, during a short stay at Marseilles for his son's wedding, touched and cured of that disease upwards of 500 persons. The kings of England had the same privilege.]

THE EGYPTIAN PRIESTS -

That which is known of the Priests of Egypt and of the ancient Brâmans, corroborated as it is by all the ancient classics and historical writers, gives us the right to believe in that which is only traditional in the opinion of sceptics. Whence the wonderful knowledge of the Egyptian Priests in every department of Science, unless they had it from a still more ancient source? The famous "Four," the seats of learning in old Egypt, are more historically certain than the beginnings of modern England. It was in the great Theban sanctuary that Pythagoras upon his arrival from India studied the Science of Occult numbers. It was in Memphis that Orpheus popularized his too-abstruse Indian metaphysics for the use of Magna Grecia; and thence Thales, and ages later Democritus, obtained all they knew. It is to Saïs that all the honour must be given of the wonderful legislation and the art of ruling people, imparted by its Priests to Lycurgus and Solon, who will both remain objects of admiration for generations to come. And had Plato and Eudoxus never gone to worship at the shrine of Heliopolis, most probably the one would have never astonished future generations with his ethics, nor the other with his wonderful knowledge of mathematics.[See Laurens' Essais Historiques for further information as to the world-wide, universal knowledge of the Egyptian Priests.]

The great modern writer on the Mysteries of Egyptian Initiation—one, however, who knew nothing of those in India—the late Ragon, has not exaggerated in maintaining that:

All the notions possessed by Hindustan, Persia, Syria, Arabia, Chaldaea, Sydonia, and the priests of Babylonia, [on the secrets of Nature], was known to the Egyptian priests. It is thus Indian philosophy, without mysteries, which, having penetrated into Chaldaea and ancient Persia, gave rise to the doctrine of Egyptian Mysteries.[Des Initiations. p.24.]

The Mysteries preceded the hieroglyphics. [The word comes from the Greek 'hieros' ("sacred") and "glupho" ("I grave"). The Egyptian characters were sacred to the Gods, as the Indian Devanâgarî is the language of the Gods.] They gave birth to the latter, as permanent records were needed to preserve and commemorate their secrets. It is primitive Philosophy [The same author had (as Occultists have) a very reasonable objection to the modern etymology of the word "philosophy," which is interpreted "love of wisdom," and is nothing of the kind. The philosophers were scientists, and philosophy was a real science—not simply verbiage, as it is in our day. The term is composed of two Greek words whose meaning is intended to convey its secret sense, and ought to be interpreted as "wisdom of love." Now it is in the last word, "love," that lies hidden the esoteric significance: for "love" does not stand here as a noun, nor does it mean "affection" or "fondness." but is the term used for Eros, that primordial principle in divine creation, synonymous with χσφοζ, the abstract desire in Nature for procreation, resulting in an everlasting series of phenomena. It means "divine love," that universal element of divine omnipresence spread throughout Nature and which is at once the chief cause and effect. The "wisdom of love" (or "philosophia,') meant attraction to and love of everything hidden beneath objective phenomena and the knowledge thereof. Philosophy meant the highest Adeptship—love of and assimilation with Deity. In his modesty Pythagoras even refused to be called a Philosopher (or one who knows every hidden thing in things visible: cause and effect, or absolute truth), and called himself simply a Sage, an aspirant to philosophy, or to Wisdom of Love—love in its exoteric meaning being as degraded by men then as it is now by its purely terrestrial application.] that has served as the foundation-stone for modern philosophy; only the progeny, while perpetuating the features of the external body, has lost on its way the Soul and Spirit of its parent.

Initiation, though it contained neither rules and principles, nor any special teaching of Science—as now understood—was nevertheless Science, and the Science of sciences. And though devoid of dogma, of physical discipline, and of exclusive ritual, it was yet the one true Religion—that of eternal truth. Outwardly it was a school, a college, wherein were taught sciences, arts, ethics, legislation, philanthropy, the cult of the true and real nature of cosmic phenomena; secretly, during the mysteries, practical proofs of the latter were given. Those who could learn on all things—i.e., those who could look the great Isis in her unveiled face and bear the awful majesty of the Goddess—became Initiates. But the children of the Fifth Race had fallen too deeply into matter always to do so with impunity. Those who failed disappeared from the world, without leaving a trace behind. Which of the highest kings would have dared to claim any individual, however high his social standing, from the stern priests, once that the victim had crossed the threshold of their sacred Adytum?

The noble precepts taught by the Initiates of the early races passed to India, Egypt, and Greece, to China and Chaldaea, and thus spread all over the world. All that is good, noble, and grand in human nature, every divine faculty and aspiration, were cultured by the Priest-Philosophers who sought to develop them in their Initiates. Their code of ethics, based on altruism, has become universal. It is found in Confucius, the "atheist," who taught that "he who loves not his brother has no virtue in him," and in the Old Testament precept, "Thou shalt love thy neighbour as thyself." [Lev., xix. 18.] The greater Initiates became like unto Gods, and Socrates, in Plato's Phaedo, is represented as saying:

The Initiates are sure to come into the company of the Gods.

REVEALING AND REVEILING -

In the same work the great Athenian Sage is made to say:

It is quite apparent that those who have established the Mysteries, or the secret assemblies of the Initiates, were no mean persons, but powerful genii, who from the first ages had endeavoured to make us understand under those enigmas that he who will reach the invisible regions unpurified will be hurled into the abyss [the Eighth Sphere of the Occult Doctrine; that is, he will lose his personality for ever], while he who will attain them purged of the maculations of this world, and accomplished in virtues, will be received in the abode of the Gods.

Said Clemens Alexandrinus, referring to the Mysteries:
Here ends all teaching. One sees Nature and all things.

A Christian Father of the Church speaks then as did the
Pagan Pretextatus, the pro-consul of Achaia (fourth century
A.D.), "a man of eminent virtues," who remarked that to
deprive the Greeks of "the sacred Mysteries which bind in
one the whole of mankind," was to render their very lives
worthless to them. Would the Mysteries have ever obtained
the highest praise from the noblest men of antiquity had they
not been of more than human origin? Read all that is said
of this unparalleled institution, as much by those who had
never been initiated, as by the Initiates themselves. Consult
Plato, Euripides, Socrates, Aristophanes, Pindar, Plutarch,
Isocrates, Diodorus, Cicero, Epictetus, Marcus Aurelius, not
to name dozens of other famous Sages and writers. That
which the Gods and Angels had revealed exoteric religions,
beginning with that moses, reveiled and hid for ages from
the sight of the world. Joseph, the son of Jacob, was an
Initiate, otherwise he would not have married Aseneth, the
daughter of Petephre ("Potiphar"—"he who belongs to Phre,"
the Sun-God), priest of Heliopolis and governor of On. ["On,"
the "Sun," the Egyptian name of Heliopolis (the "City of the
Sun")]. Every truth revealed by Jesus, and which even the
Jews and early Christians understood, was reviled by the
Church that pretends to serve Him. Read what Seneca says,
as quoted by Dr. Kenealy:

""The world being melted and having reëntered the bosom
of Jupiter [or Parabrahman], this God continues for some
time totally concentred in himself and remains concealed,

as it were, wholly immersed in the contemplation of his own ideas. Afterwards we see a new world spring from him . . . .An innocent race of men is formed." And again, speaking of mundane dissolution as involving the destruction or death of all, he [Seneca] teaches us that when the laws of Nature shall be buried in ruin and the last day of the world shall come, the Southern Pole shall crush, as it falls, all the regions of Africa; and the North Pole shall overwhelm all the countries beneath its axis. The affrighted sun shall be deprived of its light: the palace of heaven, falling to decay, shall produce at once both life and death, and some kind of dissolution shall equally seize upon all the deities, who thus shall return to their original chaos. [Book of God, p. 160.]

One might fancy oneself reading the Purânic account by Paràshara of the great Pralaya. It is nearly the same thing, idea for idea. Has Christianity nothing of the kind? Let the reader open any English Bible and read chapter iii of the Second Epistle of Peter, and he will find there the same ideas.

There shall come in the last days scoffers, ... saying, Where is the promise of his coming? For since the fathers fell asleep all things continue as they were from the beginning of the creation. For this they willingly are ignorant of that by the word of God the heavens were of old, and the earth standing out of the water and in the water: whereby the world that then was, being overflowed with water, perished. But the heavens and the earth, which are now, by the same word are . . . .reserved unto fire, ...in the which the heavens shall pass away with a great noise, and the elements shall melt with fervent heat. . . Nevertheless we . . . .look for new heavens and a new earth.

If the interpreters chose to see in this a reference to a creation, a deluge, and a promised coming of Christ, when they will live in a New Jerusalem in heaven, that is no fault of Peter. What he meant was the destruction of the Fifth Race and the appearance of a new continent for the Sixth Race.

The Druids understood the meaning of the Sun in Taurus, therefore when all the fires were extinguished on the 1st of November their sacred and inextinguishable fire remained alone to illumine the horizon like those of the Magi and the modern Zoroastrian. And like the early Fifth Race and the later Chaldaeans and Greeks, and again like the Christians (who do it to this day without suspecting the real meaning), they greeted the "Morning-Star," the beautiful Venus-Lucifer. [Mr Kenealy quotes, in his Book of God, Vallancey, who says: "I had not been a week landed in Ireland from Gibraltar, where I had studied Hebrew and Chaldaic under Jews of various countries, when I heard a peasant girl say to a boor standing by her 'Feach an Maddin Nag'(Behold the morning star) pointing to the planet Venus, the Maddena Nag of the Chaldeans."] Strabo speaks of an island near Britannia where Ceres and Persephone were worshipped with the same rites as in Samothrace, and this was the sacred Ierna, where a perpetual fire was lit. The Druids believed in the rebirth of man, not, as Lucian explains,

That the same Spirit shall animate a new body, not here, but in a different world,

but in a series of reïncarnations in this same world; for

as Diodorus says, they declared that the souls of men after a determinate period would pass into other bodies. [There was a time when the whole world, the totality of mankind, had one religion, as they were of "one lip." "All the religions of the earth were at first one, and emanated from one centre." says Faber.]

ATLANTEANS DEGENERATING –

These tenets came to the Fifth Race Aryans from their ancestors of the Fourth Race, the Atlanteans. They piously preserved the teachings, while their parent Root-Race, becoming with every generation more arrogant, owing to the acquisition of superhuman powers, were gradually approaching their end.

SECTION XXIX

THE TRIAL OF THE SUN INITIATE

WE will begin with the ancient Mysteries—those received from the Atlanteans by the primitive Äryans—whose mental and intellectual state Professor Max Müller has described with such a masterly hand, yet left so incomplete withal.

He says: We have in it [in the Rig Veda] a period of the intellectual life of man to which there is no parallel in any other part of the world. In the hymns of the Veda we see man left to himself to solve the riddle of this world. . . .He invokes the gods around him, he praises, he worships them. But still with all these gods . . . .beneath him, and above him, the early poet seems ill at rest within himself. There, too, in his own breast, he has discovered a power that is never mute when he prays, never absent when he fears and trembles. It seems to inspire his prayers and yet to listen to them; it seems to live in him, and yet to support him and all around him. The only name he can find for this mysterious power is "Brahman;" for brahman meant originally force, will, wish, and the propulsive power of creation. But this impersonal Brahman too, as soon as it is named, grows into something strange and divine. It ends by being one of many gods, one of the great triad, worshipped to the present day. And still the thought within him has no real name; that power which is nothing but itself, which supports the gods, the heavens, and every living being, floats before his mind, conceived but not expressed. At last he calls it Ãtman," for âtman, originally breath or spirit, comes to mean Self and Self alone, whether divine or human; Self, whether creating of suffering; Self, whether One or All; but always Self, independent and free. "Who has seen the first-born?" says the poet, "when he who has no bones (i.e., form) bore him that had bones? Where was the life, the blood, the Self of the world? Who went to ask this from any one who knew it?" (Rig Veda, I, 164,4.) This idea of a divine Self once expressed, everything else must acknowledge its supremacy; Self is the Lord of all things; it is the King of all things; as all the spokes of a wheel are contained in the nave and circumference, all things are contained in this Self; all selves are contained in this Self." (Brihadâranyaka, IV. v. 15). [Chips from a German Workshop, i. 69. 70.]

VISHVAKARMA AND VIKARTTANA -

This Self, the highest, the one, and the universal, was symbolised on the plane of mortals by the Sun, its life-giving effulgence being in its turn the emblem of the Soul—killing the terrestrial passions which have ever been an impediment to the re-union of the Unit Self (the Spirit) with the All-Self. Hence the allegorical mystery, only the broad features of which may be given here. It was enacted by the "Sons of the Fire-Mist" and of "Light." The second Sun (the "second hypostasis" of Rabbi Drach) appeared as put on his trial, Vishvakarma, the Hierophant, cutting off seven of his beams, and replacing them with a crown of brambles, when the "Sun" became Vikarttana, shorn of his beams or rays. After that, the Sun,—enacted by a neophyte ready to be initiated—was made to descend into Pâtâla, the nether regions, on a trial of Tantalus. Coming out of it triumphant, he emerged from this region of lust and iniquity, to re-become Karmasâkshin, witness of the Karma of men, [Sûrya, the Sun, is one of the nine divinities that witness all human actions.] and arose once more triumphant in all the glory of his regeneration, as the Graha-Râjah, King of the Constellations, and was addressed as Gabhastiman, "re-possessed of his rays."

The "fable" in the popular Pantheon of India, founded upon, and born out of the poetical mysticism of the Rig-Veda—the sayings of which were mostly all dramatised during the religious Mysteries—grew in the course of its exoteric evolution into the following allegory. It may be found now in several of the Purânas and in other Scriptures. In the Rig-Veda and its Hymns, Vishvakarma, a Mystery-God, is the Logos, the Demiurgos, one of the greatest Gods, and spoken of in two of the hymns as the highest. He is the Omnificent (Vishvakarma) called the "Great Architect of the Universe," the all seeing God, ...the father, the generator, the disposer, who gives the gods their names, and is beyond the comprehension of mortals, as is every Mystery-God. Esoterically, He is the personification of the creative manifested Power; and mystically He is the seventh principle in man, in its collectivity. For He is the son of Bhuvana, the self-created, luminous Essence, and of the virtuous, chaste and lovely Yoga-Siddhâ, the virgin Goddess, whose name speaks for itself, since it personified Yoga-power, the "chaste mother" that creates the Adepts. In the Rig-Vaidic Hymns, Vishvakarma performs the "great sacrifice" i.e., sacrifices himself for the world; or, as the Nirukta is made to say, translated by the Orientalists:

Vishvakarma first of all offers up all the world in a sacrifice, and then ends by sacrificing himself in the mystical representations of his character, Vishvakarma is often called Vittoba, and is pictured as the "Victim," the "Man-God," or the Avatàra crucified in space.

[Of the true Mysteries, the real Initiations, nothing of course can be said in public: they can be known only to those who are able to experience them. But a few hints can be given of the great ceremonial Mysteries of Antiquity, which stood to the public as the real Mysteries, and into which candidates were initiated with much ceremony and display of Occult Arts. Behind these, in silence and darkness, were the true Mysteries, as they have always existed and continue to exist. In Egypt, as in Chaldaea and later in Greece, the Mysteries were celebrated at stated times, and the first day was a public holiday, on which, with much pomp, the candidates were escorted to the Great Pyramid and passed thereinto out of sight. The second day was devoted to ceremonies of purification, at the close of which the candidate was presented with a white robe; on the third day] [There is a gap in H.P.B's MS., and the paragraph in brackets supplies what was missing.—A.B.] he was tried and examined as to his proficiency in Occult learning. On the fourth day, after another ceremony symbolical of purification, he was sent alone to pass through various trials, finally becoming entranced in a subterranean crypt, in utter darkness, for two days and two nights. In Egypt, the entranced neophyte was placed in an empty sarcophagus in the Pyramid, where the initiatory rites took place. In India and Central Asia, he was bound on a lathe, and when his body had become like that of one dead (entranced), he was carried into the crypt. Then the Hierophant kept watch over him "guiding the apparitional soul (astral body) from this world of Samsàra (or delusion) to the nether kingdoms, from which, if successful, he had the right of releasing seven suffering souls" (Elementaries). Clothed with his Anandamayakosha, the body of bliss—the Srotâpanna remained there where we have no right to follow him, and upon returning—received the Word, with or without the "heart's blood" of the Hierophant. [In Isis Unveiled, Vol. II., pp. 41, 42, a portion of this rite is referred to. Speaking of the dogma of Atonement, it is traced to ancient "heathendom" again. We say: "This cornerstone of a church which had believed herself built on a firm rock for long centuries, is now excavated by science and proved to come from the Gnostics. Professor Draper shows it as hardly known in the days of Tertullian, and as having originated among the Gnostic heretics' (see Conflict Between Religion and Science, p.224) . . . .But there are sufficient proofs to show that it originated among them no more than did their anointed Christos and Sophia. The former they modelled on the original of the King Messiah, the male principle of wisdom, and the latter on the third Sephiroth, from the Chaldaean Kabalah, and even from the Hindu Brahmâ and Sarasvati, and the Pagan Dionysius and Demeter. And here we are on firm ground, if it were only because it is now proved that the New Testament never appeared in its complete form, such as we find it now, till 300 years after the period of the apostles, and the Zohar and other Kabalistic books are found to belong to the first century before our era, if not to be far older still.

"The Gnostics entertained many of the Essenean ideas; and the Essenes had their greater and minor Mysteries at least two centuries before our era. They were the Isarim or Initiates, the descendants of the Egyptian Hierophants, in whose country they had been settled for several centuries before they were converted to Buddhistic monasticism by the missionaries of King Asoka, and amalgamated later with the earliest Christians; and they existed, probably, before the old Egyptian temples were desecrated and ruined in the incessant invasions of Persians, Greeks and other conquering hordes. The hierophants had their atonement enacted in the Mystery of Initiation ages before the Gnostics, or even the Essenes, had appeared. It was known among hierophants as the Baptism of Blood, and was considered not as an atonement for the 'fall of man' in Eden, but simply as an expiation for the past, present, and future sins of ignorant, but nevertheless polluted mankind. The hierophant had the option of either offering his pure and sinless life as a sacrifice for his race to the gods whom he hoped to rejoin, or an animal victim. The former depended entirely on their own will. At the last moment of the solemn 'new birth,' the Initiator passed 'the word' to the initiated, and immediately after the latter had a weapon placed in his right hand, and was ordered to strike. This is the true origin of the Christian dogma of atonement."

As Ballanche says, quoted by Ragon: "Destruction is the great God of the World, justifying therefore the philosophical conception of the Hindu Shiva. According to this immutable and sacred law, the Initiate was compelled to kill the Initiator: otherwise initiation remained incomplete . . . . It is death that generates life." Orthodoxie maçonnique, p. 104. All that, however, was emblematic and exoteric. Weapon and killing must be understood in their allegorical sense.]

THE TRANSMISSION OF LIGHT –

Only in truth the Hierophant was never killed—neither in India nor elsewhere, the murder being simply feigned—unless the Initiator had chosen the Initiate for his successor and had decided to pass to him the last and supreme WORD, after which he had to die—only one man in a nation having the right to know that word. Many are those grand Initiates who have thus passed out of the world's sight, disappearing.

As mysteriously from the sight of men as Moses from the top of Mount Pisgah (Nebo, oracular Wisdom), after he had laid his hands upon Joshua, who thus became "full of the spirit of wisdom;" i.e., initiated.

But he died, he was not killed. For killing, if really done, would belong to black, not to divine Magic. It is the transmission of light, rather than a transfer of life, of life spiritual and divine, and it is the shedding of Wisdom, not of blood. But the initiated inventors of theological Christianity took the allegorical language à la lettre ; and instituted a dogma, the crude, misunderstood expression of which horrifies and repels the spiritual "heathen."

All these Hierophants and Initiates were types of the Sun and of the Creative Principle (spiritual potency) as were Vishvakarma and Vikarttana,   from the origin of the Mysteries. Ragon, the famous Mason, gives curious details and explanations with regard to the Sun rites. He shows that the biblical Hiram, the great hero of Masonry (the "widow's son") a type taken from Osiris, is the Sun-God, the inventor of arts, and the "architect," the name Hiram, meaning the elevated," a title belonging to the Sun. Every Occultist knows how closely related to Osiris and the Pyramids are the narratives in Kings concerning Solomon, his Temple and its construction; he knows also that the whole of the Masonic rite of Initiation is based upon the Biblical allegory of the construction of that Temple, Masons conveniently forgetting, or perhaps ignoring, the fact that the latter narrative is modelled upon Egyptian and still earlier symbolisms. Ragon explains it by showing that the three companions of Hiram, the "three murderers," typify the three last months of the year; and that Hiram stands for the Sun—from its summer solstice downwards, when it begins decreasing—the whole rite being an astronomical allegory.

During the summer solstice, the Sun provokes songs of gratitude from all that breathes; hence Hiram, who represents it, can give to whomsoever has the right to it, the sacred Word, that is to say life. When the Sun descends to the inferior signs all Nature becomes mute, and Hiram can no longer give the sacred Word to the companions, who represent the three inert months of the year. The first companion strikes Hiram feebly with a rule twenty-four inches long, symbol of the twenty-four hours which make up each diurnal revolution; it is the first distribution of time, which afer the exaltation of the mighty star, feebly assails his existence, giving him the first blow. The second companion strikes him with an iron square, symbol of the last season, figured by the intersections of two right lines, which would divide into four equal parts the Zodiacal circle, whose centre symbolises Hiram's heart, where it touches the point of the four squares representing the four seasons; second distribution of time, which at that period strikes a heavier blow at the solar existence. The third companion strikes him mortally on his forehead with a heavy blow of his mallet, whose cylindrical form symbolises the year, the ring or circle: third distribution of time, the accomplishment of which deals the last blow to the existence of the expiring Sun. From this interpretation it has been inferred that Hiram, a founder of metals, the hero of the new legend with the title of architect, is Osiris (the Sun) of modern initiation; that Isis, his widow, is the Lodge, the emblem of the Earth (loka in Sanskrit, the world) and that Horus, son of Osiris (or of light) and the widow's son, is the free Mason, that is to say, the Initiate who inhabits the terrestrial lodge (the child of the Widow, and of Light.) [Orthodoxie maçonnique. pp. 102-104]

And here again, our friend the Jesuits have to be mentioned, for the above rite is of their making. To give one instance of their success in throwing dust into the eyes of ordinary individuals to prevent their seeing the truths of Occultism, we will point out what they did in what is now called Freemasonry.

MASONRY AND THE JESUITS -

This Brotherhood does possess a considerable portion of the symbolism, formulae, and ritual of Occultism, handed down from time immemorial from the primeval Initiations. To render this Brotherhood a mere harmless negation, the Jesuits sent some of their most able emissaries into the Order, who first made the simple brethren believe that the true secret was lost with Hiram Abiff; and then induced them to put this belief into their formularies. They then invented specious but spurious higher degrees, pretending to give further light upon this lost secret, to lead the candidate on and amuse him with forms borrowed from the real thing but containing no substance, and all artfully contrived to lead the aspiring Neophyte to nowhere. And yet men of good sense and abilities, in other respects, will meet at intervals, and with solemn face, zeal and earnestness, go through the mockery of revealing "substituted secrets" instead of the real thing.

If the reader turns to a very remarkable and very useful work called The Royal Masonic Cyclopaedia, Art, "Rosicrucianism," he will find its author, a high and learned Mason, showing what the Jesuits have done to destroy Masonry. Speaking of the period when the existence of this mysterious Brotherhood (of which many pretend to know "something" if not a good deal, and know in fact nothing) was first made known, he says:

There was a dread among the great masses of society in byegone days of the unseen—a dread, as recent events and phenomena show very clearly, not yet overcome in its entirety. Hence students of Nature and mind were forced into an obscurity not altogether unwelcome. . . .The Kabalistic reveries of a Johann Reuchlin led to the fiery action of a Luther, and the patient labours of Trittenheim produced the modern system of diplomatic cipher writing. . . . .It is very worthy of remark, that one particular century, and that in which the Rosicrucians first showed themselves, is distinguished in history as the era in which most of these efforts at throwing off the trammels of the past [Popery and Ecclesiasticism] occurred. Hence the opposition of the losing party, and their virulence against anything mysterious or unknown. They freely organised pseudo-Rosicrucian and Masonic societies in return; and these societies were instructed to irregularly entrap the weaker brethren of the True and Invisible Order, and then triumphantly betray anything they may be so inconsiderate as to communicate to the superiors of these transitory and unmeaning associations. Every wile was adopted to the authorities, fighting in self-defence against the progress of truth, to engage, by persuasion, interest or terror, such as might be cajoled into receiving the Pope as Master—when gained, as many converts to that faith know, but dare not own, they are treated with neglect, and left to battle of life as best they may, not even being admitted to the knowledge of such miserable aporrheta as the Romish faith considers itself entitled to withhold.

But if Masonry has been spoiled, none is able to crush the real invisible Rosicrucian and the Eastern Initiate. The symbolism of Vishvakarma and Sûrya Vikarttana has survived, where Hiram Abiff was indeed murdered, and we will now return to it. It is not simply an astronomical, but is the most solemn rite, an inheritance from the Archaic Mysteries that has crossed the ages and is used to this day. It typifies a whole drama of the Cycle of Life, of progressive incarnations, and of psychic as well as of physiological secrets, of which neither the Church nor Science knows anything, though it is this rite that has led the former to the greatest of its Christian Mysteries.

SECTION XXX

THE MYSTERY "SUN OF INITIATION"

THE antiquity of the Secret Doctrine may be better realised when it is shown at what point of history its Mysteries had already been desecrated, by being made subservient to the personal ambition of despot-ruler and crafty priest. These profoundly philosophical and scientifically composed religious dramas, in which were enacted the grandest truths of the Occult or Spiritual Universe and the hidden lore of learning, and become subject to persecution long before the days when Plato and even Pythagoras flourished. Withal, primal revelations given to Mankind have not died with the Mysteries; they are still preserved as heirlooms for future and more spiritual generations.

It has been already stated in Isis Unveiled, [Op. cit.,i. 15.] that so far back in the days of Aristotle, the great Mysteries had already lost their primitive grandeur and solemnity. Their rites had fallen into desuetude, and they had to a great degree degenerated into mere priestly speculations and had become religious shams. It is useless to state when they first appeared in Europe and Greece, since recognised history may almost be said to begin with Aristotle, everything before him appearing to be in an inextricable chronological confusion. Suffice it to say, that in Egypt the Mysteries had been known since the days of Menes, and that the Greeks received them only when Orpheus introduced them from

India. In an article "Was writing known before Pânini?" [Five Years of Theosophy, p.258. A curious question to start and to deny, when it is well-known even to the Orientalists that, to take but one case, there is Yaska, who was a predecessor of Pânini, and his work still exists; there are seventeen writers of Nirukta (glossary) known to have prescribed Yaska.] it is stated that the Pândus had acquired universal dominion and had taught the "sacrificial" Mysteries to other races as far back as 3,300 B.C. Indeed, when Orpheus, the son of Apollo or Helios, received from his father the phorminx—the seven-stringed lyre, symbolical of the sevenfold mystery of Initiation—these Mysteries were already hoary with age in Central. Asia and India. According to Herodotus it was Orpheus who brought them from India, and Orpheus is far anterior to Homer and Hesiod. Thus even in the days of Aristotle few were the true Adepts left in Europe and even in Egypt. The heirs of those who had been dispersed by the conquering swords of various invaders of old Egypt had been dispersed in their turn. As 8,000 or 9,000 years earlier the stream of knowledge had been slowly running down from the tablelands of Central Asia into India and towards Europe and Northern Africa, so about 500 years B.C. it had begun to flow backward to its old home and birthplace. During the two thousand subsequent years the knowledge of the existence of great Adepts nearly died out in Europe. Nevertheless, in some secret places the Mysteries were still enacted in all their primitive purity. The "Sun of Righteousness" still blazed high on the midnight sky; and, while darkness was upon the face of the profane world, there was the eternal light in the

Adyta on the nights of Initiation. The true Mysteries were never made public. Eleusinia and Agrae for the multitudes; the God Εὐβουλη, "of the good counsel," the great Orphic Deity for the neophyte.

This mystery God—mistaken by our Symbologists for the Sun—who was He? Everyone who has any idea of the ancient Egyptian exoteric faith is quite aware that for the multitudes Osiris was the Sun in Heaven, "the heavenly King," Ro-Imphab; that by the Greeks the Sun was called the "Eye of Jupiter," as for the modern orthodox Pârsi he is "the eye of Ormuzd:" that the Sun, moreover, was addressed as the "All-seeing God"(πολυοφθαλμος) as the "God Saviour," and the "saving God" (Αιτιον της σωτηριας). Read the papyrus of Papheronmes at Berlin, and the stela as rendered by Mariette Bey; [La Mére d'Apis, p. 47.] and see what they say:

Glory to thee, O Sun, divine child! . . . . thy rays carry life to the pure and to those ready. . . .The Gods [the "Sons of God"] who approach thee tremble with delight and awe. . . . Thou art the first born, the Son of God, the Word. [One just initiated is called the "first-born," and in India he becomes dwija, "twice-born," only after his final and supreme Initiation. Every Adept is a "Son of God" and a "Son of Light" after receiving the "Word," when he becomes the "Word" himself, after receiving the seven divine attributes or the "lyre of Apollo."]

The Church has now seized upon these terms and sees presentments of the coming Christ in these expressions in the initiatory rites and prophetic utterances of the Pagan Oracles.

THE SUN AS GOD -

They are nothing of the kind, for they were applied to every worthy Initiate. If the expressions that were used in hieratic writings and glyphs thousands of years before our era are now found in the laudatory hymns and prayers of Christian Churches, it is simply because they have been unblushingly appropriated by the Latin Christians, in the full hope of never being detected by posterity. Everything that could be done had been done to destroy the original Pagan manuscripts and the Church felt secure. Christianity has undeniably had her great Seers and Prophets, like every other religion; but their claims are not strengthened by denying their predecessors.

Listen to Plato:

Know then, Glaucus, that when I speak of the production of good, it is the Sun I mean. The Son has a perfect analogy with his Father.

Iamblichus calls the Sun "the image of divine intelligence or Wisdom." Eusebius, repeating the words of Philo, calls the rising Sun (ανατολη) the chief Angel, the most ancient, adding that the Archangel who is polyonymous (of many names) is the Verbum of Christ. The word Sol (Sun) being derived from solus, the One, or the "He alone." and its Greek name Helios meaning the "Most High," the emblem becomes comprehensible. Nevertheless, the Ancients made a difference between the Sun and its prototype.

Socrates saluted the rising Sun as does a true Pârsî or Zoroastrian in our own day; and Homer and Euripides, as Plato did after them several times, mention the Jupiter-Logos, the "Word" or the Sun. Nevertheless, the Christians maintain that since the oracle consulted on the God Iao answered: "It is the Sun," therefore

The Jehovah of the Jews was well known to the Pagans and Greeks;[See De Mirville, iv.15] and "Iao is our Jehovah." The first part of the proposition has nothing, it seems to do with the second part, and least of all can the conclusion be regarded as correct. But if the Christians are so anxious to prove the identity, Occultists have nothing against it. Only, in such case, Jehovah is also Bacchus. It is very strange that the people of civilised Christendom should until now hold on so desperately to the skirts of the idolatrous Jews— Sabaeans and Sun worshippers as they were, [II. Kings, xxiii, 4-13.] like the rabble of Chaldaea—and that they should fail to see that the later Jehovah is but a Jewish development of the Ja-va, or the Iao, of the Phoenicians; that this name, in short, was the secret name of a Mystery-God, one of the many Kabiri. "Highest God" as He was for one little nation, he never was so regarded by the Initiates who conducted the Mysteries; for them he was but a Planetary Spirit attached to the visible Sun; and the visible Sun is only the central Star, not the central spiritual Sun.

And the Angel of the Lord said unto him [Manoah] "Why askest thou thus after my name, seeing it is secret." [Judges, xiii, 18. Samson, Manoah's son, was an Initiate of that "Mystery" Lord, Ja-va: he was consecrated before his birth to become a "Nazarite" (a chela), an Adept. His sin with Delilah, and the cropping of his long hair that "no razor was to touch" shows how well he kept his sacred vow. The allegory of Samson proves the Esotericism of the Bible, as also the character of the "Mystery Gods" of the Jews. True, Môvers gives a definition of the Phoenician idea of the ideal sunlight as a spiritual influence issuing from the highest God, Iao, "the light conceivable only by intellect—the physical and spiritual Principle of all things: out of which the soul emanates." It was the male Essence or Wisdom, while the primitive matter or Chaos was the female. Thus the first two principles, co-eternal and infinite, were already with the primitive Phoenicians, spirit and matter. But this is the echo of Jewish thought, not the opinion of Pagan Philosophers.]

However this may be, the identity of the Jehovah of Mount Sinai with the God Bacchus is hardly disputable, and he is surely—as already shown in Isis Unveiled—Dionysos. [See Isis Unveiled. ii. 526] Wherever Bacchus was worshipped there was a tradition of Nyssa, [Beth-San or Scythopolis in Palestine had that designation: so had a spot on Mount Parnassus. But Diodorus declares that Nyssa was between Phoenicia and Egypt: Euripides states that Dionysos came to Greece from India: and Diodorus adds his testimony: "Osiris was brought up in Nyssa, in Arabia the Happy: he was the son of Zeus, and was named from his father (nominative Zeus, genitive Dios) and the place Dio-Nysos"—the Zeus or Jove of Nyssa. This identity of name or title is very significant. In Greece Dionysos was second only to Zeus, and Pindar says: "So Father Zeus governs all things, and Bacchus he governs also."] and a cave where he was reared. Outside Greece, Bacchus was the all-powerful "Zagreus, the highest of Gods," in whose service was Orpheus, the founder of the

Mysteries. Now, unless it be conceded that Moses was an initiated Priest, an Adept, whose actions are all narrated allegorically, then it must be admitted that he personally, together with his hosts of Israelites, worshipped Bacchus.

And Moses built an altar, and called the name of it Jehovah Nissi [or, Iao-nisi, or again Dionisi]. [Ex., xvii. 15.]

To strengthen the statement we have further to remember that the place where Osiris, the Egyptian Zagreus or Bacchus, was born, was Mount Sinai, which is called by the Egyptians Mount Nissa. The brazen serpent was a nis, ⸻, and the month of the Jewish Passover is Nisan.

SECTION XXXI

THE OBJECTS OF THE MYSTERIES

THE earliest Mysteries recorded in history are those of Samothrace. After the distribution of pure Fire, a new life began. This was the new birth of the Initiate, after which, like the Brâhmans of old in India, he became a dwija—a "twice born,"

Initiated into that which may be rightly called the most blessed of all Mysteries . . . being ourselves pure,[Phaedrus, Cary's translation, p.326.]

says Plato. Diodorus Siculus, Herodotus and Sanchoniathon the Phoenician—the oldest of Historians— say that these Mysteries originated in the night of time, thousands of years probably before the historical period. Iamblichus informs us that Pythagoras

Was initiated in all the Mysteries of Byblus and Tyre, in the sacred operations of the Syrians, and in the Mysteries of the Phœnicians. [Life of Pythagoras, p.297. "Since Pythagoras, "he adds," "also spent two and twenty years in the adyta of the temples in Egypt, associated with the Magians in Babylon, and was instructed by them in their venerable knowledge, it is not at all wonderful that he was skilled in Magic or Theurgy, and was therefore able to perform things which surpass merely human power, and which appear to be perfectly incredible to the vulgar." (p.298).]

As was said in Isis Unveiled:

When men like Pythagoras, Plato and Iamblichus, renowned for their severe morality, took part in the mysteries and spoke of them with veneration, it ill behoves our modern critics to judge them [and their Initiates] upon their merely external aspect.

Yet this is what has been done until now, especially by the Christian Fathers. Clement Alexandrinus stigmatises the Mysteries as "indecent and diabolical" though his words, showing that the Eleusinian Mysteries were identical with, and even, as he would allege, borrowed from, those of the Jews, are quoted elsewhere in this work. The Mysteries were composed of two parts, of which the Lesser were performed at Agrae, and the Greater at Eleusis, and Clement had been himself initiated. But the Katharsis, or trials of purification, have ever been misunderstood. Iamblichus explains the worst; and his explanation ought to be perfectly satisfactory, at any rate for every unprejudiced mind.

He says:--

Exhibitions of this kind in the Mysteries were designed to free us from licentious passions, by gratifying the sight, and at the same time vanquishing all evil thought, through the awful sanctity with which these rites were accompanied.

Dr. Warburton remarks:

The wisest and best men in the Pagan world are unanimous in this, that the Mysteries were instituted pure, and proposed the noblest ends by the worthiest means.

Although persons of both sexes and all classes were

allowed to take part in the Mysteries, and a participation in them was even obligatory, very few indeed attained the higher and final Initiation in these celebrated rites. The gradation of the Mysteries is given us by Proclus in the fourth book of his Theology of Plato.

The perfective rite, precedes in order the initiation Telete, Muesis, and the initiation , Epopteia, or the final apocalypse [revelation].

Theon of Smyrna, in Mathematica, also divides the mystic rites into five parts:

The first of which is the previous purification; for neither are the Mysteries communicated to all who are willing to receive them; but there are certain persons who are prevented by the voice of the crier. . . . . . Since it is necessary that such as are not expelled from the mysteries should first be refined by certain purifications; but after purification the reception of the sacred rites succeeds. The third part is denominated epopteia or reception. And the fourth, which is the end and design of the revelation, is (the investiture) the binding of the head and fixing of the crowns [This expression must not be understood simply literally: for, as in the initiation of certain Brotherhoods, it has a secret meaning that we have just explained; it was hinted at by Pythagoras, when he describes his feelings after the Initiation, and says that he was crowned by the Gods in whose presence he had drunk "the waters of life"—in the Hindu Mysteries there was the fount of life, and soma, the sacred drink.]. . . Whether after this he [the initiated person] becomes a torchbearer, or an hierophant of the Mysteries, or sustains some other part of the sacerdotal office. But the fifth, which is produced from all these, is friendship and interior communion with God. And this was the last and most awful of all the Mysteries. [Eleusinian and Bacchic Mysteries, T.Taylor, p.46, 47.]

The chief objects of the Mysteries, represented as diabolical by the Christian Fathers and ridiculed by modern writers, were instituted with the highest and most moral purpose in view.

MYSTERIES AND THEOPHANY

There is no need to repeat here that which has been already described in Isis Unveiled [ii. III, 113] that whether through temple Initiation or the private study of Theurgy, every student obtained the proof of the immortality of his Spirit, and the survival of his Soul. What the last epopteia was is alluded to by Plato in Phaedrus:

Being initiated in those Mysteries which it is lawful to call the most blessed of all mysteries. . . . we were freed from the molestations of evils, which otherwise await us in a future period of time. Likewise in consequence of this divine initiation, we become spectators of entire, simple, immovable, and blessed visions, resident in a pure light. [Eleusinian and Bacchic Mysteries, p.63.]

This veiled confession shows that the Initiates enjoyed Theophany—saw visions of Gods and of real immortal spirits. As Taylor correctly infers:

The most sublime part of the epopteia or final revealing, consisted in beholding the Gods [the high Planetary Spirits] themselves, invested with a resplendent light. [Op.cit, p.65]

The statement of Proclus upon the subject is unequivocal:

In all the Initiations and Mysteries, the Gods exhibit many forms of themselves, and appear in a variety of shapes; and sometimes indeed a formless light of themselves if held forth to the view; sometimes this light is according to a human form and sometimes it proceeds into a different shape. [Quoted by Taylor. p.66.]

Again we have...

Whatever is on earth is the resemblance and shadow of something that is in the sphere, while that resplendent thing [the prototype of the Soul-Spirit] remaineth in unchangeable condition, it is well also with its shadow. When that resplendent one removeth far from its shadow life removeth [from the latter] to a distance. Again that light is the shadow of something more resplendent than itself. [Verses 35-38]

Thus speaks the Desatir, in the Book of Shet (the prophet Zirtusht), thereby showing the identity of its Esoteric doctrines with those of the Greek Philosophers.

The second statement of Plato confirms the view that the Mysteries of the Ancients were identical with the Initiations practised even now among the Buddhist and the Hindu Adepts. The higher visions, the most truthful, were produced through a regular discipline of gradual Initiations, and the development of psychical powers. In Europe and Egypt the Mystæ were brought into close union with those whom Proclus calls "mystical natures," resplendent Gods," because, as Plato says:

[We] were ourselves pure and immaculate, being liberated

from this surrounding vestment, which we denominate body, and to which we are now bound like an oyster to its shell. [Phaedrus, 64, quoted by Taylor, p.64.]

As to the East,

The doctrine of planetary and terrestrial Pitris was revealed entirely in ancient India, as well as now, only at the last moment of initiation, and to the adepts of superior degrees. [Isis Unveiled, ii, 114.]

The word Pitris may now be explained and something else added. In India the chela of the third degree of Inititation has two Gurus: One, the living Adept; the other the disembodied and glorified Mahâtmâ, Who remains the adviser or instructor or even the high Adepts. Few are the accepted chelas who even see their living Master, their Guru, till the day and hour of their final and for ever binding vow. It is this that was meant in Isis Unveiled, when it was stated that few of the fakirs (the word chela being unknown to Europe and America in those days) however

Pure, and honest, and self-devoted, have yet ever seen the astral form of a purely human pitar (an ancestor or father), otherwise than at the solemn moment of their first and last initiation. It is in the presence of his instructor, the Guru, and just before the vatou-fakir [the just initiated chela] is despatched into the world of the living, with his seven-knotted bamboo wand for all protection, that he is suddenly placed face to face with the unknown PRESENCE [of his Pitar or Father, the glorified invisible Master, or disembodied Mahâtmâ]. He sees it, and falls prostrate at the feet of the evanescent form, but is not entrusted with the great secret of its evocation, for it is the supreme mystery of the holy syllable.

The Initiate, says Éliphas Lévi, knows; therefore, "he dares all and keeps silent." Says the great French Kabalist:

You may see him often sad, never discouraged or desperate; often poor, never humbled or wretched; often persecuted, never cowed down or vanquished. For he remembers the widowhood and the murder of Orpheus, the exile and solitary death of Moses, the martyrdom of the prophets, the tortures of Apollonius, the Cross of the Savior. He knows in what forlorn state died Agrippa, whose memory is slandered to this day; he knows the trials that broke down the great Paracelsus, and all that Raymond Lully had to suffer before he arrived at a bloody death.

THE MYSTERIES AND MASONRY -

He remembers Swedenborg having to feign insanity, and losing even his reason before his knowledge was forgiven to him; St. Martin, who had to hide himself all life; Cagliostro, who died forsaken in the cells of the inquisition; [This is false, and the Abbé Constant (Éliphas Lévy) knew it was so. Why did he promulgate the untruth?] Cazotte, who perished on the guillotine. Successor of so many victims, he dares, nevertheless, but understands the more the necessity to keep silent. [Dogme de la Haute Magie, i. 219. 220.]

Masonry—not the political institution known as the Scotch Lodge, but real Masonry, some rites of which are still preserved in the Grand Orient of France, and that Elias

Ashmole, a celebrated English Occult Philospher of the XVIIth century, tried in vain to remodel, after the manner of the Indian and Egyptian Mysteries—Masonry rests, according to Ragon, the great authority upon the subject, upon three fundamental degrees: the triple duty of a Mason is to study whence he comes, what he is, and whither he goes; the study that is, of God, of himself, and of the future transformation. [Orthodoxie Maconnique, p.99.] Masonic Initiation was modelled on that in the lesser mysteries. The third degree was one used in both Egypt and India from time immemorial, and the remembrance of it lingers to this day in every Lodge, under the name of the death and resurrection of Hiram Abiff, the "Widow's Son." In Egypt the latter was called "Osiris;" in India "Loka-chakshu" (Eye of the World), and "Dinakara" (day-maker) or the Sun—and the rite itself was everywhere named the "gate of death." The coffin, or sarcophagus, of Osiris, killed by Typhon, was brought in and placed in the middle of the Hall of the Dead, with the Initiates all around it and the candidate near by. The latter was asked whether he had participated in the murder, and notwithstanding his denial, and after sundry and very hard trials, the Initiator feigned to strike him on the head with a hatchet; he was thrown down, swathed in bandages like a mummy, and wept over. Then came lightening and thunder, the supposed corpse was surrounded with fire, and was finally raised.

Ragon speaks of a rumour that charged the Emperor Commodus—when he was at one time enacting the part of the Initiator—with having played this part in the initiatory drama so seriously that he actually killed the postulant when dealing him the blow with the hatchet. This shows that the lesser Mysteries had not quite died out in the second century A.D.

The Mysteries were carried into South and Central America, Northern Mexico and Peru by the Atlanteans in those days when

A pedestrian from the North [of what was once upon a time also India] might have reached—hardly wetting his feet—the Alaskan Peninsula, through Manchooria, across the future Gulf of Tartary, the Kurile and Aleutian Islands; while another traveller, furnished with a canoe and starting from the South, could have walked over from Siam, crossed the Polynesian Islands and trudged into any part of the continent of South America.[Five Years of Theosophy. p.214.]

They continued to exist down to the day of the Spanish invaders. These destroyed the Mexican and Peruvian records, but were prevented from laying their desecrating hands upon the many Pyramids—the lodges of an ancient Initiation—whose ruins are scattered over Puente Nacional, Cholula, and Teotihuacan. The ruins of Palenque of Ococimgo in Chiapas, and others in Central America are known to all. If the pyramids and temples of Guiengola and Mitla ever betray their secrets, the present Doctrine will then be shown to have been a forerunner of the grandest truths in Nature. Meanwhile they have all a claim to be called Mitla, "the place of sadness" and "the abode of the (desecrated) dead."

SECTION XXXII

TRACES OF THE MYSTERIES

SAYS the Royal Masonic Cyclopædia, art, "Sun:"

In all times, the Sun has necessarily played an important part as a symbol, and especially in Freemasonry. The W.M. represents the rising sun, the J.W. the sun at the meridian, and the S.W. the setting sun. In the Druidical rites, the Arch-Druid represents the sun, and was aided by two other officers, one representing the Moon in the West, and the other the Sun at the South in its meridian. It is quite unnecessary to enter into any lengthened discussion on this symbol.

It is the more "unnecessary" since J.M. Ragon has discussed it very fully, as one may find at the end of Section XXIX., where part of his explanations have been quoted. Freemasonry derived her rights from the East, as we have said. And if it be true to say of the modern Rosicrucians that "they are invested with a knowledge of chaos, not perhaps a very desirable acquisition," the remark is still more true when applied to all the other branches of Masonry, since the knowledge of their members about the full signification of their symbol is nil. Dozens of hypotheses are resorted to, one more unlikely than the other, as to the "Round Towers" of Ireland; one fact is enough to show the ignorance of the Masons, namely, that, according to the Royal Masonic Encylopædia, the idea that they were connected with Masonic

Initiation, may be at once dismissed as unworthy of notice. The "Towers," which are found throughout the East in Asia were connected with the Mystery-Initiations, namely, with the Vishvakarma and the Vikarttana rites. The candidates for Initiation were placed in them for three days and three nights, whenever there was no temple with a subterranean crypt close at hand. These round towers were built for no other purposes. Discredited as are all such monuments of Pagan origin by the Christian clergy, who thus "soil their own nest," they are still the living and indestructible relics of the Wisdom of old. Nothing exists in this objective and illusive world of ours that cannot be made to serve two purposes—a good and a bad one. Thus in later ages, the Initiates of the Left Path and the anthropomorphists took in hand most of those venerable ruins, then silent and deserted by their first wise inmates, and turned them indeed into phallic monuments. But this was a deliberate, wilful, and vicious misinterpretation of their real meaning, a deflection from their first use. The Sun—though ever, even for the multitudes, μονος ουρανου φεος, "the only and one King and God in heaven, and the Ευβουλη, "the God of Good Counsel" of Orpheus—had in every exoteric popular religion a dual aspect which was anthropomorphised by the profane. Thus the Sun was Osiris-Typhon, Ormuzd-Ahriman, Bel-Jupiter and Baal, the life-giving and the death-giving luminary. And thus one and the same monolith, pillar, pyramid, tower or temple, originally built to glorify the first principle or aspect, might become in time an idol-fane, or worse, a phallic emblem in its crude and brutal form. The Lingam of the Hindus has a spiritual and highly philosophical meaning, while the missionaries see in it but an "indecent emblem;" it has just the meaning which is to be found in all those baalim, chammanim, and the bamoth with the pillars of unhewn stone of the Bible, set up for the glorification of the male Jehovah. But this does not alter the fact that the pureia of the Greeks, the nur-hags of Sardinia, the teocalli of Mexico etc., were all in the beginning of the same character as the "Round Towers" of Ireland. They were sacred places of Initiation.

In 1877, the writer, quoting the authority and opinions of some most eminent scholars, ventured to assert that there was a great difference between the terms Chrestos and Christos, a difference having a profound and Esoteric meaning. Also that while Christos means "to live" and "to be born into a new life," Chrestos, in "Initiation" phraseology, signified the death of the inner, lower, or personal nature in man; thus is given the key to the Bràhmanical title, the twice-born; and finally,

There were Chrestians long before the era of Christianity, and the Essenes belonged to them. [In I Peter. ii. 3, Jesus is called "the Lord Chrestos."]

For this epithets sufficiently opprobrious to characterise the writer could hardly be found. And yet then as well as now, the author never attempted a statement of such a serious nature without showing as many learned authorities for it as could be mustered.

CHRISTOS AND CHRESTOS -

Thus on the next page it was said:

Lepsius shows that the word Nofre means Chrestos, "good," and that one of the titles of Osiris, "Onnofre," must be translated "the goodness of God made manifest." "The worship of Christ was not universal at this early date," explains Mackenzie, "by which I mean that Christolatry had not been introduced; but the worship of Chrestos—the Good Principle—had preceded it by many centuries, and even survived the general adoption of Christianity, as shown on monuments still in existence . . . .Again we have an inscription which is pre-Christian on an epitaphial tablet, (Spon. Misc. Frud. Ant. x xviii. 2) Ταχινθε Λαρισαιων Δησμοσιε. Πρως Χρηστε Χαιρε, ., and de Rossi (Roma Sotteranea, tome i., tav. xxi.) gives us another example from the catacombs—" Ælia Chreste, in Pace." [Isis Unveiled. ii. 323.]

Today the writer is able to add to all those testimonies the corroboration of an erudite author, who proves whatever he undertakes to show on the authority of geometrical demonstration. There is a most curious passage with remarks and explanations in the Source of Measures, whose author has probably never heard of the "Mystery-God" Visvakarma of the early Âryans. Treating on the difference between the terms Chrest and Christ, he ends by saying that:

There were two Messiahs: one who went down into the pit for the salvation of this world; this was the Sun shorn of his golden rays, and crowned with blackened ones (symbolising this loss), as the thorns: the other was the triumphant Messiah mounting up to the summit of the arch of heaven, and personified as the Lion of the Tribe of Judah. In both instances he had the cross; once in humiliation and once holding it in his control as the law of creation, He being Jehovah.

And then the author proceeds to give "the fact" that "there were two Messiahs," etc., as quoted above. And this—leaving the divine and mystic character and claim for Jesus entirely independent of this event of His mortal life—shows Him beyond any doubt, as an Initiate of the Egyptian Mysteries, where the same rite of Death and of spiritual Resurrection for the neophyte, or the suffering Chrestos on his trial and new birth by Regeneration, was enacted—for this was a universally adopted rite.

The "pit" into which the Eastern Initiate was made to descend was, as shown before, Pâtâla, one of the seven regions of the nether world, over which rules Vâsuki, the great "snake God." This pit, Pâtâla, has in the Eastern Symbolism precisely the same manifold meaning as is found by Mr. Ralston Skinner in the Hebrew word shiac in its application to the case in hand. For it was the synonym of Scorpio— Pâtâla's depths being "impregnated with the brightness of the new Sun"—represented by the "newly born" into the glory; and Pâtâla was and is in a sense, "a pit, a grave, the place of death, and the door of Hades or Sheol" —as, the partially exoteric Initiations in India, the candidate had to pass through the matrix of the heifer before proceeding to Pâtâla. In its non-mystic sense it is the Antipodes—America being referred to in India as Pâtâla. But in its symbolism it meant all that, and much more. The fact alone that Vâsuki, the ruling Deity of Pâtâla, is represented in the Hindu Pantheon as the great Nâga (Serpent) —who was used by the Gods and Asuras as a rope round the mountain Mandara, at the churning of the ocean for Amrita, the water of immortality—connects him directly with Initiation

For he is Shesha Nâga also, serving as a couch for Vishnu, and upholding the seven worlds; and he is also Ananta, "the endless," and the symbol of eternity—hence the "God of Secret Wisdom," degraded by the Church to the rôle of the tempting Serpent, of Satan. That what is now said is correct may be verified by the evidence of even the exoteric rendering of the attributes of various Gods and Sages both in the Hindu and the Buddhist Pantheons. Two instances will suffice to show how little our best and most erudite Orientalists are capable of dealing correctly and fairly with the symbolism of Eastern nations, while remaining ignorant of the corresponding points to be found only in Occultism and the Secret Doctrine.

(1) The learned Orientalist and Tibetan traveller, Professor Emil Schlagintweit, mentions in one of his works on Tibet, a national legend to the effect that

Nâgârjuna [a "mythological" personage "without any real existence," the learned German scholar thinks] received the book Paramârtha, or according to others, the book Avatamsaka, from the Nâgas, fabulous creatures of the nature of serpents, who occupy a place among the beings superior to man, and are regarded as protectors of the law of Buddha. To these spiritual beings Shâkyamuni is said to have taught a more philosophical religious system than to men, who were not sufficiently advanced to understand it at the time of his appearance. [Buddhism in Tibet, p.31.]

THE SYMBOLISM OF NARADA –

Nor are men sufficiently advanced for it now; for "the more philosophical religious system" is the Secret Doctrine, the Occult Eastern Philosophy, which is the corner-stone of all sciences rejected by the unwise builders even at this day, and more today perhaps than ever before, in the great conceit of our age. The allegory means simply that Nâgârjuna having been initiated by the "Serpents"—the Adepts, "the wise ones"—and driven out from India by the Brâhmans, who dreaded to have their Mysteries and sacerdotal Science divulged (the real cause of their hatred of Buddhism), went away to China and Tibet, where he initiated many into the truths of the hidden Mysteries taught by Gautama Buddha.

(2) The hidden symbolism of Nârada—the great Rishi and the author of some of the Rig-Vaidic hymns, who incarnated again later on during Krishna's time—has never been understood. Yet, in connection with the Occult Sciences, Nârada, the son of Brahmâ, is one of the most prominent characters; he is directly connected in his first incarnation with the "Builders"—hence with the seven "Rectors" of the Christian Church, who "helped God in the work of creation." This grand personification is hardly noticed by our Orientalists, who refer only to that which he is alleged to have said of Pâtâla, namely, "that it is a place of sexual and sensual gratifications." This is thought to be amusing, and the reflection is suggested that Nârada, no doubt, "found the place delightful." Yet this sentence simply shows him to have been an Initiate, connected directly with the Mysteries, and walking, as all the other neophytes, before and after him,

had to walk, in "the pit among the thorns" in the "sacrificial Chrest condition," as the suffering victim made to descend thereinto—a mystery, truly!

Nârada is one of the seven Rishis, the "mind-born sons" of Brahmâ. The fact of his having been during his incarnation a high Initiate—he, like Orpheus, being the founder of the Mysteries—is corroborated, and made evident by his history. The Mahâbhârata states that Nârada, having frustrated the scheme formed for peopling the universe, in order to remain true to his vow of chastity, was cursed by Daksha, and sentenced to be born once more. Again, when born during Krishna's time, he is accused of calling his father Brahmâ "a false teacher," because the latter advised him to get married, and he refused to do so. This shows him to have been an Initiate, going against the orthodox worship and religion. It is curious to find this Rishi and leader among the "Builders" and the "Heavenly Host" as the prototype of the Christian "leader" of the same "Host"—the Archangel Mikael. Both are the male "Virgins," and both are the only ones among their respective "Hosts" who refuse to create. Nârada is said to have dissuaded the Hari-ashvas, the five thousand sons of Daksha, begotten by him for the purpose of peopling the Earth, from producing offspring. Since then the Hari-ashvas have "dispersed themselves through the regions, and have never returned." The Initiates are, perhaps, the incarnations of these Hari-ashvas?

It was on the seventh day, the third of his ultimate trial, that the neophyte arose, a regenerated man, who, having passed through his second spiritual birth, returned to earth a glorified and triumphant conqueror of Death, a Hierophant.

An Eastern neophyte in his Chrest condition may be seen in a certain engraving in Moor's Hindu Pantheon, whose author mistook another form of the crucified Sun or Vishnu, Vittoba, for Krishna, and calls it "Krishna crucified in space." The engraving is also given in Dr. Lundy's Monumental Christianity, in which work the reverend author has collected as many proofs as his ponderous volume could hold of "Christian symbols before Christianity," as he expresses it. Thus he shows us Krishna and Apollo as good shepherds, Krishna holding the cruciform Conch and the Chakra, and Krishna "crucified in Space," as he calls it. Of this figure it may be truly said, as the author says of it himself:

This representation I believe to be anterior to Christianity . . . . It looks like a Christian crucifix in many respects . . . . The drawing, the attitude, the nail marks in hands and feet, indicate a Christian origin, while the Parthian coronet of seven points, the absence of the wood, and of the usual inscription, and the rays of glory above, would seem to point to some other than a Christian origin. Can it be the victim-man, or the priest and victim both in one, of the Hindu Mythology, who offered himself a sacrifice before the worlds were?

It is surely so.

Can it be Plato's Second God who impressed himself on the universe in the form of the cross? Or is it his divine man, who would be scourged, tormented, fettered, have his eyes burnt out; and lastly . . .would be crucified?

It is all that and much more; archaic religious Philosophy was universal, and its Mysteries are as old as man. It is the eternal symbol of the personified Sun—astronomically purified—in its mystic meaning regenerated, and symbolised by all the Initiates in memory of a sinless Humanity when all were "Sons of God."

EGYPTIAN INITIATION –

Now, mankind has become the "Son of Evil" truly. Does all this take anything away from the dignity of Christ as an ideal, or of Jesus as a divine man? Not at all. On the contrary, made to stand alone, glorified above all other "Sons of God," He can only forment evil feelings in all those many millioned nations who do not believe in the Christian system, provoking their hatred and leading to iniquitous wars and strifes. If, on the other hand, we place Him among a long series of "Sons of God" and Sons of divine Light, every man may then be left to choose for himself, among those many ideals, which he will choose as a God to call to his help, and worship on earth as in Heaven.

Many among those called "Saviours" were "good shepherds," as was Krishna for one, and all of them are said to have "crushed the serpent's head"—in other words to have conquered their sensual nature and to have mastered divine and Occult Wisdom. Apollo killed Python, a fact which exonerates him from the charge of being himself the great dragon, Satan: Krishna slew the snake Kalinâga, the Black Serpent; and the Scandinavian Thor bruised the head of the symbolical reptile with his crucifixion mace.

In Egypt every city of importance was separated from its burial-place by a sacred lake. The same ceremony of judgement, as is described in The Book of the Dead—"that precious and mysterious book" (Bunsen)—as taking place in the world of Spirit, took place on earth during the burial of the mummy. Forty-two judges or assessors assembled on the shore and judged the departed "Soul" according to its actions when in the body. After that the priests returned within the sacred precincts and instructed the neophytes upon the probable fate of the Soul, and the solemn drama that was then taking place in the invisible realm whither the Soul had fled. The immortality of the Spirit was strongly inculcated on the neophytes by the Al-om-jalt—the name of the highest Egyptian Hierophant. In the Crata Nepoa—the priestly Mysteries in Egypt—the following are described as four out of the seven degrees of Initiation.

After a preliminary trial at Thebes, where the neophyte had to pass through many probations, called the "Twelve Tortures," he was commanded, in order that he might come out triumphant, to govern his passions and never lose for a moment the idea of his inner God or seventh Principle. Then, as a symbol of the wanderings of the unpurified Soul, he had to ascend several ladders and wander in darkness in a cave with many doors, all of which were locked. Having overcome all, he received the degree of Pastophoris, after which he became, in the second and third degrees, the Neocoris and Melancphoris. Brought into a vast subterranean chamber, thickly furnished with mummies lying in state, he was placed in presence of the coffin which contained the mutilated body of Osiris. This was the hall called the "Gates of Death," whence the verse in Job:

> Have the gates of Death been
opened to thee,
> Hast thou seen the doors of the
shadow of death?

Thus asks the "Lord," the Hierophant, the Al-om-jah, the Initiator of Job, alluding to this third degree of Initiation. For the Book of Job is the poem of Initiation par excellence.

When the neophyte had conquered the terrors of this trial, he was conducted to the "Hall of Spirits," to be judged by them. Among the rules in which he was instructed, he was commanded:

Never to either desire or seek revenge; to be always ready to help a brother in danger, even unto the risk of his own life; to bury every dead body; to honour his parents above all; to respect old age, and protect those weaker than himself; and finally, to ever bear in mind the hour of death, and that of resurrection in a new and imperishable body.

Purity and chastity were highly recommended, and adultery was threatened with death. Thus the Egyptian neophyte was made a Kristophoros. In this degree the mystery-name of IAO was communicated to him.

Let the reader compare the above sublime precepts with the precepts of Buddha, and the noble commandments in the "Rule of Life" for the ascetics of India, and he will understand the unity of the Secret Doctrine everywhere.

It is impossible to deny the presence of a sexual element in many religious symbols, but this fact is not in the least open to censure, once it becomes generally known that—in the religious traditions of every country—man was not born in the first "human" race from father and mother. From the bright "mind-born Sons of Brahmâ," the Rishis, and from Adam Kadmon with his Emanations, the Sephiroth, down to the "parentless," the Anupâdaka, or the Dhyâni Buddhas, from whom sprang the Bodhisattvas and Manushi-Buddhas, the earthly Initiates—men—the first race of men was with every nation held as being born without father or mother. Man, the "Manushi Buddha," the Manu, the "Enosh," son of Seth, or the "Son of Man" as he is called—is born in the present way only as the consequence, the unavoidable fatality, of the law of natural evolution.

THE SELF-SACRIFICING VICTIM –

Mankind—having reached the last limit, and that turning point where its spiritual nature had to make room for mere physical organization—had to "fall into matter" and generation. But man's evolution and involution are cyclic. He will end as he began. Of course to our grossly material minds even the sublime symbolism of Kosmos conceived in the matrix of Space after the divine Unit had entered into and fructified it with Its holy fiat, will no doubt suggest materiality. Not so with primitive mankind. The initiatory rite in the Mysteries of the self-sacrificing Victim that dies a spiritual death to save the world from destruction—really from depopulation—was established during the Fourth Race, to commemorate an event, which, physiologically, has now become the Mystery of Mysteries among the world-problems. In the Jewish script it is Cain and the female Abel who are the sacrificed and sacrificing couple—both immolating themselves (as permutations of Adam and Eve, or the dual Jehovah) and shedding their blood "of separation and union," for the sake of and to save mankind by inaugurating a new physiological race. Later still, when the neophyte, as already mentioned, in order to be re-born once more into his lost spiritual state, had to pass through the entrails (the womb) of a virgin heifer [The Aryans replaced the living cow by one made of gold, silver or any other metal, and the rite is preserved to this day, when one desires to become a Brâhman, a twice-born, in India.] killed at the moment of the rite, it involved again a mystery and one as great, for it referred to the process of birth, or rather the first entrance of man on to this earth, through Vâch—"the melodious cow who milks forth sustenance and water"—and who is the female Logos. It had also reference to the same self-sacrifice of the "divine Hermaphrodite"—of the third Root-Race—the transformation of Humanity into truly physical men, after the loss of spiritual potency. When, the fruit of evil having been tested along with the fruit of good, there was as a result the gradual atrophy of spirituality and a strengthening of the materiality in man, then he was doomed to be born thenceforth through the present process. This is the Mystery of the Hermaphrodite, which the Ancients kept so secret and veiled. It was neither the absence of moral feeling, nor the presence of gross sensuality in them that made them imagine their Deities under a dual aspect; but rather their knowledge of the mysteries and processes of primitive Nature. The Science of Physiology was better known to them than it is to us now. It is in this that lies buried the key to the Symbolism of old, the true focus of national thought, and the strange dual-sexed images of nearly every God and Goddess in both pagan and monotheistic Pantheons.

Says Sir William Drummond in Œdipus Judaïcus:

The truths of science were the arcana of the priests because these truths were the foundations of religion.

But why should the missionaries so cruelly twit the Vaishnavas and Krishna worshippers for the supposed grossly indecent meaning of their symbols, since it is made clear beyond the slightest doubt, and by the most unprejudiced writers, that Chrestos in the pit—whether the pit to be taken as meaning the grave or hell—had likewise a sexual element in it, from the very origin of the symbol.

This fact is no longer denied today. The "Brothers of the Rosy Cross of the Middle Ages were as good Christians as any to be found in Europe, nevertheless, all their rites were based on symbols whose meaning was pre-eminently phallic and sexual. Their biographer, Hargrave Jennings, the best modern authority on Rosicrucianism, speaking of this mystic Brotherhood, describes how

The tortures and the sacrifice of Calvary, the Passion of the Cross, were, in their [the Rose-Croix's] glorious blessed magic and triumph, the protest and appeal.

Protest—by whom? The answer is, the protest of the crucified Rose, the greatest and the most unveiled of all sexual symbols—the Yoni and Lingam, the "victim" and the "murderer," the female and male principles in Nature. Open the last work of that author, Phallicism, and see in what glowing terms he describes the sexual symbolism in that which is most sacred to the Christian:

The flowing blood streamed from the crown, or the piercing circlet of the thorns of Hell. The Rose is feminine. Its lustrous carmine petals are guarded with thorns. The Rose is the most beautiful of flowers. The Rose is the Queen of God's Garden (Mary, the Virgin). It is not the Rose alone which is the magical idea, or truth. But it is the "crucified rose," or the "martyred rose" (by the grand mystic apocalyptic figure) which is the talisman, the standard, the object of adoration of all the "Sons of Wisdom" or the true Rosicrucians. [Op. cit.,p. 141.]

Not of all the "Sons of Wisdom," by any means, not even of the true Rosicrucian. For the latter would never put in such sickening relievo, in such a purely sensual and terrestrial, not to say animal light, the grandest, the noblest of Nature's symbols.

ORPHEUS -

To the Rosicrucian, the "Rose" was the symbol of Nature, of the ever prolific and virgin Earth, or Isis, the mother and nourisher of man, considered as feminine and represented as a virgin woman by the Egyptian Initiates. Like every other personification of Nature and the Earth she is the sister and wife of Osiris, as the two characters answer to the personified symbol of the Earth, both she and the Sun being the progeny of the same mysterious Father, because the Earth is fecundated by the Sun—according to the earliest

Mysticism—by divine insufflation. It was the pure ideal of mystic Nature that was personified in the "World Virgins," the "Celestial Maidens," and later on by the human Virgin, Mary, the Mother of the Saviour, the Salvator Mundi now chosen by the Christian World. And it was the character of the Jewish maiden that was adopted by Theology to archaic Symbolism, [In Ragon's Orthodoxie Maconnique p.105, note, we find the following statement—borrowed from Albumazar the Arabian, probably: "The Virgin of the Magi and Chaldæans. The Chaldæan sphere [globe] showed in its heavens a newly-born babe, called Christ and Jesus; it was placed in the arms of the Celestial Virgin. It was to this Virgin that Eratosthenes, the Alexandrian Librarian, born 276 years before our era, gave the name of Isis, mother of Horus." This is only what Kircher gives (in Ædipus Ægypticus, iii. 5), quoting Albumazar: "In the first decan of the Virgin rises a maid, called Aderenosa, that is pure, immaculate virgin . . .sitting upon an embroidered throne nursing a boy . . . a boy, named Jesus . . . which signifies Issa, whom they also call Christ in Greek." (See Isis Unveiled, ii. 491)] and not the Pagan symbol that was modelled for the new occasion.

We know through Herodotus that the Mysteries were brought from India by Orpheus—a hero far anterior to both Homer and Hesiod. Very little is really known of him, and till very lately Orphic literature, and even the Argonauts, were attributed to Onamacritus, a contemporary of Pisistratus, Solon and Pythagoras—who was credited with their compilation in the present form toward the close of the sixth century B.C., or 800 years after the time of Orpheus.

But we are told that in the days of Pausanias there was a sacerdotal family, who, like the Brâhmans with the Vedas, had committed to memory all the Orphic Hymns, and that they were usually thus transmitted from one generation to another. By placing Orpheus so far back as 1200 B.C., official Science—so careful in her chronology to choose in each case as late a period as possible—admits that the Mysteries, or in other words Occultism dramatised, belong to a still earlier epoch than the Chaldæans and Egyptians.

The downfall of the Mysteries in Europe may now be mentioned.

SECTION XXXIII

THE LAST OF THE MYSTERIES IN EUROPE

A S was predicted by the great Hermes in his dialogue with Æsculapius, the time had indeed come when impious foreigners accused Egypt of adoring monsters, and naught but the letters engraved in stone upon her monuments survived—enigmas unintelligible to posterity. Her sacred Scribes and Hierophants became wanderers upon the face of the earth. Those who remained in Egypt found themselves obliged for fear of a profanation of the sacred Mysteries to seek refuge in deserts and mountains, to form and establish secret societies and brotherhoods—such as the Essenes; those who had crossed the oceans to India and even to the (now-called) New World, bound themselves by solemn oaths to keep silent, and to preserve secret their Sacred Knowledge and Science; thus these were buried deeper than ever out of human sight. In Central Asia and on the northern borderlands of India, the triumphant sword of Aristotle's pupil swept away from his path of conquest every vestige of a once pure Religion: and its Adepts receded further and further from that path into the most hidden spots of the globe. The cycle of* * * *being at its close, the first hour for the disappearance of the Mysteries struck on the clock of the Races, with the Macedonian conqueror. The first strokes of its last hour sounded in the year 47 B.C.. Alesia [Now called St. Reine (Cote d'Or) on the two streams, the Ose and the

511

Oserain. Its fall is a historical fact in Keltic Gaulish History.] the famous city in Gaul, the Thebes of the Kelts, so renowned for its ancient rites of Initiation and Mysteries, was, as J. M. Ragon well describes it:

The ancient metropolis and the tomb of Initiation, of the religion of the Druids and of the freedom of Gaul. [Orthodoxie Maconnique, p. 22.]

ALESIA AND BIBRACTIS –

It was during the first century before our era, that the last and supreme hour of the great Mysteries had struck. History shows the populations of Central Gaul revolting against the Roman yoke. The country was subject to Cæsar, and the revolt was crushed; the result was the slaughter of the garrison at Alesia (or Alisa), and of all its inhabitants, including the Druids, the college-priests and the neophytes; after this the whole city was plundered and razed to the ground.

Bibractis, a city as large and as famous, not far from Alesia, perished a few years later. J. M. Ragon describes her end as follows:

Bibractis, the mother of sciences, the soul of the early nations [in Europe], a town equally famous for its sacred college of Druids, its civilisation, its schools, in which 40,000 students were taught philosophy, literature, grammar, jurisprudence, medicine, astrology, occult sciences, architecture, etc. Rival of Thebes, of Memphis, of Athens and of Rome, it possessed an amphitheatre, surrounded with colossal statues, and accommodating 100,000 spectators, gladiators, a capital, temples of Janus, Pluto, Prosperpine,

Jupiter, Apollo, Minerva, Cybele, Venus and Anubis; and in the midst of these sumptuous edifices the Naumachy, with its vast basin, an incredible construction, a gigantic work wherein floated boats and galleys devoted to naval games; then a Champ de Mars, an aqueduct, fountains, public baths; finally fortifications and walls, the construction of which dated from the heroic ages.[Op. cit., p.22.]

Such was the last city in Gaul wherein died for Europe the secrets of the Initiations of the Great Mysteries, the Mysteries of Nature, and of her forgotten Occult truths. The rolls and manuscripts of the famous Alexandrian Library were burned and destroyed by the same Cæsar, [The Christian mob in 389 of our era completed the work of destruction upon what remained: most of the priceless works were saved for students of Occultism, but lost to the world.] but while History deprecates the action of the Arab general, Amrus, who gave the final touch to this act of vandalism perpetrated by the great conqueror, it has not a word to say to the latter for his destruction of nearly the same amount of precious rolls in Alesia , nor to the destroyer of Bibractis. While Sacrovir—chief of the Gauls, who revolted against Roman despotism under Tiberius, and was defeated by Silius in the year 21 of our era—was burning himself alive with his fellow conspirators on a funeral pyre before the gates of the city, as Ragon tells us, the latter was sacked and plundered, and all her treasures of literature on the Occult Sciences perished by fire. The once majestic city, Bibractis, has now become Autun, Ragon explains.

A few monuments of glorious antiquity are still there, such

as the temples of Janus and Cybele.

Ragon goes on:

Arles, founded two thousand years before Christ, was sacked in 270. This metropolis of Gaul, restored 40 years later by Constantine, has preserved to this day a few remains of its ancient splendour; amphitheatre, capitol, an obelisk, a block of granite 17 metres high, a triumphal arch, catacombs, etc. Thus ended Kelto Gaulic civilisation. Cæsar, as a barbarian worthy of Rome, had already accomplished the destruction of the ancient Mysteries by the sack of the temples and their initiatory colleges, and by the massacre of the Initiates and the Druids. Remained Rome; but she never had but the lesser Mysteries, shadows of the Secret Sciences. The Great Initiation was extinct. [Op. cit., p.23. J.M. Ragon, a Belgian by birth, and a Mason, knew more about Occultism than any other non-initiated writer. For fifty years he studied the ancient mysteries wherever he could find accounts of them. In 1805, he founded at Paris the Brotherhood of Les Trinosophes, in which Lodge he delivered for years lectures on Ancient and Modern Initiations (in 1818 and again in 1841), which were published, and now are lost. Then he became the writer in chief of Hermes, a masonic paper. His best works were La Maconnerie Occulte and the Fastes Initiatiques. After his death, in 1866, a number of his MSS, remained in the possession of the Grand Orient of France. A high Mason told the writer that Ragon had corresponded for years with two Orientalists in Syria and Egypt, one of whom is a Kopt gentleman.]

A few further extracts may be given from his Occult

Masonry, as they bear directly upon our subject. However learned and erudite, some of the chronological mistakes of that author are very great. He says:

After deified man (Hermes) came the King-Priest [the Hierophant] Menes was the first legislator and the founder of Thebes of the hundred palaces. He filled that city with magnificent splendour; it is from his day that the sacerdotal epoch of Egypt dates. The priests reigned, for it is they who made the laws. It is said that there have been three hundred and twenty-nine [Hierophants] since his time—all of whom have remained unknown.

After that, genuine Adepts having become scarce, the author shows the Priests choosing false ones from the midst of slaves, whom they exhibited, having crowned and deified them, for the adoration of the ignorant masses.

Tired of reigning in such a servile way, the kings rebelled and freed themselves. Then came Sesostris, the founder of Memphis (1613, they say before our era). To the sacerdotal election to the throne succeeded that of the warriors. . . . Cheops who reigned from 1178 to 1122 built the great Pyramid which bears his name. He is accused of having persecuted theocracy and closed the temples.

This is utterly incorrect, though Ragon repeats "History." The Pyramid called by the name of Cheops is the Great Pyramid, the building of which even Baron Bunsen assigned to 5,000 B.C. He says in Egypt's Place in Universal History:

THE LEARNING OF EGYPT -

The Origins of Egypt go back to the ninth millennium before Christ.[Op. cit., iv. 462.]

And as the Mysteries were performed and the Initiations took place in that Pyramid—for indeed it was built for that purpose—it looks strange and an utter contradiction with known facts in the history of the Mysteries to suppose that Cheops, if the builder of that Pyramid ever turned against the initiated Priests and their temples. Moreover, as far as the Secret Doctrine teaches, it was not Cheops who built the Pyramid of that name, whatever else he might have done.

Yet, it is quite true that owing to an Ethiopian invasion and the federated government of twelve chiefs, royalty fell into the hands of Amasis, a man of low birth.

This was in 570 B.C., and it was Amasis who destroyed priestly power. And thus perished that ancient theocracy which showed its crowned priests for so many centuries to Egypt and the whole world.

Egypt had gathered the students of all countries around her Priests and Hierophants before Alexandria was founded. Ennemoser asks:

How comes it that so little has become known of the Mysteries and of their particular contents, through so many ages, and amongst so many different times and people? The answer is that it is again owing to the universally strict silence of the initiated. Another cause may be found in the destruction and total loss of all the written memorials of the secret knowledge of the remotest antiquity.

Numa's books, described by Livy, consisting of natural

philosophy, were found in his tomb; but they were not allowed to be made known, lest they should reveal the most secret mysteries of the state religion. . . . The senate and the tribunes of the people determined . . . that the books themselves should be burned, which was done. [History of Magic, ii, II.]

Cassain mentions a treatise, well-known in the fourth and fifth centuries, which was accredited to Ham, the son of Noah, who in his turn was reputed to have received it from Jared, the fourth generation from Seth, the son of Adam.

Alchemy also was first taught in Egypt by her learned Priests, though the first appearance of this system is as old as man. Many writers have declared that Adam was the first Adept; but that was a blind and a pun upon the name, which is "red earth" in one of its meanings. The correct information—under its allegorical veil—is found in the sixth chapter of Genesis, which speaks of the "Sons of God" who took wives of the daughters of men, after which they communicated to these wives many a mystery and secret of the phenomenal world. The cradle of Alchemy, says Olaus Borrichius, is to be sought in the most distant times. Democritus of Abdera was an Alchemist, and a Hermetic Philosopher. Clement of Alexandria wrote considerably upon the Science, and Moses and Solomon are called proficients in it. We are told by W. Godwin;

The first authentic record on this subject is an edict of Diocletian about 300 years A.D. ordering a diligent search to be made in Egypt for all the ancient books which treated of the art of making gold and silver, that they might, without distinction, be consigned to the flames.

The Alchemy of the Chaldæans and the old Chinamen is not even the parent of that Alchemy which revived among the Arabians many centuries later. There is a spiritual Alchemy and a physical transmutation. The knowledge of both was imparted at the Initiations.

Short Bio of the Author

Annie Besant was born in 1847 in London into a middle-class family of Irish origin. She was proud of her heritage and supported the cause of Irish self-rule throughout her adult life. Her father died when she was five years old, leaving the family almost penniless. Her mother supported the family by running a boarding house for boys at Harrow School. However, she was unable to support Annie and persuaded her friend Ellen Marryat to care for her. Marryat made sure that Besant had a good education. She was given a strong sense of duty to society and an equally strong sense of what independent women could achieve. As a young woman, she was also able to travel widely in Europe. There she acquired a taste for Roman Catholic colour and ceremony that never left her.

In 1867, at age nineteen she married 26-year-old clergyman Frank Besant, younger brother of Walter Besant. He was an evangelical Anglican who seemed to share many of her concerns. On the eve of marriage, she had become more politicised through a visit to friends in Manchester, who brought her into contact with both English radicals and the Manchester Martyrs of the Irish Republican Fenian Brotherhood, as well as with the conditions of the urban poor.

Soon Frank became vicar of Sibsey in Lincolnshire. Annie moved to Sibsey with her husband, and within a few years they had two children, Arthur and Mabel; however the marriage was a disaster. The first conflict came over money and Annie's independence. Annie wrote short stories, books for children, and articles. As married women did not have the legal right to own property, Frank was able to take all the money she earned. Politics further divided the couple. Annie began to support farm workers who were fighting to unionise and to win better conditions. Frank was a Tory and sided with the landlords and farmers. The tension came to a head when Annie refused to attend Communion. In 1873 she left him and returned to London. They were legally separated and Annie took her daughter with her.

Besant began to question her own faith. She turned to leading churchmen for advice, going to see Edward Bouverie Pusey, leader of the Catholic wing of the Church of England. When she asked him to recommend books that would answer her questions, he told her she had read too many already. Besant returned to Frank to make a last unsuccessful effort to repair the marriage. She finally left for London.

She fought for the causes she thought were right, starting with freedom of thought, women's rights, secularism (she was a leading member of the National Secular Society alongside Charles Bradlaugh), birth control, Fabian socialism and workers' rights.

Divorce was unthinkable for Frank, and was not really within the reach of even middle-class people. Annie was to remain Mrs Besant for the rest of her life. At first, she was able to keep contact with both children and to have Mabel live with her; she also got a small allowance from her husband.

Once free of Frank Besant and exposed to new currents of thought, she began to question not only her long-held religious beliefs but also the whole of conventional thinking. She began to write attacks on the churches and the way they controlled people's lives. In particular she attacked the status of the Church of England as a state-sponsored faith.

Soon she was earning a small weekly wage by writing a column for the National Reformer, the newspaper of the NCS. The NCS stood for a secular state and an end to the special status of Christianity, and allowed her to act as one of its public speakers. Public lectures were very popular entertainment in Victorian times. Besant was a brilliant speaker, and was soon in great demand. Using the railway, she crisscrossed the country, speaking on all of the most important issues of the day, always demanding improvement, reform and freedom.

For many years Besant was a friend of the Society's leader, Charles Bradlaugh. It seems that they were never lovers, but their friendship was very close. Bradlaugh, a former seaman, had long been separated from his wife; Besant lived with him and his daughters, and they worked together on many issues. He was an atheist and a republican; he was also trying to get elected as Member of Parliament (MP) for Northampton.

Besant and Bradlaugh became household names in 1877 when they published a book by the American birth-control campaigner Charles Knowlton. It claimed that working-class families could never be happy until they were able to decide how many children they wanted. It suggested ways to limit the size of their families. The Knowlton book was highly controversial, and was vigorously opposed by the Church.

Besant and Bradlaugh proclaimed in the National Reformer:

We intend to publish nothing we do not think we can morally defend. All that we publish we shall defend.

The pair were arrested and put on trial for publishing the Knowlton book. They were found guilty, but released pending appeal. As well as great opposition, Besant and Bradlaugh also received a great deal of support in the Liberal press. Arguments raged back and forth in the letters and comment columns as well as in the courtroom. Besant was instrumental in founding the Malthusian League during the trial, which would go on to advocate for the abolition of penalties for the promotion of contraception. For a time, it looked as though they would be sent to prison. The case was thrown out finally only on a technical point, the charges not having been properly drawn up.

The scandal cost Besant custody of her children. Her husband was able to persuade the court that she was unfit to look after them, and they were handed over to him permanently.

Bradlaugh's political prospects were not damaged by the Knowlton scandal and he got elected to Parliament in 1881. Because of his atheism, he refused to swear the oath of loyalty. Although many Christians were shocked by Bradlaugh, others (like the Liberal leader Gladstone) spoke up for freedom of belief. It took more than six years before the whole issue was sorted out (in Bradlaugh's favor) after a series of by-elections and court appearances.

Meanwhile Besant built close contacts with the Irish Home Rulers and supported them in her newspaper columns during what are considered crucial years, when the Irish nationalists were forming an alliance with Liberals and Radicals. Besant met the leaders of the Irish home rule movement. In particular, she got to know Michael Davitt, who wanted to mobilise the Irish peasantry through a Land War, a direct struggle against the landowners. She spoke and wrote in favour of Davitt and his Land League many times over the coming decades.

However, Bradlaugh's parliamentary work gradually alienated Besant. Women had no part in parliamentary politics. Besant was searching for a real political outlet, where her skills as a speaker, writer and organiser could do some real good.

For Besant, politics, friendship and love were always closely intertwined. Her decision in favour of Socialism came about through a close relationship with a struggling young Irish author living in London, and a leading light of the Annie was impressed by his work and grew very close to him too in the early 1880s. It was Besant who made the first move, by inviting Shaw to live with her. This he refused, but it was Shaw who sponsored Besant to join the Fabian Society. In its early days, the Society was a gathering of people exploring spiritual, rather than political, alternatives to the capitalist system. Besant began to write for the Fabians. This new commitment – and her relationship with Shaw – deepened the split between Besant and Bradlaugh, who was an individualist and opposed to Socialism of any sort. While he defended free speech at any cost, he was very cautious about encouraging working-class militancy in India

Unemployment was a central issue of the time, and in 1887 some of the London unemployed started to hold protests in Trafalgar Square. Besant agreed to appear as a speaker at a meeting on 13 November. The police tried to stop the assembly, fighting broke out, and troops were called. Many were hurt, one man died, and hundreds were arrested; Besant offered herself for arrest, an offer disregarded by the police.

The events created a great sensation, and became known as Bloody Sunday. Besant was widely blamed – or credited – for it. She threw herself into organising legal aid for the jailed workers and support for their families. Bradlaugh finally broke with her because he felt she should have asked his advice before going ahead with the meeting.

Another activity in this period was her involvement in the London matchgirls strike of 1888. She was drawn into this battle of the "New Unionism" by a young socialist, Herbert Burrows. He had made contact with workers at Bryant and May's match factory in Bow, London, who were mainly young women and were very poorly paid. They were also prey to industrial illnesses, like the bone-rotting Phossy jaw, which was caused by the chemicals used in match manufacture. Some of the match workers asked for help from Burrows and Besant in setting up a union.

Besant met the women and set up a committee, which led the women into a strike for better pay and conditions, an action that won public support. Besant led demonstrations by "match-girls", who were cheered in the streets, and prominent churchmen wrote in their support. In just over a week they forced the firm to improve pay and conditions. Besant then helped them to set up a proper union and a social centre.

At the time, the matchstick industry was a very powerful lobby, since electric light was not yet widely available, and matches were an essential commodity; in 1872, lobbyists from the match industry had persuaded the British government to change its planned tax policy. Besant's campaign was the first time anyone had successfully challenged the match manufacturers on a major issue, and was seen as a landmark victory of the early years of British Socialism.

During 1884, Besant had developed a very close friendship with Edward Aveling, a young socialist teacher who lived in her house for a time. Aveling was a scholarly figure and it was he who first translated the important works of Marx into English. He eventually went to live with Eleanor Marx, daughter of Karl Marx. Aveling was a great influence on Besant's thinking and she supported his work, yet she moved towards the rival Fabians at that time. Aveling and Eleanor Marx had joined the Marxist SDF and then the Socialist League, a small Marxist splinter group which formed around the artist William Morris.

It seems that Morris played a large part in converting Besant to Marxism, but it was to the SDF, not his Socialist League, that she turned in 1888. She remained a member for a number of years and became one of its best speakers. She was still a member of the Fabian Society; neither she nor anyone else seemed to think the two movements incompatible at the time.

Soon after joining the Marxists, Besant stood for election to the London School Board. Women at that time were not able to take part in parliamentary politics, but had been brought into the local electorate in 1881.

Besant drove about with a red ribbon in her hair, speaking at meetings. "No more hungry children," her manifesto proclaimed. She combined her socialist principles with feminism: "I ask the electors to vote for me, and the non-electors to work for me because women are wanted on the Board and there are too few women candidates." Besant came out on top of the poll in Tower Hamlets, with over 15,000 votes. She wrote in the National Reformer: "Ten years ago, under a cruel law, Christian bigotry robbed me of my little child. Now the care of the 763,680 children of London is placed partly in my hands."

Besant was also involved in the London Dock Strike (1889), in which the dockers, who were employed by the day, were led by Ben Tillett in a struggle for the "Dockers' Tanner". Besant helped Tillett draw up the union's rules and played an important part in the meetings and agitation which built up the organisation. She spoke for the dockers at public meetings and on street corners. Like the match-girls, the dockers won public support for their struggle, and the strike was won.

Besant was a prolific writer and a powerful orator. In 1889, she was asked to write a review for the Pall Mall Gazette on The Secret Doctrine, a book by H.P. Blavatsky. After reading it, she sought an interview with its author, meeting Blavatsky in Paris. In this way she was converted to Theosophy. Besant's intellectual journey had always involved a spiritual dimension, a quest for transformation of the whole person. As her interest in Theosophy deepened, she allowed her membership of the Fabian Society to lapse (1890) and broke her links with the Marxists. When Blavatsky died in 1891, Besant was left as one of the leading figures in Theosophy and in 1893 she represented it at the Chicago World Fair.

In 1893, soon after becoming a member of the Theosophical Society she went to India for the first time. After a dispute the American section split away into an independent organization. The original Society, then led by Henry Steel Olcott and Besant, is today based in Chennai, India, and is known as the Theosophical Society Adyar. Following the split Besant devoted much of her energy not only to the Society, but also to India's freedom and progress. Besant Nagar, a neighborhood near the Theosophical Society in Chennai, is named in her honor.

She pursued freemasonry with equal vigour when it was mentioned to her that there was a masonry that "accepted women as well as men". She saw freemasonry, in particular co-freemasonry, as an extension of her interest in the rights of women and the greater brotherhood of man and saw co-freemasonry as a "movement which practised true brotherhood, in which women and men worked side by side for the perfecting of humanity. She immediately wanted to be admitted to this organisation", known now as The International Order of Co-Freemasonry, Le Droit Humain.

The link was made in 1902 by the Theosophist Francesca Arundale, who accompanied Besant to Paris, along with six friends. "They were all initiated, passed and raised into the first three degrees and Annie returned to England, bearing a Charter and founded there the first Lodge of International Mixed Masonry, Le Droit Humain." Besant eventually became the Order's Most Puissant Grand Commander, and was a major influence in the international growth of the Order.

Besant met fellow Theosophist Charles Webster Leadbeater in London in April 1894. They became close co-workers in the Theosophical Movement and would remain so for the rest of their lives. Leadbeater claimed clairvoyance and reputedly helped Besant become clairvoyant herself in the following year. In a letter dated 25 August 1895 to Francisca Arundale, Leadbeater narrates how Besant became clairvoyant. Together they clairvoyantly investigated the universe, matter, thought-forms, and the history of mankind, and co-authored several books.

In 1906 Leadbeater became the centre of controversy when it emerged that he had advised the practice of masturbation to some boys under his care and spiritual instruction. Leadbeater stated he had encouraged the practice in order to keep the boys celibate, which was considered a prerequisite for advancement on the spiritual path. Due to the controversy, he offered to resign from the Theosophical Society in 1906, which was accepted. The next year Besant became President of the Society and in 1908, with her express support, Leadbeater was readmitted to the Society. Leadbeater went on to face accusations of improper relations with boys, but none of the accusations were ever proven and Besant never deserted him.

Until Besant's presidency, the society had as one of its foci Theravada Buddhism and the island of Sri Lanka, where Henry Olcott did the majority of his useful work. Under Besant's leadership there was more stress on the teachings of "The Aryavarta", as she called central India, as well as on esoteric Christianity.

Besant set up a new school for boys, the Central Hindu College (CHC) at Benares which was formed on underlying Theosophical principles, and which counted many prominent Theosophists in its staff and faculty. Its aim was to build a new leadership for India. The students spent 90 minutes a day in prayer and studied religious texts, but they also studied modern science. It took 3 years to raise the money for the CHC, most of which came from Indian princes. In April 1911, Besant met Pandit Madan Mohan Malaviya and they decided to unite their forces and work for a common Hindu University at Varanasi. Besant and fellow trustees of the Central Hindu College also agreed to Government of India's precondition that the college should become a part of the new University. The Banaras Hindu University started functioning from 1 October 1917 with the Central Hindu College as its first constituent college.

Blavatsky had stated in 1889 that the main purpose of establishing the Society was to prepare humanity for the future reception of a "torch-bearer of Truth", an emissary of a hidden Spiritual Hierarchy that according to Theosophists guides the evolution of Humankind. This was repeated by

Besant as early as 1896; Besant came to believe in the imminent appearance of the "emissary", who was identified by Theosophists as the so-called World Teacher.

In 1909, soon after Besant's assumption of the presidency, Leadbeater "discovered" fourteen-year-old Jiddu Krishnamurti (1895–1986), a South Indian boy who had been living next to the headquarters of the Theosophical Society at Adyar, and declared him the probable "vehicle" for the expected World Teacher. The "discovery" and its objective received widespread publicity and attracted worldwide following, mainly among Theosophists. It also started years of upheaval, and contributed to splits in the Theosophical Society and doctrinal schisms in Theosophy. Following the discovery, Jiddu Krishnamurti and his younger brother Nityananda ("Nitya") were placed under the care of Theosophists and Krishnamurti was extensively groomed for his future mission as the new vehicle for the "World Teacher". Besant soon became the boys' legal guardian with the consent of their father, who was very poor and could not take care of them. However, his father later changed his mind and began a legal battle to regain the guardianship, against the will of the boys. Early in their relationship, Krishnamurti and Besant had developed a very close bond and he considered her a surrogate mother – a role she happily accepted. (His biological mother had died when he was ten years old).

In 1929, twenty years after his "discovery", Krishnamurti, who had grown disenchanted with the World Teacher Project, repudiated the role that many Theosophists expected him to fulfil. He dissolved the Order of the Star in the East, an organization founded to assist the World Teacher in his mission, and eventually left the Theosophical Society and Theosophy at large. He spent the rest of his life travelling the world as an unaffiliated speaker, becoming in the process widely known as an original, independent thinker on philosophical, psychological, and spiritual subjects. His love for Besant never waned, as also was the case with Besant's feelings towards him; concerned for his wellbeing after he declared his independence, she had purchased 6 acres (24,000 m2) of land near the Theosophical Society estate which later became the headquarters of the Krishnamurti Foundation India.

Along with her Theosophical activities, Besant continued to actively participate in political matters. She had joined the Indian National Congress. As the name suggested, this was originally a debating body, which met each year to consider resolutions on political issues. Mostly it demanded more of a say for middle-class Indians in British Indian government. It had not yet developed into a permanent mass movement with local organisation. About this time her co-worker Leadbeater moved to Sydney, Australia.

In 1914 World War I broke out, and Britain asked the support of its Empire in the fight against Germany. Echoing an Irish nationalist slogan, Besant declared, "England's need is India's opportunity". As editor of the New India newspaper, she attacked the colonial government of India and called for clear and decisive moves towards self-rule. As with Ireland, the government refused to discuss any changes while the war lasted.

In 1916 Besant launched the Home Rule League along with the Lokmanya Tilak, once again modeling demands for India on Irish nationalist practices. This was the first political party in India to have regime change as its main goal. Unlike the Congress itself, the League worked all year round. It built a structure of local branches, enabling it to mobilise demonstrations, public meetings and agitations. In June 1917 Besant was arrested and interned at a hill station, where she defiantly flew a red and green flag. The Congress and the Muslim League together threatened to launch protests if she were not set free; Besant's arrest had created a focus for protest.

The government was forced to give way and to make vague but significant concessions. It was announced that the ultimate aim of British rule was Indian self-government, and moves in that direction were promised. Besant was freed in September 1917 to great welcome from crowds all over India and in December she took over as President of the Indian National Congress for a year.

After the war, a new leadership emerged around Mohandas K. Gandhi – one of those who had written to demand Besant's release. He was a lawyer who had returned from leading Asians in a peaceful struggle against racism in South Africa. Jawaharlal Nehru, Gandhi's closest collaborator, had been educated by a Theosophist tutor.

The new leadership was committed to action that was both militant and nonviolent, but there were differences between them and Besant. Despite her past, she was not happy with their socialist leanings. Until the end of her life, however, she continued to campaign for India's independence, not only in India but also on speaking tours of Britain. In her own version of Indian dress, she remained a striking presence on speakers' platforms. She produced a torrent of letters and articles demanding independence.

Besant tried as a person, Theosophist, and President of the Theosophical Society, to accommodate Krishnamurti's views into her life, without success; she vowed to personally follow him in his new direction although she apparently had trouble understanding both his motives and his new message. The two remained friends until the end of her life. Besant died in 1933 and was survived by her daughter, Mabel. After her death, colleagues Jiddu Krishnamurti, Aldous Huxley, Guido Ferrando, and Rosalind Rajagopal, built Happy Valley School, now renamed Besant Hill School in her honour.

For other literary works published please visit

http://www.andras-nagy.com